# Developing Linux Applications

## with GTK+ and GDK

# New Riders Professional Library

# Developing Linux Applications

## with GTK+ and GDK

201 West 103rd Street,
Indianapolis, Indiana 46290

Eric Harlow

# Developing Linux Applications
# with GTK+ and GDK

Eric Harlow

ISBN: 0-7357-0021-4

Library of Congress Catalog Card Number: 98-89433

Printed in the United States of America

First Printing: *February, 1999*

2001　00　99　　4　3　2　1

Interpretation of the printing code: The rightmost double-digit number is the year of the book's printing; the rightmost single-digit, the number of the book's printing. For example, the printing code 99-1 shows that the first printing of the book occurred in 1999.

*Composed in Bembo and MCPdigital by Macmillan Computer Publishing*

## Trademarks

## Warning and Disclaimer

**Publisher**
David Dwyer

**Executive Editor**
Laurie Petrycki

**Acquisitions Editor**
Katie Purdum

**Development Editor**
Jim Chalex

**Managing Editor**
Sarah Kearns

**Project Editor**
Caroline Wise

**Copy Editor**
June Waldman

**Proofreader**
Jeanne Clark

**Indexers**
Joy Dean Lee
Lisa Stumpf

**Technical Reviewer**
Thomas Mailund Jensen

**Book Designer**
Ruth C. Lewis

**Cover Designer**
Brainstorm Technologies

**Production**
Cheryl Lynch

# Contents

# About the Author

**Eric Harlow** holds a Bachelor of Science Degree in Computer Science from the University of Delaware. He started writing programs beginning with the Vic-20 and has worked with various computers, including the Amiga, Atari ST, and the PC. His operating system experience includes UNIX, Windows, OS/2, and of course, Linux. He has developed everything from computer games to business applications and Web sites.

Eric is currently a consultant with RDA Consultants in Baltimore, Maryland. He develops client/server applications and Web-based applications. When not earning a living, he's busy hacking Linux and Java. He advocates Linux solutions using his Linux-based ISP as an example of the capabilities of the operating system.

He currently resides in Baltimore with his wife and his computers.

# About the Technical Reviewer

This reviewer contributed his considerable practical, hands-on expertise to the entire development process for *Developing Linux Applications*. As the book was being written, he reviewed all the material for technical content, organization, and usability. His feedback was critical to ensuring that *Developing Linux Applications* fits your need for the highest quality technical information.

**Thomas Mailund Jensen** is a computer science student at the University of Aarhus, Denmark, doing his Ph.D. work as part of the Coloured Petri Nets (CPN) group. He has also been employed as a part-time programmer in the CPN group, hacking on many UNIX systems, including Linux. His interests include model/system checking and verification, and distributed systems and distributed algorithms. Why is he hacking GTK+? "For the pure fun of it!"

*To Emily*

# Acknowledgements

Writing a book is a tedious and time-consuming task, and this book would not have been possible without the understanding of my wife, Emily. She gave me the writing time I needed, which included many weekends and late nights in the basement huddled in front of my computer. She has understood my being a computer geek and a Linux advocate despite the uphill battle towards world domination.

At Macmillan, I'd like to thank Laurie Petrycki for taking a chance on this book. In addition, I'd like to thank the development editor, Jim Chalex, for guiding me through the writing process. Seeing a book come together has been an eye-opening experience. I'd also like to thank my technical reviewer, Thomas Mailund Jensen, for adding helpful comments throughout the review process.

Thanks, also, to Don Awalt and Brian Berns from RDA Consultants: Don because he's the big boss, and you should always thank the big boss; Brian because he's been my project manager throughout the project and has covered the project during critical weekends while I was home writing to meet deadlines.

I must also thank the developers on the GTK+ mailing lists who answered all my questions and the developers of GTK+ and the GIMP that made this book possible.

Special thanks to Linus Torvalds who started this world-domination tour and to all the other people who have contributed to the growth of Linux. Thanks to `slashdot.org` for allowing me to use its site as a forum when I started this project and for keeping everyone in the Linux community informed about developments within Linux, open source, and geekdom.

Thanks to those who read through the early beta versions of the book and sent me corrections when I goofed or spent too late a night writing.

I want to thank the reader for buying this book and overlooking any imperfections within. It's hard not to make mistakes, but we can learn from them.

Finally, thanks to my mom and dad.

# Tell Us What You Think

As the reader of this book, you are our most important critic and commentator. We value your opinion and want to know what we're doing right, what we could do better, what areas you'd like to see us publish in, and any other words of wisdom you're willing to pass our way.

As the Executive Editor responsible for publishing Linux titles at New Riders, I welcome your comments. You can fax, email, or write me directly to let me know what you did or didn't like about this book—as well as what we can do to make our books stronger.

*Please note that I cannot help you with technical problems related to the topic of this book, and that due to the high volume of mail I receive, I might not be able to reply to every message.* When you write, please be sure to include this book's title and author, as well as your name and phone or fax number. I will carefully review your comments and share them with the author and editors who worked on the book.

**Fax:**    317-581-4663
**Email:**  newriders@mcp.com
**Mail:**   Laurie Petrycki
           New Riders Publishing
           201 West 103rd Street
           Indianapolis, IN 46290 USA

# I

# Programming in GTK+

# 1

# Introduction to GTK+

**G**TK+ STANDS FOR THE GIMP TOOLKIT, and GIMP stands for Graphical Image Manipulation tool. The GIMP Toolkit is a library used for developing applications with a graphical user interface (GUI). The library is currently used extensively to develop Linux GUI applications. The GIMP was developed with the GTK+ library and provides an example of a professionally developed GUI application. The GIMP is a free, open-source application available from www.gimp.org. The GTK+ library can also be used to develop applications on other platforms that support the GTK+ library. The GTK+ library is an object-oriented library written in C that supports applications written in several languages. The list of supported languages includes Ada95, C++, Eiffel, Objective C, Pascal, Perl, Python, and many more. The current list of language bindings is available at the GTK+ Web site, www.gtk.org.

## What Are the Book's Assumptions About the Reader?

This book assumes that the reader is familiar with the C programming language and knows a little about Linux. The reader should be comfortable with pointers and memory allocation. The reader should also be familiar with developing GUI applications and with event-based messaging. In short, this book is good for Linux developers who want to develop GUI applications.

This book is also good for people moving from other operating systems (like MS Windows) who want to develop GUI applications under Linux.

## What's in This Book?

This book covers the GTK+ library, including GLIB and GDK using C. This is not to
say that *everything* in GTK+ is covered in this book. GTK+ is too large for a single
book to cover the subject completely. This book is an attempt to get developers to
recognize that GTK+ is a GUI toolkit for developing applications under Linux and
other operating systems.

The GTK+ library is free, or rather, it is *open-source software*, so the entire source
code for the library is available for download. The only restriction on its use is that
any libraries created from the GTK+ library must also remain under the open-source
license.

The license that GTK+ falls under is important. Because the source code is available, the product will never be dead as long as developers are using it. With the source
code available, any developer can fix bugs in the version of the library he or she is
using, and submit the bug fixes to the maintainers of GTK+ for incorporation into
the main branch. This approach turns many developers who use GTK+ into developers of GTK+, and further enhances its stability and performance.

## Where Can I Get GTK+?

GTK+ can be downloaded from the GTK+ Web site at www.GTK.org. The version
numbers are similar to Linux in that the even numbers, 1.0 and 1.2, are the stable versions and the odd numbers, .99 and 1.1, are the development versions. Sometimes an
additional number (1.0.5) indicates that bug fixes have been added to a version.

## How Do I Build GTK+?

To build GTK+, you first need to download both GLIB and GTK+ from the GTK+
Web site. You need to build GLIB first because GTK+ uses GLIB for many of its
internals. After building GLIB and installing it, you can build GTK+.

## I'm a Novice—How Do I Build from Source?

The GLIB and GTK+ packages can be built in a few simple steps. The files you
download will be named something like GTK+-1.2.0.tar.gz—this file is a tarred and
gzipped file because the extension is .tar.gz. The file must first be gunzipped by
using gunzip at the command line, like this:

```
gunzip GTK+-1.2.0.tar.gz
```

The gunzipped file is now a much larger tar file named something like
GTK+-1.2.0.tar. This tar file can now be expanded into its directory structure
by using the following tar command:

```
tar xvf GTK+-1.2.0.tar
```

This command creates the directories required to build the library. Go into the directory that was created and type

```
./configure
```

to run the configuration utility. It builds a makefile that you can use to build the library. If it runs without errors, then you can just type

```
make
```

to build the library. The library needs to be installed, but you need to be root or have someone with the proper permissions install the library. The command to install the libraries on the system is

```
make install
```

You may need to run `/sbin/ldconfig` on your system to get the libraries recognized. Of course, GLIB needs to be built and installed before GTK+ is built and installed.

## What's Required to Run the Examples?

The examples were compiled on a 2.0 version of Linux using the 2.7.2 gcc compiler. The egcs compiler has not been tested, but it should work on the examples. The examples work on GTK+ 1.1.5 and should work on GTK+ 1.2. Many of the examples will not work on GTK+ 1.0.x without some modifications to the source code. Assuming everything is configured correctly, you should be able to go into one of the sample directories and type **make** to create the programs.

## Where Can I Get the Sample Programs?

For those  not interested in spending the day typing in the examples, they can be downloaded from the following URL:

```
http://www.mcp.com/product_support/
```

Type in the ISBN of this book (**0735700214**) in the dialog box provided. All the code required to build the examples is available. All that's needed is GTK+ 1.2.

## Where Can I Get *More* Help?

In addition to reading the book, you can turn to several places for help. The GTK+ Web site has a tutorial and a few sample programs for GTK+ in addition to a repository for other GTK+ applications that can be used to learn about GTK+. Included with the sources to GTK+ is a directory of examples that contains sample applications on different aspects of GTK+. A testGTK+ application is included with the GTK+ sources and can be used to test each widget in GTK+. The source code for the testGTK+ application is valuable when the documentation for a particular widget cannot be found, because it has probably been coded in the testGTK+. Of course, the GTK+ source code is always available for the adventurous.

If none of these sources answers your questions, you can try various GTK-oriented mailing lists. Many knowledgeable GTK+ developers are on the GTK+ mailing lists, answering questions from the simple to the very complicated. The primary mailing lists are `GTK-list@redhat.com` and `GTK-app-devel-list@redhat.com`. To subscribe to the GTK-list, send an email to `GTK-list-request@redhat.com` with "subscribe" in the subject. Likewise, to subscribe to the GTK-app-devel-list, send email to `GTK-app-devel-list-request@redhat.com` with "subscribe" in the subject. You should know that these lists, especially the GTK-list, generate a lot of traffic—about 50 emails a day, and on some days the number is even higher.

# 2

# GLIB

THE GLIB LIBRARY IS A COLLECTION OF popular functions that are used extensively by GTK+. Linked lists, trees, error handling, memory management, and timers are just a part of the library's contents. This chapter discusses the most commonly used functions in the GLIB library. GTK+ requires the GLIB library and relies on it for portability and functionality. The GLIB library can be used without GTK+ for developing nongraphical user interface (GUI) applications.

## Types

Rather than using the standard types found in the C programming language, GLIB uses its own set of types. This approach makes porting to other platforms easier and allows the data types to change without requiring an application rewrite. Because GTK+ uses the GLIB data types and functions, in theory porting GTK+ requires GLIB be ported to the destination platform as well as to the GDK library that GTK+ uses. Porting applications across platforms requires a good deal of patience in addition to a portable design, especially for software ported between dissimilar platforms (Linux→Windows as opposed to Linux→UNIX).

GLIB uses many types that are slightly different from the standard C data types. What would be a `char` data type in C is a `gchar` in GLIB. Although the `gchar` may be defined as a `char` in the GLIB headers on the Intel platform, to preserve portability the two should not be used interchangeably. Many functions have a `gchar *` as a parameter instead of a `char *`. This change is not significant, but it does require getting used to. Some of the more common data type modifications are

| C Types | GLIB Types |
|---------|------------|
| char | gchar |
| short | gshort |
| long | glong |
| int | gint |
| char | gboolean |
| void* | gpointer |

Using the GLIB data types in a GLIB/GTK+ application ensures that the application will work when the implementation of the underlying data type (say `gboolean`) changes. For example, the `gboolean` data type could be defined as an `int` in a later release; using the `gboolean` data type, instead of `char`, ensures that the application will still compile cleanly.

# Messages

GLIB has four functions to display information, and each of them can be extended on-the-fly for GUI/non-GUI development. These four different functions have four levels of message handling from the nonrecoverable error displayed by `g_error` to the standard output function `g_print`. Each message function displays a different type of message and can be passed a variable number of parameters, like the `printf` function.

### *g_error*

The `g_error` function displays a hard error in an application. It displays a message and aborts the program. This function should be used only for errors that would otherwise cause the program to exit. The `g_set_error_handler` function can override the behavior of the `g_error` function, but cannot prevent the `g_error` function from aborting.

### *g_warning*

The `g_warning` function displays a message that a recoverable error has occurred, but the program can continue running. GTK+ uses this function to display programmer errors that were successfully handled. The `g_set_warning_handler` function can override the default behavior of the `g_warning` message.

## *g_message*

The g_message function displays information not associated with an error. The g_set_message_handler function can override the behavior of the g_message function.

## *g_print*

The g_print function is used mostly for debugging. You can use the g_print function during development and override the behavior of the g_print function in production so the function does not display any message. This approach is quick and easy, and faster than going through your code to remove the debug. You can use the g_set_print_handler function to override the behavior of the g_print function.

You can override each of the messaging routines by passing in the new handler function. The new message handler could pop up a window with the message log the message/error to a file, or perform some other behavior. The behavior of the message function can be modified quickly in development to suit the needs of the developer.

## Custom Error Handling

This small example shows custom error handling. Passing in a parameter of normal uses the default messaging that comes with GLIB.

```
[brain@sharp messages]$ message normal
Here's a print
message: Here's a message


** WARNING **: Here's a warning


** ERROR **: Here's an error

Aborted (core dumped)
```

Passing in a parameter of surfer for the same program shows that the default message functions now display the same messages a bit differently. Note, however, that the program still aborts when an error occurs, even though a custom error handler was installed.

```
[brain@sharp messages]$ message surfer
Dude, Here's a print
Dude, ya got a message - Here's a message
Bad news Dude. - Here's a warning
Major wipe out, dude. - Here's an error
Aborted (core dumped)
[brain@sharp messages]$ exit
```

Here is the code that illustrates the program. If surfer is passed in, the new message handlers are set up before the message functions are called.

```
/*
 * Example showing message behavior
 */

#include <glib.h>

/*
 * Surfer Print
 *
 * Override function for the g_print function.
 */
void SurferPrint (const gchar *buf)
{
  printf ("Dude, ");
  printf (buf);
}

/*
 * Surfer Message
 *
 * Override for the g_message function
 */
void SurferMessage (const gchar *buf)
{
  printf ("Dude, ya got a message - ");
  printf (buf);
}

/*
 * SurferWarning
 *
 * Override for the g_warning function
 */
void SurferWarning (const gchar *buf)
{
  printf ("Bad news Dude. - ");
  printf (buf);
}

/*
 * SurferError
 *
 * Override for the g_error function
 */
```

```
void SurferError (const gchar *buf)
{
  printf ("Major wipe out, dude. - ");
  printf (buf);
}


/*
 * ShowParams
 *
 * Show the options available for running the program.
 */
void ShowParams ()
{
  printf ("Must pass in parameter. Valid parameters are:\n");
  printf (" 'surfer' - use surfer message handling.\n");
  printf (" 'normal' - use normal message handling.\n ");
  exit (0);
}


/*
 * main
 *
 * Program begins here
 */
int main (int argc, char *argv[])
{

  /* --- Not enough args? --- */
  if (argc <= 1) {

    ShowParams ();
  }

  /* --- Normal speech? --- */
  if (strcmp (argv[1], "normal") == 0) {

    /* --- Do nothing - just verify that parameter is valid --- */

  /* --- Surfer speech? --- */
  } else if (strcmp (argv[1], "surfer") == 0) {

    /* --- Seems that they want surfer speech for the errors. --- */
    g_set_error_handler (SurferError);
    g_set_warning_handler (SurferWarning);
    g_set_message_handler (SurferMessage);
    g_set_print_handler (SurferPrint);
```

```
} else {

  /* --- Can only pick 'normal' or 'surfer' --- */
  ShowParams ();
}

/*
 * Show functions at work. If we have custom handlers,
 * the message will be intercepted.
 */

g_print ("Here's a print\n");
g_message ("Here's a message\n");
g_warning ("Here's a warning\n");

/* --- This terminates the program - always --- */
g_error ("Here's an error\n");

}
```

# Assertions

Assertions are used in development to verify assumptions made in code. If the assertion should fail, a serious problem can result. The g_assert function checks for an assertion. For instance, if a function pointer is passed into a function and if it should have a value, you can use the g_assert function to verify the assumption. If the assertion fails, the program exits and displays an error and the line number where the assertion failed.

```
g_assert (ptr != NULL);
```

Assertions should be used only when the condition *should* never occur. They're usually used before complete error handling is in place. For instance, early in the development cycle, adding assertions in the code is easier than putting in the error checking as well as the corresponding error handling. When the software is released, many of the assertions should be modified to a more graceful way of handling error conditions. The assertions in release code should be used on a limited basis only, and only for conditions that should not occur; if one does, this indicates a severe problem.

You can insert the g_assert_not_reached function into blocks of code that should never be reached. If they are reached, the program halts and displays an error.

Both these assertions can be removed from production code by defining the G_DISABLE_ASSERT during compile time.

# String Functions

GLIB has its own `GString` data type that can be used instead of `char` and `gchar` to manipulate strings. The best part about `GString` is that the functions handle the memory allocation for you. `GString`s are created by using the `g_string_new` function and passing in a string.

```
gStr = g_string_new ("Hello");
```

The `GString` is really a structure that contains information about the string (a `gchar *` called `str`) and the length (`len`). The string and length are accessible from the structure for viewing, but any manipulation should be done through the wrapper classes. Freeing the created string requires the `g_string_free` function that takes the created string and frees the memory associated with it. The `g_string_free` function takes a second parameter that determines whether the `GString`'s string memory should be freed. Usually, this should be set to `TRUE` because the `GString` functions are allocating the memory, and it should be released when the data structure is released. This should be set to `FALSE` if a reference to the `GString`'s (`char *`) is used somewhere else.

```
g_string_free (gStr, TRUE);
```

You can assign a new value to an existing `GString` by using the `g_string_assign` function. The new string replaces the existing value and handles any new memory allocation.

```
g_string_assign (gStr, "New String Value");
```

The string can be truncated to a particular length by using the `g_string_truncate` function. Passing in a zero for the new length effectively sets the string to `""`.

```
g_string_truncate (gStr, 0);
```

The `g_string_append` function enables you to append a string to the `GString`. The additional memory allocation is done automatically.

```
g_string_append (gStr, "Adding more");
```

You can also add a string to the beginning of the `GString` by using the `g_string_prepend` function. The parameters are the same as the parameters for the `g_string_append` function except that for prepend the string is inserted before the existing string.

```
g_string_prepend (gStr, "Adding before");
```

Characters can be appended or prepended to the `GString`s by using the `g_string_append_c` or `g_string_prepend_c` functions.

```
/* --- Append a 'z' to the end --- */
g_string_append_c (gStr, 'z');

/* --- Put an 'a' on the beginning --- */
g_string_prepend_c (gStr, 'a');
```

You can convert the string to uppercase by using the g_string_up function or convert the string to lowercase by using the g_string_down functions. These two functions convert the GString and return the GString that was passed in with the string in the appropriate case.

```
/* --- Convert the string to upper case --- */
g_string_up (gStr);

/* --- Convert the string to lower case --- */
g_string_down (gStr);
```

# Singly Linked Lists

The GLIB library has useful functions for storing data in linked lists. The linked-list data type is a GSList, and the functions that modify the linked list either by adding or deleting elements return a GSList pointer. The GSList data structure has two parts defined as follows:

```
gpointer data;
GSList  *next;
```

The data field in the structure stores the data, which is usually a pointer to another structure. The next field is a pointer to the next element in the linked list. Figure 2.1 illustrates this arrangement.

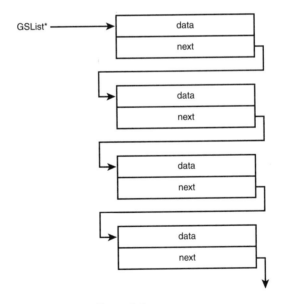

**Figure 2.1**   GSList.

In the following examples, you are passing in a string, but in reality the data you are storing in the linked list can be anything. The GSList * should always be initialized to NULL. Failure to do so causes problems because a non-NULL pointer appears as a linked list, resulting in memory problems or abnormal program terminations.

## Adding Items to the List

One way to add an item into a list is to use the g_slist_append function to create a node, and add it to the end of the linked list. For example, you can add "Wilma" to the end of the list as

```
GSList *list = NULL;

sName = "Wilma";
list = g_slist_append (list, sName);
```

or alternatively:

```
list = g_slist_append (list, "Wilma");
```

The return value from the g_slist_append function is the new linked list. Inserting or deleting items from the list always results in a new list being returned in case the head of the list changes. You can add "Joe" to the beginning of the list with the g_slist_prepend function.

```
list = g_slist_prepend (list, "Joe");
```

You can insert items at a particular position in the list by using the g_slist_insert function and providing an index of the position to insert the item. For example, you can add "Mary" after the first item in the list.

```
list = g_slist_insert (list, "Mary", 1);
```

If the position does not exist, the item is added to the end of the list.

The linked-list routines have no knowledge about the type of the data being stored in each node of the list. The developer must allocate and free the memory for the data if necessary.

## Keeping the List Sorted

Trying to keep the items in a list sorted is difficult because the data element of the list can represent any type of data and the linked list does not have intimate knowledge of the structure of that data. Fortunately, you can use a comparison function to add elements into a sorted list. The comparison function takes two data elements, compares them, and returns 1 if the first item is greater than the second, 0 if the data elements are the same, and -1 if the first item is less than the second item. You can create a small comparison function to compare the string data elements to sort the elements.

```
gint CompareNames (gconstpointer sName1, gconstpointer sName2)
{
    return ((gint) strcmp ((char *) sName1, (char *) sName2));
}
```

After the comparison function is in place, you can use it with the g_slist_insert_sorted function to insert items into a sorted list. The comparison function is called with data elements of the list to find the proper insertion point for the data element.

```
list = g_slist_insert_sorted (list,
                "Anne",
                CompareNames);
```

## Finding Elements in the List

The g_slist_find function looks for the data in the list. The return value is NULL if the data is not found in the list.

```
item = g_slist_find (list, "Joe");
```

The g_slist_find function has no intimate knowledge of the data elements of the nodes; therefore, it compares the values of the data elements, which are usually pointers. This technique can be a problem because of the following situation:

```
char szMary[20];

/* --- Put "Mary" into a string --- */
strcpy (szMary, "Mary");

/* --- Add "Mary" to the list --- */
list = g_slist_append (list, "Mary");

/* --- Look for "Mary" from the string --- */
item = g_slist_find (list, szMary);

/* --- Whaddya mean it's not found? I just added it. --- */
```

In this case, "Mary" is not found in the list because the szMary array points to the wrong memory location.

## List Length

The length of the list can be calculated with the g_list_length function.

```
guint nLength = g_slist_length (list);
```

## Removing Elements from the List

An element can be removed from the list with the g_slist_remove function. If the item is not in the list, nothing happens and you do not get warnings or errors. If the data element is a pointer, the pointers have to match for the item to be removed. You can try to remove an element from the list this way:

```
list = g_slist_remove (list, data);
```

As with the g_slist_find function, the g_slist_remove function does only a data element comparison and has no knowledge of the data if the data element is a pointer. There is no problem storing integers or other simple data types, but pointers are going to have the pointers compared (data == node->data) and not the contents of the locations. This is important to know if you use the list to store strings. Also, the data element may need to be freed if the developer allocated it.

## Getting the *n*th Element

You can look up the *n*th element in a list by using the g_slist_nth function and passing in the index of the element in the list you want. The following example gets the seventh element in the list:

```
node = g_slist_nth (list, 7);
```

You can look up the index of a data element by using the g_slist_index function. Because this function does a g_slist_find, the warnings mentioned in the earlier section, "Finding Elements in the List," apply.

```
nIndex = g_slist_index (list, 22);
```

## Viewing the List

The first way to look at the elements of the linked list is to run down the list manually in a loop. The node->next gets to the next node in the linked list.

```
/* --- list is the head --- */

/* --- Loop through the list --- */
for (node = list; node; node = node->next) {

  /* --- Dump out the contents, assumes data is char --- /*
  g_print ("%s\n", (char *) node->data);
}
```

The second way is to use the g_slist_foreach function. The g_slist_foreach function calls a function and passes the data element from each node in the linked list. To use the g_slist_foreach function, you first create a function (PrintNames) to handle the data element correctly. This PrintNames function takes the data and displays it. The data parameter is the item to be displayed and is passed in with each element of the list. The user_data is additional information that can be passed in to each of the elements.

```
void PrintNames (gpointer data, gpointer user_data)
{
  gchar  *message;

  /* --- Convert the data to a string --- */
  message = (gchar *) data;
```

```
/* --- Display the string --- */
g_print ("%s\ n", message);
}
```

Although this function displays only one data element, the `g_slist_foreach` calls it with every item in the list. You can set up the `g_slist_foreach` function to call the `PrintNames` function as follows:

```
/* --- Another way to print each of the data elements --- */
/* --- Call PrintNames for each element, user_data = NULL --- */
g_slist_foreach (list, (GFunc) PrintNames, NULL);
```

In this example, the `user_data` parameter of the `PrintNames` function is going to be passed in a `NULL` for each element in the list. This parameter can easily be changed to pass in other information for the `PrintNames` function to use.

### Freeing the List

To free the entire list, use the `g_slist_free` function and pass in the list.

```
g_slist_free (list);
```

If the data elements are pointers to allocated memory, they should be freed before you call the `g_slist_free` function; otherwise, the memory is lost.

# Doubly Linked Lists

GLIB also has a set of doubly linked-list functions that use the `GList` data type. These functions are similar in operation to the single linked-list functions except that all the doubly linked-list functions have a function prefix of `g_list` instead of `g_slist`, and the doubly linked-list functions use the `GList` data type instead of the `GSList` data type. The `GList` data type has a link to both the next and the previous element in the list, making backward traversal significantly easier (see Figure 2.2).

### Linked-list Performance

Linked lists are great for stacks (which add and remove from the front of the list) and for small lists but can be expensive when used to hold lots of data. When lists are being used to store information, the data should be added to the front of the list, making for a very quick insertion into the list. Frequent searches in the list for data may be expensive and are dependent on the list length.

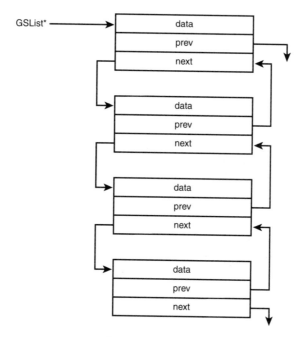

**Figure 2.2**   GList.

# Hash Tables

GLIB has a set of functions for using hash tables. *Hash tables* are a quick way to add and look up information: Items are added using a key, which can be used to retrieve the value. Figure 2.3 illustrates how hash table values are stored.

Hash tables require a callback function to compute the hashing value, and the callback function should compute a fairly unique value.

## Creating a Hash Table

Hash tables are created with the g_hash_table_new function that returns a pointer to a GHashTable. The function requires a hashing function and a comparison function. The hashing function computes the hashing value of the key that determines which bucket the key is going to be added to. The comparison function compares the keys when looking for an item. If you enter string data into a hash table, a simple function to compute the hash might take the first two characters of the string and add them together to create the hash.

```
/*
 * Make a hash from the first two characters.
 */
guint HashFunction (gpointer key)
{
```

```
    char *sKey;

  sKey = key;
  return (sKey[0] + sKey[1]);
}
```

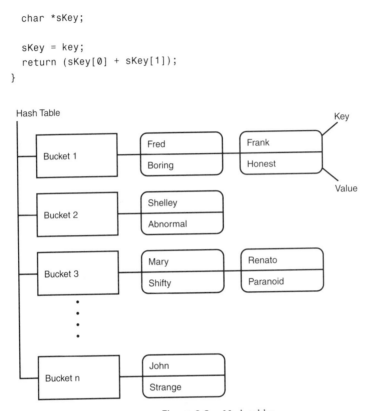

**Figure 2.3**   Hash tables.

However, this example is a bad hash function; words like *linux, linus, like,* and *list* would end up with the same hash value because the function computes the hash from the first two characters of the string. A better hash function would make better use of the data to come up with a more unique key. The next hash function uses the entire string to compute the hash. This function takes a bit longer to run than the previous hash function.

```
guint HashFunction (gpointer key)
{
  char *sKey;
  guint giHashValue = 0;
  int nIndex;

  sKey = skey;

  /* --- Some error handling --- */
  if (key == NULL) return (0);
```

```
/* --- Compute hash based on entire string --- */
for (nIndex = 0; nIndex < strlen (sKey); nIndex++) {

  /* --- Shift left because sequence is important --- */
  giHashValue = (giHashValue << 4) +
      (giHashValue ^ (guint) sKey[nIndex]);
}

return (giHashValue);
}
```

A string comparison function for the hash table would just use a string compare to determine whether the two strings are equivalent. This step is required because the hash function could return the same hash key for two separate strings. The string hash comparison function looks like this:

```
gint HashCompare (gpointer sName1, gpointer sName2)
{
  return (!strcmp ((char *) sName1, (char *) sName2));
}
```

Given these two functions, the g_hash_table_new function can be called with these two functions to create the hash table.

```
hTable = g_hash_table_new (HashFunction, HashCompare);
```

After the hash table is created, you can start to add items to it. The g_hash_table_insert function adds items to the table. The hash table takes three parameters to add an item: the hash table created with the g_hash_table_new function, a key to store the value so that the item can be looked up, and the value associated with the key. The following line of code inserts items into the hash table:

```
g_hash_table_insert (hTable, "Fred", "Boring");
```

The next example adds a value of "Boring" and associates it to the key "Fred". The g_hash_table_lookup function looks up the value of a key. The key "Fred" returns a value of "Boring".

```
sValue = g_hash_table_lookup (hTable, "Fred");
```

Like the list, the hash table has a foreach function that displays all the data elements in the table. You have to create a callback function to display the information. The callback is going to be slightly different from the list callback function because the hash callback is going to be passed both the key and the value.

```
void PrintNames (gpointer key, gpointer value, gpointer user_data)
{
  g_print ("Key: %s, Value: %s\n",
      (gchar *) key, (gchar *) value);
}
```

The g_hash_table_foreach function can then be called with this `PrintNames` function:

```
g_hash_table_foreach (hTable, (GHFunc) PrintNames, NULL);
```

You could have used the third parameter in the g_hash_table_foreach function to pass additional information into the `PrintNames` function that would appear as the user data variable of the callback function. The only guarantee about the order of the items when using the g_hash_table_foreach function is that the order is random.

### Removing Elements from the Hash Table

You can remove elements from the hash table by calling the g_hash_table_remove function and providing the key of the element that should be removed from the hash table.

```
g_hash_table_remove (hTable, "Fred");
```

### Destroying the Hash Table

When you are done with the table, you should destroy it with the g_hash_table_destroy function. As with the other destroy functions, the g_hash_table_destroy function destroys only the hash table, not any memory allocated by the user to store data in the hash table.

```
g_hash_table_destroy (hTable);
```

## Trees

Trees are great data structures for storing information. Internally, they are more complicated than linked lists or hash tables; however, trees have quicker access times than linked lists do to retrieve information, and unlike hash tables, trees can keep the information sorted.

### Comparison Function

Trees are created using the g_tree_new function that returns a pointer to a `GTree`. The function requires a comparison function as a parameter so the tree knows how to adjust itself for quick access to the information. If you store strings, the comparison function looks like this:

```
gint CompareNames (gpointer name1, gpointer name2)
{
    return (strcmp (name1, name2));
}
```

## Creating a Tree

After you create the compare function, you can use it to initialize the tree by passing it into the g_tree_new.

```
tree = g_tree_new (CompareNames);
```

## Inserting Elements

After the tree is created, you can add data into the tree. The compare function keeps the tree sorted. You add data into the tree with the g_tree_insert function, which expects the data to be passed in using a key/value combination. For example, you can add "Fred" to the tree and associate the value "Loud" with him this way:

```
g_tree_insert (tree, "Fred", "Loud");
```

## Looking Up Elements

The g_tree_lookup function looks up the value in the tree. The key is passed in, and the value for the key is returned if the value can be found in the tree. To look up the value of "Fred" that you just entered, call g_tree_lookup this way:

```
sValue = g_tree_lookup (tree, "Fred");
```

This statement returns "Loud" because it was the value you entered with the key "Fred".

## Traversing the Tree

Just as the hash and linked list types have a foreach function to traverse all the items, the tree has a function to traverse the tree, but in this case the function is a bit more complicated. The g_tree_traverse function has an additional parameter that determines how the tree is traversed. The tree can be traversed in order (G_IN_ORDER), preorder (G_PRE_ORDER), or postorder (G_POST_ORDER). Figures 2.4, 2.5, and 2.6 illustrate the different ways to traverse a tree.

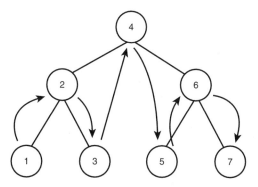

**Figure 2.4**    Traversing a tree—in order.

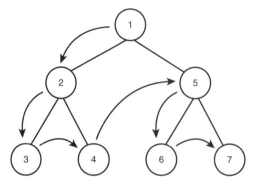

**Figure 2.5**   Traversing a tree—in preorder.

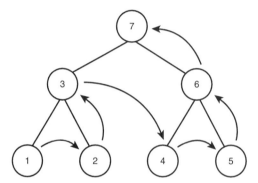

**Figure 2.6**   Traversing a tree—in postorder.

To traverse the tree alphabetically, use the `G_IN_ORDER` traversal. The following example calls the function:

```
g_tree_traverse (tree, TraverseTree, G_IN_ORDER, NULL);
```

Of course, you also need a `TraverseTree` function to display each key and value pair in the tree.

```
gint TraverseTree (gpointer key, gpointer value, gpointer data)
{
    char  *sKey = key;
    char  *sValue = value;

    g_print ("Key: %s, Value: %s\n", sKey, sValue);
    return FALSE;
}
```

# Memory Management

The GLIB library provides some memory management functions to replace the standard `malloc`/`free`. Keeping with the naming standards of the GLIB library, the `malloc` replacement is named `g_malloc`. The parameter is the size of the memory block that is being requested, which is the same as `malloc`. The library also provides a `g_free` function to replace the standard `free` function and a `g_realloc` to replace the standard `realloc` function.

```
/* --- Allocate some memory --- */
ptr = g_malloc (10 * sizeof (char));

/* --- Expand the memory --- */
ptr = g_realloc (ptr, 20 * sizeof (char));

/* --- Free the memory --- */
g_free (ptr);
```

The GLIB memory functions provide the capability to track down memory problems. When compiling GTK+/GLIB, you can define `MEM_CHECK` and/or `MEM_PROFILE` in `GLIB/gmem.c` to compile a slower and more helpful functionality into the memory management functions.

Compiling with `MEM_PROFILE` set makes GLIB keep track of memory allocations that are made through GLIB, which can be handy when tracking down a memory leak. Calling `g_mem_profile` displays information about your memory footprint similar to

```
1 allocations of 8 bytes
1 allocations of 52 bytes
2 allocations of 1024 bytes
2108 bytes allocated
0 bytes freed
2108 bytes in use
```

Using `MEM_CHECK` in GLIB keeps track of pointers that have already been freed. Attempting to free a pointer multiple times results in the following error:

```
** WARNING **: freeing previously freed memory.
```

This error usually indicates that your pointer management is not as good as you thought it was.

# Summary

The GLIB can handle many commonly used data structures, including linked lists and trees, and provides a standard set of functions for messages. These functions are used by the GTK+ library and provide a standard set of routines available on all platforms. You can use the GLIB routines with or without GTK+.

# 3

# Developing GUI Applications

**N**O SINGLE STANDARD FOR DEVELOPING GRAPHICAL user interface (GUI) applications under Linux is freely available—unless you count the X Window library, which is a very low-level library unsuitable for developing applications quickly. The Internet archives are filled with GUI toolkits designed to make application development easier, but none of these toolkits developed much of a following, and the Linux GUI community became fragmented. Things started to change when TrollTech (www.troll.no) developed a very good GUI toolkit called Qt, which is great for developing Linux GUI applications. However, Trolltech's licensing restrictions have prevented many developers from using its product. The Qt license states that developed applications must be free unless the developer purchases the commercial version of the Qt library. To me, this requirement is a restriction on the library, which prevents commercial companies from using a good toolkit to develop Linux applications. Nevertheless, Qt is free for noncommercial use.

Linux is released under the GNU General Public License (GPL), which permits anyone to take the source code, modify it, and redistribute it. Therefore, many developers believe that any toolkits that are used to develop Linux applications should also be under the GPL. This approach reduces both the need to rely on a commercial company to fix bugs, and the fear that developers have of giving any single entity too much control. This situation led to the development of the GIMP Toolkit (GTK+).

The GIMP Toolkit (GTK+) is the latest GPL GUI library for Linux; therefore it is free for both noncommercial and commercial development. GTK+ is also a cross-platform toolkit with support on many UNIX machines as well as on Microsoft Windows. With the support of some of the larger distributions of Linux software and a large base of Linux developers, GTK+ has been evolving into a very good toolkit for developing GUI applications.

GTK+ was given its name because of the use of the library to create the GIMP (which stands for Gnu Image Manipulation Project). The GIMP is an example of an excellent, commercial-quality graphical editor written using GTK+. GIMP is similar to Photoshop and can be seen at the `www.gimp.org` Web site.

GTK+ was written in C, yet is object oriented, and bindings are available to use GTK+ from many languages, including C++ (using the wrapper called, oddly enough, GTK--). Like most modern GUI toolkits, GTK+ is an event-driven toolkit. The screen is built with *widgets* (windows, combo boxes, text boxes, buttons), and *callbacks* are set up on those widgets to perform processing based on signals, which are usually mouse- or keyboard-driven events. When a callback receives notification of a signal, the application responds to those signals with some processing. The concept of a signal is similar to an event in Java or Windows.

The GTK+ is a widget library that relies on the GIMP Drawing Kit (GDK), which is a wrapper around Xlib. The GTK+ calls the GIMP Drawing Kit for anything dealing with the display of the widgets. The GDK is supposed to be a platform-dependent Application Programming Interface (API) that sits on top of the native graphics API (Xlib, Win32) and provides a graphics API. Because GDK sits as a layer between Xlib and GTK+, GTK+ can be ported to other operating systems by changing the GDK (see Figure 3.1). Both GTK+ and GDK rely heavily on the GLIB library, which provides functions for handling many common data types like lists, trees, and strings, as well as memory allocation functions and error-handling routines. Both the GLIB and the GDK libraries can be called directly without going through the GTK+.

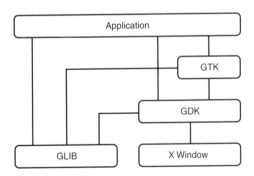

**Figure 3.1** GTK+ application layers.

# Building a GTK+ Application

To build a GTK+ application, each part of the application file that uses GTK+ function calls or definitions has to include the `gtk/gtk.h` file, which is the main include file for GTK+. In addition, you must link with a number of libraries. Fortunately, the people developing GTK+ made this task easy for you, using the gtk-config program. You can compile a simple GTK+ program with the following command line:

```
gcc -Wall -g example.c -o example 'gtk-config -cflags' 'gtk-config -libs'
```

The quotes around the `'gtk-config -cflags'` and the `'gtk-config -libs'` are single back quotes. In this example, example.c is the program you are compiling, and the `'gtk-config -cflags'` actually runs the gtk-config program, which outputs the compiler flags and puts them into the command line. The linker flags are output with `'gtk-config -libs'` and are also inserted into the command line. The gtk-config program is included with GTK+ and must be in your path. Typing `gtk-config -cflags` or `gtk-config -libs` at a Linux command prompt shows the exact parameters passed to the GNU C compiler (gcc).

## Initializing GTK+

Writing a GTK+ program requires the GTK+ library to be initialized with a call to `gtk_init` function. The arguments to the application (`argc`, `argv`) are passed into the `gtk_init` function and are parsed to look for one of the many GTK+ options that are primarily used for debugging. If any of the GTK+ parameters are found in the argument list, they are removed. They'll never be seen by the application after the `gtk_init` function returns.

```
/* --- Initalize GTK --- */
    gtk_init (&argc, &argv);
```

After GTK+ is initialized, the rest of the GTK+ library functions can be called.

## Creating Windows

A widget in GTK+ is a GUI component. Windows, check boxes, buttons, and edit fields are all widgets. Widgets and windows are always defined as pointers to a `GtkWidget` structure. The `GtkWidget` is a generic data type used by all widgets and windows in GTK+.

After the GTK+ library is initialized, most applications create a main window. In GTK+ the main window is usually called a *top-level window*. Top-level windows have no parent window, because they are not contained within any windows. In GTK+ widgets have what is called a parent/child relationship in which the parent widget is the container and the child widget is the widget within the container. Top-level windows do not have parent windows, but may be a parent for widgets.

Creating a widget in GTK+ is a two-step process in which the widget is created and then made visible. You can apply this technique to create a top-level window.

The gtk_window_new function is called with the GTK_WINDOW_TOPLEVEL parameter to create a new top-level window. The gtk_window_new function returns a pointer to a GtkWidget. The created window is not visible when created and should be made visible using the gtk_widget_show function.

```
/* --- Create a top-level window in gtk --- */
/* --- note the window is NOT visible yet --- */
window = gtk_window_new (GTK_WINDOW_TOPLEVEL);

/* --- Now, make the window visible --- */
gtk_widget_show (window);
```

## GTK+ Event Loop

After GTK+ is initialized and the windows and widgets placed on the screen, the application yields execution to GTK+ so the events (mouse movements, key presses, and so on) can be processed. The call to gtk_main does not return until the application makes a call to gtk_main_quit. But if gtk_main does not return, how can the application make a call to gtk_main_quit? In this case, before the call to gtk_main is made, callbacks should be created and set up with GTK+ so that certain signals return execution to the application for processing.

A GTK+ program can be quite small. For example, this basic GTK+ program should give you an idea about the flow of a GTK+ program. This program has no callbacks, so it will have to be killed.

```
#include <gtk/gtk.h>

int main (int argc, char *argv[])
{
    GtkWidget *window;

    /* --- Initialize gtk, handle command-line parameters --- */
    gtk_init (&argc, &argv);

    /* --- Create a window in gtk - note the window is NOT visible yet */
    window = gtk_window_new (GTK_WINDOW_TOPLEVEL);

    /* --- Now, make the window visible --- */
    gtk_widget_show (window);

    /* --- Main event loop in gtk.  We have no event handlers.  Oops  */
    gtk_main ();

    /* --- Exit status code --- */
    return 0;
}
```

Although the preceding example may be a GTK+ program, it is not an application because it has no useful function and does not exit when you try to close it. You need to add some callbacks before you can call it an application.

## GTK+ Data Types

Before you start adding events to make the small application more robust, you need a little information about GTK+ widget types. Widgets in GTK+ are usually derived from other widgets. The button widget (GtkButton) is derived from the container widget (GtkContainer), which is derived from the generic widget (GtkWidget), which is derived from a GTK+ object (GtkObject). All widget-creation functions return a pointer to a GtkWidget, which is a generic widget pointer and may need to be converted for specific widget functions. The reason for deriving one widget from another is simple: If a widget performs most of the functionality of another widget, why spend the time and effort to write a new widget? A much easier solution is to derive the new widget from an existing widget and add the necessary functionality.

Deriving widgets from each other seems to call out for the use of C++ in writing GTK+. C was chosen for GTK+ for several reasons. C is the primary language for developers on Linux. C is also more portable than C++ is and has been standardized longer. C++ is only now becoming standardized, and not all C++ compilers work on the same set of code. When GTK+ was started, C++ standardization was still a pipe dream. C++ has come a long way, but it still has some problems working across multiple compilers on multiple platforms. (There are a couple of projects to wrap GTK+ in a C++ library—visit the GTK+ Web page for more details.)

The GTK+ button-creation function returns a GtkWidget pointer, not a GtkButton function. This condition enables generic functions (like gtk_widget_show) to operate on all the widgets. The GtkWidget returned from the GTK+ button-creation function can be typecast to a GtkButton (using the GTK_BUTTON macro) for button-specific functions because it is a button. The same GtkWidget can also be typecast to a GtkContainer (using the GTK_CONTAINER macro) for container functions because the button is a container.

Although the button widget can be passed into one of the button-specific functions, the compiler complains if you pass it in as a widget. Proper GTK+ programming requires that the widget be typecast to the proper type before calling a widget function. Every widget has a conversion macro to typecast a GtkWidget to any other GTK+ widget type. A GtkWidget can be typecast to a GtkButton by using the GTK_BUTTON macro, but only if the GtkWidget can be typecast to a button, which means that the GtkWidget was created using the button-creation function or a widget derived from the button. The compiler won't complain, but the GTK+ library will complain when the program is run. The GTK+ functions check the type of the widget being passed in, so passing in a button to a container function works because a button is a container, but passing in a container to a button function fails because containers are not buttons. These error messages are dumped to the console and are very helpful in creating an error-free application.

## Signals and Callbacks

Signals are necessary in GUI-based programming because the program must be able to respond to the user. If the mouse moves, a button gets pressed, text is typed, or a window closes, a signal can be sent to an application callback function. The signal may be one that needs to be handled by the application. A word processor may have a button to make the font bold, and if the user presses that button, the code that makes the font bold needs to be called. Likewise, if the user closes the main window, some processing (saving files, cleanup) may need to occur before the window is closed.

Signals occur all the time in a GTK+ application, but most of the time the signals are ignored. Take the button widget as an example. The application has button-specific signals for when a user presses the mouse button, when a user releases the mouse button, when a user clicks on the mouse, when the mouse moves over the button, and when the mouse leaves the button. Other generic widget signals include one to signal when the mouse has moved.

In reality, the only signal worth listening for on the button widget is the "mouse clicked" signal. It is signaled when the user clicks on the button with the mouse. Most of the time, the application ignores the button's other events. It makes no sense to be notified each time the mouse is moving over the button or when the user releases the mouse button. Other widgets are similar to the button widget in that a minority of the signals are useful for the application developer, and a majority of the signals are ignored.

When a signal needs to be handled, the callback needs to be registered with GTK+ and associated with a widget. Widgets can register callbacks, and a callback can be registered with multiple widgets. Figure 3.2 illustrates the relationships between the application, GTK+, and the callback functions.

Figure 3.2 shows how signals are handled. Button5 has defined a callback that will be called when the signal occurs. Button8 has defined two different callbacks to listen to two separate signals. A widget is permitted to respond to as many signals as necessary, but it is a good idea to keep them to a minimum. When a signal occurs in a widget, the callback function for that signal in the widget is executed.

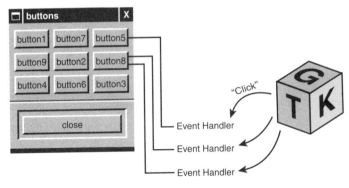

Figure 3.2    GTK+ signal execution.

## Adding Signal Handlers

Two basic signals under GTK+ are the `delete_event` and the `destroy` signal. The `delete_event` signal is sent when a window is going to be destroyed. The `destroy` signal is sent when the window is being destroyed. The top-level window should have a callback for the `delete_event` because it indicates that the user wants to shut down the application. Adding a callback for the `delete_event` signal involves two steps.

The first step is to write the callback, which this example calls `destroyapp`. The `destroyapp` function displays a message to the screen and exits out of the event loop by calling `gtk_main_quit`. The `gtk_main_quit` function must be called to break out of the application. If the top-level window closes without exiting out of the event loop, the program is actually still running processing events, which is why the previous program had to be killed. The `delete_event` callback should return a Boolean value that indicates whether the window should be prevented from closing. Returning a TRUE value keeps the window open. Returning a FALSE value means that the window can be closed. If the window can be closed, then the `destroy` signal is emitted to tell the application that the window is being destroyed.

The second step is to register the event handler with GTK+, using the `gtk_signal_connect` function. The `gtk_signal_connect` function has four parameters. The parameters tell GTK+ which widget the callback is for, which signal is being handled by the callback, the function to be used as the callback when the signal is sent, and any additional parameters to be passed in when the signal handler is called.

```
/* --- Call destroyapp when the window gets "delete_event" signal --- */
gtk_signal_connect (GTK_OBJECT (window), "delete_event",
          GTK_SIGNAL_FUNC (destroyapp), NULL);
```

Notice that the window is being typecast using `GTK_OBJECT` during the call to `gtk_signal_connect`. The `gtk_signal_connect` expects a `GtkObject` to be passed in, and because `GtkWindow` was derived from the `GtkObject` in the widget hierarchy, `GtkWindow` can be typecast to the `GtkObject`.

This code can be interpreted as follows: If the `delete_event` occurs on the widget `window`, then call the function `destroyapp` with the fourth parameter (`NULL`).

Here is the whole program with the event handler added:

```
#include <gtk/gtk.h>

gint destroyapp (GtkWidget *widget, gpointer gdata)
{
    g_print ("Quitting...\n");
    gtk_main_quit ();

    /* --- Ok to be closed.  TRUE would prevent window --- */
    /* --- from closing --- */
    return (FALSE);
}
```

```
int main (int argc, char *argv[])
{
    GtkWidget *window;

    /* --- Initialize gtk, handle command-line parameters --- */
    gtk_init (&argc, &argv);

    /* --- Create a window in gtk - note the window is NOT visible yet */
    window = gtk_window_new (GTK_WINDOW_TOPLEVEL);

    /* --- Call destroyapp when the window gets a "delete_event" signal */
    gtk_signal_connect (GTK_OBJECT (Window), "delete_event",
                GTK_SIGNAL_FUNC (destroyapp), NULL);

    /* --- Now, make the window visible --- */
    gtk_widget_show (window);

    /* --- This is the event loop in gtk --- */
    /* --- Do not return until _gtk_main_quit_ is called --- */
    gtk_main ();

    /* --- Exit status code --- */
    return 0;
}
```

Notice that when the window is destroyed, the message Quitting... is displayed on the console from which the application was started. The message gets displayed because of the callback. The gtk_main function call sits in a loop, processing events until you try to close the window. When you try to close the window, the destroyapp function is called to notify the application about the delete_event signal that was registered using the gtk_signal_connect. The destroyapp function, knowing that closing the main window should end the application, calls the gtk_main_quit function that terminates the gtk_main loop that was started in the application. The program becomes a simple and well-behaved GTK+ application. In the earlier program, the delete_event signal was being generated, but the application didn't have an event handler to process it. This time the signal is handled by the callback, and the application exits cleanly.

# Adding Widgets

A plain-vanilla window without menus or controls might be an application, but it is hardly a useful application. You can start writing an application by adding functionality to the plain window created earlier; in this case, you can add a widget to the window. Because the top-level window that gets created is also a container, widgets can be placed within it. You can use the `gtk_button_new_with_label` function to create the button and use the `gtk_container_add` function to place the button within the window. Note that both the top-level window and the button must be made visible with the `gtk_widget_show` function. The button also has to go through the additional step of being added to a container. The button is not visible on the screen until it has been added to a container, even though it has been created and made visible. Widgets need to be a top-level window (with no parent), or they must be in a visible parent to be seen. The `gtk_container_add` function sets the parent/child relationship between the top-level window and the button and places the widget in the window. You can also add an event handler to the button to process the `clicked` event so that every time the button is pressed, the `button_was_clicked` function is called to display a message to the console. Figure 3.3 shows a button that prints out a message each time the button is pressed.

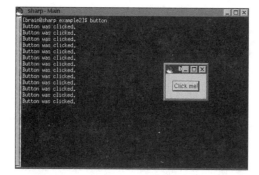

**Figure 3.3**    Simple events in a GTK+ button.

```
#include <gtk/gtk.h>

gint CloseAppWindow (GtkWidget *widget, gpointer gdata)
{
    g_print ("Quitting...\n");
    gtk_main_quit ();

    /* --- Continue closing --- */
    return (FALSE);
}

/*
 * button_was_clicked
```

```
 *
 * event handler called when the button is clicked.
 */
void button_was_clicked (GtkWidget *widget, gpointer gdata)
{
    g_print ("Button was clicked.\n");
}

int main (int argc, char *argv[])
{
    GtkWidget *window;
    GtkWidget *button;

    /* --- Initialize gtk, handle command-line parameters --- */
    gtk_init (&argc, &argv);

    /* --- Create a window in gtk - note the window is NOT visible yet */
    window = gtk_window_new (GTK_WINDOW_TOPLEVEL);

    /* --- Clean up code when the application exits --- */
    gtk_signal_connect (GTK_OBJECT (window), "delete_event",
                GTK_SIGNAL_FUNC (destroy), NULL);


    /* --- Put some breathing room around the objects in the container */
    gtk_container_border_width (GTK_CONTAINER (window), 15);

    /* --- Create a button --- */
    button = gtk_button_new_with_label ("Click me");

    /* --- Give the button an event handler - it'll call the function  */
    /* --- button_was_clicked when the button is clicked --- */
    gtk_signal_connect (GTK_OBJECT (button),
                        "clicked",
                        GTK_SIGNAL_FUNC (button_was_clicked),
                        NULL);

    /* --- The main window contains the button --- */
    gtk_container_add (GTK_CONTAINER (window), button);

    /* --- Make the button visible --- */
    gtk_widget_show (button);

    /* --- Now, make the window visible --- */
```

```
    gtk_widget_show (window);

    /* --- This is the event loop in gtk.  Do not return until "quit"  */
    gtk_main ();

    /* --- Exit status code --- */
    return 0;
}
```

Widgets are added to a window in several steps. The first step is to create the widget and get the `GtkWidget` pointer.

The second step is to set callbacks for the widget. Some widgets cannot have callbacks (like the label), and some widgets might not need to have callbacks on them, but many widgets have callbacks to interact with the user.

The third step is to set the widget's properties, for example, making a label left-justified or setting the label on a button. Sometimes, the properties can be set in the widget-creation function. For instance, a button can be created with the `gtk_button_new` function, or it can be created with a label using the `gtk_button_new_with_label`. The `gtk_button_new_with_label` is easier than creating the button and creating a label and adding the label to the button just to set the label on the button.

The fourth step is to add the widget to a container. Unless the widget is a top-level widget, it needs to be added to a visible container before it can be displayed.

The final step is to make the widget visible. Making the widget visible does not have to be the final step, but it usually is because modifying the properties of windows when they are visible causes annoying flashing to occur, especially on slower machines that cannot paint the screen quickly.

## Multiple Event Handlers

In many situations, a widget requires multiple event handlers to handle different events. The additional code is merely an extension of the existing code. This section extends the previous button example and adds event handlers for when the mouse moves onto the button and when the mouse leaves the button. The event handlers are going to print text on the console, depending on whether the mouse is moving on or off the button. The event handlers need to be created to handle the mouse entering and leaving the button.

```
    /*
     * button_entered
     *
     * Called when the mouse moves over the widget after not having
     * been on the widget.
     */
    void button_enter (GtkWidget *widget, gpointer gdata)
    {
        g_print ("Welcome to fantasy button\n");
```

```
}

/*
 * button_leave
 *
 * Called when the mouse moves off the widget.
 */
void button_leave (GtkWidget *widget, gpointer gdata)
{
    g_print ("Hey!  Where are you going?\n");
}
```

After the callbacks are written, they need to be registered with GTK+ so they will be called when the signals occur. You can use the `gtk_signal_connect` function to register the callbacks to the signals on the widgets. The `enter` event signals that the mouse has moved over the button, and the `leave` event signals that the mouse has left the button. By assigning these two events to functions, you can create a button that responds to three different events.

```
/* --- Give the button an event handler - it'll call the function ---*/
/* --- button_enter when the mouse moves over the button --- */
gtk_signal_connect (GTK_OBJECT (button),
                    "enter",
                    GTK_SIGNAL_FUNC (button_enter),
                    NULL);

/* --- Give the button an event handler - it'll call the function ---*/
/* --- button_leave when the button moves off the button --- */
gtk_signal_connect (GTK_OBJECT (button),
                    "leave",
                    GTK_SIGNAL_FUNC (button_leave),
                    NULL);
```

The button now has three callback functions, each handling different signals from GTK+ and displaying a message depending on the signal. You can see how the signals are sent and how the callbacks respond to each of the signals by moving the mouse over the button and clicking on the button.

## Containers

You've already seen how a top-level window is a container and that a widget can be placed within it. You might be surprised to learn that many widgets are containers. Because a button is a container, other widgets can be placed inside a button widget. In fact, when you create the button widget with a label, using the `gtk_create_button_with_label` function, the button widget has a label widget inside it.

The following restriction applies to containers in GTK+: The containers can have only one child widget, which is why, if you modify the earlier example to add two buttons into the parent window, only the first button is visible. A way around this restriction is to use packing widgets.

## Packing Boxes

Multiple widgets can be added to containers using packing widgets, which are also called packing boxes. Unlike button widgets, packing widgets are not visible on the screen; in fact, they are invisible containers that keep track of several child widgets at a time. The vertical packing box stacks widgets vertically, and the horizontal packing box stacks widgets horizontally. Vertical packing boxes are created with the gtk_vbox_new function, and horizontal packing boxes are created with the gtk_hbox_new function. After they are created, widgets can be added into the packing box using the gtk_box_pack_start function or the gtk_box_pack_end function. The gtk_box_pack_start function puts the widgets into the packing box at the top (for a vertical packing box) or at the left (for a horizontal packing box). The gtk_box_pack_end function puts the widgets at the bottom (for a vertical packing box) or on the right (for a horizontal packing box). For the widgets to be displayed, they must be added to the packing box and the packing box must be added to a container, effectively giving the container the ability to hold many widgets. The container and the packing box must be made visible, even though the packing box does not have any visible components. The visibility affects the widgets added to the container. Figure 3.4 shows buttons placed in vertical and horizontal packing boxes.

**Figure 3.4**    Vertical and horizontal packing boxes at work.

The functions that create packing boxes have two parameters that determine how the packing boxes will look on the screen.

```
/* --- Create a horizontal packing box --- */
hbox = gtk_hbox_new (bHomogeneous, nSpacing);

/* --- Create a vertical packing box --- */
vbox = gtk_vbox_new (bHomogeneous, nSpacing);
```

The first parameter, called `homogeneous`, determines whether all the widgets added have the same size area reserved on the screen for their use. For example, if you created five buttons on a horizontal packing box and they had labels of `fred`, `joe`, `sue`, `karen`, and `Bartholomew the Great`, a nonhomogeneous packing box would create the five buttons as big as they needed to be to fit the text in the button. A homogenous packing style would calculate the size of the largest widget (I think you can guess which one) and allocate that much space for each button whether or not the button uses the entire space. The second parameter, `spacing`, determines how much space to leave between the packed boxes as they're inserted into the packing box. Setting the spacing to `zero` leaves no extra space between the widgets as they're inserted.

The `gtk_box_pack_start` function has three parameters that determine how the individual widgets are placed in the packing boxes.

```
gtk_box_pack_start (box, widget, expand, fill, padding);
```

The `expand` flag indicates whether the box around the widgets can be expanded to fill any remaining space after all the widgets have been added to the packing box. The `expand` flag is ignored if the box was created with the `homogeneous` flag set because the homogenous flag indicates that the widgets should use an equal amount of space within the packing box.

The `fill` flag determines whether any extra space around the particular widget should be used up by the widget. Setting this flag to `TRUE` allows the widget to grow a bit bigger to fill in the entire space allocated to it by the packing box. Setting this flag to `FALSE` forces the widget to use only the space it needs, and the extra space surrounds the widget.

The `padding` flag indicates how many pixels of padding should surround the widget. Most of the time, this value is `zero`.

This example shows a window with a vertical packing box filled with five buttons. The code to create and add the button has been consolidated into a single function called `PackNewButton` to simplify the code.

```
/*
 * packbox.c
 *
 * Program illustrating the difference between vertically packed boxes
 * and horizontally packed boxes by displaying two windows each with
 * their own packing.
 */

#include <gtk/gtk.h>

/*
 * PackNewButton
 *
 * Creates a button, packs it into the box provided and makes the
 * button visible.
```

```
 *
 * box - packing box to add the button to.
 * szLabel - label the button will be created with.
 * returns - button widget that was created.
 */
GtkWidget *PackNewButton (GtkWidget *box, char *szLabel)
{

    GtkWidget *button;

    /* --- Create a new button --- */
    button = gtk_button_new_with_label (szLabel);

    /* --- Pack the button into the box --- */
    gtk_box_pack_start (GTK_BOX (box), button, FALSE, FALSE, 0);

    /* --- Show the button --- */
    gtk_widget_show (button);

    return (button);
}


/*
 * delete_event
 *
 * Handle closing of window properly by ending gtk
 */
gint Delete (GtkWidget *widget, gpointer *data)
{
    gtk_main_quit ();

    /* --- Continue closing --- */
    return (FALSE);
}



int main (int argc, char *argv[])
{
    GList *cbitems = NULL;
    GtkWidget *window;
    GtkWidget *button;
    GtkWidget *box;

    /* --- GTK initialization --- */
    gtk_init (&argc, &argv);
```

```
/* -------------------------------------- */
/* --- Create the vertically packed box. --- */
/* -------------------------------------- */

/* --- Create the top-level window --- */
window = gtk_window_new (GTK_WINDOW_TOPLEVEL);

/* --- Give window a title --- */
gtk_window_set_title (GTK_WINDOW (window),
                        "Vertical box packing");

/* --- Want to know when the window closes --- */
/* --- to the main window --- */
gtk_signal_connect (GTK_OBJECT (window), "delete_event",
                    GTK_SIGNAL_FUNC (Delete), NULL);

/* --- Give the window a border --- */
gtk_container_border_width (GTK_CONTAINER (window), 50);

/* --- We create a vertical box to pack the buttons --- */
box = gtk_vbox_new (FALSE, 0);

/* --- Create the buttons --- */
button = PackNewButton (box, "Button1");
button = PackNewButton (box, "Button2");
button = PackNewButton (box, "Button3");
button = PackNewButton (box, "Button4");
button = PackNewButton (box, "Button5");

/* --- Make the main window visible --- */
gtk_container_add (GTK_CONTAINER (window), box);
gtk_widget_show (box);
gtk_widget_show (window);

/* -------------------------------------- */
/* --- Create a horizontally packed box. --- */
/* -------------------------------------- */

/* --- Create the top-level window --- */
window = gtk_window_new (GTK_WINDOW_TOPLEVEL);

/* --- Give the window a title --- */
gtk_window_set_title (GTK_WINDOW (window), "Horizontal box packing");

/* --- Give the window a border --- */
gtk_container_border_width (GTK_CONTAINER (window), 50);
```

```
/* --- We create a horizontal box to pack the buttons --- */
box = gtk_hbox_new (FALSE, 0);

/* --- Create the buttons --- */
button = PackNewButton (box, "Button1");
button = PackNewButton (box, "Button2");
button = PackNewButton (box, "Button3");
button = PackNewButton (box, "Button4");
button = PackNewButton (box, "Button5");

/* --- Make the main window visible --- */
gtk_container_add (GTK_CONTAINER (window), box);
gtk_widget_show (box);
gtk_widget_show (window);

/* --- Start the event loop --- */
gtk_main ();

exit (0);
}
```

Packing boxes can also be put into other packing boxes to create a screen full of
widgets that are more than just a group of widgets vertically or horizontally. Usually, a
row of widgets is placed in a horizontal packing box, and the horizontal packing box
is placed with other horizontal packing boxes into a vertical packing box. This process
creates several rows of horizontal packing boxes that contain widgets that can be used
to organize a screen.

## Packing Tables

Packing tables are like packing boxes in that they allow you to put multiple widgets
into a window, but packing boxes give you two-dimensional control over the placement of the widgets. Packing tables are like HTML tables: You can control the placement of an item by row and column, and objects can take up multiple rows or
columns. The function to create a packing table looks like this:

```
table = gtk_table_new (rows, columns, homogeneous);
```

The first two arguments are the number of rows and columns to make the table. The
number of rows and columns have to be known at table creation. The third argument,
homogeneous, has the same effect it had on packing boxes: If the homogenous flag is set to
TRUE when the table is created, the table boxes within the table are sized to be the size of
the largest widget in the table. If the homogeneous flag is set to FALSE, then the width of
each column would be set to the width of the largest widget in the column and the
height of each row would be set to the height of the largest widget in that row.

The columns are laid out from 0...columns–1, and the rows are laid out from 0...rows–1.

When the widgets are added, each widget is going to provide a starting column, an ending column, a starting row, and an ending row. If a widget is going to be placed in the top-left corner of the table, the column range would be 0 to 1 and the row range would also be 0 to 1. The xpadding and ypadding indicate how many pixels to pad around the widget.

The two functions used to add widgets to a packing table are

```
gtk_table_attach (table,
                  child,
                  left_attach,
                  right_attach,
                  top_attach,
                  bottom_attach,
                  xoptions,
                  yoptions,
                  xpadding,
                  ypadding);

gtk_table_attach_defaults (table,
                           widget
                           left_attach,
                           right_attach,
                           top_attach,
                           bottom_attach);
```

Both functions add widgets to a table. The gtk_table_attach_defaults function takes fewer parameters, and defaults the padding and options that gtk_table_attach uses. For the gtk_table_attach_defaults function, the xpadding and ypadding default to zero while the xoptions and yoptions default to (GTK_FILL ¦ GTK_EXPAND). The next program shows the difference between the different options using a 4-by-4 table (see Figure 3.5). Each window has the buttons placed on it, using one of the possible flag settings. When the windows are resized, the widgets are repainted, according to the flags that were used to add the widgets to the windows.

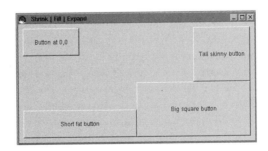

**Figure 3.5** Packing table options.

The xoptions and yoptions can GTK_FILL, GTK_SHRINK, GTK_EXPAND, or any combination of the three. The GTK_FILL flag indicates that the widget should expand to use
all the room allocated to it. The GTK_SHRINK allows the widget to shrink to a smaller
space than was originally allocated to it. The GTK_EXPAND flag causes the table to
expand to fill all the space in the window where it was inserted.

In the program, the button in the top-left corner occupies one square in the table
(0-1, 0-1), the top-right and bottom-left buttons occupy two squares, and the button
in the bottom-right corner occupies four squares. You can see the effect of the attributes by changing the size of the windows. All the window-creation code has been
placed in the CreateTable function.

```
/*
 * packtable
 *
 * Illustration of how to pack tables.
 *
 */

#include <gtk/gtk.h>

/*
 * Destroy
 *
 * Called when the main window is being closed.  Gives us the
 * opportunity to exit from the call to gtk_main ()
 */
gint Delete (GtkWidget *widget, gpointer data)
{
    gtk_main_quit ();

    /* --- Continue closing --- */
    return (FALSE);
}


/*
 * CreateTable
 *
 * Creates a top-level window with several options.  Since
 * this is going to be done many times, it's best just made
 * into a function.
 */
CreateTable (char *szTitle, gint xoptions, gint yoptions)
{
    GtkWidget *window;
    GtkWidget *button;
    GtkWidget *table;
```

```
/* --- Create the top-level window --- */
window = gtk_window_new (GTK_WINDOW_TOPLEVEL);

/* --- Give the window a title --- */
gtk_window_set_title (GTK_WINDOW (window), szTitle);

/* --- You should always remember to connect the destroy event --- */
/* --- to the main window.  Note: if any top-level window is --- */
/* --- closed, we'll shut the whole program down --- */
gtk_signal_connect (GTK_OBJECT (window), "delete_event",
                    GTK_SIGNAL_FUNC (Delete), NULL);

/* --- Give the window a border --- */
gtk_container_border_width (GTK_CONTAINER (window), 10);

/* --- Create a 4x4 table --- */
table = gtk_table_new (4, 4, TRUE);

/* --- Add a 1x1 button at 0, 0 --- */
button = gtk_button_new_with_label ("Button at 0,0");
gtk_table_attach (GTK_TABLE (table), button, 0, 1, 0, 1,
                  xoptions, yoptions, 0, 0);
gtk_widget_show (button);

/* --- Add a 2x2 button at 2-4, 2-4 --- */
button = gtk_button_new_with_label ("Big square button");
gtk_table_attach (GTK_TABLE (table), button, 2, 4, 2, 4,
                  xoptions, yoptions, 0, 0);
gtk_widget_show (button);

/* --- Add a 2x1 short wide button --- */
button = gtk_button_new_with_label ("Short fat button");
gtk_table_attach (GTK_TABLE (table), button, 0, 2, 3, 4,
                  xoptions, yoptions, 0, 0);
gtk_widget_show (button);

/* --- Add a 1x2 tall skinny button --- */
button = gtk_button_new_with_label ("Tall skinny button");
gtk_table_attach (GTK_TABLE (table), button, 3, 4, 0, 2,
                  xoptions, yoptions, 0, 0);

/* --- Make the button visible --- */
gtk_widget_show (button);

/* --- Add the table to the window --- */
gtk_container_add (GTK_CONTAINER (window), table);
```

```
    /* --- Make the table visible --- */
    gtk_widget_show (table);

    /* --- Make the window visible --- */
    gtk_widget_show (window);
}


/*
 * --- Main.
 *
 * Program begins here.
 *
 * Rather than duplicate code, the CreateTable function is
 * called.  It does the work for us - all we do is pass in
 * how we want the window to appear.
 */
int main (int argc, char *argv[])
{

    /* --- GTK initialization --- */
    gtk_init (&argc, &argv);

    /* --- No flags set --- */
    CreateTable ("Nothing", 0, 0);

    /* --- Start showing windows with flags --- */
    CreateTable ("Fill", GTK_FILL, GTK_FILL);

    CreateTable ("Shrink", GTK_SHRINK, GTK_SHRINK);

    CreateTable ("Expand",
                GTK_EXPAND,
                GTK_EXPAND);

    CreateTable ("Expand ¦ Shrink",
                GTK_EXPAND ¦ GTK_SHRINK,
                GTK_EXPAND ¦ GTK_SHRINK);

    CreateTable ("Fill ¦ Expand",
                GTK_EXPAND ¦ GTK_FILL,
                GTK_EXPAND ¦ GTK_FILL);

    CreateTable ("Shrink ¦ Fill",
                GTK_SHRINK ¦ GTK_FILL,
                GTK_SHRINK ¦ GTK_FILL);
```

```
        CreateTable ("Shrink ¦ Fill ¦ Expand",
                    GTK_EXPAND ¦ GTK_SHRINK ¦ GTK_FILL,
                    GTK_EXPAND ¦ GTK_SHRINK ¦ GTK_FILL);

        /* --- Start the gtk loop --- */
        gtk_main ();

        return (0);
}
```

## Summary

This chapter covered the basics of GTK+ programming, including writing a simple application that demonstrates a bit of the structure of GTK+ programming. The basics of GTK+ events and widgets were also covered, as well as some of the GTK+ data types. This information provides the foundation for the next chapter—"Basic Widgets."

4

# Basic Widgets

**B**UILDING APPLICATIONS REQUIRES THE USE of many different widgets. The most common widgets used are the button widgets, the entry field widget, the list box widget, and the combo box widget. These widgets make up a large percentage of the widgets in applications, and understanding these basic widgets is important to understanding the more complicated widgets. In reality, most widgets are very similar. Many are just containers for other widgets with properties that are particular to the widget; they also have common properties and functions that can be used to manipulate the widgets.

## Common Widget Functions

All button-creation functions return a pointer to a `GtkWidget`. The `GtkWidget` pointer can call generic functions that act on the widgets. One example of a generic function is the `gtk_widget_show` function. This function makes a widget visible or, at least, sets the visible attributes so that the widget can be seen on the screen if it's within a visible parent. Many other functions also act on all widgets. Some, like `gtk_widget_show`, are used more frequently than others.

## Casting Widgets

Because the widget created is a generic widget, it has to be converted to the correct type for more specific widget function calls. Creating a button widget returns a GtkWidget pointer, but the button-specific routines require a GtkButton pointer. The generic GtkWidget pointer has to be converted to a GtkButton pointer, by using the GTK_BUTTON macro, before a button function is called. By insisting that the types passed in match the types expected by the routines, this requirement helps the developer write a better program.

### Bad Casting

Only a poorly written program would pass a text widget into a function that expected a button widget. By forcing the conversion to be made, any errors in converting the widget will be reported. For instance, here is a sample piece of code to create a button widget and convert it to a text widget:

```
/* --- Create a button widget --- */
button = gtk_button_new_with_label ("Button");

/* --- Try and convert the button to a text widget --- */
text = GTK_TEXT (button);
```

If this section of code is placed in a program, it will compile cleanly because the conversion check occurs at runtime. However, running the program results in this message:

```
** WARNING **: invalid cast from "GtkButton" to "GtkText"
```

These messages should not exist. If they appear, it is usually the result of a developer error.

### Good Casting

Widgets are usually derived from other widgets. The button widget is derived from the container widget (GtkContainer) which is in turn derived from the generic widget (GtkWidget). Because of this relationship, button widgets (GtkButton) can be typecast to container widgets (GtkContainer) to use container functions. You already used the gtk_container_add function to add widgets to containers. You can also use this function to take a button widget and add a label to the button. Of course, to use the gtk_container_add function, the button must be typecast to a GtkContainer, which is possible because the GtkButton is also a GtkContainer. A widget can be cast to any type of widget within its superclass hierarchy.

```
/* --- Create a button without a label --- */
button = gtk_button_new ();

/* --- Create a label --- */
label = gtk_label_new ("Blah");
```

```
/* --- Add the label to the button --- */
gtk_container_add (GTK_CONTAINER (button), label);
```

Each widget has its own set of signals for which the developer can create a callback. The number of signals that each widget has associated with it depends on the complexity of the widget, but in general very few signals need to be handled within an application. The button widget is a good example of this. Although the button widget has many signals associated with it, the only one usually worth putting an event handler on is the "clicked" event. It's not that the other events are never used; it's more that they *usually* aren't used. Events can also be inherited, and you can see this characteristic when you look at some of the widgets that are inherited from the button widget.

# Push Buttons

Push buttons (GtkButton) are one of the simplest widgets available because their only function is to allow a user to click them. In a dialog, they usually display such text as OK or Cancel. The most important event to a push button is the "clicked" event, which indicates that the button has been clicked by the mouse. The "clicked" event is a combination of the button being pressed and released in a single motion. Usually, the button click causes some action to be performed, whether it is to save a file or get rid of the dialog. See Figure 4.1 for an example of a button.

Buttons are derived from containers (GtkContainer), so they share many characteristics of containers. An important characteristic is the capability to hold another widget. The text inside a GtkButton is really a label widget placed inside the button. A toolbar can be created from a row of buttons with images inside each button to display the function to the user. What appeared at first as a boring widget, now is seen as a very flexible widget—so flexible that other widgets actually derive themselves from the GtkButton widget.

The button can be created with or without text. The gtk_button_new_with_label function creates a button with a string caption. The gtk_button_new function creates a button with no child widget. This function can be useful if you want to create a button with a picture on it. Because you don't need the label, you can use the gtk_button_new function to create the button and add the picture to the button. The functions return a pointer to a GtkWidget, which can be converted to a GtkButton by using the GTK_BUTTON macro.

**Figure 4.1**   Push button.

Button widgets can emit several signals, but developers usually ignore most signals except for the "clicked" signal. The button signals are

| Signal | Action |
|---|---|
| pressed | The button was pressed down. |
| released | The button was released. |
| clicked | The button was clicked. This is a combination of "pressed" and "released". |
| enter | The mouse has moved over the button. |
| leave | The mouse has left the button. |

The events can be caused by a user action or simulated using one of the functions to signal an event. The signaling functions are not usually used.

| Signal | Function to Create Signal |
|---|---|
| pressed | gtk_button_pressed (button) |
| released | gtk_button_released (button) |
| clicked | gtk_button_clicked (button) |
| enter | gtk_button_enter (button) |
| leave | gtk_button_leave (button) |

This short program creates a window with a button in it and displays each of the button signals on the console as they occur.

```
/*
 * button.c
 *
 * Example showing button behavior
 */

#include <gtk/gtk.h>

/*
 * Destroy
 *
 * The app is closing down.  Need to shut down gtk.
 */
gint CloseAppWindow (GtkWidget *widget, gpointer *data)
{
    gtk_main_quit ();

    /* --- Ok to close --- */
    return (FALSE);
}
```

```
/*
 * button_event
 *
 * Some event happened and the name is passed in the
 * data field.
 */
void button_event (GtkWidget *widget, gpointer *data)
{
    g_print ("Button event: %s\n", data);
}
int main (int argc, char *argv[])
{
    GtkWidget *window;
    GtkWidget *button;

    /* --- GTK initialization --- */
    gtk_init (&argc, &argv);

    /* --- Create the top-level window --- */
    window = gtk_window_new (GTK_WINDOW_TOPLEVEL);

    gtk_window_set_title (GTK_WINDOW (window), "Push Button");

    /* You should always remember to connect the delete_event
     * to the main window
     */
    gtk_signal_connect (GTK_OBJECT (window), "delete_event",
                        GTK_SIGNAL_FUNC (CloseAppWindow), NULL);

    /* --- Give the window a border --- */
    gtk_container_border_width (GTK_CONTAINER (window), 50);

    /* --------------------- */
    /* --- Create a button --- */
    /* --------------------- */

    /* --- Create a new button --- */
    button = gtk_button_new_with_label ("Button");

    /* --- Show the button (it's not visible yet, though) --- */
    gtk_widget_show (button);

    /* ---------------------------- */
    /* --- Register event handlers --- */
    /* ---------------------------- */
    gtk_signal_connect (GTK_OBJECT (button), "pressed",
```

```
                            GTK_SIGNAL_FUNC (button_event), "pressed");
    gtk_signal_connect (GTK_OBJECT (button), "released",
                            GTK_SIGNAL_FUNC (button_event), "released");
    gtk_signal_connect (GTK_OBJECT (button), "clicked",
                            GTK_SIGNAL_FUNC (button_event), "clicked");
    gtk_signal_connect (GTK_OBJECT (button), "enter",
                            GTK_SIGNAL_FUNC (button_event), "enter");
    gtk_signal_connect (GTK_OBJECT (button), "leave",
                            GTK_SIGNAL_FUNC (button_event), "leave");

    /* --- Add the button to the window --- */
    gtk_container_add (GTK_CONTAINER (window), button);

    /*
    *--- Make the main window visible, now the button
    *    will be made visible.
    */
    gtk_widget_show (window);

    gtk_main ();
    return (0);
}
```

# Toggle Buttons

Toggle buttons (GtkToggleButton) are derived from the GtkButton and are similar in appearance to GtkButtons but behave in a slightly different fashion. Toggle buttons have a state associated with them, which can be up or down, and the appearance of the toggle button reflects its state. At first the toggle button looks like a normal button, but if the button is pressed, it stays down. The toggle button requires another press to pop back up. Figure 4.2 shows a toggle button in the up and down states.

You can create toggle buttons with a label by using the gtk_toggle_button_new_with_label function or without a label by using the gtk_toggle_button_new function. Because the toggle button is derived from a normal button, all the events and functions that can be used on a normal button can also be used on the toggle button if you use the GTK_BUTTON macro to typecast the toggle button.

The toggle button has a new signal added to those derived from the GtkButton. The "toggled" signal is sent when the state of the button changes. The state of the button can be set using the gtk_toggle_button_set_state function and passing in the state that the button should be in. The gtk_toggle_button_toggled function changes the state of the button. Functions that change the state of the button may also signal to be sent to the application. For instance, if the gtk_toggle_button_set_state function sets the state of the button to TRUE and the button is currently in the FALSE state, the "clicked" signal and the "toggled" signal would be sent to the application.

**Figure 4.2**    Toggle button.

```
/*
 * togglebutton.c
 *
 * Example showing toggle button behavior
 */

#include <gtk/gtk.h>

/*
 * Destroy
 *
 * main window closing, end gtk
 */
gint CloseAppWindow (GtkWidget *widget, gpointer *data)
{
    gtk_main_quit ();

    /* --- Ok to close --- */
    return (FALSE);
}


    /* --- Event happened --- */

void ButtonEvent (GtkWidget *widget, button_event gpointer *data)
{
    g_print ("Button event: %s\n", data);
}


int main (int argc, char *argv[])
{
    GtkWidget *window;
    GtkWidget *button;
    GtkWidget *vbox;

    /* --- GTK initialization --- */
    gtk_init (&argc, &argv);
```

```
/* --- Create the top-level window --- */
window = gtk_window_new (GTK_WINDOW_TOPLEVEL);

gtk_window_set_title (GTK_WINDOW (window), "Toggle Button");

/* --- You should always remember to connect the destroy event --- */
/*     to the main window --- */
gtk_signal_connect (GTK_OBJECT (window), "delete_event",
                    GTK_SIGNAL_FUNC (CloseAppWindow), NULL);

/* --- Give the window a border --- */
gtk_container_border_width (GTK_CONTAINER (window), 50);

/* We create a vertical box (vbox) to pack the horizontal boxes into.
vbox = gtk_vbox_new (FALSE, 0);

/* ---------------------- */
/* --- Create a button --- */
/* ---------------------- */

/* --- Create a new button --- */
button = gtk_toggle_button_new_with_label ("Top Toggle Button");

/* --- Pack the button into the vertical box (vbox box1) --- */
gtk_box_pack_start (GTK_BOX (vbox), button, FALSE, FALSE, 0);

/* --- Show the button --- */
gtk_widget_show (button);

gtk_signal_connect (GTK_OBJECT (button), "toggled",
                    GTK_SIGNAL_FUNC (ButtonEvent), "top toggled");
gtk_signal_connect (GTK_OBJECT (button), "pressed",
                    GTK_SIGNAL_FUNC (ButtonEvent), "top pressed");
gtk_signal_connect (GTK_OBJECT (button), "released",
                    GTK_SIGNAL_FUNC (ButtonEvent), "top released");
gtk_signal_connect (GTK_OBJECT (button), "clicked",
                    GTK_SIGNAL_FUNC (ButtonEvent), "top clicked");
gtk_signal_connect (GTK_OBJECT (button), "enter",
                    GTK_SIGNAL_FUNC (ButtonEvent), "top enter");
gtk_signal_connect (GTK_OBJECT (button), "leave",
                    GTK_SIGNAL_FUNC (ButtonEvent), "top leave");

/* --------------------------- */
/* --- Create another button --- */
/* --------------------------- */

/* --- Create a new button --- */
```

```
    button = gtk_toggle_button_new_with_label ("Bottom Toggle Button");

    /* --- Pack the button into the vertical box (vbox box1) --- */
    gtk_box_pack_start (GTK_BOX (vbox), button, FALSE, FALSE, 0);

    /* --- Show the button --- */
    gtk_widget_show (button);

    gtk_signal_connect (GTK_OBJECT (button), "toggled",
                        GTK_SIGNAL_FUNC (ButtonEvent), "bottom toggled");
    gtk_signal_connect (GTK_OBJECT (button), "pressed",
                        GTK_SIGNAL_FUNC (ButtonEvent), "bottom pressed");
    gtk_signal_connect (GTK_OBJECT (button), "released",
                        GTK_SIGNAL_FUNC (ButtonEvent), "bottom
                        ➥released");
    gtk_signal_connect (GTK_OBJECT (button), "clicked",
                        GTK_SIGNAL_FUNC (ButtonEvent), "bottom clicked");
    gtk_signal_connect (GTK_OBJECT (button), "enter",
                        GTK_SIGNAL_FUNC (ButtonEvent), "bottom enter");
    gtk_signal_connect (GTK_OBJECT (button), "leave",
                        GTK_SIGNAL_FUNC (ButtonEvent), "bottom leave");

    /* --------------------------------- */
    /*--- Make the main window visible --- */
    /*--------------------------------- */

    gtk_container_add (GTK_CONTAINER (window), vbox);
    gtk_widget_show (vbox);
    gtk_widget_show (window);

    gtk_main ();
    return (0);
}
```

# Check Buttons

The check button (GtkCheckButton) is derived from the GtkToggleButton, so most of
the behavior of the GtkCheckButton is similar to the GtkToggleButton. The only difference between the GtkCheckButton and the GtkToggleButton is the way the button is
displayed on the screen (see Figure 4.3). Functionally, both widgets can display text to
describe the widget, and they can both display the state of the widget, but they display
the state in different ways. The GtkToggleButton displays the widget text within the
toggle button, whereas the GtkCheckButton displays the text to the right of a small
button. The buttons perform the same function, so choosing to use one button over
the other is usually a matter of user preference.

**Figure 4.3**   `GtkCheckButton`.

The `GtkCheckButton` can be created with a label by using the `gtk_check_button_new_with_label` function or without a label by using the `gtk_check_button_new` function. Because the `GtkCheckButton` was derived from the `GtkToggleButton`, the same functions and events that apply to the `GtkToggleButton` also apply to the `GtkCheckButton`.

The toggle button code can be converted into a `GtkCheckButton` example by replacing the code that creates the toggle button. The old toggle button code

```
/* --- Create a new button --- */
button = gtk_toggle_button_new_with_label ("Top Toggle Button");
```

can be replaced with the following `GtkCheckButton` code:

```
/* --- Create check buttons --- */
check = gtk_check_button_new_with_label (szLabel);
```

The previous example is now an example of the `GtkCheckButton` instead of toggle buttons.

## Radio Buttons

At first glance, radio buttons (`GtkRadioButton`) look like the `GtkCheckButtons`. The radio buttons' appearance suggests that they are derived from the `GtkCheckButton`. The `GtkRadioButton` has a minor change to its behavior to distinguish it from the `GtkCheckButton` (see Figure 4.4). With the `GtkRadioButton`, only one of the buttons in a group can be selected at any time. Clicking one of the buttons unselects the previously selected button, and the button that was clicked becomes selected.

`GtkRadioButtons` can be created with a label by using the `gtk_radio_button_new_with_label` function or without a label by using the `gtk_radio_button_new` function. Creating the `GtkRadioButton` is only half of the work, though, because the radio button must be associated with a group so that only one of the buttons is selected at any time. Each time a radio button is created, the `gtk_radio_button_group` function needs to be called with the radio button and the group to add the button to the group. The first time a button is added to a group, `NULL` should be used as the group because it does not exist yet. The group will be created if `NULL` is used as the group. (The group is really a singly linked list [`GSList`] keeping track of the buttons in the group.)

**Figure 4.4**    Radio buttons.

Failing to call the gtk_radio_button_group to get the group after each radio button is added results in unpredictable behavior. Also, failing to initialize the group to NULL for the first call to gtk_radio_button_group usually causes a program exception.

This example shows the button being created and added to the group. After the button is created, the group that it belongs to is retrieved.

```
GtkWidget *radio;
GSList *group = NULL;

/* --- Create the radio button and add to the group --- */
/* --- if group is NULL, a new group is created --- */
radio = gtk_radio_button_new_with_label (group, szLabel);

/* Get the group from the button.  The group is a linked list
 * of the buttons - and the group changes since elements are
 * added to the head. Always get the group after adding buttons.
 */
group = gtk_radio_button_group (GTK_RADIO_BUTTON (radio));
```

Because the radio button was derived from the check button, which was derived from the toggle button, the radio button can use the toggle button events and functions to set attribute information. The same events used by the toggle button are also used by the radio button.

# Labels

Labels (GtkLabel) are static noneditable fields usually used to describe other fields on the screen. Labels describe a button by placing the label within the button, or they can be placed next to other fields, like edit fields, to provide the field with a description. Labels are created with the gtk_label_new function. Querying the label text is made with a call to the gtk_label_get function and changing the label text requires a call to the gtk_label_set function.

Unlike most other widgets, labels are not derived from GtkWidget, but are instead derived from GtkMisc. Therefore, labels cannot have events associated with them.

Labels are lightweight widgets because a window is not created when the widget is created. Instead, the label is painted onto the parent widget. This process has the advantage of reducing overhead by not keeping track of another window. The downside is that these widgets are limited.

```
GtkWidget *label;
char *buffer;

/* --- Create a new label --- */
label = gtk_label_new (_This is a label_);

/* --- set the label text to a new value --- */
gtk_label_set (label, _This is the new label_);

/* --- Get the label text --- */
gtk_label_get (label, &buffer);
```

The `gtk_label_get` function gets the reference to the text displayed within the label. You should not modify this string directly; instead, use the `gtk_label_set` function if you want to modify the text in the label. The reference to the label text prevents the memory allocated for the text from being destroyed, so you should always dereference it if it is no longer being used.

Because the label is derived from `GtkMisc`, you can use the `gtk_misc_set_alignment` function to modify the display of the text within the label. The function takes an $x$ alignment and a $y$ alignment value to compute where the text should be displayed. For the $x$ alignment value, a zero (**0**) indicates that the text should be displayed left-aligned. A **.5** value indicates that the text should be centered along the $x$, and a **1** indicates that the text should be right-aligned. For the $y$ value, **0** indicates that the text should be aligned top, **.5** indicates that the value should be centered along the $y$, and a **1** indicates that the text should be aligned on the bottom of the field.

```
/* --- Right aligned, but vertically centered --- */
Gtk_misc_set_alignment (GTK_MISC (label), 1.0, .5);
```

# Entry Widget

The entry widget (`GtkEntry`) is a single-line entry field used for entering and displaying textual information. The entry widget is derived from the editable widget and is a slimmed-down version of the more complicated text widget. The entry widget is still much more complicated than the button widgets or the label widget. The entry widget has more functions associated with it than the button or label widgets do.

In Figure 4.5, an illustration of the label and entry widget can be seen with a combo box and an option menu (described later in the chapter). The combo box looks very similar to the entry widget because the combo box uses an entry widget as well as other widgets.

**Figure 4.5**    A combo box with label widget, entry widget, and option menu.

The entry widget (GtkEntry) can be created with the gtk_entry_new function or with the gtk_entry_new_with_max_length function. The gtk_entry_new_with_max_length sets the maximum number of characters that can be entered into the widget. The text in the widget can be retrieved using the gtk_entry_get_text function, but this returns only a pointer to the string data and shouldn't be modified through the pointer. Instead, the text in the widget can be set in one of three ways:

- Text can be inserted at the beginning of the field by using gtk_entry_prepend_text.

- Text can be appended to the end of the field by using the gtk_entry_append_text.

- The text can also be set by using the gtk_entry_set_text function, which destroys any previous value of the field.

The cursor can also be manipulated in the entry widget. The current position of the cursor (and selection) can be queried using the gtk_entry_select_region. The cursor can be moved to a position in the field by using the gtk_entry_set_position function. The gtk_entry_select_region allows a range of text to be selected in the widget.

Additional properties of the entry widget include a property that indicates whether the user is allowed to modify the text in the widget. The gtk_entry_set_editable function sets this editable property. The gtk_entry_set_visibility function determines whether the text being typed into the field is visible to the user. Most of the time, the text should be visible to the user, but for fields like passwords, it is improper to display the password as the user types.

```
/* --- Create an entry field --- */
entry = gtk_entry_new ();

/* --- Set the default value --- */
gtk_entry_set_text (GTK_ENTRY (entry), "12:00");

/* --- Append some text --- */
gtk_entry_append_text (GTK_ENTRY (entry), "am");
```

```
/* --- Don't allow editing of the field --- */
gtk_entry_set_editable (GTK_ENTRY (entry), FALSE);
```

The entry box can listen for the "changed" signal, which signals that the text in the entry widget has changed.

# List Boxes

List boxes (`GtkList`) show a list of items and allow a user to pick one or more of the items in the list depending on how the `GtkList` is configured (see Figure 4.6). A `GtkList` is created using the `gtk_list_new` function, and items are added to the `GtkList` using one of several methods. The simplest way is to use a combination of `gtk_list_item_new_with_label` and `gtk_container_add`. The `gtk_container_add` function can add multiple items in the `GtkList` because the `GtkList` overrides the `GtkContainer`'s add function to handle multiple items in the container.

Figure 4.6  `GtkList`.

The following code segment illustrates how to create a `GtkList` and add a couple of items to it.

```
/* --- Create the list box --- */
listbox = gtk_list_new ();

/* --- Allow multiple items to be selected in the list box --- */
gtk_list_set_selection_mode (GTK_LIST (listbox),
                             GTK_SELECTION_MULTIPLE);

/* ------------------- */
/* --- Add one item --- */
/* ------------------- */

/* --- Create an item --- */
item = gtk_list_item_new_with_label ("Car");

/* --- Add it to the list --- */
gtk_container_add (GTK_CONTAINER (listbox), item);
```

```
/* --- Make the item visible --- */
gtk_widget_show (item);

/* --------------------- */
/* --- Add another item --- */
/* --------------------- */

/* --- Create an item --- */
item = gtk_list_item_new_with_label ("House");

/* --- Add it to the list --- */
gtk_container_add (GTK_CONTAINER (listbox), item);

/* --- Make the item visible --- */
gtk_widget_show (item);
```

Of course, in situations when you repeatedly use a multistep process to add an item to a GtkList, the best technique is to move the code that performs the adding of items to a function. This approach simplifies the code and makes it easier to read. The code above would simplify as follows:

```
/* --- Create the list box --- */
listbox = gtk_list_new ();

/* --- Allow multiple items to be selected in the list box --- */
gtk_list_set_selection_mode (GTK_LIST (listbox),
                             GTK_SELECTION_MULTIPLE);

/* ---------------- */
/* --- Add items --- */
/* ---------------- */

AddListItem (listbox, _Car_);
AddListItem (listbox, _House_);
```

Here's what the function AddListItem looks like:

```
void AddListItem (GtkWidget *listbox, char *sText)
{
    GtkWidget *item;

    /* --- Create list item from data --- */
    item = gtk_list_item_new_with_label (sText);

    /* --- Add item to listbox --- */
    gtk_container_add (GTK_CONTAINER (listbox), item);

    /* --- Make it visible --- */
    gtk_widget_show (item);
}
```

This function may not look like it is saving much work, but if the code had many more items to add, the savings would be much greater. Additional savings would occur if other `GtkList` widgets used the same function to be populated.

Items can also be added to the `GtkList` using functions that add a list of items to the `GtkList`. The list of items is a linked list (`GList *`) of widgets created by using the `gtk_list_item_new_with_label` function. These items can be inserted into the `GtkList` at the end with `gtk_list_append_items`, at the beginning with `gtk_list_prepend_items`, or at a particular position with `gtk_list_insert_items`. In each case, the data portion of the `Glist` is the `GtkListItem`.

You can add a group of widgets to the end of a `GtkList`. A `CreateListItem` function (created next) simplifies the coding. This function creates and makes visible a list item and returns the widget pointer so it can be added into the linked list.

```
/*
 * Create Item
 *
 * Creates a list item with the text passed in and
 * returns it.
 */
GtkWidget *CreateItem (char *sText)
{
    GtkWidget    *item;

    /* --- Create a list item from the data element --- */
    item = gtk_list_item_new_with_label (sText);

    /* --- Show the item --- */
    gtk_widget_show (item);

    /* --- Return the value --- */
    return (item);
}
```

You can use the `CreateList` function to create an item that is added to the linked list. The list can be created with the following code:

```
items = NULL;
items = g_list_append (items, CreateItem ("pink"));
items = g_list_append (items, CreateItem ("blue"));
items = g_list_append (items, CreateItem ("red"));
items = g_list_append (items, CreateItem ("yella"));
```

After the list is created, the list can be appended to the end of the `GtkList` this way:

```
gtk_list_append_items (GTK_LIST (listbox), items);
```

Or the items can be inserted at the top of the `GtkList` like this:

```
gtk_list_prepend_items (GTK_LIST (listbox), items);
```

The `GtkList` can be cleared with the `gtk_list_clear_items` function. To clear the `GtkList`, you must know the index of the first and last item. The entire list can be cleared with

```
gtk_list_clear_items (listbox, 0, -1);
```

where the last item is set to -1 to indicate the end of the list. This line clears all the items in the `GtkList`.

Items can be selected by using the `gtk_list_select_item` function and unselected by using the `gtk_list_unselect` function. The item to select/unselect is determined by the index passed in. The `gtk_list_select_child` and `gtk_list_unselect_child` functions perform similar tasks except that the `GtkListItem` is passed in instead of the index.

```
/* --- Selects child in the list box --- */
gtk_list_select_child (listbox, child);

/* --- Unselects child in the list box --- */
gtk_list_unselect_child (listbox, child);
```

A `GtkList` can allow multiple items to be selected or single items to be selected by setting the mode of the `GtkList`. The function `gtk_list_set_selection_mode` can be used to set the mode. The most commonly used modes are `GTK_SELECTION_SINGLE`, which allows only one of the items in the `GtkList` to be selected at a time, and the `GTK_SELECTION_MULTIPLE`, which allows multiple items to be selected at a time.

The signal used most by the `GtkList` is the `"selection_changed"` signal. The `"selection_changed"` signal is emitted when the selected items in the `GtkList` change, whether it's selecting another item or unselecting an item. Because the list items in the `GtkList` are also widgets, they can also receive signals, including the `"select"` signal, which indicates that the item was selected. Sometimes it's handy to use the `"select"` signal because individual list items can pass in additional information with the event handler. The `AddListItem` function could be modified to accept a code with the text, which would be passed to the event handler.

```
/*
 * AddListItem
 *
 * Adds text to the list box.
 */
void AddListItem (GtkWidget *listbox, char *sText, char *sCode)
{
    GtkWidget        *item;

    /* --- Create a list item from the data element --- */
    item = CreateItem (sText);

    /* --- Add it to the list box --- */
    gtk_container_add (GTK_CONTAINER (listbox), item);

    /* --- Setup signal handler.  Note that the code of the item --- */
```

```
        /* --- is going to be passed in --- */
        gtk_signal_connect (GTK_OBJECT (item), "select",
                   GTK_SIGNAL_FUNC (listitem_selected), sCode);
}


/*
 * listitem_selected
 *
 * If an item is selected in the list box, the call is made
 * here and the code is passed in as the data parameter.
 */
void listitem_selected (GtkWidget *widget, gpointer *data)
{
    g_print ("code of item selected - %s\n", (char *) data);
}
```

# Combo Boxes

A combo box (GtkCombo) is a mix between an edit field and a list box (refer to Figure 4.5). The edit field can allow entry of a value, or it can be restricted to values in the drop-down portion of the GtkCombo. A GtkCombo can be created with the gtk_combo_new function and populated with the gtk_combo_set_popdown_strings function.

```
    /* --------------------------------------- */
    /* --- Create a list of the items first --- */
    /* --------------------------------------- */
    cbitems = NULL;
    cbitems = g_list_append (cbitems, "Car");
    cbitems = g_list_append (cbitems, "House");
    cbitems = g_list_append (cbitems, "Job");
    cbitems = g_list_append (cbitems, "Computer");

    /* --- Make a combo box --- */
    combo = gtk_combo_new ();

    /* --- Create the drop-down portion of the combo --- */
    gtk_combo_set_popdown_strings (GTK_COMBO(combo), cbitems);
```

The GtkCombo can be restricted to allow only values in the drop-down list box by using the gtk_combo_set_value_in_list function, but it is not always wise to restrict the GtkCombo this way. If you don't want the user to type data in the edit portion of the GtkCombo, you can set the edit portion to read-only so that no one can type in the field. The user can still select from the drop-down list when the edit portion is read-only. The entry field can be accessed from the application by retrieving the entry from the GtkCombo and accessing it like a standard entry field. The following code prevents characters from being typed within the edit field:

```
/* --- Get the entry field portion of the combo box --- */
entry = GTK_ENTRY (GTK_COMBO (combo)->entry);

/* --- Do not allow it to be edited --- */
gtk_entry_set_editable (entry, FALSE);
```

The GtkCombo entry field can catch the "changed" signal, which would indicate that the value in the entry field of the GtkCombo has changed.

```
gtk_signal_connect (GTK_OBJECT (GTK_COMBO (combo)->entry),
                    _changed_,
                    GTK_SIGNAL_FUNC (combofunc),
                    NULL);
```

The GtkCombo has no function defined to clear the combo box, but the GtkCombo has a GtkWidget that it uses to keep track of the items in the drop-down list. We can use the list element to manipulate the items in the GtkCombo. Clearing the list is a simple matter of getting the list box and using the gtk_list_clear_items function.

```
GtkList *list;

/* --- Get the list box from the combo --- */
list = GTK_LIST (GTK_COMBO (widget)->list);

/* --- Clear the list within the combo --- */
gtk_list_clear_items (list, 0, -1);
```

You can clear the list in a single step with

```
/* --- Clear list in one step --- */
gtk_list_clear_items (GTK_LIST (GTK_COMBO(widget)->list), 0, -1);
```

# Option Menus

Option menus (GtkOptionMenu) are similar to the GtkList without the editing capability (refer to Figure 4.5). Although the behavior is similar, the look is entirely different. The option menus are sometimes used like a GtkCombo.

When the GtkOptionMenu is clicked, a menu appears to show the user the valid choices for the widget. Selecting a value causes the value to appear on the widget when the menu disappears.

The GtkOptionMenu must first be created with the gtk_option_menu_new function. Then the GtkRadioMenuItems need to be created, added to a group (like the radio buttons), and added to a GtkMenu. When the GtkMenu is populated, it can be associated with the GtkOptionMenu.

The initialization of the GtkOptionMenu looks something like this:

```
/* --- Create the option menu --- */
omenu = gtk_option_menu_new ();

/* --- Create a menu --- */
menu = gtk_menu_new ();
```

```
/* --- No group --- */
group = NULL;
```

Every item added to the option menu needs to go through the following process:

```
/* --- Value to be displayed --- */
sText = "Medium";

/* --- Create a menu item with a label --- */
menuitem = gtk_radio_menu_item_new_with_label (group, sText);

/* --- Get the group that the menu item is in --- */
group = gtk_radio_menu_item_group (GTK_RADIO_MENU_ITEM (menuitem));

/* --- Add the menu item to the menu --- */
gtk_menu_append (GTK_MENU (menu), menuitem);

/* --- Make the item visible --- */
gtk_widget_show (menuitem);

/* --- Let me know when it's selected and pass in the text --- */
/* --- to the callback function --- */
gtk_signal_connect_object (GTK_OBJECT (menuitem),
                           "activate",
                           GTK_SIGNAL_FUNC (combo_select),
                           (gpointer) sText);
```

The `"activate"` signal indicates that the `GtkRadioMenuItem` has been selected. When all the items have been added, the menu can be associated with the option menu this way:

```
/* --- Associate the menu with the option menu --- */
gtk_option_menu_set_menu (GTK_OPTION_MENU (omenu), menu);

/* --- Make it visible --- */
gtk_widget_show (omenu);
```

The `GtkOptionMenu` is great for giving the user a list of items to pick from and displaying the currently selected item.

## Containers

Containers (`GtkContainers`) are widgets that can be parents to other widgets by placing those other widgets within the container widget. You cannot create a container widget, because there is no `gtk_container_new` function, but container widgets are used all the time. The main window in earlier examples, buttons, and list boxes are some examples of container widgets. The chief purpose of the container widget is to provide common functions that can be used on all container widgets without writing a specific set of functions for each widget.

Widgets can be added to container widgets by using the `gtk_container_add` function, and they can be removed by using the `gtk_container_remove` function. Most container widgets allow only one child widget to be added. Some exceptions are widgets like the `GtkList`, but it serves the specific purpose of storing multiple items. If more than one widget needs to be in a normal container, packing boxes or packing tables are needed to hold the widgets.

To iterate through the list of child widgets stored in a container, you can use the `gtk_container_children` function to return a linked list (`GList *`) of the child widgets. The alternative is to use a `foreach` function. The `gtk_container_foreach` function performs a function on each of the child widgets and passes in a widget as a parameter.

The `gtk_container_border_width` function controls the width of the border around the widget within the container. Setting this value to zero will provide the widget within the container with no border.

# Summary

Basic widgets involve creating and setting widget properties before the widgets are shown. Widgets have attribute functions, and most signal events that can be trapped by applications. The `GtkLabel`, buttons, `GtkList`, entry field, and combo box have been covered. These are the most commonly used widgets in applications, and understanding them is essential to understanding more complicated widgets.

# 5

# Menus, Toolbars, and Tooltips

**A** GOOD FRONT END ON AN APPLICATION is sometimes as important as what is underneath. The user interface is the first thing most users see, and if the interface does not provide a quick and intuitive way for users to get at the functionality they need, the developer has not written a good application. Just as selling cars is as much about marketing as it is about engineering, the front end of an application is as important as the internal algorithms. Nonprogrammers, especially, are quick to judge an application based on its appearance and ease of use, not its algorithms.

Users have become accustomed to well-designed menus to issue commands and to toolbars that provide quick access to commonly used functions. In this chapter, you design a small front end using the GTK+ functions. The front end includes a functional menu and a toolbar.

## Starting Up

The application's top-level window should be created and have its characteristics set. Attributes such as window size, title, and border widget are commonly set on the top-level window. The application title is one item that should be set. The `gtk_window_new` function creates the top-level window, which can be used to set the characteristics of the application.

```
win = gtk_window_new (GTK_WINDOW_TOPLEVEL);
```

After the window is created, you can use the widget handle returned by gtk_window_new to set the window's characteristics. The title enables the user to distinguish the window from other windows on the screen and should be as short as possible to adequately describe the window. The title is set using the gtk_widget_set_title function.

```
gtk_widget_set_title (GTK_WINDOW (win), "Application title");
```

If the application is some type of editor, the title should include the name of the file to remind the user what is being edited. Remember that several windows can be open at any point in time, and the title helps the user identify each window.

The size of the window is determined by the size of the widgets within the window. Sometimes the size determined by the widgets is too small. The minimum size of the window can be set in advance with the gtk_widget_set_usize function. If the created window is smaller than the minimum size, the size of the window is adjusted to the minimum. This statement sets the window to 300 pixels by 200 pixels:

```
gtk_widget_set_usize (win, 300, 200);
```

The border of the window can be set with the gtk_container_border_width function. This example sets the border of the container to zero.

```
gtk_container_border_width (GTK_CONTAINER (win), 0);
```

In Chapter 3, "Developing GUI Applications," you learned how to make the window visible and how to listen for the "delete_event" signal; this step should be repeated for the application window. The "delete_event" signal indicates that the window is being closed. When the window is ready, you can add GUI components to make the application look more professional.

## Menus, the Hard Way

Menus in GTK+ are widgets and behave like other widgets. The menu that people normally think of has two parts: a menu bar that spans the top of the window and several menus that hang off the menu bar. The menu bar is usually the top-most widget within the application window. The layering of the menu bar at the top of the window followed by the toolbar suggests that the menu should be inserted into a vertical packing box. The application's vertical packing box needs to be created before you can work with the menu bar.

```
/* --- Create the application_s vertical packing box --- */
vbox_main = gtk_vbox_new (FALSE, 0);

/* --- Add the packing box to the main window --- */
gtk_container_add (GTK_CONTAINER (win), vbox_main);
```

```
/* --- Make the packing box visible --- */
gtk_widget_show (vbox_main);
```

The menu consists of the menu bar (`GtkMenuBar`) that sits along the entire top portion of the window and the menus (`GtkMenu`) that can be dropped down from the menu bar or other menus. Each individual menu choice is a `GtkMenuItem` created and inserted into a `GtkMenu`.

The first step is to create the `GtkMenuBar` and add it to the vertical packing box. The `gtk_menu_bar_new` function creates the `GtkMenuBar` widget. Here's the code to create the menu bar and put it in the vertical packing box.

```
/* --- Create a menu bar for the application --- */
menubar = gtk_menu_bar_new ();

/* --- Put the menu bar in the application packing box --- */
gtk_box_pack_start (GTK_BOX (vbox), menubar, FALSE, TRUE, 0);

/* --- Make the menu bar visible --- */
gtk_widget_show (menubar);
```

This code creates a blank `GtkMenuBar`. For the menu bar to be useful, you need to add the menu items.

When you were working with basic widgets, you created a few wrapper functions to combine several steps into a single function. You can use the same technique with the menus. To create a menu item, the first step is to create a "File" menu item (`GtkMenuItem`) with a label.

```
/* --- Create a menu item for "File" --- */
menuFile = gtk_menu_item_new_with_label ("File");
```

After the `GtkMenuItem` is created, you need to add it to the `GtkMenuBar` you created earlier and then make the `GtkMenuItem` visible.

```
/* --- Add File to the menu bar --- */
gtk_menu_bar_append (GTK_MENU_BAR (menubar), menuFile);

/* --- Make the widget visible --- */
gtk_widget_show (menuFile);
```

In most applications, the menu item "File" contains other menu items that are visible only when the menu is dropped down. When selected, the "File" menu item does not cause the application to perform an action. Instead, the "File" menu opens a submenu, which contains selectable options such as "New," "Open," and "Save." Because "File" really leads to a new menu, it needs to be associated with a new menu that contains these other items. You can use the `gtk_menu_item_set_submenu` function after creating a new `GtkMenu` that will contain the "New," "Open," and "Save" options.

```
/* --- Create the new menu for "New," "Open," etc --- */
menu = gtk_menu_new ();
```

```
/* --- Mark the submenu under the "File" menuitem --- */
gtk_menu_item_set_submenu (GTK_MENU_ITEM (menuFile), menu);
```

Now you can add GtkMenuItems to the new GtkMenu. To simplify this procedure for each submenu, you should make the process of creating a submenu into a function.

```
/*
 * CreateBarSubMenu
 *
 * Create a submenu
 *
 * menu - higher level menu
 * szName - Name of submenu item to be added to menu
 */
GtkWidget *CreateBarSubMenu (GtkWidget *menu, char *szName)
{
    GtkWidget *menuitem;
    GtkWidget *submenu;

    /* --- Create menu --- */
    menuitem = gtk_menu_item_new_with_label (szName);

    /* --- Add it to the menu bar --- */
    gtk_menu_bar_append (GTK_MENU_BAR (menu), menuitem);
    gtk_widget_show (menuitem);

    /* --- Get a menu and attach to the menu item --- */
    submenu = gtk_menu_new ();
    gtk_menu_item_set_submenu (GTK_MENU_ITEM (menuitem), submenu);

    /* --- Viola! --- */
    return (submenu);
}
```

After you add the submenu, you can add individual instances of GtkMenuItem to the submenu. You start out by first creating a GtkMenuItem.

```
menuitem = gtk_menu_item_new_with_label ("New");
```

Then you just add the GtkMenuItem to the submenu you created and make the GtkMenuItem visible.

```
gtk_menu_append (GTK_MENU (submenu), menuitem);
gtk_widget_show (menuitem);
```

Of course, the menu does not do anything yet. First you need to trap the event that indicates that the user has selected a GtkMenuItem. The GtkMenuItem has an "activate" signal that indicates that the GtkMenuItem has been selected. By putting a callback function on the "activate" signal, the application can respond to the user selecting an item in the menu.

A separator between two instances of GtkMenuItem can be inserted by calling the gtk_menu_item_new function with no label and adding the new GtkMenuItem to the sub-menu. This step adds a horizontal line in the menu that separates groups of commands. Separators are especially useful in long menus. The "Exit" menu item should be separated from the other menu choices so users do not accidentally hit "Exit" when selecting a nearby menu selection.

## Checked Menu Items

In addition to handling commands, menus can also show state information. The checked menu item (GtkCheckMenuItem) acts like a check box in the menu by allow-ing you to view and modify a Boolean value on the menu. The steps to create a GtkCheckMenuItem are similar to the steps you used to create a regular GtkMenuItem except that now you use the gtk_check_menu_item_new_with_label function and you want to trap the "toggled" signal. You can create a function that does all the work to create a GtkCheckedMenuItem:

```
/*
 * CreateMenuCheck
 *
 * Create a menu item that has a check box
 *
 * menu - parent menu to add the check menu item
 * szName - name assigned to the menu item
 * func - event handler to call when menu item is toggled
 * data - additional info to pass to the event handler
 */
GtkWidget *CreateMenuCheck (GtkWidget *menu,
                            char *szName,
                            GtkSignalFunc func,
                            gpointer data)
{
    GtkWidget *menuitem;

    /* --- Create menu item --- */
    menuitem = gtk_check_menu_item_new_with_label (szName);

    /* --- Add it to the menu --- */
    gtk_menu_append (GTK_MENU (menu), menuitem);
    gtk_widget_show (menuitem);

    /* --- Listen for "toggled" messages --- */
    gtk_signal_connect (GTK_OBJECT (menuitem), "toggled",
```

```
                          GTK_SIGNAL_FUNC(func), data);

    return (menuitem);
}
```

The check menu item can be set using the gtk_check_menu_item_set_state function.

```
/* --- Set it at false --- */
gtk_check_menu_item_set_state (GTK_CHECK_MENU_ITEM (menuitem), FALSE);
```

# Radio Menu Items

Just as menu items can act as check boxes, the menu items can also act as radio buttons (GtkRadioMenuItem) within a group. A menu item that wants to behave like a radio button needs to be created with the gtk_radio_menu_item_new_with_label function, which takes the group that the radio menu item is being added to, and the name of the menu item. The group needs to be set to NULL before adding the first radio menu item, and the new value of the group needs to be retrieved after adding each item. The following code illustrates this process:

```
GSList *group = NULL;

/* --- Add "Tall" to the group --- */
menuitem = gtk_radio_menu_item_new_with_label (group, "Tall");

/* --- Update the group that we added the item to --- */
group = gtk_radio_menu_item_group (GTK_RADIO_MENU_ITEM (menuitem));
/* --- Add the menu item to a menu --- */
gtk_menu_append (GTK_MENU (menu), menuitem);

/* --- Show the menu item --- */
gtk_widget_show (menuitem);

/* --- Connect the signal handler --- */
gtk_signal_connect (GTK_OBJECT (menuitem), "toggled",
                    GTK_SIGNAL_FUNC (TallFunc), NULL);
```

The GtkRadioMenuItem is derived from the GtkCheckMenuItem; therefore, the signals are identical, and the function to get and set the state of the GtkRadioMenuItem is identical to the function to get and set the state of the GtkCheckMenuItem. In fact, the GtkRadioMenuItem can be set by using the following code:

```
/* --- Set it at false --- */
gtk_check_menu_item_set_state (GTK_CHECK_MENU_ITEM (menuitem), FALSE);
```

# Tooltips

One other nice feature you can provide to users is the tooltip. *Tooltips* are those little pop-up text windows that appear when the mouse moves over a widget and disappear when the mouse moves off the widget. They give users additional information about the widget; that is, a tooltip explains what a widget does. (Tooltips are especially useful if an incompetent artist is drawing your toolbar pictures.) Tooltips are mostly used with toolbars but can also be used with other widgets. You can create a tooltip with the gtk_tooltips_new function.

```
/* --- Create tooltips --- */
tooltips = gtk_tooltips_new ();
```

After you create the tooltips, you can use the gtk_tooltips_set_tip function to add them to a menu item.

```
/* --- Add the tip to a menu item --- */
gtk_tooltips_set_tip (tooltips, menuitem,
        "An apple a day keeps the doctor away", NULL);
```

You can make tooltips quite colorful by using the gtk_tooltips_set_colors function. By passing in a background and a foreground GdkColor, the colors on the tooltips can be modified.

```
/* --- Change the color --- */
gtk_tooltips_set_colors (tooltips, background, foreground);
```

You can also set the delay on the tooltips by using the gtk_tooltips_set_delay function. The tooltips can be disabled by using the gtk_tooltips_disable function and reenabled by using the gtk_tooltips_enable function.

# Accelerator Keys

Many people do not like to use the mouse to select menus, and they stick with keyboard shortcuts for many commands. Good menu developers keep these people in mind by creating keyboard shortcuts for the commonly used commands. Before accelerators are used, they need to be created and associated with a window. The gtk_accel_group_new function creates the GtkAccelGroup, and the gtk_window_add_accelerator_table function associates the accelerator table with the window.

```
/* --- Create the accelerator table --- */
accel_group = gtk_accel_group_new ()

/* --- Add the accelerator table to the application window --- */
gtk_accel_group_attach (accel_group, GTK_OBJECT (win_main));
```

Although the accelerator table has been created, you have not mapped the shortcut keys to the menus yet. The gtk_widget_add_accelerator function maps a keyboard command to the menu. The function takes a GtkMenuItem, the accelerator group, the signal (usually "activate"), and the keys used to generate the signal.

This example maps the Control-C (GDK_CONTROL_MASK, 'C') key sequence to the GtkMenuItem and makes the accelerator visible on the menu (GTK_ACCEL_VISIBLE). The "activate" signal will be sent when the Control-C key sequence is hit.

```
/* --- The Control-C key activates this menu --- */
gtk_widget_install_accelerator (menuitem,
                                "activate",
                                accel_group,
                                'C',
                                GDK_CONTROL_MASK,
                                GTK_ACCEL_VISIBLE);
```

# Consolidating the Code

You can consolidate all these steps to create a GtkMenuItem (the menu, the accelerator, and the tooltips) into a single function. This function replaces 10 to 15 lines of code per menu item and makes the code a bit easier to write.

The function has parameters for the tooltips and the accelerator, but if they're not provided, they are not set up. If no name is provided for the menu label, a separator is created instead. The whole function looks like this:

```
/*
 * CreateMenuItem
 *
 * Creates an item and puts it in the menu and returns the item.
 *
 * menu - container menu
 * szName - Name of the menu - NULL for a separator
 * szAccel - Acceleration string - "^C" for Control-C
 * szTip - Tooltips
 * func - Callback function
 * data - Callback function data
 *
 * returns new menu item
 */
GtkWidget *CreateMenuItem (GtkWidget *menu,
                           char *szName,
                           char *szAccel,
                           char *szTip,
                           GtkSignalFunc func,
                           gpointer data)
{
    GtkWidget *menuitem;

    /* --- If there's a name, create the item and put a
     *     signal handler on it.
```

```
   */
if (szName && strlen (szName)) {
    menuitem = gtk_menu_item_new_with_label (szName);
    gtk_signal_connect (GTK_OBJECT (menuitem), "activate",
                GTK_SIGNAL_FUNC(func), data);
} else {
    /* --- Create a separator --- */
    menuitem = gtk_menu_item_new ();
}

/* --- Add menu item to the menu and show it. --- */
gtk_menu_append (GTK_MENU (menu), menuitem);
gtk_widget_show (menuitem);

if (accel_group == NULL) {
    accel_group = gtk_accel_group_new ();
    gtk_accel_group_attach (accel_group, GTK_OBJECT (win_main));
}

/* --- If there was an accelerator --- */
if (szAccel && szAccel[0] == '^') {
    gtk_widget_add_accelerator (menuitem,
                            "activate",
                            accel_group,
                            szAccel[1],
                            GDK_CONTROL_MASK,
                            GTK_ACCEL_VISIBLE);
}

/* --- If there was a tooltip --- */
if (szTip && strlen (szTip)) {
    gtk_tooltips_set_tip (tooltips, menuitem, szTip, NULL);
}

return (menuitem);
}
```

When you have the submenu, you can use the preceding function to create the
menu items. We can create the "New" and "Open" menu items with tooltips and
accelerator keys using the following:

```
/* --- Create "New" --- */
menuitem = CreateMenuItem (menu, "New", "^N",
                "Create a new item",
                GTK_SIGNAL_FUNC (NewFunc), "new");

/* --- Create "Open" --- */
menuitem = CreateMenuItem (menu, "Open", "^O",
                "Open an existing item",
                GTK_SIGNAL_FUNC (OpenFunc), "open");
```

Using a single function makes the code easy to read. In addition, it is easy to change the code later because the code that does the menu creation is all in one place. This function could be expanded by moving the data into a structure and reading the information from the structure, but that's left as an exercise to the reader.

# Item Factories (Menus the Easy Way)

Menus can be created easily using the item factory (`GtkItemFactoryEntry`). The item factory uses a prefilled structure as the basis for the menu. The structure consists of five parts—the *menu path*, the *accelerator*, the *callback*, the *extra parameter to the callback*, and the *flags* that indicate what the item is. The flags can be any of the following:

- `<Title>`. Creates a title item.
- `<Item>`. Creates a simple menu item.
- `<CheckItem>`. Creates a check menu item.
- `<ToggleItem>`. Creates a toggle menu item.
- `<RadioItem>`. Creates a radio menu item.
- `<Separator>`. Creates a separator to separate items in the menu.
- `<Branch>`. Creates an item to hold submenus.
- `<LastBranch>`. Creates a right-justified item to hold submenus.

Using `NULL`, `0`, or `""` for the flag just creates a simple menu item.

For instance, a "New" submenu in the "File" menu might have the following line to define that one menu item:

```
"/File/New", "<control>N", FileNew, NULL, 0"
```

`"/File/New"` is parsed to identify the path. In this case, the first slash indicates the root menu or the menu bar. The `File` is the item in the menu bar, and `"New"` is the menu item within the "File" menu. The `"<control>N"` indicates that the accelerator key to call this menu is the Ctrl+N sequence. Accelerators can use a `<shift>` sequence (`"<shift>b"`) to indicate that the shift key is pressed or an `<alt>` sequence (`"<alt>q"`) to indicate that the alt key is pressed. The callback is a standard callback function that is called when the user picks the menu item using the mouse or hits the accelerator sequence. The extra parameter field is passed in when the callback is called. Setting it to `NULL` passes in a `NULL`. The callback for the item factory is a bit different in the parameters that it sends. The callback is called with the callback data from the table, the callback action, and the widget—in that order.

## Coding the Item Factories

Once the `GtkItemFactory` table has been created, the code required to use the table is small. The first step is to create the `GtkItemFactory` with the `gtk_item_factory_new` function. The item factory is created with the `GTK_TYPE_MENU_BAR` as the type, a name, and an accelerator group created using the `gtk_accel_group_new` function. The menu items from the `GtkItemFactory` are added using the `gtk_item_factory_create_items` function and passing in the table information. The following example uses an item factory to create a menu for a window. The routine implements some callbacks for displaying the action, and implements the `Quit` action to exit from the application.

```c
/*
 * menu.c
 *
 * Menus using the item factory
 */

#include <gtk/gtk.h>

static void QuitApp (gpointer callback_data,
                     guint callback_action,
                     GtkWidget *widget);
static void ShowMenu (gpointer callback_data,
                      guint callback_action,
                      GtkWidget *widget);


/*
 * Structure to build the menus
 */
static GtkItemFactoryEntry menu_items[] = {
  {"/_File",               NULL,          0,         0, "<Branch>" },
  {"/File/tearoff1",       NULL,          ShowMenu, 0, "<Tearoff>" },
  {"/File/_New",           "<control>N", ShowMenu, 0 },
  {"/File/_Open",          "<control>O", ShowMenu, 0 },
  {"/File/_Save",          "<control>S", ShowMenu, 0 },
  {"/File/Save _As...",    NULL,          ShowMenu, 0 },
  {"/File/sep1",           NULL,          ShowMenu, 0, "<Separator>" },
  {"/File/_Quit",          "<control>Q", QuitApp,  0 },

  {"/_Edit",               NULL,          0,         0, "<Branch>" },
  {"/_Edit/Cut",           "<control>X", 0,         0, 0},
  {"/_Edit/_Copy",         "<control>C", 0,         0, 0},
  {"/_Edit/_Paste",        "<control>V", 0,         0, 0},
  {"/_Edit/_Font",         NULL,          0,         0, "<Branch>" },
  {"/_Edit/Font/_Bold",    NULL,          ShowMenu, 0, "<RadioItem>" },
  {"/_Edit/Font/_Italics", NULL,          ShowMenu, 0, "<RadioItem>" },
  {"/_Edit/Font/_Underline", NULL,        ShowMenu, 0, "<RadioItem>" },
  {"/_Edit/_Color",        NULL,          0,         0, "<Branch>" },
  {"/_Edit/Color/_Red",    NULL,          ShowMenu, 0, "<CheckItem>" },
  {"/_Edit/Color/_Blue",   NULL,          ShowMenu, 0, "<CheckItem>" },
  {"/_Edit/Color/_Green",  NULL,          ShowMenu, 0, "<CheckItem>" },
```

```
    {"/_Help",                      NULL,       0,        0, "<LastBranch>" },
    {"/Help/_About",                NULL,       ShowMenu, 0 },
};


/*
 * FactoryQuit
 *
 * Quit the app when called from the menu.
 */
static void QuitApp (gpointer callback_data,
                         guint callback_action,
                         GtkWidget *widget)
{
    /* --- Display a message about the menu --- */
    g_message ("ItemFactory: activated \"%s\"",
                 gtk_item_factory_path_from_widget (widget));

    /* --- Exit the application --- */
    gtk_main_quit ();
}



/*
 * ShowMenu
 *
 * Display the item that was selected
 */
static void ShowMenu (gpointer  callback_data,
                         guint     callback_action,
                         GtkWidget *widget)
{
    g_message ("ItemFactory: activated \"%s\", action %d",
                 gtk_item_factory_path_from_widget (widget), (int)
callback_action);
}



/*
 * --- Number of items in the menu
 */
static int nmenu_items = sizeof (menu_items) / sizeof (menu_items[0]);


/*
 * CloseApp
```

```
 *
 * Close down GTK when they close the application
 * window
 */
static gint CloseApp (GtkWidget *widget, gpointer data)
{
    gtk_main_quit ();
    return (TRUE);
}



/*
 *
 */
static void CreateItemFactory ()
{
    GtkWidget *window = NULL;
    GtkWidget *box1;
    GtkWidget *box2;
    GtkWidget *separator;
    GtkWidget *label;
    GtkWidget *button;
    GtkAccelGroup *accel_group;
    GtkItemFactory *item_factory;

    /* --- Create the window --- */
    window = gtk_window_new (GTK_WINDOW_TOPLEVEL);

    /* --- Set the minimum size --- */
    gtk_widget_set_usize (window, 200, 200);

    /* --- Connect signals for destruction --- */
    gtk_signal_connect (GTK_OBJECT (window), "destroy",
            GTK_SIGNAL_FUNC (gtk_widget_destroyed),
            &window);
    gtk_signal_connect (GTK_OBJECT (window), "delete-event",
            GTK_SIGNAL_FUNC (CloseApp),
            NULL);

    /* --- Create a new accel group --- */
    accel_group = gtk_accel_group_new ();

    /* --- Create a new item factory --- */
    item_factory = gtk_item_factory_new (GTK_TYPE_MENU_BAR,
                                "<blah>",
                                accel_group);
```

```
        /* --- Create the items in the factory using data --- */
        gtk_item_factory_create_items (item_factory,
                                       nmenu_items,
                                       menu_items,
                                       NULL);

        /* --- Attach the accel group to app window --- */
        gtk_accel_group_attach (accel_group, GTK_OBJECT (window));

        /* --- Set the title of the window --- */
        gtk_window_set_title (GTK_WINDOW (window), "Item Factory");

        /* --- No border --- */
        gtk_container_border_width (GTK_CONTAINER (window), 0);

        /* --- Vertical packing box. --- */
        box1 = gtk_vbox_new (FALSE, 0);
        gtk_container_add (GTK_CONTAINER (window), box1);

        /* --- Put menu in the vertical packing box --- */
        gtk_box_pack_start (GTK_BOX (box1),
                gtk_item_factory_get_widget (item_factory, "<blah>"),
                FALSE, FALSE, 0);

        /* --- Make everything visible --- */
        gtk_widget_show_all (window);
}

int main (int argc, char *argv[])
{

  gtk_init (&argc, &argv);

  CreateItemFactory ();

  gtk_main ();

  return 0;
}
```

# Item Factories Versus Hand-Coding Menus

Item factories are a great way to make quick menus, but they are somewhat limited in what they can create in a menu. For instance, they cannot be used to add widgets to menus, like pixmaps. However, for most purposes, the item factories are a quick and simple method of adding menus to an application. The hand-coding of menus is more complicated, but also more flexible.

# Pixmaps

Displaying graphical images in buttons and other widgets requires pixmaps. *Pixmaps* are image widgets frequently used as icons on buttons or other widgets to provide a graphical illustration of what the button or widget does. Toolbars within applications have a whole row of graphical buttons because they take up less space than text-based buttons do and provide a quick way for a user to find the toolbar version of a command. One way to create a pixmap is to create it from a graphical editor (like the GIMP) and save the file as an xpm file. Here's an xpm file created from the GIMP (comments added):

```
static const gchar *xpm_open[] = {
"16 16 4 1",             /* 16 x 16 bitmap, 4 colors, 1 char/color */
"  c None",              /* color 1 - ' ' = transparent color */
"B c #000000000000",     /* color 2 - 'B' = black */
"Y c #FFFFFFFF0000",     /* color 3 - 'Y' = yellow */
"y c #999999990000",     /* color 4 - 'y' = dark yellow */
"                ",      /* image data begins here */
"          BBB   ",
"  BBBBB  B  BB  ",
"  BYYYB     BB  ",
"  BYYYYYBBBBB   ",
"  BYYYYYYYYYB   ",
"  BYYYYYYYYYB   ",
"  BYYYYYYYYYB   ",
"  BYYBBBBBBBBBB ",
"  BYYByyyyyyyyB ",
"  BYByyyyyyyyyB ",
"  BYByyyyyyyyyB ",
"  BByyyyyyyyyB  ",
"  BByyyyyyyyyB  ",
"  BBBBBBBBBBB   ",
"                ",      /* image data ends here */
};
```

The xpm file consists of three sections: the *header*, the *color table*, and the *bitmap data*. The header is the first string in the array. The string looks something like "16 16 4 1" where the first two numbers are the height and width of the image, the third number is the number of colors defined in the string array, and the fourth number is the number of characters per color. In the example, "16 16 4 1" indicates that the image has a height of 16 pixels and a width of 16 pixels. The third number defines the number of strings after the header that make up the color data. This example, therefore, has four lines of color data:

```
"  c None",
"B c #000000000000",
"Y c #FFFFFFFF0000",
"y c #999999990000",
```

Each color data line defines a color in the image. The header specifies how many characters (usually one) define a single color.

Each color data line has the character being defined, the character c, and a hex value representing the color or None for no color (transparent). The color value is in RGB format. In the preceding example, spaces represent no color, the character B represents black (#000000000000), Y represents yellow (#FFFFFFFF0000), and y represents a darker yellow (#999999990000). The hex values representing the colors here are 8-byte color values. A 4-byte color value could be used instead. The darker yellow would be represented by #999900 instead of by #999999990000.

The image data immediately follows the color data. Using the defined color data, the image can be seen as the "open" icon, which looks like a slightly open, yellow file folder. The spaces usually mean that no color is to be used, which makes it easy to see the outline of the image in the code.

Defining the image is just the beginning. To use the image, you need to convert it into a widget so that you can then treat the image like any other widget. You can create a function to take the data and create a pixmap widget. To create a pixmap widget, you need a GdkPixmap to pass into the gtk_pixmap_new function with a mask. Fortunately, you can call the GDK function gdk_pixmap_create_from_xpm_d, which takes the xpm data structure and provides the mask and a GdkPixmap.

```
/*
 * CreateWidgetFromXpm
 *
 * Convert an xpm string into a pixmap widget
 * Uses (win_main) which is a global.
 */
GtkWidget *CreateWidgetFromXpm (GtkWidget *window, gchar **xpm_data)
{
    GdkBitmap *mask;
    GdkPixmap *pixmap_data;
    GtkWidget *pixmap_widget;

    /* --- Convert the string to a gdk_pixmap --- */
    pixmap_data = gdk_pixmap_create_from_xpm_d (
                            win_main->window,
                            &mask,
                            NULL,
                            (gchar **) xpm_data);

    /* --- Convert the pixmap to a pixmap widget --- */
    pixmap_widget = gtk_pixmap_new (pixmap_data, mask);

    /* --- Make the widget visible --- */
    gtk_widget_show (pixmap_widget);
```

```
/* --- Return it so it can be used --- */
return (pixmap_widget);
}
```

This code creates a pixmap widget that will be visible when it is added to a container. You can also create a button and add the pixmap to the button; then you have a button with the pixmap in it. This technique enables you to put icons on the toolbar buttons.

# Toolbars

Toolbars provide users with menu shortcuts to commonly used commands. Toolbars usually contain buttons with icons representing the commands but can contain other widgets as well. The toolbar widget is created with the gtk_toolbar_new function and takes two parameters that determine the style of the toolbar. The first parameter determines whether the icons are laid out horizontally (GTK_ORIENTATION_HORIZONTAL) or vertically (GTK_ORIENTATION_VERTICAL), and the second parameter indicates whether the buttons are to display icons (GTK_TOOLBAR_ICONS), text (GTK_TOOLBAR_TEXT), or both (GTK_TOOLBAR_BOTH). The toolbar in this example is a horizontal toolbar with icons going across the main window. You will add the toolbar to the vertical packing box created earlier for the application.

```
/* --- Create a horizontal toolbar with icons --- */
toolbar = gtk_toolbar_new (GTK_ORIENTATION_HORIZONTAL,
                           GTK_TOOLBAR_ICONS);

/* --- Add the toolbar to the application vertical --- */
/* --- packing box. This is right under the menu --- */
gtk_box_pack_start (GTK_BOX (vbox), toolbar, FALSE, TRUE, 0);

/* --- Make the toolbar visible --- */
gtk_widget_show (toolbar);
```

Now you have a toolbar without the buttons. Adding widgets to the toolbar and formatting the toolbar requires one of several functions. The three mostly commonly used are gtk_toolbar_append_item, gtk_toolbar_append_element, and gtk_toolbar_append_space.

## Adding Toolbar Buttons

The gtk_toolbar_append_item adds a button to the toolbar. The gtk_toolbar_append_item has parameters for the button pixmap, tooltips, the callback function, and more. The function prototype is

```
GtkWidget *gtk_toolbar_append_item (
            GtkToolbar *toolbar,
            const char *text,
```

```
                 const char *tooltip_text,
                 const char *tooltip_private_text,
                 GtkWidget *widget,
                 GtkSignalFunc callback,
                 gpointer userdata);
```

The `toolbar` is the toolbar that the button is being added to. The `text` is for textual buttons. This toolbar was defined as a graphical button, so this field is ignored. The `tooltip_text` defines the tooltip text displayed when the user moves over the button with the mouse. The `tooltip_private_text` can be ignored for now. The `widget` is usually a pixmap widget used to put an image on the button. The `callback` is the function called when the button is pressed, and the `userdata` is the additional parameter to be passed into the callback function.

You can use the `CreateWidgetFromXpm` function created earlier to create a widget from the xpm data so that you can create a button with an icon in it. Passing the pixmap in adds the pixmap to the button.

```
/* --- Create the "new" button on the toolbar --- */
gtk_toolbar_append_item (GTK_TOOLBAR (toolbar),
         NULL, "New window", NULL,
         CreateWidgetFromXpm (vbox_main, (gchar **) xpm_new),
         (GtkSignalFunc) ButtonEvent,
         NULL);
```

The button displays the passed-in pixmap as the button's icon. When the button in the toolbar is pressed, the `ButtonEvent` function is notified so that you can put code in the function to perform processing. The standard approach here is to call the same function as the menu command `"New Window"` calls for the same event. The nice thing about the `gtk_toolbar_append_item` function is that it also does the setup of the event handler and the tooltip (`"New Window"`) without any additional calls. When you were creating a menu, you had to do each little step manually, so you created a function to do the work. Here, there's only one function, which makes the function easier to use.

## Adding Other Items to the Toolbar

The `gtk_toolbar_append_element` is similar to the `gtk_toolbar_append_item` function but more flexible and therefore more complicated. Instead of just supporting plain toolbar buttons, the `gtk_toolbar_append_element` has support for buttons (`GTK_TOOLBAR_CHILD_BUTTON`), toggle buttons (`GTK_TOOLBAR_CHILD_TOGGLEBUTTON`), radio buttons (`GTK_TOOLBAR_CHILD_RADIOBUTTON`), and widgets (`GTK_TOOLBAR_CHILD_WIDGET`) and for creating gaps (`GTK_TOOLBAR_CHILD_SPACE`) between logical widget groups. The function adds two parameters: a type and a widget. The type parameter determines what kind of widget is inserted into the toolbar and whether the type is set to `GTK_TOOLBAR_CHILD_WIDGET`; then the widget parameter is used as the widget is inserted.

```
GtkWidget *gtk_toolbar_append_element (
                    GtkToolbarChildType type,
                    GtkWidget *widget,
                    GtkToolbar *toolbar,
                    const char *text,
                    const char *tooltip_text,
                    const char *tooltip_private_text,
                    GtkWidget *icon,
                    GtkSignalFunc callback,
                    gpointer userdata);
```

For instance, adding toggle buttons requires the gtk_toolbar_append_element function.

```
/* --- Create a bold button on the toolbar --- */
tool_bold = gtk_toolbar_append_element (GTK_TOOLBAR (toolbar),
              GTK_TOOLBAR_CHILD_TOGGLEBUTTON,
              NULL,
              NULL, "Bold", NULL,
              CreateWidgetFromXpm (vbox_main,
                                   (gchar **) xpm_bold),
              (GtkSignalFunc) BoldClicked,
              NULL);
```

Alternatively, you could have created a GtkToggleButton, passed it in as the widget parameter, and changed the type to GTK_TOOLBAR_CHILD_WIDGET. This instruction tells GTK+ that you're passing in a custom widget and not to create a widget, as it would for the GTK_TOOLBAR_CHILD_TOGGLEBUTTON type.

A shorter version of this function is the gtk_toolbar_append_widget. It requires more setup but provides more flexibility. The function is defined as follows:

```
void gtk_toolbar_append_widget (GtkToolbar **toolbar,
                    GtkWidget *widget,
                    Const gchar *tooltip_text,
                    Const gchar *tooltip_private_text);
```

Because the function does not set up callbacks or icons, these items should be done programmatically. This method may increase the amount of code you have to write but provides flexibility when it's necessary to step outside the box.

## Adding Spacing to the Toolbar

The gtk_toolbar_append_space function adds a space at the end of the toolbar. The only parameter required is the toolbar to which you want to add the spacing.

```
/* --- Add a gap between widgets --- */
gtk_toolbar_append_space (toolbar);
```

The `gtk_toolbar_append_space` inserts space after the last button. The insertion of spaces can help group logical sets of buttons. Grouping buttons into logical groups (font buttons might be a group, file operations another) helps users pick out a button to perform a specific task.

In addition to the append functions, equivalent prepend functions allow items to be inserted on the toolbar in the front of any widgets instead of the back (`gtk_toolbar_prepend_item`, `gtk_toolbar_prepend_element`, `gtk_toolbar_prepend_space`, and `gtk_toolbar_prepend_widget`). The parameters to the functions are the same as for the append versions of the functions.

Sometimes it's necessary to insert widgets into the middle of a group of widgets in the toolbar—usually when modifying an existing toolbar. The buttons/widgets can be inserted into any position in the toolbar by using the insert functions. Similar to the append and prepend functions, insert functions add a parameter that determines the position to insert the button/widget. The parameter is an integer index representing the position where the item should be inserted. Passing in a `zero` indicates that the item should be added as the first item, and `toolbar->num_children` indicates that the item should be added as the last item (`toolbar->num_children` is the current number of items in the toolbar).

# Building the Application's User Interface

With all this information in hand, you can create a sample front end that can be modified for all kinds of applications. In creating the application, try to consolidate functions where it makes sense to simplify the coding. If you are constantly calling three or four GTK+ functions to perform an action, then consolidate those steps into a single function. In the menu section, for instance, you consolidated many of the steps required to create a menu into a single function.

You are now ready to build a front-end application from the ground up; this section shows you how to do so quickly and easily. You need to create two menus. The "File" menu has "New," "Open," "Save," "Save As…," a separator, and "Quit." The "Edit" menu has "Cut," "Copy," "Paste," and a "Font" submenu, which contains the toggle menu items "Bold," "Italics," and "Underline."

### Creating the Application Window and Menus

The main program is small, and its only interesting aspects are that the tooltips are created in it and that the `CreateMainWindow` function is called to do most of the work.

```
/*
 * main
 *
 * --- Program begins here
 */
int main(int argc, char *argv[])
{
```

```
    /* --- Initialize GTK --- */
    gtk_init (&argc, &argv);

    /* --- Initialize tooltips --- */
    tooltips = gtk_tooltips_new();

    /* --- Create application --- */
    CreateMainWindow ();

    /* --- Let GTK do its processing --- */
    gtk_main();

    return 0;
}
```

The `CreateMainWindow` function handles most of the widget creation and does so in a few stages. The first part is the window creation and the setting of the main window attributes. Attributes like the title and size are set up before the window is made visible. The acceleration table is initialized and assigned to the main window so that you can use the acceleration keys in the menu, and you add an event handler to listen for the `"delete_event"` signal. With the window created, a vertical packing box will be added so that the menu can be stacked on the top and anything else can go beneath it. The packing box is added to the main window, and the main window is made visible.

```
/*
 * CreateMainWindow
 *
 * Create the main window and the menu/toolbar associated with it
 */
static void CreateMainWindow ()
{
    GtkWidget *vbox_main;
    GtkWidget *menubar;
    GtkWidget *menu;
    GtkWidget *menuitem;
    GtkWidget *menufont;
    GtkWidget *toolbar;
    GtkWidget *button;

    /* --- Create the top window and size it --- */
    win_main = gtk_window_new(GTK_WINDOW_TOPLEVEL);
    gtk_widget_set_usize(win_main, 360, 260);

    /* --- Set the title and border width --- */
    gtk_window_set_title (GTK_WINDOW (win_main), "Menu test");
    gtk_container_border_width (GTK_CONTAINER (win_main), 0);
```

```
/* --- Create accel table --- */
accelerator_table = gtk_accelerator_table_new();
gtk_window_add_accelerator_table(GTK_WINDOW(win_main),
➥accelerator_table);

/* --- Top-level window should listen for the "delete_event" --- */
gtk_signal_connect (GTK_OBJECT (win_main), "delete_event",
        GTK_SIGNAL_FUNC(EndProgram), NULL);

/* --- Create v-box for menu, toolbar --- */
vbox_main = gtk_vbox_new (FALSE, 0);

/* --- Put up v-box --- */
gtk_container_add (GTK_CONTAINER (win_main), vbox_main);
gtk_widget_show (vbox_main);
gtk_widget_show (win_main);

/* --- Menu bar --- */
menubar = gtk_menu_bar_new ();
gtk_box_pack_start (GTK_BOX (vbox_main), menubar, FALSE, TRUE, 0);
gtk_widget_show (menubar);
```

The "File" submenu is added to the menu bar, and the items that fall under the
"File" menu are added. Here you add (in order) "New," "Open," "Save," "Save As...," a
separator, and "Quit." In each case, you are giving the menu item an event-handler
function and a tooltip, and in most cases, an accelerator key string also. For most of the
functions, you are setting the callback to be the PrintFunc function that displays on
the console a message to show the menu that was selected. If this example were an
application, the callback would perform some action. The last parameter to
CreateMenuItem is the data that ends up being passed to the PrintFunc event handler
when it is called, which is how most menu items can end up using the same event
handler.

```
/* ----------------
 * --- File menu ---
 * ---------------- */
menu = CreateBarSubMenu (menubar, "File");

/* --- _New_ menu item--- */
menuitem = CreateMenuItem (menu, "New", "^N",
                "Create a new item",
                GTK_SIGNAL_FUNC (PrintFunc), "new");

/* --- _Open_ menu item--- */
menuitem = CreateMenuItem (menu, "Open", "^O",
                "Open an existing item",
                GTK_SIGNAL_FUNC (PrintFunc), "open");
```

```
/* --- _Save_ menu item --- */
menuitem = CreateMenuItem (menu, "Save", "^S",
                "Save current item",
                GTK_SIGNAL_FUNC (PrintFunc), "save");

/* --- _Save as__ menu item ---*/
menuitem = CreateMenuItem (menu, "Save As...", "",
                "Save current item with new name",
                GTK_SIGNAL_FUNC (PrintFunc), "save as");

/* --- Separator --- */
menuitem = CreateMenuItem (menu, NULL, NULL,
                NULL, NULL, NULL);

/* --- Quit --- */
menuitem = CreateMenuItem (menu, "Quit", "",
                "What's more descriptive than quit?",
                GTK_SIGNAL_FUNC (PrintFunc), "quit");
```

The "Edit" menu is smaller and has the following items: "Cut," "Copy," "Paste," and "Font." The "Font" menu item is really a submenu, and the function you use to create it is different from the function that you used to create the other menu items.

```
/* ----------------
 * --- Edit menu ---
 * ---------------- */
menu = CreateBarSubMenu (menubar, "Edit");

/* --- Cut menu item --- */
menuitem = CreateMenuItem (menu, "Cut", "^X",
                "Remove item and place into clipboard",
                GTK_SIGNAL_FUNC (PrintFunc), "cut");

/* --- Copy menu item --- */
menuitem = CreateMenuItem (menu, "Copy", "^C",
                "Place a copy of the item in the clipboard",
                GTK_SIGNAL_FUNC (PrintFunc), "copy");

/* --- Paste menu item --- */
menuitem = CreateMenuItem (menu, "Paste", "^V",
                "Paste item",
                GTK_SIGNAL_FUNC (PrintFunc), "paste");
```

Finally, you add the "Font" menu items: "Bold," "Italics," and "Underline." These are going to be check menu items so that they display either checked or unchecked in the menu. The toolbar is created after all the menu items are created. Unlike when you created the previous set of buttons, now you need to keep track of the widgets for the toolbar. The reason will be apparent later.

```
/* --------------------
 * --- Font sub menu ---
 * -------------------- */
menufont = CreateSubMenu (menu, "Font");

menuBold = CreateMenuCheck (menufont,
    "Bold", GTK_SIGNAL_FUNC (SelectMenu), "bold");

menuItalics = CreateMenuCheck (menufont,
    "Italics", GTK_SIGNAL_FUNC (SelectMenu), "italics");

menuUnderline = CreateMenuCheck (menufont,
    "Underline", GTK_SIGNAL_FUNC (SelectMenu), "underline");

/* --- Create the toolbar --- */
CreateToolbar (vbox_main);
}
```

Note that the Item Factory could not have been used in this example because of the check boxes in the menu. Without check boxes, it would probably be easier to use the Item Factory.

## Creating the Toolbar

The CreateToolbar function creates the toolbar with all the icons on the buttons. As an added bonus, a font combo box on the toolbar will give it a professional look. First, the toolbar needs to be created and added to the vertical packing box.

```
/*
 * CreateToolbar
 */
void CreateToolbar (GtkWidget *vbox_main)
{
  GtkWidget *widget;

    /* --- Create the toolbar and add it to the window --- */
    toolbar = gtk_toolbar_new (GTK_ORIENTATION_HORIZONTAL,
➥GTK_TOOLBAR_ICONS);
    gtk_box_pack_start (GTK_BOX (vbox_main), toolbar, FALSE, TRUE, 0);
    gtk_widget_show (toolbar);

    /* --- Create "new" button --- */
    gtk_toolbar_append_item (GTK_TOOLBAR (toolbar),
                        NULL, "New window", NULL,
                        CreateWidgetFromXpm (vbox_main, (gchar **)
➥xpm_new),
```

```
                                (GtkSignalFunc) ButtonClicked,
                                NULL);

    /* --- Create "open" button --- */
    gtk_toolbar_append_item (GTK_TOOLBAR (toolbar),
                                "Open Dialog", "Open dialog", "",
                                CreateWidgetFromXpm (vbox_main, (gchar **)
➥xpm_open),
                                (GtkSignalFunc) ButtonClicked,
                                NULL);

    /* --- Little gap --- */
    gtk_toolbar_append_space (GTK_TOOLBAR (toolbar));


    /* --- The _Cut_ button --- */
    gtk_toolbar_append_item (GTK_TOOLBAR (toolbar),
                                "Cut", "Cut", "",
                                CreateWidgetFromXpm (vbox_main, (gchar **)
➥xpm_cut),
                                (GtkSignalFunc) ButtonClicked,
                                NULL);

    /* --- The _Paste_ button --- */
    gtk_toolbar_append_item (GTK_TOOLBAR (toolbar),
                                "Paste", "Paste", "",
                                CreateWidgetFromXpm (vbox_main, (gchar **)
➥xpm_copy),
                                (GtkSignalFunc) ButtonClicked,
                                NULL);

    /* --- Add a gap --- */
    gtk_toolbar_append_space (GTK_TOOLBAR (toolbar));

    /* --- Create a font combo box. The CreateCombobox
     *     function creates the combo box and puts an event
     *     handler on the combo box. */
    widget = CreateCombobox ();

    /* --- Add the combo box to the toolbar --- */
    gtk_toolbar_append_widget (GTK_TOOLBAR (toolbar),
                                widget,
                                "Font", "Pick a font");

    /* --- A little gap --- */
    gtk_toolbar_append_space (GTK_TOOLBAR (toolbar));
```

```
        /*
         * --- Create a toggle button for the Bold
         */
        tool_bold = gtk_toolbar_append_element (GTK_TOOLBAR (toolbar),
                        GTK_TOOLBAR_CHILD_TOGGLEBUTTON,
                        NULL,
                        NULL, "Bold", NULL,
                        CreateWidgetFromXpm (vbox_main,
                                        (gchar **) xpm_bold),
                        (GtkSignalFunc) ButtonClicked,
                        "bold");

      /*
       * --- Create a toggle button for the Italics
       */
      tool_italics = gtk_toolbar_append_element (GTK_TOOLBAR (toolbar),
                        GTK_TOOLBAR_CHILD_TOGGLEBUTTON,
                        NULL,
                        "Italics", "Italics", "Italics",
                        CreateWidgetFromXpm (vbox_main,
                                        (gchar **) xpm_italics),
                        (GtkSignalFunc) ButtonClicked,
                        "italics");

      /*
       * --- Create a toggle button for the Underline
       */
      tool_underline = gtk_toolbar_append_element (GTK_TOOLBAR (toolbar),
                        GTK_TOOLBAR_CHILD_TOGGLEBUTTON,
                        NULL,
                        "Underline", "Underline", "Underline",
                        CreateWidgetFromXpm (vbox_main,
                                        (gchar **) xpm_underline),
                        (GtkSignalFunc) ButtonClicked,
                        "underline");

}
```

## Synchronizing Toolbar and Menu Items

The font buttons on the toolbar and the font menu selections are totally distinct and separate as far as GTK+ is concerned. No association exists between the two elements unless you put an association in the code. The association usually involves the menu item and the toolbar buttons having the same callback, which causes both the toolbar button and the menu item to have the same effect in the application.

In some applications, state information is shown in several places. In the application you are creating, font information is shown on the toolbar and on a checked menu item. If the toolbar "Bold" button is selected, the "Bold" menu selection should also reflect the state change. However, synchronization between the toolbar toggle buttons and the menu toggle items is not an automatic process, because the application has no knowledge of the relationship between the two items.

To achieve the necessary synchronization, recall that the toolbar font buttons set the callback to a function called `ButtonClicked`. This function knows which button was pressed and sets the equivalent menu item state. Also recall that you stored the font menu item widget pointer when you created the menu item. This makes it easy to update the menu when the toolbar button is clicked. You can check the toggled state of the toggled button by using the following code:

```
/* --- Is the button up or down? --- */
nState = GTK_TOGGLE_BUTTON (widget)->active;
```

The widget is converted into a toggle button so that you can check on the state of the button. You can create the small `ButtonClicked` function that does the following:

```
/*
 * --- ButtonClicked
 */
void ButtonClicked (GtkWidget *widget, gpointer data)
{
    /* --- Get the button state --- */
    int nState = GTK_TOGGLE_BUTTON (widget)->active;

    /* --- Synchronize the menu state with the button --- */
    SetMenuButton ((char *) data, nState);
}
```

The `data` variable was set up when you created the widget so the value gets passed into this function. In this case, the `data` variable tells you which button was pressed. Recall that you can use the `gtk_check_menu_item_set_state` function to set the check button's state. The button that was selected passes in the `data` parameter with text that describes which button was pressed.

```
/*
 * SetMenuButton
 *
 * Set the menu button based on the name and state.
 *
 * szButton _ name of the button to change
 * nState _ State to set the button
 */
void SetMenuButton (char *szButton, int nState)
{
    GtkCheckMenuItem *check = NULL;
```

```
/* --- Show how we're changing the button --- */
printf ("check_menu_set_state - %d\n", nState);

/* --- Bold button? --- */
if (!strcmp (szButton, "bold")) {

    check = GTK_CHECK_MENU_ITEM(menuBold);

/* --- Italic button? --- */
} else if (!strcmp (szButton, "italics")) {

    check = GTK_CHECK_MENU_ITEM(menuItalics);

/* --- Underline button? --- */
} else if (!strcmp (szButton, "underline")) {

    check = GTK_CHECK_MENU_ITEM(menuUnderline);
}

/* --- If we found a button --- */
if (check) {

    /* --- Set the state --- */
    gtk_check_menu_item_set_state (check, nState);
}
}
```

In turn, the menu needs to set the state of the toolbar button if it is selected. The differences are that the `gtk_toggle_button_set_state` function sets the button state, and you need to convert the widget into a `GTK_CHECK_MENU_ITEM` to determine whether the button is selected.

```
void SelectMenu (GtkWidget *widget, gpointer data)
{
    GtkToggleButton *button = NULL;
    char *szButton;

    /* --- Get state of the menu --- */
    int nState = GTK_CHECK_MENU_ITEM (widget)->active;

    /* --- Show param and button state --- */
    szButton = (char *) data;
    printf ("select menu %s - %d\n", szButton, nState);

    /* --- Toggle the toolbar button ---*/
    if (!strcmp (szButton, "bold")) {
```

```
        button = GTK_TOGGLE_BUTTON (tool_bold);
    } else if (!strcmp (szButton, "italics")) {

        button = GTK_TOGGLE_BUTTON (tool_italics);
    } else if (!strcmp (szButton, "underline")) {

        button = GTK_TOGGLE_BUTTON (tool_underline);
    }
    if (button) {
        gtk_toggle_button_set_state (button, nState);
    }
}
```

The two routines are very similar. Now, when the toolbar button for the font styles is clicked, the menu is updated; and when the menu is clicked, the toolbar is updated with the correct state. These small touches make an application feel solid. Nothing is worse than having the toolbar show one state and having the menu items show a different state. Well, okay, maybe there are worse things, but it sure doesn't look very good to the application user.

## Summary

Applications require a good user interface. Menus, toolbars, pixmaps, and tooltips help make a professional-looking application. There is a hard way and an easy way to create menu items; the hard way is more flexible and enables you to do more, such as add check boxes to the menu. Many functions are available to help you add items to the toolbar. Pixmaps are images that can be made into pixmap widgets and inserted into buttons to provide a button with an icon. Small applications are created to illustrate how to create a shell application using the item factory and by hand coding all the elements.

6

# More Widgets: Frames, Text, Dialog Boxes, File Selection Dialog Box, Progress Bar

Sᴌᴍᴘʟᴇ ᴡɪᴅɢᴇᴛs ᴀʀᴇ ᴏɴʟʏ ᴛʜᴇ ʙᴇɢɪɴɴɪɴɢ of GTK+. GTK+ has many widgets to help developers write complete applications. This chapter covers some of these additional widgets, including the frame widget, dialog widget, progress bar and the powerful text widget.

## Frames

Frames are containers that usually have a border around them as well as a title that is used to group widgets. Frames help to distinguish between different fields on a screen. Frames are created with the `gtk_frame_new` function that creates the default frame. The standard creation sequence for a frame is

```
/* --- Create the frame --- */
frame = gtk_frame_new ("Title");

/* --- Set any attributes --- */

/* --- Make it visible --- */
gtk_widget_show (frame);

/* --- Add it to a container or a box or something --- */
gtk_container_add (window, frame);
```

After you create the frame, you can use the gtk_frame_set_label function to change the label on the frame.

```
gtk_frame_set_label (frame, "Hey, new title");
```

The frame border characteristics can be set by using the gtk_frame_set_shadow function. It specifies how the frame looks to the viewer. Setting the frame with the GTK_SHADOW_IN makes the whole frame appear to be depressed, whereas the GTK_SHADOW_OUT makes the frame appear higher up than the other widgets. This color effect is achieved by using colors to trick the eyes. The more commonly used GTK_SHADOW_ETCHED_OUT and GTK_SHADOW_ETCHED_IN only draw a border around the frame, and GTK_SHADOW_ETCHED_NONE draws no border. Figure 6.1 shows the different types of frames.

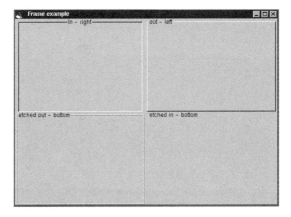

Figure 6.1 Frames.

The title can appear in the frame in one of three ways: on the left, in the middle, or on the right. You can use the gtk_frame_set_label_align function to change the alignment. The parameters you used to set the label alignment are also used to set the frame's label alignment. Left alignment is 0, centered is .5, and right alignment is 1. You can see the alignment parameters here:

```
/* --- Set frame label to the left --- */
gtk_frame_set_label_align (GTK_FRAME (frame), 0, 0);

/* --- Center the frame label --- */
gtk_frame_set_label_align (GTK_FRAME (frame), .5, 0);

/* --- Put the frame label on the right --- */
gtk_frame_set_label_align (GTK_FRAME (frame), 1, 0);
```

After they are created, widgets can be added to the frame. The frame should be treated like a container widget that happens to have a border and a title. If you want to add more than one widget to the frame, you need a packing box or packing table widget.

# Text Widget

The text widget (see Figure 6.2) is similar to the entry widget (see Chapter 4, "Basic Widgets"), but the text widget supports multiple lines of text, making it ideally suited for an editor. In fact, later you explore the creation of an editor using the text widget. The text widget is considerably more complicated than the smaller widgets, as it has many attributes that can be set.

The text widget supports a series of shortcuts, including the standard cut, copy, and paste shortcuts. These shortcuts are also supported by the entry widget because they're both derived from `GtkEditable`. Here are some of the text widget shortcuts:
Motion shortcuts:

- Ctrl+A—Beginning of line
- Ctrl+E—End of line
- Ctrl+N—Next line
- Ctrl+P—Previous line
- Ctrl+B—Backward one character
- Ctrl+F—Forward one character
- Alt+B—Backward one word
- Alt+F—Forward one word

Editing shortcuts:

- Ctrl+H—Delete backward character (backspace)
- Ctrl+D—Delete forward character (delete)
- Ctrl+W—Delete backward word
- Alt+D—Delete forward word
- Ctrl+K—Delete to end of line
- Ctrl+U—Delete line

Selection shortcuts:

- Ctrl+X—Cut to clipboard
- Ctrl+C—Copy to clipboard
- Ctrl+V—Paste from clipboard

The text widget is virtually an editor right out of the box. Using the text widget to make an editor application does not take much work. You can see how easy the process is in Chapter 8, "Developing a Simple Word Processor," when you use the text widget to make a small editor.

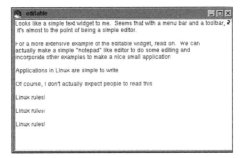

Figure 6.2    Text widget.

## Creating a Text Widget

Creating a text widget is done by using the `gtk_text_new` function and passing in a `GtkAdjustment` value that specifies the horizontal and vertical adjustment values. Usually, these can be passed in with NULL, and the default adjustments will be used. You can create the text widget with

```
text = gtk_text_new (NULL, NULL);
```

The text widget can be set to *read-only* by using the `gtk_text_set_editable` function. The function sets the field to "read-only" if FALSE is passed in; otherwise, the widget is made editable. The default setting is to allow editing.

```
/* --- Allow the text widget to be edited --- */
gtk_text_set_editable (GTK_TEXT (text), TRUE);

/* --- Set the widget to 'read-only' mode --- */
gtk_text_set_editable (GTK_TEXT (text), FALSE);
```

The cursor position can be set by using the `gtk_text_set_point` function. The `gtk_text_set_point` function expects an index that determines where the cursor is positioned. The index is a character-based index. For example:

```
/* --- Set the cursor after the tenth character --- */
gtk_text_set_point (GTK_TEXT (text), 10);
```

The cursor position can also be queried by using the `gtk_text_get_point` function. An index is returned that represents the offset into the text where the cursor is positioned.

```
/* --- Find out where the cursor is --- */
nPos = gtk_text_get_point (GTK_TEXT (text));
```

The text widget can be queried to find out how many characters are in the widget by using `gtk_text_get_length` function. You can use the `gtk_editable_get_chars` function to get the text within the text widget. For instance, to get all the characters in the text widget, the following code would suffice:

```
/* --- Get the number of chars in the widget --- */
nLength = gtk_text_get_length (GTK_TEXT (text));

/* --- Get the text in the widget --- */
buffer = gtk_editable_get_chars (GTK_EDITABLE (text),
                                 (gint) 0,
                                 (gint) nLength);
```

Rather than calculate the length of the text within the widget, the value -1 can be used to indicate the last character.

```
/* --- Get the text in the widget --- */
buffer = gtk_editable_get_chars (GTK_EDITABLE (text),
                                 (gint) 0,
                                 (gint) -1);
```

The buffer returned in the `gtk_editable_get_chars` function is a new block of memory allocated specifically for the return value. It would be bad programming practice to leave the memory floating around until the application exited. (What? Do you think this is a Microsoft application?) The `g_free` function should be used to free up the memory when it is no longer needed.

```
/* --- Done with the memory, free it --- */
g_free (buffer);
```

A single character in the text widget can be retrieved with the `GTK_TEXT_INDEX` macro. By passing in the index, the character at the position is retrieved.

```
/* --- Get the 101st character in the widget --- */
ch = GTK_TEXT_INDEX (GTK_TEXT (text), 101);
```

The text in the widget can also be inserted into the widget using the `gtk_text_insert_text` function. The `gtk_text_insert_text` function inserts the text at the current cursor position. If the text is going to be added using a particular font or color, the `gtk_text_insert` function is used with the font and color information. Passing in a `NULL` uses the current font and color.

```
/* --- Add some text without a font/color --- */
gtk_text_insert (GTK_TEXT (text), NULL, NULL, NULL,
                 buffer, strlen (buffer));

/* --- Add some text with a font/color --- */
gtk_text_insert (GTK_TEXT (text), font,
                 foreColor, backColor,
                 buffer, strlen (buffer));

/* --- Add some text and use current font/color --- */
gtk_text_insert_text (GTK_TEXT (text), buffer,
                      strlen (buffer), &nPosition);
```

Deleting text is done relative to the current cursor position. The text can be deleted from the current cursor position to a point before or after the cursor position.

The gtk_text_forward_delete function deletes characters from the cursor position forward and the gtk_text_backward_delete function deletes characters from the cursor position going back.

```
/* --- Delete the ten characters after the cursor --- */
bSuccess = gtk_text_forward_delete (GTK_TEXT (text), (guint) 10);

/* --- Delete the ten characters before the cursor --- */
bSuccess = gtk_text_backward_delete (GTK_TEXT (text), (guint) 10);
```

The return value is TRUE if the delete was successful and FALSE otherwise.

## Inserting and Deleting Text

Inserting and deleting text can be slow when a large amount of text is being inserting or deleted. The widget wants to repaint itself after every insertion or deletion of text and that is not always a good idea, especially when several strings are being inserted and deleted together. Sometimes the best approach is to suspend the painting of the widget until the insertion or deletion of text occurs. You can suspend automatic updating by calling the gtk_text_freeze function and restart updating by calling the gtk_text_thaw function. The gtk_text_freeze function is called before the updates to the widget are made. When the updates are complete, you can use the gtk_text_thaw function to "unfreeze" the widget, which causes it to repaint if it changed while frozen. The code looks like this:

```
/* --- Freeze the widget --- */
gtk_text_freeze (GTK_TEXT (text));

/* --- Put the updates here --- */

/* --- Un-freeze the widget --- */
gtk_text_thaw (GTK_TEXT (text));
```

Failing to use the gtk_text_freeze and gtk_text_thaw functions when inserting and deleting a lot of text causes the widget to repaint itself after every insertion or deletion. So instead of [insert text][insert text][insert text][paint], the widget would end doing [insert text][paint][insert text][paint][insert text][paint]. The two additional paints are unnecessary, because the widget is going to have additional operations done that will cause the widget to repaint further. It's better to tell the widget not to update itself until all the insertion and deletion operations have been completed. This situation might happen if you used the editor to implement a search and replace. It would be better to freeze the screen while the updates were occurring and display the finished product, rather than to slow down the search and replace by having the widget repaint itself with the new text every time the text is fixed within the widget.

Text widgets that are editors of some kind have to support the cut, copy, and paste options. The text widget automatically supports the cut (Ctrl+X), copy (Ctrl+C), and paste (Ctrl+V) within the widget. However, many people tend to enjoy using the mouse to handle functions such as copy, cut, and paste. You can implement these functions in the widget by calling the functions that handle the copy, cut, and paste functionality.

The `gtk_editable_copy_clipboard` function copies the selected text from the widget and moves it to the clipboard. The text remains in the clipboard until needed or overwritten.

```
/* --- Copy selected text and move to the clipboard --- */
gtk_editable_copy_clipboard (GTK_EDITABLE (text), GDK_CURRENT_TIME);
```

The `gtk_editable_cut_clipboard` function removes the selected text from the widget and moves it into the clipboard.

```
/* --- Remove the selected text from the widget and put in the
➥clipboard */
gtk_editable_cut_clipboard (GTK_EDITABLE (text), GDK_CURRENT_TIME);
```

The `gtk_editable_paste_clipboard` function pastes the text from the clipboard and inserts it into the cursor position within the widget.

```
/* --- Copy the text from the clipboard and insert it into --- */
/* --- the widget at the cursor position --- */
gtk_editable_copy_clipboard (GTK_EDITABLE (text), GDK_CURRENT_TIME);
```

## Scrollbars

Scrollbars are useful in a text widget. They are good for instances when a user enters more text than the widget can display on the screen, which, surprisingly, seems to happen quite often. Although the text fits in the widget, a user may want to use the mouse to scroll through the data but will find that it's difficult without scrollbars. The text widget is certainly more useful with scrollbars that allow the user to scroll through the text with the mouse.

The scrollbars can be created and attached to the text control easily. The following code creates a text widget within a table and adds scrollbars to the edit control. A 2×2 packing table is created so that the text can be placed in it with the vertical scrollbar next to it on the right side and the horizontal scrollbar right beneath the text widget. In terms of the packing table, the text widget is in the upper-left corner (0-1,0-1) of the packing table. The vertical scrollbar goes in the upper-right corner (1-2,0-1) of the packing table, and the horizontal scrollbar goes at the bottom-left corner (0-1,1-2) of the packing table.

```
/* --- Create the widget --- */
table = gtk_table_new (2, 2, FALSE);

/* --- Make it visible --- */
gtk_widget_show (table);
```

```
/* --- Create the widget --- */
text = gtk_text_new (NULL, NULL);
/* --- Add the widget to the packing table --- */
gtk_table_attach (GTK_TABLE (table), text, 0, 1, 0, 1,
        GTK_EXPAND ¦ GTK_SHRINK ¦ GTK_FILL,
        GTK_EXPAND ¦ GTK_SHRINK ¦ GTK_FILL, 0, 0);

/* --- Make it visible --- */
gtk_widget_show (text);
```

When the text widget is in the packing table, the scrollbars can be added to the widget. The scrollbars should be added to the text widget's structure. The structure has a hadj field and a vadj field, which are GtkAdjustment pointers. To create a scrollbar and associate the text field's GtkAdjustment to the scrollbar, just pass in the GtkAdjustment when the scrollbar is created.

```
/* -------------------------------- */
/* --- Create a horizontal scrollbar --- */
/* -------------------------------- */
hscroll = gtk_hscrollbar_new (GTK_TEXT (text)->hadj);

/* --- Put the horizontal scrollbar beneath the text widget --- */
gtk_table_attach (GTK_TABLE (table), hscroll, 0, 1, 1, 2,
        GTK_EXPAND ¦ GTK_FILL ¦ GTK_SHRINK, GTK_FILL, 0, 0);

/* --- Display the widget---*/
gtk_widget_show (hscroll)

/* -------------------------------- */
/* --- Create a vertical scrollbar --- */
/* -------------------------------- */
vscroll = gtk_vscrollbar_new (GTK_TEXT (text)->vadj);

/* --- Put the vertical scrollbar to the right of the text --- */
gtk_table_attach (GTK_TABLE (table), vscroll, 1, 2, 0, 1,
        GTK_FILL, GTK_EXPAND ¦ GTK_SHRINK ¦ GTK_FILL, 0, 0);

/* --- Make it visible --- */
gtk_widget_show (vscroll);
```

If the horizontal scrollbar is not needed then you can simply create a packing box and put the vertical scrollbar next to the text widget. The following code shows an example:

```
/* --- Create the widget --- */
text = gtk_text_new (NULL, NULL);

/* --- Add the text widget to the packing box --- */
gtk_box_pack_start (GTK_BOX (hbox), text, FALSE, FALSE, 0);
```

```
/* --- Create a vertical scrollbar --- */
vscroll = gtk_vscrollbar_new (GTK_TEXT(text)->vadj);

/* --- Add scrollbar.  Should be to the right of text widget --- */
gtk_box_pack_start(GTK_BOX(hbox), vscroll, FALSE, FALSE, 0);

/* --- Make the scrollbar visible --- */
gtk_widget_show (vscroll);
```

# Dialog Boxes

Dialog boxes can be used to display information to the user ("Your disk is getting full.") or to ask a user a question ("Are you sure you want to do this?") or to get other information from the user ("What do you want to save the file as?").

Dialog boxes are created by using the `gtk_dialog_new` function, which creates the basic dialog box with no buttons or text. The created dialog box has two packing boxes (`vbox`, `action_area`) where other widgets can be added. The box is used to place labels or other information, and the buttons are placed in the `action_area`. The plain-vanilla dialog box is not usable until you add a text widget and a button or two and is useless unless it conveys information to the user. The easiest way to make the dialog box useful is to display some text with an "Ok" button. We can create the label and add it to the dialog box's `vbox` packing box using

```
/* --- Create the label --- */
label = gtk_label_new (szMessage);

/* --- Give it a little breathing room --- */
gtk_misc_set_padding (GTK_MISC (label), 10, 10);

/* --- Add it to the dialog box's vbox area --- */
gtk_box_pack_start (GTK_BOX (GTK_DIALOG (dialog_window)->vbox),
                    label, TRUE, TRUE, 0);

/* --- Always make it visible --- */
gtk_widget_show (label);
```

Nice, but it still does not provide for any user interaction. To do that, you should add a button to the `action_area`. When you add a button to a dialog box, it's usually good to set the `GTK_CAN_DEFAULT` flag on the button. The `GTK_CAN_DEFAULT` flag specifies that the widget can be the default action for a dialog box and allows the user to press the Enter key instead of click the button. The `gtk_widget_grab_default` function sets the default widget to the widget specified. This simple example has only one button; therefore, we can make it the default button for the dialog box so that the user can just press the Enter key when the dialog box pops up. The default button has a wide border around it to indicate that it is the default widget. Adding an "Ok" button for the user to press is as simple as

```
/* --- Create the button --- */
button = gtk_button_new_with_label ("Ok");

/* --- Allow the button to be defaulted --- */
GTK_WIDGET_SET_FLAGS (button, GTK_CAN_DEFAULT);

/* --- Add widget to the action area --- */
gtk_box_pack_start (GTK_BOX (GTK_DIALOG (dialog_window)->action_area),
                    button, TRUE, TRUE, 0);

/* --- Grab the focus --- */
gtk_widget_grab_default (button);

/* --- Make it visible --- */
gtk_widget_show (button);

/* --- Wait for the button to be clicked --- */
gtk_signal_connect (GTK_OBJECT (button), "clicked",
                    GTK_SIGNAL_FUNC (OkClicked),
                    &return_value);
```

Linux supports several types of dialog boxes. Some are modal dialog boxes, and some are modeless. Modal dialog boxes put the focus of the application on the dialog box and keeps it there so the user cannot use any other window until that dialog box disappears. The only events that the application allows to be processed are for the modal dialog box. In Linux the application may want to display modal dialog boxes to make sure that the user has viewed information or when the information in the dialog box is critical to moving to the next step in a series. Many times the File Selection dialog box is modal because the user has specified that he or she wants to load up a file. It makes no sense to do anything until the file has been selected and the user presses the "Ok" button or decides to cancel the dialog box by pressing the "Cancel" button. Figure 6.3 shows some dialog boxes in action.

Modeless dialog boxes have no serial dependencies. A color chart might be displayed in a dialog box that gives the user a color choice. Other windows and dialog boxes can be displayed at the same time without dedicating the focus to the color dialog.

The Popup function created here displays a simple dialog box and waits for the user to hit the "Ok" button. This is accomplished by creating the dialog box, creating the label for the message and putting it in the dialog box, and creating the "Ok" button and putting it in the dialog box. The button has an event handler on it that closes the dialog box when it is pressed. This dialog box is a modal one because it calls the gtk_grab_add function. The function makes sure that only the dialog box gets events.

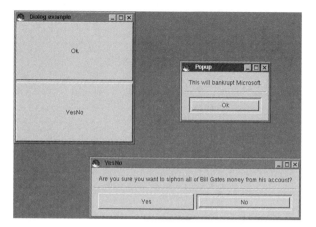

**Figure 6.3**   Dialog widget.

```
/*
 * Popup
 *
 * Display a popup dialog window with a message and an
 * "Ok" button
 */
void Popup (char *szMessage)
{
    static GtkWidget *label;
    GtkWidget *button;
    GtkWidget *dialog_window;

    /* --- Create a dialog window --- */
    dialog_window = gtk_dialog_new ();

    /* --- Trap the window close signal to release the grab --- */
    gtk_signal_connect (GTK_OBJECT (dialog_window), "destroy",
                    GTK_SIGNAL_FUNC (ClosingDialog),
                    &dialog_window);

    /* --- Add a title to the window --- */
    gtk_window_set_title (GTK_WINDOW (dialog_window), "Popup");

    /* --- Create a small border --- */
    gtk_container_border_width (GTK_CONTAINER (dialog_window), 5);

    /* ------------------------ */
    /* --- Create the message --- */
```

```
/* ------------------------ */

/* --- Create the message in a label --- */
label = gtk_label_new (szMessage);

/* --- Put some room around the label --- */
gtk_misc_set_padding (GTK_MISC (label), 10, 10);

/* --- Add the label to the dialog box --- */
gtk_box_pack_start (GTK_BOX (GTK_DIALOG (dialog_window)->vbox),
                    label, TRUE, TRUE, 0);

/* --- Make the label visible --- */
gtk_widget_show (label);

/* ------------------- */
/* --- "Ok" button --- */
/* ------------------- */

/* --- Create the "Ok" button --- */
button = gtk_button_new_with_label ("Ok");

/* --- Need to close the window if they press "Ok" --- */
gtk_signal_connect (GTK_OBJECT (button), "clicked",
                    GTK_SIGNAL_FUNC (CloseDialog),
                    dialog_window);

/* --- Allow it to be the default button --- */
GTK_WIDGET_SET_FLAGS (button, GTK_CAN_DEFAULT);

/* --- Add the button to the dialog box --- */
gtk_box_pack_start (GTK_BOX (
                GTK_DIALOG (dialog_window)->action_area),
                button, TRUE, TRUE, 0);

/* --- Make the button the default button --- */
gtk_widget_grab_default (button);

/* --- Make the button visible --- */
gtk_widget_show (button);

/* --- Make the dialog box visible --- */
gtk_widget_show (dialog_window);

gtk_grab_add (dialog_window);
}
```

The CloseDialog button that is mapped to the "OK" button calls the `gtk_grab_remove` function to release the modal mode that the dialog box is in and then closes the dialog window. The dialog box's `GtkWidget` pointer is passed in as the data field because the callback doesn't know which dialog box the signal came from, just that it came from the widget. The `gtk_signal_connect` function set up the passing of the dialog window into the callback, and here it is used to close the dialog window.

```
/*
 * CloseDialog
 *
 * Close the dialog window.  The dialog handle is passed
 * in as the data.
 */
void CloseDialog (GtkWidget *widget, gpointer data)
{

    /* --- Close it --- */
    gtk_widget_destroy (GTK_WIDGET (data));

}
```

When the dialog window was created, the `gtk_grab_add` function was called to make the dialog window modal. On closing the dialog window, the corresponding `gtk_grab_remove` should be called to release the dialog window grab. The `"destroy"` signal is the perfect place to do so because it signals that the window is closing.

```
/*
 * ClosingDialog
 *
 * Calls when window is about to close.  Returns FALSE
 * to let it close.  Releases the grab which made the dialog
 * window modal.
 */
void ClosingDialog (GtkWidget *widget, gpointer data)
{
    gtk_grab_remove (GTK_WIDGET (widget));
}
```

Slightly more complicated examples are the "Yes/No" or "Ok/Cancel" types of dialog boxes. They present the user with a message and provide a choice. They are along the lines of "Are you sure you want to do this?" where the choices in the dialog box cause different things to happen. You can create these types of dialog boxes by extending the previous example to give each button in the dialog box its own event handler that can be passed into the function.

Notice that both the "Yes" button and the "No" button in the following example have the `GTK_CAN_DEFAULT` flag set on them. Consequently, either one can be the default action for the dialog box. If you click on either button and hold down the mouse, the border around the button moves to that particular button.

Pressing Enter at that point is the equivalent of pressing the default button. The dialog box starts with the "No" button defaulted with the `gtk_widget_grab_default` function. You should usually set the default action to a nondestructive action. For instance, a program that reformats your hard drive and asks, "Are you sure you want to do this?" should probably default to the "No" button.

The `YesNo` function takes a message ("Are you sure you want to do this?") and two functions. The `YesFunc` function should be called when the user presses the "Yes" button and the `NoFunc` function should be called when the user presses the "No" button.

```
/*
 * YesNo
 *
 * Function to display a yes/no window
 */
void YesNo (char *szMessage, void (*YesFunc)(), void (*NoFunc)())
{
    GtkWidget *label;
    GtkWidget *button;
    GtkWidget *dialog_window;

    /* --- Create the dialog box --- */
    dialog_window = gtk_dialog_new ();

    /* --- Trap the window close signal to release the grab --- */
    gtk_signal_connect (GTK_OBJECT (dialog_window), "destroy",
                GTK_SIGNAL_FUNC (ClosingDialog),
                &dialog_window);

    /* --- Set the title --- */
    gtk_window_set_title (GTK_WINDOW (dialog_window), "YesNo");

    /* --- Add a small border --- */
    gtk_container_border_width (GTK_CONTAINER (dialog_window), 5);

    /* ------------------------ */
    /* --- Create the message --- */
    /* ------------------------ */

    /* --- Create a label with the message --- */
    label = gtk_label_new (szMessage);

    /* --- Give the label some room --- */
    gtk_misc_set_padding (GTK_MISC (label), 10, 10);

    /* --- Add label to the dialog box --- */
```

```
gtk_box_pack_start (GTK_BOX (GTK_DIALOG (dialog_window)->vbox),
                    label, TRUE, TRUE, 0);

/* --- Show the widget --- */
gtk_widget_show (label);

/* ----------------- */
/* --- Yes button --- */
/* ----------------- */

/* --- Create the "Yes" button --- */
button = gtk_button_new_with_label ("Yes");

gtk_signal_connect (GTK_OBJECT (button), "clicked",
                    GTK_SIGNAL_FUNC (YesFunc),
                    dialog_window);

GTK_WIDGET_SET_FLAGS (button, GTK_CAN_DEFAULT);

/* --- Add the button to the dialog box --- */
gtk_box_pack_start (GTK_BOX (GTK_DIALOG (dialog_window)
➥->action_area),
            button, TRUE, TRUE, 0);

/* --- Make the button visible --- */
gtk_widget_show (button);

/* ----------------- */
/* --- No button --- */
/* ----------------- */

/* --- Create the "No" button --- */
button = gtk_button_new_with_label ("No");

gtk_signal_connect (GTK_OBJECT (button), "clicked",
                    GTK_SIGNAL_FUNC (NoFunc),
                    dialog_window);

/* --- Allow "No" to be a default --- */
GTK_WIDGET_SET_FLAGS (button, GTK_CAN_DEFAULT);

/* --- Add the "No" button to the dialog box --- */
gtk_box_pack_start (GTK_BOX (GTK_DIALOG (dialog_window)
➥->action_area),
            button, TRUE, TRUE, 0);
```

```
    /* --- Make the "No" the default --- */
    gtk_widget_grab_default (button);

    /* --- Make the button visible --- */
    gtk_widget_show (button);

    /* --- Show the dialog box --- */
    gtk_widget_show (dialog_window);

    /* --- Only this window can be used for now --- */
    gtk_grab_add (dialog_window);
}
```

The YesNo function can now be used by applications to create stunning dialog
boxes. The call to the function would look like this:

```
YesNo ("Are you sure you want to siphon all of"
       "Bill Gates money from his account?",
       DisplayYes, DisplayNo);
```

The DisplayYes and DisplayNo functions should destroy the dialog box when they
have completed processing. The YesNo function passes the dialog box's GtkWidget parameter as the gpointer in the clicked callback. The DisplayYes and DisplayNo functions are quite small here, but they could be bigger to perform more processing.

```
/*
 * DisplayYes
 *
 * Show that the Yes button was pressed
 */
void DisplayYes (GtkWidget *widget, gpointer data)
{
    /* --- Display message --- */
    g_print ("Withdrawing $60,000,000,000.00\n");

    /* --- Close it --- */
    gtk_widget_destroy (GTK_WIDGET (data));
}

/*
 * DisplayNo
 *
 * Show that the No button was pressed
 */
void DisplayNo (GtkWidget *widget, gpointer data)
{
    /* --- Display message --- */
    g_print ("Money can't buy you happiness.\n");
```

```
/* --- Close it --- */
gtk_widget_destroy (GTK_WIDGET (data));


}
```

# File Selection Dialog Box

The file selection dialog box is a specialized dialog box that is already coded to provide standard "file selection" similar to the way Windows has generic "file selection." This feature gives GTK+ applications their own common look and feel. The file selection dialog box allows a user to select a file and perform some action with the file (see Figure 6.4).

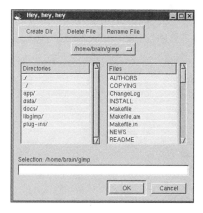

**Figure 6.4**   File selection dialog box.

The file selection dialog box in GTK+ is created using the `gtk_file_selection_new` function and passing in a title for the dialog window. Setting the title to something like `Save As` or `Open` is probably a good idea in case the user forgets what he or she is doing or is interrupted after the dialog box comes up.

```
/* --- Create the dialog box with a title --- */
filew = gtk_file_selection_new ("Save as");
```

If the dialog box is displayed because the user chose a "Save As" menu, the filename in the dialog box should be filled with the current filename. (There may be other reasons to default the field.) The dialog box can have the filename default to a particular filename by using the `gtk_file_selection_set_filename` function.

```
/* --- Set the default filename --- */
gtk_file_selection_set_filename (
                GTK_FILE_SELECTION (filew),
                "problems.txt");
```

The file selection dialog box has a series of widgets that the developer can access. The GtkFileSelection structure in gtkfilesel.h is defined as

```
struct _GtkFileSelection
{
  GtkWindow window;

  GtkWidget *dir_list;
  GtkWidget *file_list;
  GtkWidget *selection_entry;
  GtkWidget *selection_text;
  GtkWidget *main_vbox;
  GtkWidget *ok_button;
  GtkWidget *cancel_button;
  GtkWidget *help_button;
  GtkWidget *history_pulldown;
  GtkWidget *history_menu;
  GList     *history_list;
  GtkWidget *fileop_dialog;
  GtkWidget *fileop_entry;
  gchar     *fileop_file;
  gpointer   cmpl_state;

  GtkWidget *fileop_c_dir;
  GtkWidget *fileop_del_file;
  GtkWidget *fileop_ren_file;

  GtkWidget *button_area;
  GtkWidget *action_area;

};
```

The widgets that are usually used are the ok_button, the cancel_button, and the help_button. Most of the other widgets have default behaviors defined, and they usually don't need changing. The buttons are all a part of the file selection dialog box, and they can be used to register your own events. For instance, if you wanted to know when the "Cancel" button was pressed, you could put in a little bit of code that set up an event handler for the cancel_button in the GtkFileSelection structure.

```
gtk_signal_connect_object (
        GTK_OBJECT (GTK_FILE_SELECTION (filew)->cancel_button),
        "clicked",
        (GtkSignalFunc) gtk_widget_destroy,
        GTK_OBJECT (filew));
```

The gtk_signal_connect_object function is similar to the gtk_signal_connect function in that they both set up callback functions for signals. The gtk_signal_connect_object function sets up a callback for a signal, but when it calls the callback function, the only parameter it takes is the fourth parameter in the gtk_signal_connect_object function. This effectively removes the callback from knowing the widget that caused the callback to be called. The callback function in this case would look like

```
gint CallbackFunction (GtkObject *object)
{
}
```

The object sent in to the callback function would be the file selection widget (filew) that was configured in the gtk_signal_connect_object. Any reference to the widget that caused the event (in this case, the "Cancel" button) has been removed. But in this case, it's not important.

The "Ok" button can be set up to perform an action on a file using a similar event handler, and if the application is going to be user-friendly, the "Help" button can also be configured to do something. (It could also be made to disappear so the user has no preconceived notion of getting help, but that would not be user-friendly.)

# Progress Bar

The progress bar (GtkProgressBar) is a nifty little widget that is commonly used to display the current status of a time-consuming function. Displaying the progress of an action is certainly better than allowing the user to wonder about how long the operation is going to take to complete. The developer has total control of the progress bar widget because he or she has to write the code to update the widget so that it displays correctly.

The GtkProgressBar inherits much of its functionality from the GtkProgress widget. The GtkProgress widget and GtkProgressBar widget have a lot of functionality in them that doesn't need to be covered. We're going to create a basic progress bar for use throughout the book when we're doing time-consuming operations (see Figure 6.5).

Creating a progress bar widget is done with the gtk_progress_bar_new or the gtk_progress_bar_new_with_adjustment function. After it is created, the progress bar widget can be updated with the gtk_progress_set_percent function, and by passing in a new completion value where zero is not complete at all and one is totally complete.

The widget is going to use a data structure to keep track of information about the progress bar. This information includes the dialog widget, the progress bar widget, a flag that indicates whether the dialog box can be closed, and information about the last known percentage shown on the progress bar widget.

```
typedef struct {

    GtkWidget *progressbar;
    GtkWidget *window;
    int bProgressUp;
    int nLastPct;

} typProgressData;
```

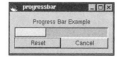

**Figure 6.5**   Progress bar.

Our progress bar is going to have three functions for it to be used. The first is going to be the `StartProgress` function. This is going create the progress bar in a dialog box.

```
/*
 * StartProgress
 *
 * Create a window for the progress bar
 */
void StartProgress ()
{
    GtkWidget *label;
    GtkWidget *table;
    GtkWidget *window;
    GtkAdjustment *adj;

    pdata = g_malloc (sizeof (typProgressData));
    pdata->nLastPct = -1;
    pdata->bProgressUp = TRUE;
    /*
     * --- Create the top-level window
     */
    window = gtk_window_new (GTK_WINDOW_TOPLEVEL);
    pdata->window = window;

    /* --- Hook up the destroy  --- */
    gtk_signal_connect (GTK_OBJECT (window), "delete_event",
                    GTK_SIGNAL_FUNC (CanWindowClose), pdata);

    gtk_container_border_width (GTK_CONTAINER (window), 10);

    /* --- Create a table --- */
    table = gtk_table_new (3, 2, TRUE);
    gtk_container_add (GTK_CONTAINER (window), table);

    /* --- Add a label to the table --- */
    label = gtk_label_new ("Loading...");
    gtk_table_attach_defaults (GTK_TABLE (table), label, 0,2,0,1);
    gtk_widget_show (label);
```

```
    /* --- Add the progress bar to the table --- */
    adj = (GtkAdjustment *) gtk_adjustment_new (0, 0, 400, 0, 0, 0);
    pdata->progressbar = gtk_progress_bar_new_with_adjustment (adj);
    gtk_table_attach_defaults (GTK_TABLE (table),
                                   pdata->progressbar, 0,2,1,2);
    gtk_widget_show (pdata->progressbar);

    /* --- Show everything --- */
    gtk_widget_show (table);
    gtk_widget_show (window);
}
```

The UpdateProgress function is going to update the progress bar with the current state of the time-consuming operation. It's going to take two numeric values—a current state value and the final state value. When the current state value equals the final state value, the operation should be done. This could be used when reading in a large file. The final state would be the file size and the current state would be the file position as the file is read in.

```
/*
 * UpdateProgress
 *
 * Update the progress window to reflect the state
 * of the file that is being loaded.
 *
 * pos - how much of the file has been loaded.
 * len - length of the file
 * (pos / len) = % file has been loaded.
 */
void UpdateProgress (long pos, long len)
{
    gfloat pvalue;
    int pct;

    /* --- Prevent divide by zero errors --- */
    if (len > 0) {

        /* --- Calculate the percentage --- */
        pvalue = (gfloat) pos / (gfloat) len;

        pct = pvalue * 100;

        if (pdata->nLastPct != pct) {

            /* --- Update the displayed value --- */
            gtk_progress_set_percentage (GTK_PROGRESS (pdata-
            ➡>progressbar),
```

```
                                            pvalue);

            /* --- Repaint any windows - like the progress bar --- */
            while (gtk_events_pending ()) {
                gtk_main_iteration ();
            }
            pdata->nLastPct = pct;
        }
    }
}
```

The `EndProgress` function closes the dialog box with the progress bar within it. This should be called at the end of the operation to close the dialog box.

```
/*
 * EndProgress
 *
 * Close down the progress bar.
 */
void EndProgress ()
{
    /* --- Allow it to close --- */
    pdata->bProgressUp = FALSE;

    /* --- Destroy the window --- */
    gtk_widget_destroy (pdata->window);

    /* --- Free used memory. --- */
    g_free (pdata);

    pdata = NULL;
}
```

The `CanCloseWindow` function prevents the user from closing the window until the operation is done. It is called by the `"delete_event"` which is sent when the user tries to close the dialog box. The return value indicates whether the window can be closed.

```
/*
 * CanWindowClose
 *
 * Function that determines that if the dialog
 * window can be closed.
 */
gint CanWindowClose (GtkWidget *widget)
{
    /* --- TRUE => cannot close --- */
    /* --- FALSE => can close --- */
    return (pdata->bProgressUp);
}
```

To illustrate the progress bar, the following example creates a window and a button in a window. When the button is pressed, the dialog box with the progress bar is created using the StartProgress and updated every 100ms using a timer.

## Using a Timer

The timer is created using gtk_timeout_add. The function takes an interval frequency, a function, and a data parameter. The function passed into the gtk_timeout_add is going to be called using the frequency interval passed in. The data parameter is going to be passed into the function. For instance, the following function call:

```
ptimer = gtk_timeout_add (100, UpdateProgressTimer, data);
```

calls the UpdateProgressTimer function every 100ms, passing in the data as the parameter. The return value is the timer ID and is needed to end the timer. The gtk_timeout_remove function is used to end the function from being called. The value passed in is the value returned from the gtk_timeout_add function.

```
gtk_timeout_remove (ptimer);
```

## Testing the Progress Bar

The entire program used to test the progress bar is as follows:

```
/*
 * Application code begins here.
 */


#include <gtk/gtk.h>

int ptimer;
int nValue;

/*
 * UpdateProgressTimer
 *
 * This is the timer callback function.   It updates the
 * progress bar and closes it when it reaches the end.
 */
UpdateProgressTimer (gpointer data)
{

    /* --- Increment value --- */
    nValue += 1;

    /* --- Update the progress bar --- */
    UpdateProgress (nValue, 100);
```

```c
    /* --- Close if it's at the end. --- */
    if (nValue == 100) {
        EndProgress ();
        gtk_timeout_remove (ptimer);
    }
}


/*
 * ButtonClicked
 *
 * Called to create the progress bar and the time when
 * the button has been clicked.
 */
gint ButtonClicked (GtkWidget *widget, gpointer data)
{
    /* --- Do some initialization --- */
    nValue = 0;
    StartProgress ();

    /* --- Call the timer. --- */
    ptimer = gtk_timeout_add (100, UpdateProgressTimer, data);
}



/*
 * CloseAppWindow
 *
 * Close down the application
 */
gint CloseAppWindow ()
{
    gtk_main_quit ();
    return (FALSE);
}

/*
 * main
 *
 * program begins here.
 */
main (int argc, char *argv[])
{
    GtkWidget *window;
    GtkWidget *button;
```

```
    gtk_init (&argc, &argv);

    /* --- Create main window and give it a title --- */
    window = gtk_window_new (GTK_WINDOW_TOPLEVEL);
    gtk_window_set_title (GTK_WINDOW (window), "Progress bar");

    /* --- End app when close window detected --- */
    gtk_signal_connect (GTK_OBJECT (window), "delete_event",
                        GTK_SIGNAL_FUNC (CloseAppWindow), NULL);

    /* --- Create a button to bring up the progress bar --- */
    button = gtk_button_new_with_label ("Progress bar");
    gtk_widget_show (button);

    /* --- This is where we handle it --- */
    gtk_signal_connect (GTK_OBJECT (button), "clicked",
                        GTK_SIGNAL_FUNC (ButtonClicked), NULL);

    gtk_container_add (GTK_CONTAINER (window), button);
    gtk_widget_show (window);

    /* --- Let GTK take over --- */
    gtk_main ();
    exit (0);
}
```

# Summary

The widgets in this chapter are more complicated than the simple widgets described in the previous chapters. Dialog boxes are used extensively in GTK+, and the file selection widget shows how dialog boxes can be used. The file selection dialog box is a standard dialog box to allow users to select files. The text widget is virtually a text editor by itself. The progress bar can help show the progress of a time-consuming operation. All of these widgets help to make an application in Linux easy to write.

# II

# Example Applications using GTK+

7

# Writing a Calculator Application

THIS CHAPTER USES THE KNOWLEDGE YOU already have to create a simple calculator. A calculator is a good starter application because it consists of a group of buttons and a display area for the results. The buttons are organized neatly in a packing table, along with the display area. The application accepts both key press and mouse click events to enter information into a calculator that performs simple arithmetic operations.

## The Calculator Program

It's important to provide feedback to users as they perform operations in an application. If the user uses a mouse to click on the calculator buttons, he or she should see the buttons as they are clicked—that is, a button should go down and come back up to provide visual feedback. In addition, the display area should be updated based on the button that was clicked. However, some users prefer to use the keyboard instead of the mouse. They, too, should receive some feedback as they are typing on the keyboard. This application shifts the focus to the key that the user pressed on the keyboard. A user who enters information this way should see the key he or she pressed get the focus highlight and also see the display area get updated.

## Data Structures

Each button in the calculator has a set of characteristics associated with it. Each button has a widget pointer as well as a label and a position expressed in row and column format to determine where to place the button in the packing table.

The data structure for each button looks like this:

```
/*
 * --- Data structure to keep track of the calculator buttons.
 */
typedef struct {

    char      *szLabel;    /* --- Label display on button --- */
    int       row;         /* --- Row to place the button --- */
    int       col;         /* --- Column to place the button --- */
    GtkWidget *widget;     /* --- The button pointer --- */

} typCalculatorButton;
```

You can use this structure to define the buttons in a table. The table is an array of `typCalculatorButton` elements. The benefit of defining the buttons in a table like this is that you can easily add or remove buttons to the table without significant code modifications. In fact, you can even move the buttons around in this table without changing any other lines of code. The buttons are defined as follows:

```
/*
 * --- This is the button list.  Each button is documented here so
 *     we can access it.
 */
typCalculatorButton buttonList [] = {
    {"C",   1, 0, NULL},    /* --- Clear --- */
    {"CE",  1, 1, NULL},    /* --- Clear --- */
    {"/",   1, 3, NULL},    /* --- Division --- */

    {"7",   2, 0, NULL},    /* --- Digit --- */
    {"8",   2, 1, NULL},    /* --- Digit --- */
    {"9",   2, 2, NULL},    /* --- Digit --- */
    {"*",   2, 3, NULL},    /* --- Multiplication --- */
    {"%",   2, 4, NULL},    /* --- Percent --- */

    {"4",   3, 0, NULL},    /* --- Digit --- */
    {"5",   3, 1, NULL},    /* --- Digit --- */
    {"6",   3, 2, NULL},    /* --- Digit --- */
    {"-",   3, 3, NULL},    /* --- Subtraction --- */
    {"1/x", 3, 4, NULL},    /* --- 1/x --- */

    {"1",   4, 0, NULL},    /* --- Digit --- */
    {"2",   4, 1, NULL},    /* --- Digit --- */
```

```
  {"3",   4, 2, NULL},      /* --- Digit --- */
  {"+",   4, 3, NULL},      /* --- Addition --- */
  {"sqrt",4, 4, NULL},      /* --- Square root --- */

  {"+/-", 5, 0, NULL},      /* --- Negate value --- */
  {"0",   5, 1, NULL},      /* --- zero --- */
  {".",   5, 2, NULL},      /* --- Decimal --- */
  {"=",   5, 3, NULL},      /* --- Equals/total --- */
  {"x^2", 5, 4, NULL},      /* --- Square --- */
};
```

The following formula calculates the number of buttons in the array:

```
int nButtons = sizeof (buttonList) /
               sizeof (typCalculatorButton);
```

This formula automatically calculates the number of buttons in the array at compile time so that you don't have to adjust the number as you add or delete buttons. This method is certainly better than defining the array with a constant and updating the constant each time buttons are added or deleted.

In addition to the table with the button information (buttonList), the application needs other global variables, for example, the label used to display results. A label represents the LCD screen of the calculator, because controlling what gets typed into the LCD is easier if the user cannot actually type directly into the widget. Any key press is trapped by the application window. The application window updates the label after filtering out characters that don't belong in the field.

## Main Program

Now that the data calculator and the data structures have been explained, you can start to write the code. The main function performs the setup required to start the calculator. Windows have to be created and positioned, and the signal callbacks have to be placed so that the gtk_main function can be called to start processing signals. The first step is to initialize GTK+ and create the application window.

```
int main (int argc, char *argv[])
{
    GtkWidget *window;
    GtkWidget *table;

    /* --- GTK initialization --- */
    gtk_init (&argc, &argv);

    /* --- Create the calculator window --- */
    window = gtk_window_new (GTK_WINDOW_TOPLEVEL);
```

Ideally, you should give the application window a descriptive title as well as set the minimum window size because the default size of the application is a little too small for the user to be able to click on the buttons with a mouse.

```
/* --- Give the window a title. --- */
gtk_window_set_title (GTK_WINDOW (window), "Calculator");

/* --- Set the window size. --- */
gtk_widget_set_usize (window, 200, 200);
```

As always, you should remember to listen for the closing of the application window. The application window also listens for the key_press event in case the user decides to use the keyboard instead of the mouse. The keystrokes have to be mapped to the appropriate button, using the table defined earlier, and handled as if the user clicked on the particular button with the mouse.

```
/* --- We care if a key is pressed --- */
gtk_signal_connect (GTK_OBJECT (window), "key_press_event",
                    GTK_SIGNAL_FUNC (key_press), NULL);

/* --- You should always remember to connect the "delete_event"
 *     to the main window. --- */
gtk_signal_connect (GTK_OBJECT (window), "delete_event",
                    GTK_SIGNAL_FUNC (CloseAppWindow), NULL);
```

The table that contains the buttons is a five-by-five table with the first row being used for the display screen. A CreateCalculatorButtons function uses the button array and places the buttons in the table at the correct positions. The function also adds a common event handler for all the buttons for actions such as the button click and keystrokes.

```
/* --- Create a 5x5 table for the items in the calculator. --- */
table = gtk_table_new (5, 5, TRUE);

/* --- Create the calculator buttons. --- */
CreateCalculatorButtons (table);
```

The display screen is a label control with the text aligned to the right side of the label in calculator fashion. The display screen is added to the table on the first row but goes across all the columns of the packing table.

```
/* --- Create the calculator LED --- */
label = gtk_label_new ("0");
gtk_misc_set_alignment (GTK_MISC (label), 1, .5);

/* --- Add label to the table --- */
gtk_table_attach_defaults (GTK_TABLE (table), label,
                           0, 4, 0, 1);
```

Next, all the widgets are made visible and added to the main window.

```
gtk_widget_show (label);

/* --- Make them visible --- */
gtk_container_add (GTK_CONTAINER (window), table);
```

```
    gtk_widget_show (table);
    gtk_widget_show (window);
```

Finally, a call to `gtk_main` is made to start the event loop processing.

```
    gtk_main ();
    exit (0);
}
```

The event handler for the `"delete_event"` is necessary to shut down GTK+ when the calculator is closed.

```
/*
 * CloseAppWindow
 *
 * The window is closing down, end the gtk loop
 */
gint CloseAppWindow (GtkWidget *widget, gpointer data)
{
    gtk_main_quit ();

    return (FALSE);
}
```

## *CreateCalculatorButtons*

The `CreateCalculatorButtons` function creates the buttons from the array of buttons described earlier in the chapter. Each button is created with the label, row, and column defined in the table, and the `GtkWidget` representing the newly created button is stored in the table. The `CreateCalculatorButtons` function relies on `CreateButton` to actually create the buttons.

```
    void CreateCalculatorButtons (GtkWidget *table)
    {
        int nIndex;

        /* --- Run through the list of buttons. --- */
        for (nIndex = 0; nIndex < nButtons; nIndex++) {

            /* --- Create a button and store the widget --- */
            buttonList[nIndex].widget =
                    CreateButton (table,
                                  buttonList[nIndex].szLabel,
                                  buttonList[nIndex].row,
                                  buttonList[nIndex].col);
        }
    }
```

### *CreateButton*

The CreateButton function creates a button in the packing table with a label. This function also sets up an event handler for the button_clicked event. Notice that every button uses the same button_clicked callback function. Rather than try to extract the label from the button to determine which button got the event, it's easier to configure the callback to receive the button's label as a parameter. When the button_clicked callback is set up with the gtk_signal_connect function, the button's label is passed in as the gpointer data value. When an event occurs on the button, the callback function receives the information as the data parameter.

```
/*
 * CreateButton
 *
 * Create a button, assign event handlers, and attach the button to the
 * table in the proper place.
 */
GtkWidget *CreateButton (GtkWidget *table, char *szLabel, int row, int
➥column)
{
    GtkWidget *button;

    /* --- Create the button --- */
    button = gtk_button_new_with_label (szLabel);

    /* --- We care if the button is clicked --- */
    gtk_signal_connect (GTK_OBJECT (button), "clicked",
                        GTK_SIGNAL_FUNC (button_clicked), szLabel);

    /* --- Put the button in the table in the right place. --- */
    gtk_table_attach (GTK_TABLE (table), button,
                        column, column+1,
                        row, row + 1,
                        GTK_FILL ¦ GTK_EXPAND,
                        GTK_FILL ¦ GTK_EXPAND,
                        5, 5);

    /* --- Make the button visible --- */
    gtk_widget_show (button);

    /* --- return the button. --- */
    return (button);
}
```

The event handlers to process the mouse and key press events must figure out which button was pressed and then update the display in the calculator based on that button.

For the mouse click events, the button that the mouse event occurred on gets the event. For the `key_press` events, the button that gets the event is probably not the button that the user wanted to press. For instance, if the focus is on the "3" button and the user types a "5", the "3" button is going to get the signal that the "5" key was pressed. Ideally, the key handling should be like the `"button_clicked"` signal where the button that was pressed gets the signal. (Press the "5" button; the "5" button should get the signal that the "5" key was pressed.) In addition, if the user is using the keyboard, the focus should change to the button that the user has typed. In the previous example, the focus should change to the "5" button because the "5" key was pressed. This action provides additional visible feedback to the user and is more of an aesthetic issue than a programming issue.

Rather than put a `key_press` event callback on the button, we can put it on the application window where the signal will end up if it's not handled by the button with the focus. The application window's `key_press` event callback will send a `"button_clicked"` signal to the button based on the key that was pressed.

The mouse click event and the `key_press` event do the same type of processing. The `key_press` event handler can take advantage of this condition by calling the same functions that get called when the `"button_clicked"` signal is processed.

The `key_press` callback is quite small because it only needs to figure out which button should be clicked based on the key that was pressed. The callback looks up the key in the table and tries to match the key to the string in the button label. This process compares only a single character, so this doesn't work for more complicated functions such as `1/x`, which are hard to express in terms of a single keystroke. It does work on the commonly used characters in the calculator, such as the digits and the simple operations (`+-/*`). After the button is found, the focus is shifted to the button to provide visual feedback and `gtk_button_clicked` is called to signal a `clicked` signal on the button.

```
 * key_press
 *
 * Handle the button "key_press" event.
 *
 * Function looks for the keystroke in the calculator
 * data structure and (if a match is found) presses the
 * button that matches the keystroke for the user.  It
 * keeps our code small because we only have to handle the
 * button_clicked events.
 */
void key_press (GtkWidget *widget,
                GdkEventKey *event,
                gpointer data)
{
    int nIndex;

    /* --- Search through the buttons --- */
    for (nIndex = 0; nIndex < nButtons; nIndex++) {
```

```
            /* --- If the keystroke is the first character of a button AND ---
➡*/
            /* --- the button label length is one. --- */
            if (event->keyval == buttonList[nIndex].szLabel[0] &&
                buttonList[nIndex].szLabel[1] == (char) 0) {

                /* --- Set focus to that button --- */
                gtk_widget_grab_focus (buttonList[nIndex].widget);

                /* --- Make like the button was clicked to do processing. ---
➡*/
                gtk_button_clicked (GTK_BUTTON (buttonList[nIndex].widget));
                return;
            }
        }
    }
}
```

If a button is pressed or a key on the keyboard is pressed, the `button_clicked` event handler will be called. The `button_clicked` function keeps track of the state of the calculator and performs any operations or just adds digits to the LED display using the `gtk_label_set` function. Sure, the `button_clicked` function could have been written to handle operator precedence, parentheses, more calculations (sin, cos, tan), and hex and binary conversions, but doing so is left as an exercise for the reader.

The `button_clicked` function has two distinct cases. The user is either going to press a digit (0–9) or call for an operation. If the user presses a digit, it usually means that the digit needs to be added to the display. For instance, if the display shows "45" and the user presses "2", then the display should read "452". The exception is when the previous command was a binary operator. If the user typed in a binary operator (+-/*), the display still shows the first part of the number, but the digit should not be added. Instead, the display should be replaced with the new number, as it is the first digit of the second number that makes up the binary operation.

The second case is when the user enters an operator. If an operator is entered, then the number saved in the buffer is used with the number in the display. For instance, a user types in "235+111". So far, no calculations are performed. But when the user types in "=", the calculator looks up the previous command ("+"), the number saved in the buffer ("235"), and the number in the display "111". The calculator must then perform the addition of "235" and "111". This same situation would occur if the user typed in the "+" instead of the "=" after entering "235+111". The difference is that the second "+" would put the calculator in a mode to add the next number that would be entered.

```
/*
 * button_clicked
 *
 * widget - button pressed.
```

```c
 * data - button label.
 *
 * Button was pressed, handle it.
 */
void button_clicked (GtkWidget *widget, gpointer data)
{
    char ch = *((char *) data);
    int len;
    char *str;

    /* --- Get the button label --- */
    str = (char *) data;

    /* --- Entering a number... --- */
    if (FloatingPointChar (ch) && strlen (str) == 1) {

        HandleDigit (str, ch);

    } else {

        /* --- Clear? --- */
        if (strcmp (str, "CE") == 0) {
            gtk_label_set (GTK_LABEL (label), "0");
            return;

        /* --- BIG clear? --- */
        } else if (strcmp (str, "C") == 0) {
            prevCmd = (char) 0;
            lastChar = (char) 0;
            gtk_label_set (GTK_LABEL (label), "0");
            return;

        } else {

            /* --- Maybe it's a unary operator? --- */
            MaybeUnaryOperation (str);
        }

        /* --- See if there's a binary operation to do --- */
        HandleBinaryOperation ();

        prevCmd = ch;
    }
    lastChar = ch;
}
```

The code that handles digits adds the digit to the end of the digits in the field unless the preceding key was a command. In that case, the digit becomes the first digit in the field.

```
/*
 * HandleDigit
 *
 * Digit button was pressed, deal with it.  How it
 * is dealt with depends on the situation.
 */
void HandleDigit (char *str, char ch)
{
    char *labelText;
    char buffer[BUF_SIZE];
    int  len;

    /* --- And they just did a command --- */
    if (Command (lastChar)) {

        /* --- Clear the digit field --- */
        gtk_label_set (GTK_LABEL (label), "");

        /* --- If they did a computation --- */
        if (lastChar == '=') {

            /* --- Clear out the command --- */
            lastChar = (char) 0;
            prevCmd = (char) 0;
        }
    }

    /* --- Get the buffer in the LED --- */
    gtk_label_get (GTK_LABEL (label), &labelText);
    strcpy (buffer, labelText);

    /* --- Add the new character on it. --- */
    len = strlen (buffer);
    buffer[len] = (gchar) ch;
    buffer[len+1] = (gchar) 0;

    /* --- Trim leading zeros. --- */
    TrimLeadingZeros (buffer);

    /* --- Add digit to field. --- */
    gtk_label_set (GTK_LABEL (label), (char *) buffer);
}
```

The calculator handles two types of commands: those that take two numbers to perform an operation and those that take one number to perform an operation. The `MaybeUnaryOperation` function determines whether the command is a unary operator and tries to perform the unary operation if it is.

```c
/*
 * MaybeUnaryOperation
 *
 * str - label on button that describes operation.
 *
 * Check to see if the user hit a unary operator button -
 * like %, sqrt, 1/x, etc that should be dealt with NOW
 * not later.
 */
void MaybeUnaryOperation (char *str)
{
    char *labelText;
    char buffer[BUF_SIZE];
    float num2;

    /* --- Get number in the field. --- */
    gtk_label_get (GTK_LABEL (label), &labelText);
    num2 = atof (labelText);

    /* --- Percentage? --- */
    if (strcmp (str, "%") == 0) {
        num2 = num2 / 100;

    /* --- Trying for 1/x? --- */
    } else if (strcmp (str, "1/x") == 0) {

        /* --- Can't divide by zero. --- */
        if (num2 == 0) {
            return;
        }
        num2 = 1 / num2;

    /* --- Calculate sqrt --- */
    } else if (strcmp (str, "sqrt") == 0) {
        num2 = sqrt ((double) num2);

    /* --- Calculate square --- */
    } else if (strcmp (str, "x^2") == 0) {
        num2 = num2 * num2;
    }
```

```
    /* --- Put the number back. --- */
    sprintf (buffer, "%f", (float) num2);
    TrimTrailingZeros (buffer);
    TrimLeadingZeros (buffer);
    gtk_label_set (GTK_LABEL (label), buffer);
}
```

The HandleBinaryOperation function checks to see whether a binary operation needs to be performed. The global variable num1 stores the first part of the number that is used in the calculation. The second part of the number is in the LED display. When the calculation is complete, the number is stored in the global variable num1 because it becomes the first part of the next binary calculation.

```
/*
 * HandleBinaryOperation
 *
 * Perform a calculation with two sets of digits.  One set
 * is in the LED display and the other set is saved in
 * a global variable (num1).
 */
void HandleBinaryOperation ()
{
    char buffer[BUF_SIZE];
    char *labelText;
    float num2;

    /* --- Get number in the field. --- */
    gtk_label_get (GTK_LABEL (label), &labelText);
    num2 = atof (labelText);

    /* --- Calculate based on previous command. --- */
    switch (prevCmd) {
        case '+':
            num1 = num1 + num2;
            break;

        case '-':
            num1 = num1 - num2;
            break;

        case '*':
            num1 = num1 * num2;
            break;

        case '/':
            num1 = num1 / num2;
            break;
```

```
        case '=':
            num1 = num2;
            break;

        default:
            num1 = num2;
            break;
    }

    /* --- Put the number back. --- */
    sprintf (buffer, "%f", (float) num1);
    TrimTrailingZeros (buffer);
    TrimLeadingZeros (buffer);
    gtk_label_set (GTK_LABEL (label), buffer);
}
```

The remaining functions are support functions. They help to make the previous blocks of code readable by using function names that help to document the code. For instance, the function FloatingPointChar determines whether a character is a floating-point character (0–9 or the '.' character). It's certainly easier to read a line of code that says

```
if (FloatingPointChar (ch)) {
```

instead of a line of code that says

```
if (isdigit (ch) ¦¦ ch == ".") {

/*
 * TrimTrailingZeros
 *
 * Get rid of trailing zeros
 * Takes the string and removes the trailing zeros.
 */
void TrimTrailingZeros (char *szDigits)
{
    int nIndex;
    int bDecimal = FALSE;
    int nPos = -1;

    /* --- Loop through the string. --- */
    for (nIndex = 0; nIndex < strlen (szDigits); nIndex++) {

        /* --- Is this a decimal? --- */
        if (szDigits[nIndex] == '.') {
            bDecimal = TRUE;
        }

        /* --- If we're on the right side of the decimal... --- */
```

```c
        if (bDecimal) {

            /* --- A zero?  Hmm... from this point on? --- */
            if (szDigits[nIndex] == '0') {

                /* --- If we don't have a point yet... --- */
                if (nPos < 0) {

                    /* --- Save this as a point. --- */
                    nPos = nIndex;
                }
            } else {

                /* --- Clear it.  Bad point. --- */
                nPos = -1;
            }
        }
    }

    /* --- Truncate the field. --- */
    if (nPos > 0) {
        szDigits[nPos] = (char) 0;
    }
}
/*
 * TrimLeadingZeros
 *
 * Trim the leading zeros.
 *
 * Converts numbers like "0000012" to "12"
 */
void TrimLeadingZeros (char *szDigits)
{
    int nPos;

    if (szDigits == NULL) return;

    /* --- While we have a combination, a digit in front --- */
    for (nPos = 0; (szDigits[nPos] && szDigits[nPos] == '0'); nPos++) {

        /* --- If the digit is a zero and next char is a digit --- */
        if (isdigit (szDigits[nPos+1])) {

            /* --- Blank the field. --- */
            szDigits[nPos] = ' ';
        }
```

```
        }
}
/*
 * Command
 *
 * Returns true if the character is a two-digit command.
 */
int Command (char ch)
{
    switch (ch) {
        case '+':
        case '-':
        case '/':
        case '*':
        case '=':
            return (TRUE);
    }
    return (FALSE);
}



/*
 * FloatingPointChar
 *
 * Returns true if the character is any of [0123456789.]
 */
int FloatingPointChar (char ch)
{

    return (isdigit (ch) || ch == '.');
}
```

# Summary

Creating a simple calculator using the button widget and the label widget is quite
easy. Mix in a little event handling with some widgets, and you have an application.
You are already well on the way to creating larger applications.

# 8

# Developing a Simple Word Processor

T HIS CHAPTER FOCUSES ON USING THE MATERIAL covered earlier to put together a small word processor similar to the Notepad on Windows machines. Again, using an existing application as a design and trying to duplicate it is easier than writing it from scratch. The Windows Notepad enables users to edit simple text files and save them but is otherwise quite limited in its capabilities. Still, it is a good application for putting together a few widgets to create a small and robust application.

The notepad application (see Figure 8.1) illustrates many concepts of putting an application together from widgets, including menus, toolbars, various dialog boxes, and an area used for editing the information. Again, the notepad is loosely based on the application that comes with Microsoft Windows. You can customize it to suit your needs, or you can just use it as a quick and small editor.

The top-level menus consist of the menu titles "File," "Edit," "Search," and "Help." The "File" menu has a "New" menu choice to create new documents, an "Open" menu choice to load existing files, a "Save" menu choice to save the current document, a "Save As…" menu choice to save the current document using another name, and a "Quit" menu choice to exit the application. The "Edit" menu consists of the clipboard commands "Cut," "Copy," and "Paste." The "Search" menu has only a "Find" menu choice, and the "Help" menu has only an "About…" menu to display the author and version information.

**Figure 8.1**    The Gnotepad.

In addition to the menus, the application has a toolbar so that users can access most of these commands quickly. The original notepad didn't have a toolbar, but adding one here to make the notepad more functional is not difficult.

## *main.c*

This program starts like most GTK+ applications—by creating a window and giving it a title, as well as creating a vertical packing box so that the menu and toolbar can be placed within it above the text widget that is used to display and edit the file. The code that creates the menu and toolbar is encapsulated within the `CreateMenu` function, and the actual text widget used for editing goes in the `CreateText` function.

The one problem here involves creating the toolbar in the application. Creating the toolbar icons requires converting the pixmap text data to a `GdkPixmap` so that it can be converted into a pixmap widget. The conversion of the pixmap text data requires an X Window as one of the parameters. Rather than make the window visible (which would create the X Window) and then load up the toolbar information and display it, you can keep the window invisible while you configure it by using the `gtk_realize_widget` function. The `gtk_realize_widget` function creates an X Window for the widget that can be used without making the window visible. Usually, the realization occurs as part of the `gtk_widget_show` function, but here you want to have the X Window created for the application window *before* the window is made visible. You can eliminate the `gtk_realize_widget` by putting the `CreateMenu` function in after making the application window visible, but that solution is not ideal, because the window would be displayed without being finished (that is, without menus/toolbars).

```
/*
 * --- main
 *
 * program begins here.
 */
int main(int argc, char *argv[])
{
    GtkWidget *window;
    GtkWidget *main_vbox;

    /* --- Start up GTK --- */
    gtk_init(&argc, &argv);

    /* --- Create the top-level window --- */
    window = gtk_window_new(GTK_WINDOW_TOPLEVEL);

    /* --- Title and border --- */
    gtk_window_set_title (GTK_WINDOW (window), "Gnotepad");
    gtk_container_border_width (GTK_CONTAINER (window), 0);

    /* --- Listen for the main window being closed --- */
    gtk_signal_connect (GTK_OBJECT(window), "delete_event",
                GTK_SIGNAL_FUNC (ClosingAppWindow),
                NULL);

    /* --- Set the window title and size --- */
    gtk_widget_set_usize (GTK_WIDGET(window), 200, 200);

    /* --- Create a new vertical box for storing widgets --- */
    main_vbox = gtk_vbox_new (FALSE, 1);

    /* --- border width is 1 --- */
    gtk_container_border_width (GTK_CONTAINER(main_vbox), 1);

    /* --- Add the vertical box to the main window --- */
    gtk_container_add (GTK_CONTAINER(window), main_vbox);

    /* --- Make the vertical box visible --- */
    gtk_widget_show (main_vbox);

    /* --- Associate window with X Window to create pixmaps. --- */
    gtk_widget_realize (window);

    /* --- Create the menu/toolbar. --- */
    CreateMenu (window, main_vbox);
    CreateText (window, main_vbox);
```

```
/* --- Show the top-level window --- */
gtk_widget_show (window);

/* --- Loop and process messages --- */
gtk_main();

return(0);
}
```

## *menu.c*

The code that defines the toolbar icons and creates the menu and toolbar buttons goes in this file. Much of this code is the same as the simple front end that was created earlier.

The first block of code in menu.c defines the bitmaps for the toolbars. The bitmaps should be easily recognizable and clear. Generally, you should limit the number of colors used in the bitmap to four—usually less. Too many colors distract from the purpose of the bitmap, which should be to provide a recognizable function. Because many applications use familiar icons to perform functions, you should stick to standards. Nothing confuses a user more than a new set of icons. The icons for the toolbar buttons are being reused from earlier chapters.

The CreateMenu code called from main sets up the accelerator table and the menus and ends up calling the CreateToolbar function to (obviously) create the toolbars. The callbacks for the menu items have the prefix menu in front of them to distinguish them from normal functions. For example, the menu_New function is going to be called when the File→New menu is selected.

```
/*
 * CreateMenu
 *
 * Create the main window and the menu/toolbar associated with it
 */
void CreateMenu (GtkWidget *window, GtkWidget *vbox_main)
{
    GtkWidget *menubar;
    GtkWidget *menu;
    GtkWidget *menuitem;

    win_main = window;

    /* --- Create accel table --- */
    accel_group = gtk_accel_group_new ();
    gtk_accel_group_attach (accel_group, GTK_OBJECT (window));

    /* --- Menu bar --- */
    menubar = gtk_menu_bar_new ();
```

```
gtk_box_pack_start (GTK_BOX (vbox_main), menubar, FALSE, TRUE, 0);
gtk_widget_show (menubar);

/* -----------------
   --- File menu ---
   ----------------- */
menu = CreateBarSubMenu (menubar, "File");

menuitem = CreateMenuItem (menu, "New", "^N",
                "Create a new item",
                GTK_SIGNAL_FUNC (menu_New), "new");

menuitem = CreateMenuItem (menu, "Open", "^O",
                "Open an existing item",
                GTK_SIGNAL_FUNC (menu_Open), "open");

menuitem = CreateMenuItem (menu, "Import RTF", "",
                "Import RTF file",
                GTK_SIGNAL_FUNC (menu_ImportRTF), "import rtf");

menuitem = CreateMenuItem (menu, "Save", "^S",
                "Save current item",
                GTK_SIGNAL_FUNC (menu_Save), "save");

menuitem = CreateMenuItem (menu, "Save As...", "",
                "Save current item with new name",
                GTK_SIGNAL_FUNC (menu_SaveAs), "save as");

menuitem = CreateMenuItem (menu, NULL, NULL,
                NULL, NULL, NULL);

menuitem = CreateMenuItem (menu, "Quit", "",
                "What's more descriptive than quit?",
                GTK_SIGNAL_FUNC (menu_Quit), "quit");

/* -----------------
   --- Edit menu ---
   ----------------- */
menu = CreateBarSubMenu (menubar, "Edit");

menuitem = CreateMenuItem (menu, "Cut", "^X",
                "Remove item and place into clipboard",
                GTK_SIGNAL_FUNC (menu_Cut), "cut");

menuitem = CreateMenuItem (menu, "Copy", "^C",
                "Place a copy of the item in the clipboard",
```

```
                          GTK_SIGNAL_FUNC (menu_Copy), "copy");

    menuitem = CreateMenuItem (menu, "Paste", "^V",
                        "Paste item",
                        GTK_SIGNAL_FUNC (menu_Paste), "paste");



    /* --------------------
       --- Find submenu ---
       -------------------- */
    menu = CreateBarSubMenu (menubar, "Search");

    menuitem = CreateMenuItem (menu, "Find", "^F",
                        "Find item",
                        GTK_SIGNAL_FUNC (menu_Find), "find");


    /* -------------------
       --- Help menu ---
       -------------------- */
    menu = CreateBarSubMenu (menubar, "Help");

    menuitem = CreateMenuItem (menu, "About", "",
                        "About",
                        GTK_SIGNAL_FUNC (menu_About), "about");

    /* --- Create the toolbar --- */
    CreateToolbar (vbox_main);
}
```

The last part of the `CreateMenu` function is the `CreateToolbar` function that creates the toolbar. Most of the toolbar bitmaps are reused from the earlier example showing how to create a front-end GUI. The buttons put into the toolbar are simple buttons placed into a toolbar. The buttons set up the same functions that the menu items set up. In fact, the New button sets up GTK+ to call the `menu_New` function when pressed, which is the same function called by the File→New menu choice.

```
/*
 * CreateToolbar
 *
 * Create the toolbar for commonly used options
 */
void CreateToolbar (GtkWidget *vbox_main)
{

    /* --- Create the toolbar and add it to the window --- */
    toolbar = gtk_toolbar_new (GTK_ORIENTATION_HORIZONTAL,
➥GTK_TOOLBAR_ICONS);
```

```
    gtk_box_pack_start (GTK_BOX (vbox_main), toolbar, FALSE, TRUE, 0);
    gtk_widget_show (toolbar);


    /*             -------
     * --- Create ¦ new ¦ button
     *             -------
     */
    gtk_toolbar_append_item (GTK_TOOLBAR (toolbar),
                    NULL, "New window", NULL,
                CreateWidgetFromXpm (win_main, (gchar **) xpm_new),
                    (GtkSignalFunc) menu_New,
                        NULL);


    /*             --------
     * --- Create ¦ open ¦ button
     *             --------
     */
    gtk_toolbar_append_item (GTK_TOOLBAR (toolbar),
                    "Open Dialog", "Open dialog", "",
                CreateWidgetFromXpm (win_main, (gchar **) xpm_open),
                    (GtkSignalFunc) menu_Open,
                        NULL);


    /* --- Little gap --- */
    gtk_toolbar_append_space (GTK_TOOLBAR (toolbar));


    /*             -------
     * --- Create ¦ cut ¦ button
     *             -------
     */
    gtk_toolbar_append_item (GTK_TOOLBAR (toolbar),
                    "Cut", "Cut", "",
                CreateWidgetFromXpm (win_main, (gchar **) xpm_cut),
                    (GtkSignalFunc) menu_Cut,
                        NULL);


    /*             --------
     * --- Create ¦ copy ¦ button
     *             --------
     */
    gtk_toolbar_append_item (GTK_TOOLBAR (toolbar),
                    "Copy", "Copy", "",
                CreateWidgetFromXpm (win_main, (gchar **) xpm_copy),
                    (GtkSignalFunc) menu_Copy,
                        NULL);
```

```
/*               - - - - - - - - - -
 * --- Create ¦ paste ¦ button
 *               - - - - - - - - - -
 */
gtk_toolbar_append_item (GTK_TOOLBAR (toolbar),
                "Paste", "Paste", "",
          CreateWidgetFromXpm (win_main, (gchar **) xpm_paste),
              (GtkSignalFunc) menu_Paste,
                  NULL);


}
```

## misc.c

This file contains the lower-level functions called from CreateMenu and CreateToolbar. This file, plucked from the earlier example on menus and toolbars, has no new elements. The code to create bitmaps, menus, and submenus is easily reused here.

## showmessage.c

Several areas of the application require displaying a message to the user. To prevent duplication of code, a single function called showmessage was created to display a dialog box for the user. This function also calls the gtk_grab_add to make sure that the dialog box that pops up gets the user's attention.

The gtk_grab_add function keeps the user from performing other functions until he or she dismisses the dialog box. After the user presses the OK button, the dialog box grab is released, using the gtk_grab_remove function in the destroy callback. The code is put in the destroy callback because the dialog box could be dismissed without pressing the OK or Cancel buttons.

The ShowMessage function takes a title and a message, puts the title in the dialog window, and puts the message in the dialog box with an OK button.

```
/*
 * ShowMessage
 *
 * Show a popup message to the user.
 */
void ShowMessage (char *szTitle, char *szMessage)
{
    GtkWidget *label;
    GtkWidget *button;
    GtkWidget *dialog_window;
```

```
    /* --- Create a dialog window --- */
    dialog_window = gtk_dialog_new ();

    gtk_signal_connect (GTK_OBJECT (dialog_window), "destroy",
            GTK_SIGNAL_FUNC (ClearShowMessage),
            NULL);

    /* --- Set the title and add a border --- */
    gtk_window_set_title (GTK_WINDOW (dialog_window), szTitle);
    gtk_container_border_width (GTK_CONTAINER (dialog_window), 0);

    /* --- Create an "OK" button with the focus --- */
    button = gtk_button_new_with_label ("OK");

    gtk_signal_connect (GTK_OBJECT (button), "clicked",
            GTK_SIGNAL_FUNC (CloseShowMessage),
            dialog_window);

    /* --- Default the "OK" button --- */
    GTK_WIDGET_SET_FLAGS (button, GTK_CAN_DEFAULT);
    gtk_box_pack_start (GTK_BOX (GTK_DIALOG (dialog_window)
➥->action_area),
            button, TRUE, TRUE, 0);
    gtk_widget_grab_default (button);
    gtk_widget_show (button);

    /* --- Create a descriptive label --- */
    label = gtk_label_new (szMessage);

    /* --- Put some room around the label text --- */
    gtk_misc_set_padding (GTK_MISC (label), 10, 10);

    /* --- Add label to designated area on dialog box --- */
    gtk_box_pack_start (GTK_BOX (GTK_DIALOG (dialog_window)->vbox),
            label, TRUE, TRUE, 0);

    /* --- Show the label --- */
    gtk_widget_show (label);


    /* --- Show the dialog box --- */
    gtk_widget_show (dialog_window);

    /* --- Only this window can have actions done. --- */
    gtk_grab_add (dialog_window);
}
```

To get the ShowMessage function to work flawlessly, two situations need to be handled through events. The user may click the OK button or may just close the dialog box. These actions generate different events. Clicking the button generates a clicked event, but doesn't do anything. Closing the window generates a destroy event that doesn't clean up the fact that the gtk_grab_add function was called. To close the window when the user clicks the OK button, the clicked event for the OK was set up to call the CloseShowMessage function when it was created. The function needs to call the gtk_grab_remove function and to destroy the dialog window. Note that the dialog widget is passed in the data parameter of the function because the dialog window was configured to be passed in as the data parameter when the clicked event was set up with gtk_signal_connect.

```
/*
 * --- CloseShowMessage
 *
 * Routine to close the about dialog window.
 */
void CloseShowMessage (GtkWidget *widget, gpointer data)
{
    GtkWidget *dialog_widget = (GtkWidget *) data;

    /* --- Close the widget --- */
    gtk_widget_destroy (dialog_widget);
}
```

If the user closes the window without clicking OK, the dialog box is dismissed, but not before the destroy signal is sent. The ClearShowMessage function cleans up anything that was set up when the dialog box was created. Here, it only calls the gtk_grab_remove function.

```
/*
 * ClearShowMessage
 *
 * Release the window "grab"
 * Clear out the global dialog_window since that
 * is checked when the dialog box is brought up.
 */
void ClearShowMessage (GtkWidget *widget, gpointer data)
{
    gtk_grab_remove (widget);
}
```

## *about.c*

You can use the ShowMessage code to create the simple dialog boxes within the application. For instance, the "About…" menu choice that displays some information about the application is displayed in a dialog box. The information usually includes the company, author, and version information. The entire "About…" code is just a call to the ShowMessage function to display the message.

```
/*
 * ShowAbout
 *
 * Show the about dialog box.  Reuse existing code.
 */
void ShowAbout ()
{
    ShowMessage ("About...",
                 "GtkNotepad v.07\n - "
                 "Eric Harlow\n");

}
```

# *filesel.c*

The file selection dialog box is called by the routines that load and save files. The title of the dialog box is passed into the `GetFilename` function to remind the user which function he or she is performing. A function is also passed in so that the dialog box can be a generic file dialog box. If the user clicks the OK button, the function is called with the name of the file that was selected. This technique allows the same file selection code to work for either the loading or the saving of a file.

Again, the `gtk_grab_add` function keeps the user from performing other functions until he or she dismisses the dialog box. By trapping the `destroy` signal, the proper cleanup code is performed in one place.

The file selection code relies on a structure allocated by `GetFilename` and passed to all the callbacks in the dialog box. This code contains information about the dialog widget and the action to be performed if the OK button is selected. The structure follows.

```
typedef struct {

    void (*func) (gchar *);
    GtkWidget *filesel;

} typFileSelectionData;

/*
 * GetFilename
 *
 * Show a dialog box with a title and if "OK" is selected
 * call the function with the name of the file.
 */
void GetFilename (char *sTitle, void (*callback) (char *))
{
    GtkWidget *filew = NULL;
    typFileSelectionData *data;
```

```
        /* --- Create a new file selection widget --- */
        filew = gtk_file_selection_new (sTitle);

        data = g_malloc (sizeof (typFileSelectionData));
        data->func = callback;
        data->filesel = filew;

        gtk_signal_connect (GTK_OBJECT (filew), "destroy",
                (GtkSignalFunc) destroy, data);

        /* --- Connect the "OK" button --- */
        gtk_signal_connect (GTK_OBJECT
                (GTK_FILE_SELECTION (filew)->ok_button),
                "clicked", (GtkSignalFunc) FileOk, data);

        /* --- Connect the Cancel button --- */
        gtk_signal_connect_object (
                GTK_OBJECT (GTK_FILE_SELECTION (filew)->cancel_button),
                "clicked", (GtkSignalFunc) gtk_widget_destroy,
                (gpointer) filew);

        if (sFilename) {

            /* --- Set the default filename --- */
            gtk_file_selection_set_filename (GTK_FILE_SELECTION (filew),
                                                sFilename);
        }

        /* --- Show the dialog box --- */
        gtk_widget_show (filew);

        /* --- Grab the focus. --- */
        gtk_grab_add (filew);
    }
```

If the OK button was pressed, then the callback function passed into the GetFilename function is executed using the filename from the file selection dialog box. For this application, the function passed in is either going to be a function to load a file or save a file. The code also uses a static variable (sFilename) to keep track of the filename. If the user wants to load a file or uses "Save As" to save the file, the filename is populated into the dialog box and the user has the opportunity to change it.

The FileOk function is called when the button is clicked. The function gets the filename from the widget, passes the filename to a function to get the work done, and destroys the widget. The function that does the work depends on the function that the user used to make the call to GetFilename. The function is stored in a global variable.

This approach is possible because only one file selection dialog box is up at any time—a condition guaranteed by the `gtk_grab_add` function. You cannot create another file selection dialog box without closing the current file selection dialog box.

```
/*
 * FileOk
 *
 * The "OK" button has been clicked.
 * Call the function (func) to do what is needed
 * to the file.
 */
void FileOk (GtkWidget *w, gpointer data)
{
    char *sTempFile;
    typFileSelectionData *localdata;
    GtkWidget *filew;

    localdata = (typFileSelectionData *) data;
    filew = localdata->filesel;

    /* --- Which file? --- */
    sTempFile = gtk_file_selection_get_filename (
                        GTK_FILE_SELECTION (filew));

    /* --- Free old memory --- */
    if (sFilename) g_free (sFilename);

    /* --- Duplicate the string --- */
    sFilename = g_strdup (sTempFile);

    /* --- Call the function that does the work. --- */
    (*(localdata->func)) (sFilename);

    /* --- Close the dialog box--- */
    gtk_widget_destroy (filew);
}
```

The `destroy` function cleans up by calling the `gtk_grab_remove` function. This function should begin to look familiar for dialog boxes.

```
/*
 * destroy
 *
 * Function to handle the destroying of the dialog box. We must
 * release the focus that we grabbed.
 */
static void destroy (GtkWidget *widget, gpointer *data)
{
```

```
    /* --- Remove the focus. --- */
    gtk_grab_remove (widget);

    g_free (data);
}
```

## *notepad.c*

The functions in `notepad.c` deal primarily with interactions with the text widget. Functions for loading the file into the text widget and saving the file from the text widget are here, as well as functions to cut and paste text.

The `CreateText` function is called from `main.c` to create the widget and configure it to be used in the editor. The text widget is in a two-by-two packing table with vertical and horizontal scrollbars. The text widget is stored in a static variable to give the functions within this module access to the widget. Direct access to the widget from outside this module is not permitted.

```
/*
 * CreateText
 *
 * Creates the text widget for the editor.
 *
 */
void CreateText (GtkWidget *window, GtkWidget *container)
{
    GtkWidget *table;
    GtkWidget *hscrollbar;
    GtkWidget *vscrollbar;

    /* --- Create a table to put text widget and scrollbars --- */
    table = gtk_table_new (2, 2, FALSE);

    /* --- Add table to container --- */
    gtk_container_add (GTK_CONTAINER (container), table);

    /* --- No gaps so the scrollbars look like they are a
           part of the widget. --- */
    gtk_table_set_row_spacing (GTK_TABLE (table), 0, 2);
    gtk_table_set_col_spacing (GTK_TABLE (table), 0, 2);

    /* --- Add packing table to the container and make visible --- */
    gtk_widget_show (table);

    /* --- Create the text widget --- */
    text = gtk_text_new (NULL, NULL);
```

```
    /* --- Allow it to be edited --- */
    gtk_text_set_editable (GTK_TEXT (text), TRUE);

    /* --- Insert the text widget into the table --- */
    gtk_table_attach (GTK_TABLE (table), text, 0, 1, 0, 1,
            GTK_EXPAND ¦ GTK_SHRINK ¦ GTK_FILL,
            GTK_EXPAND ¦ GTK_SHRINK ¦ GTK_FILL, 0, 0);

    /* --- Make it visible --- */
    gtk_widget_show (text);

    /* --- Add a horizontal scrollbar --- */
    hscrollbar = gtk_hscrollbar_new (GTK_TEXT (text)->hadj);
    gtk_table_attach (GTK_TABLE (table), hscrollbar, 0, 1, 1, 2,
            GTK_EXPAND ¦ GTK_FILL ¦ GTK_SHRINK, GTK_FILL, 0, 0);
    gtk_widget_show (hscrollbar);

    /* --- Add a vertical scrollbar --- */
    vscrollbar = gtk_vscrollbar_new (GTK_TEXT (text)->vadj);
    gtk_table_attach (GTK_TABLE (table), vscrollbar, 1, 2, 0, 1,
            GTK_FILL, GTK_EXPAND ¦ GTK_SHRINK ¦ GTK_FILL, 0, 0);
    gtk_widget_show (vscrollbar);

}
```

## Cut, Copy, and Paste

The text widget automatically supports the clipboard commands "Cut," "Copy," and
"Paste," but generally the user will not use the keyboard (Ctrl+X, Ctrl+C, Ctrl+V) to
perform the clipboard operation. The menu and toolbar clipboard operations should
appear to the user as integrated as the keyboard shortcuts are. The menu and toolbar
commands are mapped to a series of functions that perform the same work as the
keyboard commands. For instance, the "Cut" on the menu is going to call the
gtk_editable_cut_clipboard function to remove the text and place it in the clipboard.

```
    /*
     * TextCut
     *
     * Cut the selected text from the text widget and
     * put it in the clipboard.
     */
    void TextCut (GtkWidget *widget, gpointer data)
    {
        gtk_editable_cut_clipboard (GTK_EDITABLE (text));
    }
```

In fact, the Copy and Paste commands can be done just as easily.

```
/*
 * TextCopy
 *
 * Copy the selected text in the widget into the
 * clipboard.
 */
void TextCopy (GtkWidget *widget, gpointer data)
{
    gtk_editable_copy_clipboard (GTK_EDITABLE (text));
}


/*
 * TextPaste
 *
 * Paste the text in the clipboard into the text widget
 */
void TextPaste (GtkWidget *widget, gpointer data)
{
    gtk_editable_paste_clipboard (GTK_EDITABLE (text));
}
```

## Creating a Clean Slate

The editor now has full cut, copy, and paste functionality. The text widget needs to handle other commands. The File→New option should clear the text in the widget. This operation can also be done in a single step.

```
/*
 * ClearFile
 *
 * Called to clear all the text in the text widget
 */
void ClearFile (GtkWidget *widget, gpointer data)
{
    gtk_editable_delete_text (GTK_EDITABLE (text), 0, -1);
}
```

## Loading Files

Loading a file into the widget requires the use of the file selection dialog box. The LoadFile function is passed into the GetFilename function, and if the OK button is clicked, the function is called.

```
/*
 * menu_Open (main.c)
 *
 * Give the user a dialog box to read a file.
 */
void menu_Open (GtkWidget *widget, gpointer data)
{
    GetFilename ("Open", LoadFile);
}
```

The `LoadFile` function reads a file into the widget while displaying the status using a progress bar. Three progress bar functions show the status of the file load. `StartProgress` creates the progress bar, `UpdateProgress` updates the status of the load, and `EndProgress` closes the progress bar. To prevent the widget from spending time drawing the text while the file is loaded into the widget, the `gtk_text_freeze` function is used. The file is read using small blocks of `BUF_SIZE` length. The `BUF_SIZE` constant can be adjusted to a larger size to increase the speed of the load. In this case, it was set to a small size; otherwise, the files are loaded so fast that the progress bar doesn't even get displayed.

```
/*
 * LoadFile
 *
 * sFilename - file to load
 *
 * Reads in the file and places it in the text widget.
 */
void LoadFile (char *sFilename)
{
    char buffer[BUF_SIZE];
    int nchars;
    FILE *infile;
    struct stat fileStatus;
    long fileLen = 0;

    /* --- Freeze the widget --- */
    gtk_text_freeze (GTK_TEXT (text));

    /* --- Empty the widget --- */
    gtk_editable_delete_text (GTK_EDITABLE (text), 0, -1);

    /* --- Get file information --- */
    stat (sFilename, &fileStatus);
    fileLen = fileStatus.st_size;

    StartProgress ();
```

```
/* --- Open the file --- */
infile = fopen (sFilename, "r");

/* --- If we open the file. --- */
if (infile) {

    /* --- Read a chunk... --- */
    while ((nchars = fread (buffer, 1, BUF_SIZE, infile)) > 0) {

        /* --- Update the progress bar --- */
        UpdateProgress (ftell (infile), fileLen);

        /* --- Insert the text --- */
        gtk_text_insert (GTK_TEXT (text), NULL, NULL,
                NULL, buffer, nchars);

        /* --- Less than buffer means EOF --- */
        if (nchars < BUF_SIZE)
            break;
    }

    /* --- Close file  --- */
    fclose (infile);
}
EndProgress ();

/* --- Unfreeze the text widget - it'll repaint now --- */
gtk_text_thaw (GTK_TEXT (text));
}
```

## Saving Files

Saving the file is similar to loading the file except that the file can be written out as
one large block of memory. The block of memory, which is retrieved from the widget
using gtk_editable_get_chars, should be released using the g_free function.

```
/*
 * SaveFile
 *
 * sFilename - filename to load
 *
 * Save the file.
 */
void SaveFile (char *sFilename)
{
    FILE *outfile;
```

```
        char *buffer;
        int nchars;

        gtk_text_freeze (GTK_TEXT (text));

        /* --- Open the file --- */
        outfile = fopen (sFilename, "w");

        if (outfile) {

            /* --- Get the string from the widget --- */
            buffer = gtk_editable_get_chars (
                        GTK_EDITABLE (text),
                        (gint) 0,
                        (gint) gtk_text_get_length (GTK_TEXT (text)));

            /* --- Write the buffer to disk --- */
            nchars = fwrite (buffer, sizeof (char), strlen (buffer), outfile);

            /* --- Close the file --- */
            fclose (outfile);

            if (nchars != strlen (buffer)) {

                ShowMessage ("Save", "Error: Can't write file.");
            }

            /* --- Free up the memory --- */
            g_free (buffer);

        } else {

            ShowMessage ("Save", "Error: Can't save file.");
        }

        gtk_text_thaw (GTK_TEXT (text));
    }
```

## Searching for Text

The search capability is implemented using a nonmodal dialog box. Whereas the About box and the file selection window do not allow other access to the application while those windows are up, the search window allows other windows to be brought up. The search window, however, allows only one copy of the search dialog box to be used at any given time.

The "Find" menu is mapped to the menu_Find function that creates a dialog box and allows the user to search for a string from the current cursor position to the end of the file. The two functions passed into the dialog box correspond to the two buttons on the dialog box. If the Find Next button is clicked, the FindFunction is called to look for the string in the widget. If the Cancel button is clicked, the CancelFunction function is called to close the window.

```
/*
 * menu_Find
 *
 * Find a string in the editor
 */
void menu_Find (GtkWidget *widget, gpointer data)
{
    FindStringDialog ("Find", FindFunction, CancelFunction);
}
```

The FindStringDialog creates the dialog box and assigns the FindFunction and CancelFunction to the Find Next and Cancel buttons. The function does a check on a global variable (dialog_window) before creating the dialog box to ensure that only one copy of the dialog box is open.

```
/*
 * FindStringDialog
 *
 * Function to display a search dialog box
 */
void FindStringDialog (char *szMessage, void (*YesFunc)(), void
(*NoFunc)())
{
    GtkWidget *label;
    GtkWidget *button;
    GtkWidget *hbox;

    /* --- If window is already open, just return --- */
    if (dialog_window) return;

    /* --- Create the dialog box--- */
    dialog_window = gtk_dialog_new ();

    gtk_signal_connect (GTK_OBJECT (dialog_window), "destroy",
                    GTK_SIGNAL_FUNC (CloseFindDialog),
                    dialog_window);

    /* --- Set the title --- */
    gtk_window_set_title (GTK_WINDOW (dialog_window), "Find");
```

```c
/* --- Add a small border --- */
gtk_container_border_width (GTK_CONTAINER (dialog_window), 5);


/*
 * --- Create the message
 */

hbox = gtk_hbox_new (TRUE, TRUE);

/* --- Create a label with the message --- */
label = gtk_label_new ("Find What:");
gtk_widget_show (label);

/* --- Create the entry field --- */
entry = gtk_entry_new ();
gtk_widget_show (entry);

/* --- If they've searched before --- */
if (szNeedle) {

    /* --- Prefill with the value they looked for last time --- */
    gtk_entry_set_text (GTK_ENTRY (entry), szNeedle);
}

gtk_box_pack_start (GTK_BOX (hbox),
                    label, TRUE, TRUE, 0);

gtk_box_pack_start (GTK_BOX (hbox),
                    entry, TRUE, TRUE, 0);
gtk_widget_show (hbox);

/* --- Add label to the dialog box--- */
gtk_box_pack_start (GTK_BOX (GTK_DIALOG (dialog_window)->vbox),
                    hbox, TRUE, TRUE, 0);

/* --- Create the "yes" button --- */
button = gtk_button_new_with_label ("Find Next");

gtk_signal_connect (GTK_OBJECT (button), "clicked",
                    GTK_SIGNAL_FUNC (YesFunc),
                    dialog_window);

/* --- Add the button to the dialog box--- */
gtk_box_pack_start (GTK_BOX (GTK_DIALOG (dialog_window)-
➡>action_area),
                    button, TRUE, TRUE, 0);
```

```
/* --- Make the button visible --- */
gtk_widget_show (button);


/*
 * --- Cancel button
 */

/* --- Create the "Cancel" button --- */
button = gtk_button_new_with_label ("Cancel");

gtk_signal_connect (GTK_OBJECT (button), "clicked",
                    GTK_SIGNAL_FUNC (NoFunc),
                    dialog_window);

/* --- Allow "Cancel" to be a default --- */
GTK_WIDGET_SET_FLAGS (button, GTK_CAN_DEFAULT);

/* --- Add the "Cancel" button to the dialog box--- */
gtk_box_pack_start (GTK_BOX
                (GTK_DIALOG (dialog_window)->action_area),
                    button, TRUE, TRUE, 0);

/* --- Make the "Cancel" the default --- */
gtk_widget_grab_default (button);

/* --- Make the button visible. --- */
gtk_widget_show (button);

/* --- Show the dialog box--- */
gtk_widget_show (dialog_window);
}
```

The CancelFunction routine destroys the dialog and clears the global variable so that it can be created again.

```
/*
 * CancelFunction
 *
 * Close the find dialog window.
 */
void CancelFunction (GtkWidget *widget, gpointer data)
{
    /* --- Close it. --- */
    gtk_widget_destroy (GTK_WIDGET (data));

    dialog_window = NULL;
}
```

Rather than creating and destroying the dialog box every time it is used, you can create it once and then make it visible whenever it's used. When the user is done with the dialog box, it is hidden so that it appears to have been closed. Although this method requires more memory when the machine is running, the dialog box comes up more quickly because it doesn't have to be created.

The FindFunction does a search for the string in the file. The function starts from the current cursor position and searches from that point. Rather than use the gtk_text_get_point function to get the cursor position, the selection_end_pos field in the widget is used. The reasoning here is that when a search is performed, the value found will be highlighted, and finding the next value in the file needs to start at the end of the selected area. After you find the string in the field, a little trick is required to get the text widget to actually scroll to the position where the text is highlighted (highlighting the text doesn't actually scroll the text to bring the widget into view). Fortunately, inserting a character into the widget scrolls the widget to the point where the text is inserted, but because you are just searching for a string, you can insert a character, let the widget scroll to the position, and then delete the character.

```
/*
 * FindFunction
 *
 * Looks for the string in the notepad
 */
void FindFunction (GtkWidget *widget, gpointer data)
{
    int nIndex;
    GtkWidget *text = GetTextWidget ();
    char *szHaystack;

    /* --- Get the text from the widget --- */
    szHaystack = GetText ();

    /* --- Free up the old needle (text) --- */
    if (szNeedle) {
        g_free (szNeedle);
    }

    /* --- Get text to search for.  --- */
    szNeedle = gtk_editable_get_chars (
                    GTK_EDITABLE (entry), 0, -1);

    /* --- Get cursor position --- */
    nIndex = GTK_EDITABLE (text)->selection_end_pos;

    /* --- Find the string --- */
    nIndex = LookForString (szHaystack, szNeedle, nIndex);
```

```
        if (nIndex >= 0) {

            /* --- Move the cursor to a position --- */
            gtk_text_set_point (GTK_TEXT (text), nIndex);

            /* --- These two lines will force the widget to --- */
            /*     scroll to the position where the text is. --- */
            gtk_text_insert (GTK_TEXT (text), NULL, NULL, NULL, " ", 1);
            gtk_text_backward_delete (GTK_TEXT (text), 1);

            /* --- Select the field found. --- */
            gtk_editable_select_region (GTK_EDITABLE (text),
                                nIndex, nIndex + strlen (szNeedle));

            /* --- Allow it to be created again --- */
            dialog_window = NULL;
        } else {

            ShowMessage ("Find...", "Not found.  Reached the end of the
    ➥file.");
        }

        /* --- Release memory. --- */
        g_free (szHaystack);
    }
```

Don't forget that the string you got with the GetText function needs to be freed because the function makes a call to the gtk_editable_get_chars function, which returns an allocated block of memory for the string. The function LookForString does a brute force search for the string from the position passed in and returns the index of the position, or -1 if the string cannot be found in the text widget.

```
/*
 * LookForString
 *
 * Search for a string (szNeedle) in a larger
 * string (szHaystack) starting at a given position (nStart)
 * in the large string.
 *
 * This is referred to as the brute force algorithm.
 */
int LookForString (char *szHaystack, char *szNeedle, int nStart)
{
    int nHaystackLength;
    int nNeedleLength;
    int nPos;

    /* --- Get the length of the strings. --- */
```

```
nHaystackLength = strlen (szHaystack);
nNeedleLength = strlen (szNeedle);

/* --- Check each string --- */
for (nPos = nStart; nPos < nHaystackLength; nPos++) {

    /* --- Did we find it here? --- */
    if (strncmp (&szHaystack[nPos], szNeedle, nNeedleLength) == 0) {

        /* --- yes, return index --- */
        return (nPos);
    }
}

/* Didn't find string, return -1 --- */
return (-1);
}
```

## Progress Bar

The progress bar functions are reused from Chapter 6, "More Widgets: Frames, Text, Dialog Boxes, File Selection Dialog Box, Progress Bar." You can use the progress bar to display information to a user about the status of operations that may take a long time to perform. Again, the loading of a file is intentionally hindered, using a small buffer in a loop to slow down the loading of a file. If the loading of a file occurred too quickly, the progress bar would not get a chance to be displayed. You can easily change the buffer size to speed up the file load.

# Summary

You can use GTK+ to create applications quickly. In this chapter, the widgets within GTK+ did most of the work to develop the editor. By combining a menu, a toolbar, and an edit widget, you were able to create a simple editor application.

# 9

# Minesweeper

**M**INESWEEPER IS A SIMPLE GAME THAT became popular when Microsoft included it with Windows. The idea of the game is to uncover all the squares on the board that do not have bombs underneath. Although the first few choices are pretty much random, the uncovered squares provide clues to assist you in defusing the rest of the squares. Each square "knows" how many bombs are in the adjacent squares, so uncovering a square that has no bomb provides a clue to help you figure out which of that square's neighbors might be harboring a bomb. Of course, to make it interesting, a timer tells you how long you're taking, so that once you clear the board, the challenge is to clear the board in less time. The Minesweeper playing field is shown in Figure 9.1.

Minesweeper reinforces most of the topics we've discussed already. In fact, the basics of the minesweeper application look a lot like the calculator application. They both use buttons in a packing table, but minesweeper is a bit more involved than the calculator. Minesweeper features a menu with some choices about game complexity (beginner, intermediate, and advanced), and a toolbar that displays a timer and the number of undiscovered bombs. It also uses xpm images for the bombs, the smiley button, the colorful digits, and the flags.

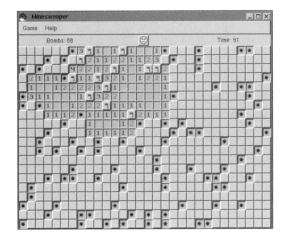

**Figure 9.1**   The minesweeper application.

All the buttons are stored in a two-dimensional array of `typMinesweeperButton`. This structure stores the button widget as well as whether the button has a bomb underneath and how many of the button's neighbors have a bomb.

```
/*
 * --- data structure to keep track of the Minesweeper buttons.
 */
typedef struct {
    int       buttonState;    /* --- Column to place the button --- */
    GtkWidget *widget;        /* --- Handle to the button --- */
    int       nBombsNearby;   /* --- How many near this cell? --- */
    int       bHasBomb;       /* --- Does it have a bomb? --- */
    int       nRow;           /* --- Row of button --- */
    int       nCol;           /* --- Column of button --- */
} typMinesweeperButton;
```

When the user starts a game, the computer quickly generates the game by placing the appropriate number of bombs under some of the buttons. The computer also calculates how many bombs are adjacent to each button in the game. This information is initially hidden from the user, but the number of bombs adjacent to a given button is displayed if the player clicks on a button that does not contain a bomb.

The first step is to create the image data. The images are simple and intuitive. They consist of several smiley faces for the button, a flag so the user can mark where the bombs are, a bomb (in case the user makes a mistake), and a series of colorful digits that display the number of bombs near any particular square.

# *bitmaps.h*

Pictures used by the Minesweeper game are in the `bitmaps.h` file. The colorful digit bitmaps are not included in this file. Notice that the smiley face has three distinct images—one for the game while it's being played, one for losing the game, and one for winning the game. These three images don't require much code, and they add to the character of the game.

```
/*
 * --- Flag for marking the bombs.
 */
static char *xpm_flag[] = {
"12 12 4 1",
"  c None",
"X c #000000",
"R c #FF0000",
"r c #AA0000",
"            ",
"   RRRRRR   ",
"   RRRRRrr  ",
"   RRRrrrr  ",
"   Rrrrrrr  ",
"        X   ",
"        X   ",
"        X   ",
"        X   ",
"        X   ",
"       XXX  ",
"            ",
};


/*
 * --- A bomb.  Oops, you're not as smart as you thought.
 */
static char *xpm_bomb[] = {
"12 12 4 1",
"  c None",
"X c #000000",
"R c #FF0000",
"r c #AA0000",
"            ",
"     X      ",
"  X  X  X   ",
"    XXXXX   ",
"    XXXXX   ",
" XXXXXXXX   ",
```

```
"    XXXXX      ",
"    XXXXX      ",
"  X  X  X      ",
"       X       ",
"               ",
"               ",
};


/*
 * --- Wrong move!
 */
static char *xpm_bigx[] = {
"12 12 4 1",
"  c None",
"X c #000000",
"R c #FF0000",
"r c #AA0000",
"RRR        RRR",
" RRR      RRR ",
"  RRR    RRR  ",
"   RRRRRR     ",
"     RRRR      ",
"     RRRR      ",
"     RRRR      ",
"    RRRRRR     ",
"   RRR  RRR   ",
" RRR      RRR ",
"RRR        RRR",
"              ",
};


/*
 * --- Bitmap of a smile
 */
static char *xpm_smile[] = {
"16 16 4 1",
"  c None",
". c #000000",
"X c #FFFF00",
"r c #AA0000",
"     ......     ",
"   ..XXXXXX..   ",
"  ..XXXXXXXXXX. ",
" .XXXXXXXXXXXX. ",
```

```
"  .XX..XXXX..XX.  ",
".XXX..XXXX..XXX.",
".XXXXXXXXXXXXXX.",
".XXXXXXXXXXXXXX.",
".XXXXXXXXXXXXXX.",
".XXXXXXXXXXXXXX.",
"  .XX.XXXXXX.XX.  ",
"  .XXX......XXX.  ",
"   .XXXXXXXXXX.    ",
"     ..XXXXXX..     ",
"          ......      ",
"                      ",
};


/*
 * --- frown.  You lost.
 */
static char *xpm_frown[] = {
"16 16 4 1",
"   c None",
".  c #000000",
"X  c #FFFF00",
"r  c #AA0000",
"          ......      ",
"     ..XXXXXX..     ",
"   ..XXXXXXXXXX.    ",
"   .XXXXXXXXXXXX.   ",
"   .XX.X.XX.X.XX.   ",
".XXXX.XXXX.XXXX.",
".XXX.X.XX.X.XXX.",
".XXXXXXXXXXXXXX.",
".XXXXXXXXXXXXXX.",
".XXXXXXXXXXXXXX.",
"  .XXX......XXX.  ",
"  .XX.XXXXXX.XX.  ",
"   .XXXXXXXXXX.    ",
"     ..XXXXXX..     ",
"          ......      ",
"                      ",
};


/*
 * --- We have a winner.
 */
```

```
static char *xpm_winner[] = {
"16 16 4 1",
"   c None",
".  c #000000",
"X  c #FFFF00",
"r  c #AA0000",
"     ......     ",
"    ..XXXXXX..   ",
"  ..XXXXXXXXXX.  ",
"  .XXXXXXXXXXXX. ",
"  .XX...XX...XX. ",
" .XX.........XX.",
" .X.X...XX...X.X.",
"  ..XXXXXXXXXXX..",
"  .XXXXXXXXXXXXX.",
"  .XXXXXXXXXXXXX.",
"  .XX.XXXXX.XX.  ",
"  .XXX......XXX. ",
"   .XXXXXXXXX.   ",
"    ..XXXXX..    ",
"     ......      ",
"                ",
};
```

## *digits.h*

The digits that display the number of bombs in the squares next to one of the squares are pixmaps. Because all the button data is in pixmaps, the routines that put the bombs, flags, or digits on the buttons can all be in the same set of code—only the image changes.

```
/*
 * 1 - light blue
 * 2 - green
 * 3 - red
 * 4 - dark blue
 * 5 - brownish purple
 */

static const char *xpm_one[] = {
"12 12 2 1",
"   c None",
"X  c #3333CC",
"            ",
"     XX     ",
"     XXX    ",
```

```
"    X XX      ",
"       XX      ",
"       XX      ",
"       XX      ",
"       XX      ",
"       XX      ",
"     XXXXXX     ",
"                ",
"                ",
};


static const char *xpm_two[] = {
"12 12 2 1",
"  c None",
"X c #009900",
"                ",
"    XXXXXX      ",
"   X        X   ",
"            XX  ",
"           XX   ",
"          XX    ",
"         XX     ",
"        XX      ",
"      XX        ",
"     XXXXXXXX   ",
"                ",
"                ",
};


static const char *xpm_three[] = {
"12 12 2 1",
"  c None",
"X c #AA0000",
"                ",
"    XXXXX       ",
"          XX    ",
"          XX    ",
"     XXXXXX     ",
"          XX    ",
"          XX    ",
"          XX    ",
"          XX    ",
"     XXXXXX      ",
"                ",
```

```
"            ",
};


static const char *xpm_four[] = {
"12 12 2 1",
"  c None",
"X c #000066",
"            ",
"  XX    XX  ",
"  XX    XX  ",
"  XX    XX  ",
"  XX    XX  ",
"  XXXXXXX   ",
"        XX  ",
"        XX  ",
"        XX  ",
"        XX  ",
"            ",
"            ",
};


static const char *xpm_five[] = {
"12 12 2 1",
"  c None",
"X c #992299",
"            ",
"  XXXXXXX   ",
"  XX        ",
"  XX        ",
"  XXXXXX    ",
"        XX  ",
"        XX  ",
"        XX  ",
"  XX    XX  ",
"  XXXXXX    ",
"            ",
"            ",
};


static const char *xpm_six[] = {
"12 12 2 1",
"  c None",
```

```
"X c #550055",
"               ",
"    XXXXXX     ",
"    XX        ",
"    XX        ",
"    XXXXXXX    ",
"    XX    XX   ",
"    XX    XX   ",
"    XX    XX   ",
"    XX    XX   ",
"    XXXXXX     ",
"               ",
"               ",
};


static const char *xpm_seven[] = {
"12 12 2 1",
"  c None",
"X c #550000",
"               ",
"    XXXXXXXX   ",
"          XX   ",
"         XX    ",
"         XX    ",
"        XX     ",
"        XX     ",
"       XX      ",
"       XX      ",
"       XX      ",
"               ",
"               ",
};


static const char *xpm_eight[] = {
"12 12 2 1",
"  c None",
"X c #441144",
"               ",
"    XXXXXX     ",
"    XX    XX   ",
"    XX    XX   ",
"    XXXXXX     ",
```

```
"  XX    XX  ",
"  XX    XX  ",
"  XX    XX  ",
"  XX    XX  ",
"    XXXXXX    ",
"              ",
"              ",
};
```

## *timer.c*

The game needs to keep track of and update the number of seconds since the user first clicked on a button on the page. The StartTimer function gets called when the user first clicks on a button—actually, it gets called *each* time the user clicks on a button; however, if the timer is already running, StartTimer ignores the call. The StartTimer function starts up a callback (TimerCallback) that gets called every second to update and display the time. The StopTimer function gets called when the user hits a bomb, wins the game, or resets the game by clicking on the smiley button.

```
/*
 * Timer.c
 *
 * Auth: Eric Harlow
 *
 * Routines to update something every second.
 */

#include <gtk/gtk.h>


static int nSeconds = 0;
static gint timer = 0;
static int bTimerRunning = FALSE;

void UpdateSeconds (int);

/*
 * TimerCallback
 *
 * Every second, this will be called to update the time
 * in the clock window.
 */
gint TimerCallback (gpointer data)
{
    /* --- Another second has gone by --- */
    nSeconds++;
```

```
    UpdateSeconds (nSeconds);
}


/*
 * StartTimer
 *
 * Starts up the time.  Happens when the user first
 * clicks on a button.
 */
void StartTimer ()
{

    /* --- If the timer isn't already running --- */
    if (!bTimerRunning) {

        /* --- Start at zero --- */
        nSeconds = 0;

        /* --- Call function 'TimerCallback' every 1000ms --- */
        timer = gtk_timeout_add (1000, TimerCallback, NULL);

        /* --- Timer is running. --- */
        bTimerRunning = TRUE;
    }
}


/*
 * StopTimer
 *
 * Stops the timer.  User probably hit a bomb.
 */
void StopTimer ()
{
    /* --- If the time is running. --- */
    if (bTimerRunning) {

        /* --- Stop the timer. --- */
        gtk_timeout_remove (timer);

        /* --- Fix the flag. --- */
        bTimerRunning = FALSE;
    }
}
```

## *minesweeper.c*

The game itself is an N × M grid of toggle buttons represented by the data structure `typMinesweeperButton`. Each button has a row (`nRow`) and column (`nCol`) in the grid and a flag that indicates whether it has a bomb underneath (`bHasBomb`). In addition, a widget variable stores the toggle button when it's created, and a counter displays the number of bombs next to this square (the count is used only if the square does not have a bomb). A `buttonState` reflects one of several states that the button is in. The button starts out in the `BUTTON_UNKNOWN` state, but the user can change the state to `BUTTON_FLAGGED` by clicking on the right mouse button. This action also puts a flag on the button to indicate the state to the user. The `BUTTON_DOWN` state indicates that the button has been pressed down. If the button had a bomb underneath, this state would cause the game to end. The final state (`BUTTON_QUESTION`) is for the user to mark a button as questionable. A question mark appears on the button to mark it as possibly having a bomb underneath. This button state is not implemented at this time, although it is easy to add. Adding the button is left as an exercise for the reader.

Some recursion simplifies the coding. For instance, if the user clicks on a button without a bomb and the nearby bomb count is zero, it recursively opens the nearby squares as if the user had clicked on them. If one of those squares has a zero nearby bomb count, all the nearby squares of that square get opened.

When the buttons are created, each one is given the same callback function for the button click. The callback data parameter is configured with the button's data from the `typMinesweeperButton` array. Although the callback data is the data associated with the button that was clicked, the data contains the row and column of the button that can be used to figure out which buttons in the table are neighbors.

```
/*
 * File: minesweeper.c
 * Auth: Eric Harlow
 *
 * Similar to the Windows Minesweeper game.
 */

#include <gtk/gtk.h>
#include <stdlib.h>
#include <time.h>
#include "misc.h"
#include "bitmaps.h"
#include "digits.h"

void SetStartButtonIcon (gchar **xpm_data);

/*
 * --- Want the buttons to be a particular size.
 */
```

```
#define BUTTON_WIDTH 18
#define BUTTON_HEIGHT 19


/*
 * --- Each of the digits showing the number of bombs
 *     has a colorful bitmap showing the count.  This
 *     array makes the looking up of the digits happen
 *     very quickly.
 */
gpointer digits[] = {
    NULL,
    xpm_one,
    xpm_two,
    xpm_three,
    xpm_four,
    xpm_five,
    xpm_six,
    xpm_seven,
    xpm_eight
};



/*
 * --- These are the available button states.
 *
 * Unknown - Empty.  Don't know what it could be.
 * Flagged - User has put a flag on it, suspecting
 *           there's a bomb underneath.
 * Question - not implemented.
 * Down - Button has been pressed.
 */
enum {
    BUTTON_UNKNOWN,
    BUTTON_FLAGGED,
    BUTTON_QUESTION,
    BUTTON_DOWN
};

/*
 * --- data structure to keep track of the minesweeper buttons.
 */
typedef struct {
    int        buttonState;  /* --- Column to place the button --- */
    GtkWidget *widget;       /* --- Handle to the button --- */
```

```
      int       nBombsNearby; /* --- How many are near this cell? --- */
      int       bHasBomb;     /* --- Does it have a bomb? --- */
      int       nRow;         /* --- Row of button --- */
      int       nCol;         /* --- Column of button --- */
} typMinesweeperButton;

/*
 * --- Default values for the size of the grid
 *     and number of bombs.
 */
static int nRows = 10;
static int nCols = 10;
static int nTotalBombs = 10;


/*
 * --- Use a 2-d array for the grid.  This is just
 *     the maximum size.
 */
#define MAX_ROWS 35
#define MAX_COLS 35
/*
 * Globals.
 */

/* --- Just allocate the MAX for now.  This really should be dynamic,
 *     but using a two-dimensional array is easy when dealing with a
 *grid.
 */
typMinesweeperButton mines[MAX_COLS][MAX_ROWS];

/* --- Flags for the game --- */
int bGameOver = FALSE;          /* --- Game is over? --- */
int bResetGame = FALSE;         /* --- Game is over? --- */
int nBombsLeft;                 /* --- Undiscovered bombs --- */

GtkWidget *table = NULL;        /* --- Table with the grid in it. */
GtkWidget *button_start;        /* --- Start button --- */
GtkWidget *label_bombs;         /* --- Label showing # of bombs left */
GtkWidget *label_time;          /* --- Label showing # of bombs left */
GtkWidget *vbox;                /* --- main window's vbox --- */

/*
```

```
 * --- Prototypes.
 */
void DisplayHiddenInfo (typMinesweeperButton *mine);
void CreateMinesweeperButtons (GtkWidget *table, int c, int r, int flag);
void FreeChildCallback (GtkWidget *widget);




/*
 * CheckForWin
 *
 * Check to see if the game has been won.  Game has been won when the
 * number of unclicked squares equals the number of total bombs.
 */
void CheckForWin ()
{
    int i, j;
    int nMines = 0;

    /* --- Run through all the squares --- */
    for (i = 0; i <  nCols; i++) {
        for (j = 0; j < nRows; j++) {

            /* --- If square is unclicked or has a flag on it... --- */
            if (mines[i][j].buttonState == BUTTON_UNKNOWN ||
                mines[i][j].buttonState == BUTTON_FLAGGED) {

                /* --- Could be a bomb. --- */
                nMines ++;
            }
        }
    }

    /* --- As many bombs as there are squares left? --- */
    if (nMines == nTotalBombs) {

        /* --- Stop the game.  We have a winner. --- */
        StopTimer ();
        SetStartButtonIcon ((gchar **) xpm_winner);
        bGameOver = TRUE;
    }
}



/*
 * AddImageToMine
```

```
 *
 * Change the image on the button to be that of the xpm.
 *
 * mine - square on the grid
 * xpm - image data
 */
void AddImageToMine (typMinesweeperButton *mine, char *xpm[])
{
    GtkWidget *widget;

    /* --- Create a widget from the xpm file --- */
    widget = CreateWidgetFromXpm (table, (gchar **) xpm);

    /* --- Put the bitmap in the button --- */
    gtk_container_add (GTK_CONTAINER (mine->widget), widget);

    /* --- deref image so when button is destroyed, image is destroyed.*/
    gdk_pixmap_unref ((GdkPixmap *) widget);
}


/*
 * UpdateSeconds
 *
 * Refresh the seconds display in the toolbar.
 *
 * nSeconds - how many seconds to display.
 */
void UpdateSeconds (int nSeconds)
{
    char buffer[44];

    /* --- Change the label to show new time --- */
    sprintf (buffer, "Time: %d", nSeconds);
    gtk_label_set (GTK_LABEL (label_time), buffer);
}


/*
 * DisplayBombCount
 *
 * Show number of bombs remaining.
 */
void DisplayBombCount ()
{
```

```
    char buffer[33];

    /* --- You have XX bombs left --- */
    sprintf (buffer, "Bombs: %d", nBombsLeft);
    gtk_label_set (GTK_LABEL (label_bombs), buffer);
}



/*
 * FreeChild
 *
 * Free all the children of the widget
 * This is called when the button has to display a new image.
 * The old image is destroyed here.
 */
void FreeChild (GtkWidget *widget)
{
    /* --- Free button children --- */
    gtk_container_foreach (
                GTK_CONTAINER (widget),
                (GtkCallback) FreeChildCallback,
                NULL);

}

/*
 * delete_event
 *
 * The window is closing down, end the gtk loop
 *
 */
void delete_event (GtkWidget *widget, gpointer *data)
{
    gtk_main_quit ();
}



/*
 * ShowBombs
 *
 * They clicked on a bomb, so now we have to show them where the
 * bombs really are.  (At least those they didn't find already.)
 * We display the bombs they didn't find as well as the bombs
 * they think they found that were not bombs.
 */
void ShowBombs (typMinesweeperButton *minefound)
```

```
{
    int i, j;
    typMinesweeperButton *mine;
    GtkWidget *widget_x;

    /* --- Run through all the squares --- */
    for (i = 0; i <  nCols; i++) {
        for (j = 0; j < nRows; j++) {

            /* --- Get the datastructure --- */
            mine = &mines[i][j];

            /* --- If there's a button here and there's a bomb --- */
            /* --- underneath --- */
            if (mine->buttonState == BUTTON_UNKNOWN &&
                mine->bHasBomb) {

                /* --- Display the bomb. --- */
                DisplayHiddenInfo (mine);

            /* --- If they marked it as a bomb and there is
             *     no bomb here... --- */
            } else if (mine->buttonState == BUTTON_FLAGGED &&
                       !mine->bHasBomb) {

                /* --- Free the flag --- */
                FreeChild (mine->widget);

                /* --- Show the X at the location --- */
                AddImageToMine (mine, xpm_bigx);
            }
        }
    }
}


/*
 * OpenNearbySquares
 *
 * Open up all squares around this square.
 *
 * col, row - position to open up the square
 * Open all squares near this one - X represents
 * the current square.
 *
 *      |---|---|----
```

```
*        |   |   |   |
*        -------------
*        |   | X |   |
*        -------------
*        |   |   |   |
*        |---|---|----
*/
void OpenNearbySquares (int col, int row)
{
    int i, j;

    /* --- Look one column back and one column ahead --- */
    for (i = MAX (col-1, 0); i <= MIN (col+1, nCols-1); i++) {

        /* --- Check one row back and one row ahead --- */
        for (j = MAX (row-1, 0); j <= MIN (row+1, nRows-1); j++) {

            /* --- Display what's underneath --- */
            DisplayHiddenInfo (&mines[i][j]);
        }
    }
}



/*
 * DisplayHiddenInfo
 *
 * Display what's hidden underneath the button.
 * Could be a bomb -
 * Could be a square with a count of the bombs
 *  nearby.
 * Could be an empty square
 */
void DisplayHiddenInfo (typMinesweeperButton *mine)
{
    char     buffer[88];
    GtkWidget *widget;

    /* --- If it's already down, just return --- */
    if (mine->buttonState == BUTTON_DOWN) {
        gtk_toggle_button_set_state (GTK_TOGGLE_BUTTON (mine->widget),
➥TRUE);
        return;
    }

    /* --- If the button is flagged, don't fix it for them --- */
```

```
        if (mine->buttonState == BUTTON_FLAGGED) {

            /* --- They said there's a bomb here - so don't
             *     open it up even if logically, there
             *     can't be a bomb.
             */
            gtk_toggle_button_set_state (GTK_TOGGLE_BUTTON (mine->widget),
➥FALSE);

        } else {

            /* --- Put the button in the "down" state --- */
            mine->buttonState = BUTTON_DOWN;
            gtk_toggle_button_set_state (GTK_TOGGLE_BUTTON (mine->widget),
➥TRUE);

            /* --- If there's a bomb at the location --- */
            if (mine->bHasBomb) {

                /* --- Show the bomb at the location --- */
                AddImageToMine (mine, xpm_bomb);

            /* --- No bombs, but there are bombs near this one --- */
            } else if (mine->nBombsNearby) {

                /* --- Show the count of nearby bombs. --- */
                AddImageToMine (mine, digits[mine->nBombsNearby]);

            } else {

                /* --- Hmm.  Clicked here, but no bombs and no count. --- */
                /* --- Open up all squares near here - may cascade. --- */
                OpenNearbySquares (mine->nCol, mine->nRow);
            }
        }
    }


/*
 * ResetGame
 *
 * Reset the game so it can be replayed.  Reset bomb
 * count and create a nice empty field of bombs.
 */
void ResetGame (int nGridColumns, int nGridRows, int nBombs,
➥int bNewButtons)
```

```
{
    /* --- Reset the number of bombs in grid  --- */
    nTotalBombs = nBombs;

    /* --- Reset the number of bombs undiscovered --- */
    nBombsLeft = nBombs;

    /* --- Create the minesweeper buttons. --- */
    CreateMinesweeperButtons (table, nGridColumns, nGridRows,
➥bNewButtons);

    /* --- Stop the timer. --- */
    StopTimer ();

    UpdateSeconds (0);

    SetStartButtonIcon ((gchar **) xpm_smile);
}


/*
 * FreeChildCallback
 *
 * Free the widget.
 */
void FreeChildCallback (GtkWidget *widget)
{
    gtk_widget_destroy (widget);
}


/*
 * SetStartButtonIcon
 *
 * Set the start button to have the image based on
 * the data passed in.  Usually, this is going to be
 * either the happy face or the frown.
 */
void SetStartButtonIcon (gchar **xpm_data)
{
    GtkWidget *widget;

    /* --- Create a widget from the xpm --- */
    widget = CreateWidgetFromXpm (button_start, xpm_data);
```

```
    /* --- Free any children the button has --- */
    FreeChild (button_start);

    /* --- Make this the current image --- */
    gtk_container_add (GTK_CONTAINER (button_start), widget);
}


/*
 * start_button_clicked
 *
 * Event handler for the clicking of the start
 * button
 */
void start_button_clicked (GtkWidget *widget, gpointer *data)
{
    SetStartButtonIcon ((gchar **) xpm_smile);
    ResetGame (nCols, nRows, nTotalBombs, FALSE);
}


/*
 * mine_button_clicked
 *
 * Event handler for one of the mine buttons being
 * clicked.
 *
 * widget - button pressed.
 * data - button label.
 */
void mine_button_clicked (GtkWidget *widget, gpointer *data)
{
    typMinesweeperButton *mine;
    GtkWidget *label;

    mine = (typMinesweeperButton *) data;

    printf ("button clicked - game over = %d\n", bGameOver);

    /* --- If the game is over --- */
    if (bGameOver) {
        /* --- Leave the button as it was. --- */
        gtk_toggle_button_set_state (GTK_TOGGLE_BUTTON (widget),
                        (mine->buttonState == BUTTON_DOWN));
        return;
    }
```

```
    /* --- If game is being reset --- */
    if (bResetGame) return;

    /* --- Start the time ... now --- */
    StartTimer ();

    /* --- If they clicked on a mine button... --- */
    if (mine->bHasBomb) {

        /* --- Game over, dude! --- */
        bGameOver = TRUE;

        /* --- Smiley face is frowning. --- */
        SetStartButtonIcon ((gchar **) xpm_frown);

        /* --- Display all unseen bombs. --- */
        StopTimer ();
        ShowBombs (mine);

    } else {

        /* --- Create a label for the cell and put the  --- */
        /* --- number of nearby bombs in it. --- */
        DisplayHiddenInfo (mine);
        CheckForWin ();
    }
}


/*
 * button_press
 *
 * The button press could be a right mouse button
 * that needs to be handled by rotating the
 * image in the button.
 */
void button_press (GtkWidget *widget, GdkEventButton *event, gpointer
➥*data)
{
    typMinesweeperButton *mine;
    GtkWidget *pixmapWidget;

    /* --- Ignore if game is already over--- */
    if (bGameOver) {
        return;
    }
```

```
        /* --- Which mine was clicked? --- */
        mine = (typMinesweeperButton *) data;

        /* --- Make sure it's a button event --- */
        if (event->type == GDK_BUTTON_PRESS) {

            /* --- Was it the right mouse button? --- */
            if (event->button == 3) {

                switch (mine->buttonState) {

                    case BUTTON_UNKNOWN:

                        /* --- Free button children --- */
                        FreeChild (widget);

                        mine->buttonState = BUTTON_FLAGGED;
                        AddImageToMine (mine, xpm_flag);
                        nBombsLeft --;
                        break;

                    case BUTTON_FLAGGED:

                        /* --- Free button children --- */
                        FreeChild (widget);

                        /* --- Free button children --- */
                        mine->buttonState = BUTTON_UNKNOWN;
                        nBombsLeft ++;
                        break;
                }
                DisplayBombCount ();
                CheckForWin ();
            }
        }
}


/*
 * CreateButton
 *
 * Create a button, assign event handlers, and attach the button to the
 * table in the proper place.
 */
GtkWidget *CreateButton (GtkWidget *table,
                         typMinesweeperButton *mine,
```

```
                              int row,
                              int column)
{
    GtkWidget *button;

    /* --- Create the button --- */
    button = gtk_toggle_button_new ();

    /* --- Init the button fields --- */
    mine->buttonState = BUTTON_UNKNOWN;
    mine->nRow = row;
    mine->nCol = column;

    /* --- We care if the button is clicked --- */
    gtk_signal_connect (GTK_OBJECT (button), "clicked",
                        GTK_SIGNAL_FUNC (mine_button_clicked), mine);

    /* --- We care about other mouse events. --- */
    gtk_signal_connect (GTK_OBJECT (button), "button_press_event",
                        GTK_SIGNAL_FUNC (button_press), mine);

    /* --- Put the button in the table in the right place. --- */
    gtk_table_attach (GTK_TABLE (table), button,
                      column, column+1,
                      row + 1, row + 2,
                      GTK_FILL | GTK_EXPAND,
                      GTK_FILL | GTK_EXPAND,
                      0, 0);

    /* --- Set the button to a uniform size --- */
    gtk_widget_set_usize (button, BUTTON_WIDTH, BUTTON_HEIGHT);

    /* --- Make the button visible --- */
    gtk_widget_show (button);

    /* --- return the button. --- */
    return (button);
}



/*
 * CountNearbyBombs
 *
 * Count the number of bombs this square is next to.
 */
```

```
int CountNearbyBombs (int col, int row)
{
    int i, j;
    int nCount = 0;

    /* --- Every square that would be at most 1 square away --- */
    for (i = MAX (col-1, 0); i <= MIN (col+1, nCols-1); i++) {
        for (j = MAX (row-1, 0); j <= MIN (row+1, nRows-1); j++) {

            /* --- If it's got a bomb --- */
            if (mines[i][j].bHasBomb) {

                /* --- Keep track of the count. --- */
                nCount++;
            }
        }
    }
    return (nCount);
}



/*
 * CreateMinesweeperButtons
 *
 * Create the buttons on the minesweeper from the table we defined at the
 * beginning of this program.  The button pointers (handles) are stored
 * back in the table so they can be referenced later.
 */
void CreateMinesweeperButtons (GtkWidget *table,
                               int nGridColumns,
                               int nGridRows,
                               int bNewButtons)
{
    int ci;
    int ri;
    GtkWidget *button;
    int nBombs;
    typMinesweeperButton *mine;

    /* --- Update the global variables --- */
    nCols = nGridColumns;
    nRows = nGridRows;

    bGameOver = FALSE;
    bResetGame = TRUE;
```

```
/* --- Update bomb count. --- */
DisplayBombCount ();

/* --- Check each button --- */
for (ci = 0; ci < nCols; ci++) {
    for (ri = 0; ri < nRows; ri++) {

        /* --- The button has nothing at all. --- */
        mine = &mines[ci][ri];
        mine->bHasBomb = 0;
        mine->buttonState = BUTTON_UNKNOWN;

        /* --- Widget assoc to the mine? --- */
        if (bNewButtons) {

            /* --- Create a button --- */
            mine->widget = CreateButton (table, mine, ri, ci);
        } else {

            /* --- Reuse button --- */

            /* --- Free any existing xpm/label --- */
            FreeChild (mine->widget);

            /* --- Put button up. --- */
            gtk_toggle_button_set_state (
                    GTK_TOGGLE_BUTTON (mine->widget),
                    FALSE);
        }
    }
}

/* --- Place the bombs. --- */
nBombs = nTotalBombs;

/* --- While we have bombs to deliver --- */
while (nBombs > 0) {

    /* --- Calculate a row/col position --- */
    ci = rand () % nCols;
    ri = rand () % nRows;

    /* --- If no bomb exists, create one! --- */
    if (mines[ci][ri].bHasBomb == 0) {
        mines[ci][ri].bHasBomb = 1;
        nBombs--;
```

```
            }
        }

        /* --- Once all bombs have been distributed, calculate
         *     how many bombs are adjacent to each button.
         */

        /* --- Check every button --- */
        for (ci = 0; ci < nCols; ci++) {
            for (ri = 0; ri < nRows; ri++) {

                mine = &mines[ci][ri];

                /* --- How many buttons? --- */
                mine->nBombsNearby = CountNearbyBombs (ci, ri);
            }
        }
        bResetGame = FALSE;
}


/*
 * SetGrid
 *
 * Sets the game grid to the size specified with the
 * number of bombs.
 */
void SetGrid (int nGridColumns, int nGridRows, int nBombs)
{
    int row, col;

    /* --- If the packing table exists. --- */
    if (table) {

        /* --- Destroy it and all the buttons. --- */
        gtk_widget_destroy (table);
    }

    /* --- Create a table for the buttons --- */
    table = gtk_table_new (nGridColumns, nGridRows, FALSE);

    /* --- Add it to the vbox --- */
    gtk_box_pack_start (GTK_BOX (vbox), table, FALSE, FALSE, 0);

    /* --- Show the table. --- */
    gtk_widget_realize (table);
```

```c
    /* --- Do a game reset with the numbers --- */
    ResetGame (nGridColumns, nGridRows, nBombs, TRUE);

    /* --- Show the table. --- */
    gtk_widget_show (table);
}



/*
 * main
 *
 * Program begins here
 */
int main (int argc, char *argv[])
{
    GtkWidget *window;
    GdkBitmap *mask;
    GtkStyle  *style;
    GtkWidget *widget_smile;
    GtkWidget *hbox;

    /* --- GTK initialization --- */
    gtk_init (&argc, &argv);

    /* --- Create the top window --- */
    window = gtk_window_new (GTK_WINDOW_TOPLEVEL);

    /* --- Don't allow window to be resized.  --- */
    gtk_window_set_policy (GTK_WINDOW (window), FALSE, FALSE, TRUE);

    /* --- Give the window a title. --- */
    gtk_window_set_title (GTK_WINDOW (window), "Minesweeper");

    /* --- You should always remember to connect the destroy event
     *      to the main window.
     */
    gtk_signal_connect (GTK_OBJECT (window), "delete_event",
                        GTK_SIGNAL_FUNC (delete_event), NULL);

    vbox = gtk_vbox_new (FALSE, 1);
    gtk_widget_show (vbox);

    /* --- Create the application menu --- */
    CreateMenu (window, vbox);
```

```
/* --- Horizontal box for score/start button --- */
hbox = gtk_hbox_new (TRUE, 1);
gtk_widget_show (hbox);

gtk_box_pack_start (GTK_BOX (vbox), hbox, FALSE, FALSE, 0);

/*
 * --- Bombs left on the page is a label
 */

/* --- Add label with # of bombs left. --- */
label_bombs = gtk_label_new ("");
gtk_box_pack_start (GTK_BOX (hbox), label_bombs, FALSE, FALSE, 0);
gtk_widget_show (label_bombs);

/*
 * --- Create the start button with smilely face on it
 */
button_start = gtk_button_new ();

/* --- We care if the button is clicked --- */
gtk_signal_connect (GTK_OBJECT (button_start),
                    "clicked",
                    GTK_SIGNAL_FUNC (start_button_clicked),
                    NULL);

gtk_box_pack_start (GTK_BOX (hbox), button_start, FALSE, FALSE, 0);
gtk_widget_show (button_start);

/*
 * --- Time on the right
 */

/* --- Add label with # of bombs left --- */
label_time = gtk_label_new ("");
gtk_box_pack_start (GTK_BOX (hbox), label_time, FALSE, FALSE, 0);
gtk_widget_show (label_time);

/* --- Make them visible --- */
gtk_widget_show (vbox);

/* --- Add application vbox to main window --- */
gtk_container_add (GTK_CONTAINER (window), vbox);
gtk_widget_show (window);

/* --- Create the *smile* and put it on the start button --- */
```

```
    SetStartButtonIcon ((gchar **) xpm_smile);

    /* --- Create 10x10 grid. --- */
    SetGrid (10, 10, 10);

    /* --- Start gtk event processing --- */
    gtk_main ();
    exit (0);
}
```

## *menu.c*

The functions within `menu.c` handle the creation and selection of the menu items. The interface to the minesweeper code is kept to a minimum.

```
/*
 * Minesweeper GUI application front end.
 *
 * Auth: Eric Harlow
 *
 */


#include <sys/stat.h>
#include <unistd.h>
#include <errno.h>
#include <gtk/gtk.h>
#include "misc.h"


void SetGrid (int nColumns, int nRows, int nBombs);


/*
 * --- Global variables
 */
GtkWidget          *win_main;
GtkAccelGroup      *accel_group;
GtkWidget          *toolbar;


/*
 * menu_New
 *
 * Called when the "new" menu is selected.
 * Creates a new game for the user.
```

```
 */
void menu_New (GtkWidget *widget, gpointer data)
{
    /* --- Parameters are not used... --- */

    /* --- Pretend the start button was clicked. --- */
    start_button_clicked (NULL, NULL);
}

/*
 * funcBeginner
 *
 * Picked the "beginner" option from the menu.
 * Create a small grid.
 */
void funcBeginner (GtkWidget *widget, gpointer data)
{
    if (GTK_CHECK_MENU_ITEM (widget)->active) {
        SetGrid (10, 10, 10);
    }
}

/*
 * funcIntermediate
 *
 * Picked the "intermediate" option from the menu.
 * Creates a medium-sized grid.
 */
void funcIntermediate (GtkWidget *widget, gpointer data)
{
    if (GTK_CHECK_MENU_ITEM (widget)->active) {
        SetGrid (20, 15, 40);
    }
}

/*
 * funcAdvanced
 *
 * User picked the "advanced" option in the menu.
 * Make the largest grid with the most bombs.
 */
void funcAdvanced (GtkWidget *widget, gpointer data)
{
    /* --- If this item is now active --- */
    if (GTK_CHECK_MENU_ITEM (widget)->active) {
```

```
        /* --- Set the grid size --- */
        SetGrid (30, 20, 100);
    }
}


/*
 * menu_Quit
 *
 * Choose quit in the menu.
 * Exit the game.
 */
void menu_Quit (GtkWidget *widget, gpointer data)
{
    gtk_main_quit ();
}


/*
 * menu_About ()
 *
 * User chose the "about" menu item.
 * Show information about the application.
 */
void menu_About (GtkWidget *widget, gpointer data)
{

    ShowAbout ();
}


/*
 * CreateMainWindow
 *
 * Create the main window and the menu/toolbar associated with it
 */
void CreateMenu (GtkWidget *window, GtkWidget *vbox_main)
{
    GtkWidget *menubar;
    GtkWidget *menu;
    GtkWidget *menuitem;
    GSList *group = NULL;

    win_main = window;

    /* --- Create accel table --- */
    accel_group = gtk_accel_group_new ();
    gtk_accel_group_attach (accel_group, GTK_OBJECT (window));
```

```
/* --- Menu Bar --- */
menubar = gtk_menu_bar_new ();
gtk_box_pack_start (GTK_BOX (vbox_main), menubar, FALSE, TRUE, 0);
gtk_widget_show (menubar);

/* ----------------
   --- File menu ---
   ---------------- */
menu = CreateBarSubMenu (menubar, "Game");

menuitem = CreateMenuItem (menu, "New", "^N",
               "New Game",
               GTK_SIGNAL_FUNC (menu_New), NULL);

menuitem = CreateMenuItem (menu, NULL, NULL,
               NULL, NULL, NULL);

menuitem = CreateMenuRadio (menu, "Beginner", &group,
               GTK_SIGNAL_FUNC (funcBeginner), NULL);

menuitem = CreateMenuRadio (menu, "Intermediate", &group,
               GTK_SIGNAL_FUNC (funcIntermediate), NULL);

menuitem = CreateMenuRadio (menu, "Advanced", &group,
               GTK_SIGNAL_FUNC (funcAdvanced), NULL);

menuitem = CreateMenuItem (menu, NULL, NULL,
               NULL, NULL, NULL);

menuitem = CreateMenuItem (menu, "Quit", "",
               "What's more descriptive than quit?",
               GTK_SIGNAL_FUNC (menu_Quit), "quit");

/* ----------------
   --- Help menu ---
   ---------------- */
menu = CreateBarSubMenu (menubar, "Help");

menuitem = CreateMenuItem (menu, "About Minesweeper", NULL,
               "About the Minesweeper",
               GTK_SIGNAL_FUNC (menu_About), "about");


}
```

# Remainder of the Files

The remainder of the files have already been covered and can be downloaded from www.mcp.com (refer to Chapter 1, "Introduction to GTK+"). These other files handle the support functions for the menus and the Help dialog box. The dialog boxes were covered in Chapter 6, "More Widgets: Frames, Text, Dialog Boxes, File Selection Dialog Box, Progress Bar," and the menu support functions were covered in Chapter 5, "Menus, Toolbars, and Tooltips."

# Summary

Writing the minesweeper application should have further solidified your understanding of how to put together a small application using toolbars, menus, and other widgets. The GTK+ library is flexible in the types of applications that can be created using the widgets.

# Drawing, Color, and GDK

# 10

# Graphics Drawing Kit

T HE GRAPHICS DRAWING KIT (GDK) IS A low-level drawing layer that sits between GTK+ and the operating-system-specific Application Programming Interface (API)—Xlib in the case of Linux. Because GTK has no direct interaction with the machine's API, porting GTK+ should be a matter of porting GDK and GLIB. GDK provides the capability to do drawing down to a pixel level as well as low-level window creation and manipulation functions. Using widgets is fine for many applications, but if you want to write an analog clock application using GTK+, it's going to be difficult without the capability to draw a clock face. Using the drawing area widget with GDK allows you to draw whatever you want, instead of using the canned widgets.

## Drawing Routines

Using GDK routines to write an application is not much better than using Xlib directly. Fortunately, GTK+ provides a widget that you can use to create applications that need to do manual drawing. The drawing area widget can be used like other GTK+ widgets and is flexible enough to create applications that are dependent on graphics. The advantage of this approach is that you can use GTK+ as well as GDK within the same application. GTK+ provides menus, toolbars, and other widgets to support the drawing being done within the drawing area widget. The GDK provides an API for drawing lines, pixels, boxes, circles, and more.

Each GDK routine takes at least two parameters—a drawable (GdkDrawable) area and a GdkGC. The GdkDrawable represents the area that is going to be drawn on, and the GdkGC contains color and font information as well as other drawing information.

## Drawing Pixels

The GDK provides routines to draw within a window and widgets (such as the drawing area). The simplest routine that is used is the gdk_draw_point for drawing a single pixel in the drawable area.

```
/* --- Draw a point at 10, 10 --- */
gdk_draw_point (drawable, gc, 10, 10);
```

In this example and the others, drawable represents the area being drawn into and gc usually represents the color information. Later in this chapter, you learn how to get and set these parameters.

## Drawing Lines

The gtk_draw_line function can be used to draw a line between two points.

```
/* --- Draw a diagonal line --- */
gdk_draw_line (drawable, gc, 0, 0, 10, 10);
```

## Drawing Rectangles

The gdk_draw_rectangle function draws a box within the drawable region. The box can be filled in, a technique that is frequently used to erase a region of the screen that needs repainting. The first two numbers in the coordinates represent the upper-left side of the box, and the last two numbers in the coordinates represent the width and height of the box. The third parameter indicates whether the rectangle should be filled in or left hollow. A value of TRUE indicates that the rectangle should be filled in.

```
/*--- Draw a box on the screen (0,0), (20,20) --- */
gdk_draw_rectangle (drawable, gc, FALSE, 0, 0, 20, 20);

/* --- Fill in a box on the screen (10,10)-(30,30) --- */
gdk_draw_rectangle (drawable, gc, TRUE, 10, 10, 20, 20);
```

## Drawing Polygons

Drawing odd shapes (like the shape of my head or an octagon) requires drawing many lines. Rather than use gdk_draw_line multiple times, it's usually easier to use the gdk_draw_polygon function and pass in an array of points to connect. The first and last points in the array will be connected if they are not the same point. The polygon can be filled by setting the filled parameter to TRUE.

Here's one way to draw a triangle:

```
GdkPoint points[4];

/* --- Top point of triangle --- */
points[0].x = 50;
points[0].y = 0;

/* --- Bottom-left side of triangle --- */
points[1].x = 0;
points[1].y = 50;

/* --- Bottom-right side of triangle --- */
points[2].x = 100;
points[2].y = 50;

/* --- Close the triangle --- */
points[3].x = 50;
points[3].y = 0;

/* --- Draw a polygon (don't fill it in) --- */
gdk_draw_polygon (drawable, gc, FALSE, points, 4);

/* --- Or... fill in the triangle --- */
gdk_draw_polygon (drawable, gc, TRUE, points, 4);
```

## Drawing Multiple Lines

Two functions can speed up the drawing of multiple lines. The `gdk_draw_lines` function takes a list of points and connects the dots. The `gdk_draw_segments` function takes an array of line segments and draws them as independent lines. This example uses both functions and draws the same triangle you drew earlier.

```
/*
 * --- First try using gdk_draw_lines to draw the triangle
 */

/* --- Top point of triangle --- */
points[0].x = 50;
points[0].y = 0;

/* --- Bottom-left side of triangle --- */
points[1].x = 0;
points[1].y = 50;

/* --- Bottom-right side of triangle --- */
points[2].x = 100;
points[2].y = 50;
```

```
/* --- Close the triangle --- */
points[3].x = 50;
points[3].y = 0;

/* --- Draw lines between four points --- */
gdk_draw_lines (drawable, gc, points, 4);

/*
 * --- Then use gdk_draw_segments to draw the triangle
 */

/* --- Set up the segments of the triangle --- */
segment[0].x1 = 50;
segment[0].y1 = 0;
segment[1].x2 = 0;
segment[1].y2 = 50;

segment[1].x1 = 0;
segment[1].y1 = 50;
segment[1].x2 = 100;
segment[1].y2 = 50;

segment[2].x2 = 100;
segment[2].y2 = 50;
segment[2].x2 = 50;
segment[2].y2 = 0;

/* --- Draw three line segments --- */
gdk_draw_segments (drawable, gc, segment, 3);
```

Figure 10.1 shows the difference between drawing multiple lines and multiple segments.

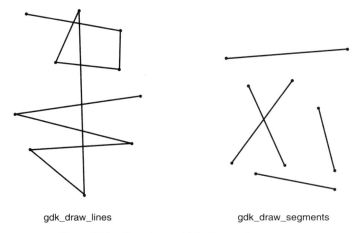

gdk_draw_lines                    gdk_draw_segments

**Figure 10.1**   Drawing multiple lines and segments.

You can also use the `gdk_draw_points` function to draw multiple points in a drawable widget. This method is faster than calling `gdk_draw_point` multiple times, but any drawing that requires drawing single pixels from an application is going to be slow. Consider using pixmaps if possible.

## Drawing Circles and Arcs

The `gdk_draw_arc` function draws an arc or circle within the drawable area. This function needs a more detailed explanation than the other functions because it has quite a few parameters. The prototype is defined as follows:

```
gdk_draw_arc (GdkDrawable *drawable,     /* --- Drawing area --- */
              GdkGC       *gc,           /* --- How (color/font) --- */
              gint        filled,        /* --- Fill it in? --- */
              gint        x,             /* --- Left side --- */
              gint        y,             /* --- Top side --- */
              gint        width,
              gint        height,
              gint        angle1,        /* --- Start angle --- */
              gint        angle2);       /* --- End angle --- */
```

The start angle and end angle of the arc are a bit confusing because unlike most arc functions, they are not in degrees or radians. The angle should be converted to degrees and then multiplied by 64. The angle 0 is at three o'clock, and the angle increases counterclockwise. If you wanted to draw an arc from the top of the box to the bottom of the box, the angle would be from (90 ★ 64) to (180 ★ 64). Figure 10.2 illustrates this condition.

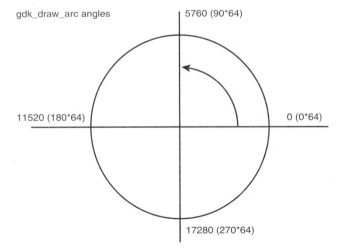

Figure 10.2   gdk_draw_arc.

```
/* --- Draw a complete circle --- */
gdk_draw_arc (drawable, gc, FALSE, 0, 0, 30, 30, 0, (360 * 64));

/* --- Draw a 90 degree arc from 12 o'clock to 9 o'clock --- */
gdk_draw_arc (drawable, gc, FALSE, 0, 0, 30, 30, (90 * 64), (180 * 64));
```

# Displaying Text

Text can be drawn in a drawable area with the `gdk_draw_string` function. The function requires the font in addition to the drawable widget and the `GdkGC`. Otherwise, it's similar to the other functions.

```
/* --- Display "Hey!" --- */
gdk_draw_string (drawable, font, gc, 50, 50, "Hey!");
```

The `gdk_draw_text` function does the same thing as the `gdk_draw_string` function except that the `gdk_draw_text` function takes the string length as a parameter.

```
/* --- Display "Hey!" --- */
szMessage = "Hey!";
gdk_draw_string (drawable, font, gc, 50, 50,
                 szMessage, strlen (szMessage));
```

# Drawing Pixmaps

For the times when drawing lines and dots just won't do, the `gdk_draw_pixmap` allows you to copy an entire image onto the drawable area. This method is handy for copying images onto the drawing area. See the section "Eliminating Flicker" later in the chapter for more information on this handy function.

```
/* --- Copy a 40x40 pixmap to the drawable widget --- */
gdk_draw_pixmap (drawable, gc, pixmap, 0, 0, 0, 0, 40, 40);
```

# The Drawing Area Widget

The drawing area widget is a very simple widget. Most of the widgets we've discussed are containers or have properties associated with them. The drawing area widget has few of the properties that the other widgets have. The widget does have a size property that can be set with the `gtk_drawing_area_size` function, but that's about it. The whole purpose of this widget is to provide an area to use GDK functions to draw into the widget. The widget is created with the `gtk_drawing_area_new` function.

```
/* --- Create the widget --- */
drawable = gtk_drawing_area_new ();

/* --- Size the widget appropriately --- */
gtk_drawing_area_size (drawable, 200, 200);
```

# Drawable Area Events

The two events that are important to a drawing area are the `configure_event` and the `expose_event`. The `configure_event` is sent to indicate that the drawing area has either been created or has been resized. The `expose_event` is sent when the drawing area needs to repaint itself. The `expose_event` is sent when the widget is drawn, when another window is moved off of it (exposing it), or by an application-generated repaint message.

# The Simple Clock Application

This simple clock application illustrates the use of the drawing area widget and the GDK. The clock needs to be drawn on the screen (an arc and some lines for the tick marks), and the clock hands need to be drawn and updated every second. The clock uses a timer to update itself every second and to repaint the whole area. Figure 10.3 shows what you are trying to create.

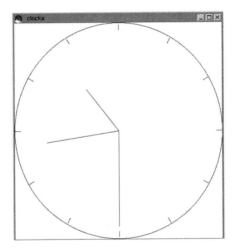

**Figure 10.3** Clock application.

Right away, it's obvious that you need a timer to run and repaint the clock every second with the most current time. This simple clock application sets a timer using `gtk_timeout_add` to call the `Repaint` function every second. The `Repaint` function clears the drawing area and redraws the entire clock every second. First the code:

```
/*
 * Auth: Eric Harlow
 * Linux Application Development
 *
 *
 */
```

```c
#include <gtk/gtk.h>
#include <time.h>

int radius;

static GdkColor clrBlue = { 0, 0x0000, 0x0000, 0xffff };

/*
 * DrawTickAt
 *
 * Draw a tick mark on the clock's face.  The tick marks
 * are drawn at the hour marks to help people read the
 * time on the clock.
 *
 * pixmap - drawing area
 * gc - pen
 * nHour - 1-12, what time to draw the tick mark
 * cx - width of clock
 * cy - height of clock
 */
void DrawTickAt (GdkDrawable *pixmap, GdkGC *gc, int nHour, int cx,
➥int cy)
{

    /* --- Convert time to radians --- */
    double dRadians = nHour * 3.14 / 6.0;

    /* --- Draw line from .95 * rad to 1.0 * rad --- */
    gdk_draw_line (pixmap, gc,
                    cx+(int) ((0.95 * radius * sin (dRadians))),
                    cy-(int) ((0.95 * radius * cos (dRadians))),
                    cx+(int) ((1.0 * radius * sin (dRadians))),
                    cy-(int) ((1.0 * radius * cos (dRadians)))));
}

/*
 * Repaint
 *
 * data - widget to repaint
 */
gint Repaint (gpointer data)
{
    GtkWidget*  drawing_area = (GtkWidget *) data;
```

```
int i;
    int midx, midy;
    int nHour;
    float dRadians;
    time_t now;
    struct tm *now_tm;
    GdkDrawable *drawable;

    /* --- Get drawing area window --- */
    drawable = drawing_area->window;

    /* --- Clear rectangle --- */

    gdk_draw_rectangle (drawable,
                        drawing_area->style->white_gc,
                        TRUE,
                        0, 0,
                        drawing_area->allocation.width,
                        drawing_area->allocation.height);

    /* --- Get the midpoint --- */
    midx = drawing_area->allocation.width / 2;
    midy = drawing_area->allocation.height / 2;

    /* --- Find smaller radius to make round clock --- */
    radius = min (midx, midy);

    /* --- Draw clock face (circle) --- */
    gdk_draw_arc (drawable,
                  drawing_area->style->black_gc,
                  0,
                  0, 0, midx + midx, midy + midy, 0, 360 * 64);

    /* --- Draw tickmarks at each hour --- */
    for (nHour = 1; nHour <= 12; nHour++) {

        DrawTickAt (drawable,
                    drawing_area->style->black_gc,
                    nHour, midx, midy);
    }

    /* --- Get time --- */
    time (&now);

    /* --- Convert time --- */
    now_tm = localtime (&now);
```

```
    /*
     * --- Draw the second hand
     */

    /* --- Get radians from seconds --- */
    dRadians = now_tm->tm_sec * 3.14 / 30.0;

    /* --- Draw seconds --- */
    gdk_draw_line (drawable, drawing_area->style->black_gc,
                   midx, midy,
                   midx + (0.9 * radius * sin (dRadians)),
                   midy - (0.9 * radius * cos (dRadians)));

    /*
     * --- Draw the minute
     */

    /* --- Get radians from minutes and seconds --- */
    dRadians = (now_tm->tm_min * 3.14 / 30.0) +
               (3.14 * now_tm->tm_sec / 1800.0);

    /* --- Draw minutes --- */
    gdk_draw_line (drawable, drawing_area->style->black_gc,
                   midx, midy,
                   midx+(int) (0.7 * radius * sin (dRadians)),
                   midy-(int) (0.7 * radius * cos (dRadians)));

    /*
     * --- Draw the hour hand
     */

    /* --- Calculate hours to the time in radians --- */
    dRadians = (now_tm->tm_hour % 12) * 3.14 / 6.0 +
               (3.14 * now_tm->tm_min / 360.0);

    /* --- Draw the hour hand --- */
    gdk_draw_line (drawable, drawing_area->style->black_gc,
                   midx, midy,
                   midx + (int) (radius * 0.5 * sin (dRadians)),
                   midy - (int) (radius * 0.5 * cos (dRadians)));

}

/*
 * quit
 *
 * exit gtk message loop
 */
```

```
void quit ()
{
    gtk_exit (0);
}



/*
 * main
 *
 * Program begins here.
 */
int main (int argc, char *argv[])
{
    GtkWidget *window;
    GtkWidget *drawing_area;
    GtkWidget *vbox;

    /* --- Initialize GTK --- */
    gtk_init (&argc, &argv);

    /* --- Create a top-level window --- */
    window = gtk_window_new (GTK_WINDOW_TOPLEVEL);

    /* --- Get a packing box --- */
    vbox = gtk_hbox_new (FALSE, 0);

    /* --- Add packing box to window --- */
    gtk_container_add (GTK_CONTAINER (window), vbox);

    /* --- Make packing box visible --- */
    gtk_widget_show (vbox);

    /* --- Listen for the destroy --- */
    gtk_signal_connect (GTK_OBJECT (window), "destroy",
                        GTK_SIGNAL_FUNC (quit), NULL);

    /* --- Create the drawing area ---*/
    drawing_area = gtk_drawing_area_new ();

    /* --- Set the size --- */
    gtk_drawing_area_size (GTK_DRAWING_AREA (drawing_area), 200, 200);

    /* --- Add drawing area to packing box --- */
    gtk_box_pack_start (GTK_BOX (vbox), drawing_area, TRUE, TRUE, 0);
```

```
    /* --- Make drawing area visible --- */
    gtk_widget_show (drawing_area);

    /* --- Make the window visible --- */
    gtk_widget_show (window);

    /* --- Repaint every 1000ms (every second) --- */
    gtk_timeout_add (1000, Repaint, (gpointer) drawing_area);

    /* --- Start gtk message loop --- */
    gtk_main ();

    return 0;
}
```

So, what problems exist? Well, for one thing, the clock is going to flicker on slow machines and will probably flicker a little even on faster machines. The flicker is caused by the repainting routine. The computer screen is refreshed constantly (many times a second), and if the hardware refreshes the monitor display right after the code clears the drawing area, a blank (or partially redrawn) drawing area is displayed briefly on the screen. Of course, by the next hardware refresh, the repainting should be done, but it's too late. The human eye will not see the blank clock that was drawn, but it will see the clock flicker. Fortunately, the clock only has a chance of flickering every second when the clock is redrawn. The more complicated the drawing, the more likely the drawing will not be completed between the screen refreshes and the more likely the user will see flickering. Flicker is not a good feature, and we'll have to work to eliminate it.

The second problem is noticeable if you repeatedly move a window over the clock and then move the item away. You should eventually detect a bit of a lag between when the window is moved and when the screen actually updates the image in the window. This delay is never more than a second, and occurs because the application is not listening to the expose_event, which tells it when the window is exposed and needs to be repainting. A well-behaved GDK application would add a callback to the expose_event and repaint the clock immediately, instead of waiting for the next timer tick to occur.

## Eliminating Flicker

The big problem with the clock is the flicker that occurs every second as the clock is redrawn. The best way to eliminate flicker is to use a technique called *double buffering*. Double buffering involves a buffer that is used as a canvas for all the drawing that takes place. The image on the screen is not modified by the drawing. Instead, all the drawing takes place in the buffer. In this example, you can create a buffer the same size as the window and draw the clock in the buffer instead of in the window. When the clock has been completely drawn in the buffer, the buffer is copied right into the window. Because the transfer of the buffer into the window doesn't involve clearing the screen, no flickering occurs.

The first step required to make the clock animation flicker free is to listen for the expose_event and the configure_event. The configure_event is sent when the drawing area is created or has its size modified. This situation provides an opportunity to create a background buffer that is the same size as the drawing area. If the window is resized, the configure_event callback re-creates the buffer with the appropriate size.

## configure_event

The configure_event callbackcreates the background buffer so it can be used to draw the clock without disturbing the image displayed on the screen. The background buffer is going to be a pixmap, and you can create the pixmap with the gdk_pixmap_new function and get a pixmap with the same size as the drawing area widget. If the size of the drawing area widget changes, the pixmap has to be reallocated. The configure_event callback is called when the widget is resized, giving you the opportunity to create a new background pixmap with a new size. Because the old pixmap is no longer needed, you can call the gdk_pixmap_unref function to tell GDK that you are no longer referencing the pixmap and that it can be freed if no one else is referencing it. The configure_event function ends up looking like this:

```
static gint configure_event (GtkWidget *widget, GdkEventConfigure *event)
{
    /* --- Free background if we created it --- */
    if (pixmap) {
        gdk_pixmap_unref (pixmap);
    }

    /* --- Create a new pixmap with new size --- */
    pixmap = gdk_pixmap_new (widget->window,
            widget->allocation.width,
            widget->allocation.height,
            -1);

    return TRUE;
}
```

## expose_event

The expose_event is actually quite simple. Because you are drawing the clock onto the background pixmap, the expose_event's only function is to copy the background image into the window using the gdk_draw_pixmap. Using the expose_event also eliminates the second problem with the clock: not repainting immediately after another window is moved off the clock. Now, if a window is moved off the clock, the application callback hears the expose_event and copies the last known clock image (pixmap) into the window. The expose_event is sent with the event parameter whose area field indicates the area of the window that was exposed and needs to be redrawn.

This is usually for cases where you have overlapping windows and you move one off another window. The quickest solution is to redraw only the area that was hidden beneath another window. For this clock, we would have to force the whole clock to be redrawn. The entire expose_event function ends up as follows:

```
gint expose_event (GtkWidget *widget, GdkEventExpose *event)
{

    /* --- Copy pixmap to the window --- */
    gdk_draw_pixmap (widget->window,
            widget->style->fg_gc[GTK_WIDGET_STATE (widget)],
            pixmap,
            event->area.x, event->area.y,
            event->area.x, event->area.y,
            event->area.width, event->area.height);


    return FALSE;
}
```

So, you're probably still a little confused. If you are drawing in the background pixmap, how is the screen going to be updated? After the clock has been drawn into the pixmap, you just need to have the expose_event callback copy the pixmap into the window. You do so by defining the area that is going to be exposed (the entire drawing area) and calling gtk_widget_draw with the widget and the area that needs updating.

```
/* --- Define the area to be redrawn --- */
update_rect.x = 0;
update_rect.y = 0;
update_rect.width = drawing_area->allocation.width;
update_rect.height = drawing_area->allocation.height;

/* --- And then draw it (calls expose_event) --- */
gtk_widget_draw (drawing_area, &update_rect);
```

The new version of the clock that implements the double buffering follows. Most of the code is very similar to the original. The changes may be minor, but the effect is major.

```
/*
 * Auth: Eric Harlow
 * File: dblclock.c
 * Linux application development
 *
 * Double buffered clock (no flickering)
 */

#include <gtk/gtk.h>
#include <time.h>
#include <stdlib.h>
```

```
/* --- Backing pixmap for drawing area --- */
static GdkPixmap *pixmap = NULL;

int radius;

/*
 * DrawTickAt
 *
 * Draw a tick mark on the clock's face.
 * pixmap - drawing area
 * gc - pen
 * nHour - 1-12, what time to draw the tick mark
 * cx - width of clock
 * cy - height of clock
 */
void DrawTickAt (GdkDrawable *pixmap, GdkGC *gc, int nHour, int cx,
➡int cy)
{
    /* --- Convert time to radians --- */
    double dRadians = nHour * 3.14 / 6.0;

    /* --- Draw line from .95 * rad to 1.0 * rad --- */
    gdk_draw_line (pixmap, gc,
                   cx+(int) ((0.95 * radius * sin (dRadians))),
                   cy-(int) ((0.95 * radius * cos (dRadians))),
                   cx+(int) ((1.0 * radius * sin (dRadians))),
                   cy-(int) ((1.0 * radius * cos (dRadians))));
}


/*
 * Repaint
 *
 * data - widget to repaint
 */
gint Repaint (gpointer data)
{
    GtkWidget*    drawing_area = (GtkWidget *) data;
    GdkRectangle  update_rect;
    char buffer[88];
    int i;
    int prevx = 0;
    int prevy = 0;
    int x = 0;
    int y = 0;
    int midx, midy;
```

```
int nHour;
float dRadians;
time_t now;
struct tm *now_tm;

/* --- Clear pixmap (background image) --- */
gdk_draw_rectangle (pixmap,
          drawing_area->style->white_gc,
          TRUE,
          0, 0,
          drawing_area->allocation.width,
          drawing_area->allocation.height);

/* --- Calculate midpoint of clock --- */
midx = drawing_area->allocation.width / 2;
midy = drawing_area->allocation.height / 2;

/* --- Calculate radius --- */
radius = MIN (midx, midy);

/* --- Draw circle --- */
gdk_draw_arc (pixmap,
            drawing_area->style->black_gc,
            0,
            0, 0, midx + midx, midy + midy, 0, 360 * 64);

/* --- Draw tickmarks --- */
for (nHour = 1; nHour <= 12; nHour++) {

    DrawTickAt (pixmap, drawing_area->style->black_gc,
              nHour, midx, midy);
}

/* --- Get time --- */
time (&now);
now_tm = localtime (&now);

/*
 * --- Draw the second hand
 */

/* --- Get radians from seconds --- */
dRadians = now_tm->tm_sec * 3.14 / 30.0;

/* --- Draw seconds --- */
gdk_draw_line (pixmap, drawing_area->style->black_gc,
```

```
                    midx, midy,
                    midx + (0.9 * radius * sin (dRadians)),
                    midy - (0.9 * radius * cos (dRadians))));

    /*
     * --- Draw the minute
     */


    /* --- Get radians from minutes and seconds --- */
    dRadians = (now_tm->tm_min * 3.14 / 30.0) +
               (3.14 * now_tm->tm_sec / 1800.0);

    /* --- Draw minutes --- */
    gdk_draw_line (pixmap, drawing_area->style->black_gc,
                    midx, midy,
                    midx+(int) (0.7 * radius * sin (dRadians)),
                    midy-(int) (0.7 * radius * cos (dRadians)));

    /*
     * --- Draw the hour hand
     */


    /* --- Calculate hours to the time in radians --- */
    dRadians = (now_tm->tm_hour % 12) * 3.14 / 6.0 +
               (3.14 * now_tm->tm_min / 360.0);

    /* --- Draw the hour hand --- */
    gdk_draw_line (pixmap, drawing_area->style->black_gc,
                    midx, midy,
                    midx + (int) (radius * 0.5 * sin (dRadians)),
                    midy - (int) (radius * 0.5 * cos (dRadians)));

    /* --- Set the rect up
     * --- The entire pixmap is going to be copied
     * --- onto the window so the rect is configured
     * --- as the size of the window.
     */
    update_rect.x = 0;
    update_rect.y = 0;
    update_rect.width = drawing_area->allocation.width;
    update_rect.height = drawing_area->allocation.height;

    /* --- And then draw it (calls expose_event) --- */
    gtk_widget_draw (drawing_area, &update_rect);
}
```

```
/*
 * configure_event
 *
 * Create a new backing pixmap of the appropriate size
 * Of course, this is called whenever the window is
 * resized.  We have to free up things we allocated.
 */
static gint configure_event (GtkWidget *widget, GdkEventConfigure *event)
{
    /* --- Free background if we created it --- */
    if (pixmap) {
        gdk_pixmap_unref (pixmap);
    }

    /* --- Create a new pixmap with new size --- */
    pixmap = gdk_pixmap_new (widget->window,
                widget->allocation.width,
                widget->allocation.height,
                -1);

    return TRUE;
}


/*
 * expose_event
 *
 * When the window is exposed to the viewer or
 * the gdk_widget_draw routine is called, this
 * routine is called.  Copies the background pixmap
 * to the window.
 */
gint expose_event (GtkWidget *widget, GdkEventExpose *event)
{

    /* --- Copy pixmap to the window --- */
    gdk_draw_pixmap (widget->window,
            widget->style->fg_gc[GTK_WIDGET_STATE (widget)],
            pixmap,
            event->area.x, event->area.y,
            event->area.x, event->area.y,
            event->area.width, event->area.height);

    return FALSE;
}
```

```
/*
 * quit
 *
 * Get out of the application
 */
void quit ()
{
    gtk_exit (0);
}

/*
 * main
 *
 * Program begins here.
 */
int main (int argc, char *argv[])
{
    GtkWidget *window;
    GtkWidget *drawing_area;
    GtkWidget *vbox;

    gtk_init (&argc, &argv);

    window = gtk_window_new (GTK_WINDOW_TOPLEVEL);

    vbox = gtk_hbox_new (FALSE, 0);
    gtk_container_add (GTK_CONTAINER (window), vbox);
    gtk_widget_show (vbox);

    gtk_signal_connect (GTK_OBJECT (window), "destroy",
                GTK_SIGNAL_FUNC (quit), NULL);

    /* --- Create the drawing area --- */
    drawing_area = gtk_drawing_area_new ();
    gtk_drawing_area_size (GTK_DRAWING_AREA (drawing_area), 200, 200);
    gtk_box_pack_start (GTK_BOX (vbox), drawing_area, TRUE, TRUE, 0);

    gtk_widget_show (drawing_area);

    /* --- Signals used to handle backing pixmap --- */
    gtk_signal_connect (GTK_OBJECT (drawing_area), "expose_event",
                (GtkSignalFunc) expose_event, NULL);
    gtk_signal_connect (GTK_OBJECT(drawing_area),"configure_event",
                (GtkSignalFunc) configure_event, NULL);

    /* --- Show the window --- */
    gtk_widget_show (window);
```

```
        /* --- Repaint every second --- */
        gtk_timeout_add (1000, Repaint, drawing_area);

        /* --- Call gtk-main loop --- */
        gtk_main ();

        return 0;
}
```

# System Monitor

We're going to reuse some of the earlier code to create a little program that monitors the machine and displays a graph showing the state of the CPU and the ethernet connection (see Figure 10.4). The only problem is how to get information about the system.

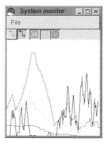

**Figure 10.4**   System monitor.

### Using the */proc* File System

Much of the information available about Linux is available from the /proc file system. The "files" in the /proc directory can be opened and parsed like ordinary files and provide plenty of information about the machine. For instance, the /proc/loadavg file has information about the CPU load. If you're curious about other files, you can type in **man proc** to get a summary of all the files in the /proc system.

If you cat the /proc/loadavg file, you end up with something like the following:

```
[brain@sharp /proc]$ cat loadavg
0.00 0.00 0.00 2/47 649
```

The first three numbers are the load average of the processor in the last minute, last 5 minutes, and last 15 minutes. If you use the w command at the Linux prompt, you get something like this:

```
   4:15pm  up  3:44,  4 users,  load average: 0.00, 0.00, 0.00
```

The preceding line displays the load average as the last three numbers. (Hmm…
machine seems a bit idle.)

Another example of /proc system is the /proc/net/dev file which has information
about the packets sent and received for every device. On my machine, the results look
something like this:

```
Inter-¦   Receive                    ¦  Transmit
  face ¦packets errs drop fifo frame¦packets errs drop fifo colls carrier
    lo:   103    0    0    0     0    103    0    0    0     0      0
  eth0:  9600    0    0    0     0   6487    0    0    0     1      0
```

Of course, the packets sent and received change each time. If I type the command a
little later, I get the following:

```
Inter-¦   Receive                    ¦  Transmit
  face ¦packets errs drop fifo frame¦packets errs drop fifo colls carrier
    lo:   104    0    0    0     0    104    0    0    0     0      0
  eth0:  9639    0    0    0     0   6513    0    0    0     1      0
```

The device I want to monitor here is the eth0: device. The eth0: device is the
ethernet card on my machine, and I want to know how much traffic is going through
the card at any given time. By comparing the total packet traffic to the last time I read
the file, I can figure out how much traffic there was since the last time I read the file.

## Description

The application uses a timer to update the screen every few seconds. It reads the /proc
file system for statistics about the system and displays the information in a graph with
a different color for each item in the graph. The graph is configurable using toolbar
buttons.

Upon experimenting, I found the network usage graph tended to fluctuate wildly,
making it hard to gauge actual throughput. It was easier to add a button to display the
average throughput as well as the actual throughput. The average is computed using
the last N samples and provides a graph with fewer fluctuations.

The code for the system monitor is broken down into several modules. Each module has specific code to handle its share of the application. The description of the files
begins with frontend.c.

### *frontend.c*

frontend.c creates the application window, the toolbar (with pixmaps), and the small
menu. It also has routines for other functions that query for information about the user
interface. For instance, the CPUButton15Down function can be called to ask whether the
toolbar button that displays the CPU state every 15 minutes has been pressed. This
approach is better than allowing the tool_cpu15 variable to be used outside of this file.

(Data encapsulation for C.) Note that the toolbar buttons are different colors. The color each is displayed in in the toolbar is going to be the color that the item is graphed in to make it easy for the user to turn items off and on. Visual color cues help to make the association between the graph and its toolbar buttons.

```c
/*
 * Sample GUI application front end.
 *
 * Auth: Eric Harlow
 * File: frontend.c
 *
 */


#include <sys/stat.h>
#include <unistd.h>
#include <errno.h>
#include <gtk/gtk.h>

/*
 * --- Function prototypes
 */
GtkWidget *CreateDrawingArea ();
static void CreateMainWindow ();
void CreateToolbar (GtkWidget *vbox_main);
void SetToolbarButton (char *szButton, int nState);
void SelectMenu (GtkWidget *widget, gpointer data);
void DeSelectMenu (GtkWidget *widget, gpointer data);
void SetMenuButton (char *szButton, int nState) ;
GtkWidget *CreateWidgetFromXpm (GtkWidget *window, gchar **xpm_data);
GtkWidget *CreateMenuItem (GtkWidget *menu,
                           char *szName,
                           char *szAccel,
                           char *szTip,
                           GtkSignalFunc func,
                           gpointer data);
GtkWidget *CreateMenuCheck (GtkWidget *menu,
                            char *szName,
                            GtkSignalFunc func,
                            gpointer data);
GtkWidget *CreateSubMenu (GtkWidget *menubar, char *szName);
GtkWidget *CreateBarSubMenu (GtkWidget *menu, char *szName);
void Repaint ();


/*
 * --- Global variables
 */
```

```
GtkWidget               *win_main;
GtkTooltips             *tooltips;
GtkAccelGroup           *accel_group;
GtkWidget               *toolbar;

static GtkWidget            *tool_cpu1;
static GtkWidget            *tool_cpu5;
static GtkWidget            *tool_cpu15;
static GtkWidget            *tool_network;
static GtkWidget            *tool_network_avg;


/*
 * --- Bitmap for "network"
 */
static const gchar *xpm_network[] = {
"16 16 4 1",
"  c None",
"B c #888888",
"                ",
"                ",
"   BBB          ",
"   BBBBBBB      ",
"   BBB   B      ",
"         B      ",
"         B      ",
"         B      ",
"         B      ",
"         B      ",
"         B      ",
"         B  BBB ",
"         BBBBBB ",
"            BBB ",
"                ",
"                ",
};


/*
 * --- Bitmap for "network"
 */
static const gchar *xpm_network_avg[] = {
"16 16 4 1",
"  c None",
"B c #000000",
```

```
"                   ",
"                   ",
"  BBB              ",
"  BBBBBBB          ",
"  BBB   B          ",
"        B          ",
"        B          ",
"        B          ",
"        B          ",
"        B          ",
"        B          ",
"        B  BBB     ",
"        BBBBBB     ",
"            BBB    ",
"                   ",
"                   ",
};


/*
 * --- Bitmap for "cpu" over last minute
 */
static const char *xpm_cpu1[] = {
"16 16 2 1",
"  c None",
"B c #FF0000",
"                 ",
"   B B B B B B   ",
"  BBBBBBBBBBBB   ",
" BB          B   ",
"  B     B    BB",
" BB    BB    B ",
"  B    B    BB",
" BB    B    B ",
"  B    B    BB",
" BB    B    B ",
"  B    B    BB",
" BB   BBB   B ",
"  B         BB",
"  BBBBBBBBBBBB   ",
"   B B B B B B   ",
"                 ",
};


/*
 * --- Bitmap for "cpu" over 5 minutes
```

```
 */
static const char *xpm_cpu5[] = {
"16 16 2 1",
"  c None",
"B c #00FF00",
"                ",
"   B B B B B B  ",
"  BBBBBBBBBBBB  ",
" BB          B ",
"  B   BBBBB  BB",
" BB   B      B ",
"  B   B      BB",
" BB   BBBB   B ",
"  B      B   BB",
" BB      B  B ",
"  B   B  B   BB",
" BB   BBB    B ",
"  B          BB",
"  BBBBBBBBBBBB  ",
"   B B B B B B  ",
"                ",
};


/*
 * --- Bitmap for "cpu" over 15 minutes
 */
static const char *xpm_cpu15[] = {
"16 16 2 1",
"  c None",
"B c #0000FF",
"                ",
"   B B B B B B  ",
"  BBBBBBBBBBBB  ",
" BB          B ",
"  B B BBBBB BB",
" BB BB B     B ",
"  B B B     BB",
" BB B BBBB  B ",
"  B B     B BB",
" BB B     B B ",
"  B B B   B BB",
" BB BBB  BBB B ",
"  B          BB",
"  BBBBBBBBBBBB  ",
"   B B B B B B  ",
```

```
            "                 ",
};


/*
 * RepaintGraph
 *
 * Called when the user toggles buttons on the
 * toolbar to change the information being displayed
 * in the graph.  Called "Repaint" to force a repaint
 * of the graph.
 */
void RepaintGraph (GtkWidget *widget, gpointer data)
{
    Repaint ();
}

/*
 * NetworkButtonDown
 *
 * Is the network button down on the toolbar.
 */
int NetworkButtonDown ()
{
    return (GTK_TOGGLE_BUTTON (tool_network)->active);
}

/*
 * NetworkAvgButtonDown
 *
 * Is the network button down on the toolbar.
 */
int NetworkAvgButtonDown ()
{
    return (GTK_TOGGLE_BUTTON (tool_network_avg)->active);
}

/*
 * CPUButton1Down
 *
 * Is the CPU-1 button down on the toolbar?
 */
int CPUButton1Down ()
{
    return (GTK_TOGGLE_BUTTON (tool_cpu1)->active);
}
```

```
/*
 * CPUButton5Down
 *
 * Is the CPU-5 button down on the toolbar?
 */
int CPUButton5Down ()
{
    return (GTK_TOGGLE_BUTTON (tool_cpu5)->active);
}


/*
 * CPUButton15Down
 *
 * Is the CPU-15 button down on the toolbar?
 */
int CPUButton15Down ()
{
    return (GTK_TOGGLE_BUTTON (tool_cpu15)->active);
}


/*
 * EndProgram
 *
 * Exit from the program
 */
void EndProgram ()
{
    gtk_main_quit ();
}




/*
 * CreateMainWindow
 *
 * Create the main window and the menu/toolbar associated with it
 */
static void CreateMainWindow ()
{
    GtkWidget *widget;
    GtkWidget *vbox_main;
    GtkWidget *menubar;
    GtkWidget *menu;
    GtkWidget *menuitem;

    /* --- Create the top window and size it. --- */
    win_main = gtk_window_new(GTK_WINDOW_TOPLEVEL);
```

```
    /* --- Don't let the window be resized. --- */
    gtk_window_set_policy (GTK_WINDOW (win_main), FALSE, FALSE, TRUE);

    /* --- Title --- */
    gtk_window_set_title (GTK_WINDOW (win_main), "System monitor");
    gtk_container_border_width (GTK_CONTAINER (win_main), 0);

    /* --- Create accel table --- */
    accel_group = gtk_accel_group_new ();
    gtk_accel_group_attach (accel_group, GTK_OBJECT (win_main));

    /* --- Top-level window should listen for the destroy --- */
    gtk_signal_connect (GTK_OBJECT (win_main), "destroy",
            GTK_SIGNAL_FUNC(EndProgram), NULL);

    /* --- Create v-box for menu, toolbar --- */
    vbox_main = gtk_vbox_new (FALSE, 0);

    /* --- Put up v-box --- */
    gtk_container_add (GTK_CONTAINER (win_main), vbox_main);

    gtk_widget_show (vbox_main);
    gtk_widget_show (win_main);

    /* --- Menu bar --- */
    menubar = gtk_menu_bar_new ();
    gtk_box_pack_start (GTK_BOX (vbox_main), menubar, FALSE, TRUE, 0);
    gtk_widget_show (menubar);

    /* ----------------
       --- File menu ---
       ---------------- */
    menu = CreateBarSubMenu (menubar, "File");

    menuitem = CreateMenuItem (menu, "Quit", "",
                    "What's more descriptive than quit?",
                    GTK_SIGNAL_FUNC (EndProgram), "quit");

    /* --- Create the toolbar --- */
    CreateToolbar (vbox_main);

    /* --- Create area to display information --- */
    widget = CreateDrawingArea ();
    gtk_box_pack_start (GTK_BOX (vbox_main), widget, TRUE, TRUE, 0);
}
```

```
/*
 * CreateToolbar
 *
 * Create the toolbar buttons that will show or
 * hide items from being graphed in the drawing area.
 */
void CreateToolbar (GtkWidget *vbox_main)
{
    /* --- Create the toolbar and add it to the window --- */
    toolbar = gtk_toolbar_new (GTK_ORIENTATION_HORIZONTAL,
➥GTK_TOOLBAR_ICONS);
    gtk_box_pack_start (GTK_BOX (vbox_main), toolbar, FALSE, TRUE, 0);
    gtk_widget_show (toolbar);

    /* --- Show network packet information --- */
    tool_network = gtk_toolbar_append_element (GTK_TOOLBAR (toolbar),
                        GTK_TOOLBAR_CHILD_TOGGLEBUTTON,
                        NULL,
                        "Network", "Network", "Network",
                        CreateWidgetFromXpm (vbox_main, (gchar **)
➥xpm_network),
                        (GtkSignalFunc) RepaintGraph,
                        NULL);

    /* --- Show network packet information --- */
    tool_network_avg = gtk_toolbar_append_element (GTK_TOOLBAR (toolbar),
                        GTK_TOOLBAR_CHILD_TOGGLEBUTTON,
                        NULL,
                        "Network (avg)", "Network (avg)", "Network
➥(avg)",
                        CreateWidgetFromXpm (vbox_main, (gchar **)
➥xpm_network_avg),
                        (GtkSignalFunc) RepaintGraph,
                        NULL);

    /* --- Little gap --- */
    gtk_toolbar_append_space (GTK_TOOLBAR (toolbar));

    /* --- Show cpu utilization in last minute --- */
    tool_cpu1 = gtk_toolbar_append_element (GTK_TOOLBAR (toolbar),
                        GTK_TOOLBAR_CHILD_TOGGLEBUTTON,
                        NULL,
                        "CPU 1", "CPU 1", "CPU 1",
                        CreateWidgetFromXpm (vbox_main, (gchar **)
➥xpm_cpu1),
                        (GtkSignalFunc) RepaintGraph,
```

```
                                      NULL);

        /* --- Show cpu utilization in last five minutes --- */
        tool_cpu5 = gtk_toolbar_append_element (GTK_TOOLBAR (toolbar),
                          GTK_TOOLBAR_CHILD_TOGGLEBUTTON,
                          NULL,
                          "CPU 5", "CPU 5", "CPU 5",
                          CreateWidgetFromXpm (vbox_main, (gchar **)
➥xpm_cpu5),
                          (GtkSignalFunc) RepaintGraph,
                          NULL);

        /* --- Show cpu utilization in last 15 minutes --- */
        tool_cpu15 = gtk_toolbar_append_element (GTK_TOOLBAR (toolbar),
                          GTK_TOOLBAR_CHILD_TOGGLEBUTTON,
                          NULL,
                          "CPU 15", "CPU 15", "CPU 15",
                          CreateWidgetFromXpm (vbox_main, (gchar **)
➥xpm_cpu15),
                          (GtkSignalFunc) RepaintGraph,
                          NULL);
}


/*
 * main
 *
 * --- Program begins here
 */
int main(int argc, char *argv[])
{
    gtk_init (&argc, &argv);

    tooltips = gtk_tooltips_new();

    CreateMainWindow ();

    gtk_main();

    return 0;
}
```

## *device.c*

The device.c file has routines to keep track of devices and the numeric data that represents a possible graph. The devices are stored in a GSList (see Chapter 2, "GLIB").

This routine was written so that the various devices can store their information with just a name and a set of values, instead of having to maintain a separate data format for every device. The `typDevice` used by `device.c` is in `device.h`.

```
/*
 * device.h
 * Defines typDevice
 */
#define DELTA 1
#define ACTUAL 2

#define MAX_VALUES 200

typedef long typHistoryValue;

typedef struct {
    char            *sName;      /* --- Device name --- */
    int             nType;       /* --- Type - DELTA or ACTUAL --- */
    typHistoryValue nLast;       /* --- Last value (for DELTA) --- */
    typHistoryValue nMax;        /* --- Max value --- */
    typHistoryValue nValues[MAX_VALUES]; /* --- Values saved --- */
} typDevice;



/*
 * File: device.c
 * Auth: Eric Harlow
 *
 * Linux development
 */

#include <stdio.h>
#include <strings.h>
#include <gtk/gtk.h>
#include "device.h"

static GSList *devlist = NULL;

/*
 * LookupDevice
 *
 * Look up the device in the list of devices
 */
typDevice *LookupDevice (char *sName)
{
    GSList    *node;
```

```
        typDevice *dev;

        /* --- Go through the list of nodes. --- */
        for (node = devlist; node; node = node->next) {

            /* --- Get the data --- */
            dev = (typDevice *) node->data;

            /* --- This what we're looking for? --- */
            if (!strcmp (dev->sName, sName)) {
                return (dev);
            }
        }
        return (NULL);
    }


    /*
     * AddDevice
     *
     * Add a new device to the list of devices and
     * return it so it can be initialized.
     */
    typDevice *AddDevice ()
    {
        typDevice *dev;

        /* --- Create the new device --- */
        dev = (typDevice *) g_malloc (sizeof (typDevice));

        /* --- Add the item to the list --- */
        devlist = g_slist_append (devlist, dev);

        /* --- Return the new item --- */
        return (dev);
    }


    /*
     * UpdateDevice
     *
     * Updates the information about a device.  If the
     * device does not currently exist, it's created and
     * initialized.
     *
     * sDevName - device name.  "eth0:", "cpu1", etc.
```

```
 * nValue - value at this time.
 * nType - DELTA/ACTUAL.
 *         ACTUAL means the value is "as is"
 *         DELTA means that the value is relative to
 *                 the previous value and needs to be
 *                 computed knowing that.
 * nMax - This is the normal max value to be displayed.
 */
void UpdateDevice (char *sDevName, long nValue, int nType, long nMax)
{
    typDevice  *dev;
    int        i;

    /* --- No name?  Get outta here! --- */
    if (sDevName == NULL) return;

    /* --- Look up the device by its name --- */
    dev = LookupDevice (sDevName);

    /* --- Do we have information about the device? --- */
    if (dev) {

        /* --- Just add a value. --- */
        NewValue (dev, nValue, FALSE);
    } else {
        /* --- Don't have the device! --- */

        /* --- Create a new device. --- */
        dev = AddDevice ();

        /* --- Initialize the values. --- */
        dev->sName = strdup (sDevName);
        dev->nType = nType;
        dev->nMax = nMax;

        /* --- Clear out values. --- */
        for (i = 0; i < MAX_VALUES; i++) {

            dev->nValues[i] = (typHistoryValue) 0;
        }

        /* --- Update with current position --- */
        NewValue (dev, nValue, TRUE);
    }
}
```

```
/*
 * UpdateExistingDevice
 *
 * If we know that the device exists, we use this
 * routine because it requires fewer parameters for me
 * to type and for the computer to push/pull from the
 * stack.
 */
void UpdateExistingDevice (char *sDevName, long nValue)
{
    typDevice  *dev;

    /* --- Name has to have a value. --- */
    if (sDevName == NULL) return;

    /* --- Look up the device name --- */
    dev = LookupDevice (sDevName);

    /* --- If the device exists... --- */
    if (dev) {

        /* --- Add the value. --- */
        NewValue (dev, nValue, FALSE);
    }
}


/*
 * NewValue
 *
 * Routine to add a value to the list of values
 * being stored for the device.  Also must shift the
 * values over by one every time we add another value.
 *
 * dev - device to add a value to
 * value - value to add to the device.
 * bInit - Is this the first value to be added to the device?
 */
void NewValue (typDevice *dev,
               typHistoryValue value,
               int bInit)
{
    int    i;

    /* --- Shift values down --- */
    for (i = MAX_VALUES-2; i >=0; i--) {
```

```
            dev->nValues[i+1] = dev->nValues[i];
        }

        /* --- If this is NOT initialization --- */
        if (!bInit) {

            /* --- Add new value to the end --- */
            if (dev->nType == DELTA) {

                /* --- New value is a delta - diff between
                 *     current value and previous value.
                 */
                dev->nValues[0] = value - dev->nLast;
            } else {
                /* --- Use value as-is. --- */
                dev->nValues[0] = value;
            }
        }

        /* --- Store last value. --- */
        dev->nLast = value;

        /* --- Calculate the max value. --- */
        if (dev->nValues[0] > dev->nMax) {
            dev->nMax = dev->nValues[0];
        }
    }
```

## sys.c

The sys.c file has the routines that parse the /proc files (for network utilization and CPU utilization). It updates the information for each device by calling the routines in the device.c file. Other parsers could be added easily by using the existing code as an example. The flow for adding a new device is to read the information in, parse it, and update the device information (in device.c). It will then be accessed from the generic data structure.

```
/*
 * File: sys.c
 * Auth: Eric Harlow
 *
 * Linux development
 */

#include <stdio.h>
#include <string.h>
```

```c
#include <gtk/gtk.h>
#include "device.h"

#define SEPARATORS " |\n"
void GetPacketInfo ();

/*
 * GetPacketInfo
 *
 * Get information about the packets going across the
 * ethernet.  Packet information is in /proc/net/dev if
 * the machine supports the /proc file system.
 */
void GetPacketInfo ()
{

    char *szFilename = "/proc/net/dev";
    char szBuffer[132];
    int  nLineNo = 0;
    FILE *fp;
    char *sToken;
    char *sDevName;
    int  nWord;
    long nIncoming;
    long nOutgoing;
    typDevice *dev;

    /* --- Open the file to get the information --- */
    fp = fopen (szFilename, "r");
    if (fp) {

        /* --- While we have information to read --- */
        while (!feof (fp)) {

            nLineNo++;

            /* --- Read in a line of text --- */
            fgets (szBuffer, sizeof (szBuffer), fp);

            /* --- After 3rd line are the devices --- */
            if (nLineNo >= 3) {

                nWord = 0;
                sDevName = NULL;
                sToken = strtok (szBuffer, SEPARATORS);
                while (sToken) {
```

```
                switch (nWord) {
                    case 0:
                        sDevName = sToken;
                        break;
                    case 1:
                        nIncoming = atoi (sToken);
                        break;
                    case 6:
                        nOutgoing = atoi (sToken);
                        break;
                }

                nWord++;
                sToken = strtok (NULL, SEPARATORS);
            }

            /* --- Got a name --- */
            if (sDevName) {

                /* --- Look it up --- */
                dev = LookupDevice (sDevName);

                /* --- Add/Update it --- */
                if (dev) {
                    UpdateExistingDevice (sDevName,
                            (long) (nIncoming + nOutgoing));
                } else {
                    UpdateDevice (sDevName,
                            (long) (nIncoming + nOutgoing), DELTA, 1);
                }
            }
            szBuffer[0] = (char) 0;
        }
    }

    /* --- All done --- */
    fclose (fp);
} else {

    /* --- Uh... error! --- */
    printf ("Unable to open file %s.", szFilename);
}
}
```

```
/*
 * GetCPUInfo
 *
 * Read in the /proc/loadavg file and parse for the cpu information.
 */
void GetCPUInfo ()
{
    static char *szFile = "/proc/loadavg";
    char szBuffer[88];
    FILE *fp;
    float cpu1, cpu2, cpu3;
    long lcpu1, lcpu2, lcpu3;
    typDevice *dev;

    /* --- Open the file with cpu info --- */
    fp = fopen (szFile, "r");

    /* --- If it's opened... --- */
    if (fp) {

        fgets (szBuffer, sizeof (szBuffer), fp);

        /* --- Get CPU utilization numbers --- */
        sscanf (szBuffer, "%f %f %f", &cpu1, &cpu2, &cpu3);

        /* --- Want range of 1-100+ instead of .01 to 1.0+ --- */
        lcpu1 = cpu1 * 100;
        lcpu2 = cpu2 * 100;
        lcpu3 = cpu3 * 100;

        /* --- Look up device --- */
        dev = LookupDevice ("cpu1");
        if (dev) {

            /* --- Already exists, update devices --- */

            UpdateExistingDevice ("cpu1", lcpu1);
            UpdateExistingDevice ("cpu5", lcpu2);
            UpdateExistingDevice ("cpu15", lcpu3);
        } else {

            /* --- First time, create devices --- */

            UpdateDevice ("cpu1", lcpu1, ACTUAL, 100);
            UpdateDevice ("cpu5", lcpu2, ACTUAL, 100);
            UpdateDevice ("cpu15", lcpu3, ACTUAL, 100);
```

```
            }
            /* --- Clean up. --- */
            fclose (fp);
        } else {
            printf ("Unable to open file %s.\n", szFile);
        }
    }
```

## graph.c

Everything dealing with the drawing widget goes into this file. The information is queried using the invented names for the devices that were used in sys.c. The UpdateDevice and UpdateExistingDevice created a device and associated numeric information with it. The routines in graph.c access the information by calling the routines in device.c. Because graph.c has no knowledge of the /proc file system, you can change the implementation details (sys.c) later if the kernel changes (not likely) or you port the application to an operating system that does not support the /proc file system.

Many of the routines are similar to the routines that update the clock. The big difference here is in the use of color in the drawing. When the application is created, several "pens" (actually GdkGC) are created to allow the drawing to occur in particular colors. These pens are allocated up-front to speed up the drawing. (Otherwise, you would have to create a new GdkGC every time you wanted to repaint the screen.) The pens are created in the GetPen function, which makes the code more readable than it would be if the pens were in a GetGdkGC function.

```
/*
 * File: graph.c
 * Auth: Eric Harlow
 *
 *
 */

#include <gtk/gtk.h>
#include "device.h"

void DrawDevice (GtkWidget *drawing_area, char *szName, GdkGC *pen,
➥int bAvg);
int NetworkButtonDown ();
int NetworkAvgButtonDown ();
int CPUButton15Down ();
int CPUButton5Down ();
int CPUButton1Down ();
void Repaint ();

GtkWidget *drawing_area;
```

```
typedef struct {

    GdkDrawable *pixmap;
    GdkGC *gc;

} typGraphics;

static typGraphics *g;
static GdkGC *penBlack = NULL;
static GdkGC *penRed = NULL;
static GdkGC *penBlue = NULL;
static GdkGC *penGreen = NULL;
static GdkGC *penGray = NULL;


/*
 * NewGraphics
 *
 * Create a new graphics data element to keep track
 * of the pixmap and the gc.
 */
typGraphics *NewGraphics ()
{
    typGraphics *gfx;

    /* --- Allocate the space --- */
    gfx = (typGraphics *) g_malloc (sizeof (typGraphics));

    /* --- Initialize --- */
    gfx->gc = NULL;
    gfx->pixmap = NULL;

    /* --- Hand back, ready to use. --- */
    return (gfx);
}


/*
 * GetPen
 *
 * Get a pen using the GdkColor passed in.  The "pen"
 * (just a GdkGC) is created and returned ready for
 * use.
 */
GdkGC *GetPen (GdkColor *c)
{
```

```
    GdkGC *gc;

    /* --- Create a gc --- */
    gc = gdk_gc_new (g->pixmap);

    /* --- Set the foreground to the color --- */
    gdk_gc_set_foreground (gc, c);

    /* --- Return it. --- */
    return (gc);
}



/*
 * NewColor
 *
 * Create and allocate a GdkColor with the color
 * specified in the parameter list.
 */
GdkColor *NewColor (long red, long green, long blue)
{
    /* --- Get the color --- */
    GdkColor *c = (GdkColor *) g_malloc (sizeof (GdkColor));

    /* --- Fill it in. --- */
    c->red = red;
    c->green = green;
    c->blue = blue;

    gdk_color_alloc (gdk_colormap_get_system (), c);

    return (c);
}



/*
 * UpdateAndRepaint
 *
 * Routine to poll for the latest stats on network
 * traffic and cpu utilization and repaint the
 * screen with the information
 */
gint UpdateAndRepaint (gpointer data)
{
    /* --- Get information about networking --- */
    GetPacketInfo ();
```

```
    /* --- Get information about the CPU --- */
    GetCPUInfo ();

    /* --- Repaint. --- */
    Repaint ();

    return (1);
}


/*
 * Repaint
 *
 * Update the screen with the latest numbers.
 */
void Repaint ()
{
    GdkRectangle    update_rect;

    /* --- Clear pixmap so we can draw on it. --- */
    gdk_draw_rectangle (g->pixmap,
            drawing_area->style->white_gc,
            TRUE,
            0, 0,
            drawing_area->allocation.width,
            drawing_area->allocation.height);

    /* --- If they want to see the actual network usage --- */
    if (NetworkButtonDown ()) {
        DrawDevice (drawing_area, "eth0:", penGray, 0);
    }

    /* --- If they want to see the averaged network usage --- */
    if (NetworkAvgButtonDown ()) {
        DrawDevice (drawing_area, "eth0:", penBlack, 1);
    }
    /* --- If they want to see the 15 minute cpu util --- */
    if (CPUButton15Down ()) {
        DrawDevice (drawing_area, "cpu15", penBlue, 0);
    }
    /* --- If they want to see the 5 minute cpu util --- */
    if (CPUButton5Down ()) {
        DrawDevice (drawing_area, "cpu5", penGreen, 0);
    }
    /* --- If they want to see the 1 minute cpu util --- */
    if (CPUButton1Down ()) {
```

```
        DrawDevice (drawing_area, "cpu1", penRed, 0);
    }

    /* --- Update the screen with the background pixmap --- */
    update_rect.x = 0;
    update_rect.y = 0;
    update_rect.width = drawing_area->allocation.width;
    update_rect.height = drawing_area->allocation.height;

    gtk_widget_draw (drawing_area, &update_rect);
}



/*
 * DrawDevice
 *
 * Draw a graph with the device's information
 *
 * drawing_area - widget
 * szName - name of the device being monitored
 * pen - GC with the color information
 * bAvg - Average plot indicator.  True => do some averaging
 */
void DrawDevice (GtkWidget *drawing_area, char *szName, GdkGC *pen, int
➥bAvg)
{
    typDevice  *dev;
    int     prevx = 0;
    int     prevy = 0;
    int     x = 0;
    int     y = 0;
    int     i;
    int     nLast;

    /* --- Look up the device by the name --- */
    dev = LookupDevice (szName);

    /* --- If we found it --- */
    if (dev) {

        /* --- If they're averaging --- */
        if (bAvg) {
            nLast = MAX_VALUES-4;
        } else {
            nLast = MAX_VALUES;
        }
```

```
            /* --- Go across the widget and plot --- */
            for (i = 0; i < drawing_area->allocation.width && i < nLast;
➡i++) {

                x = i;
                if (dev->nMax != 0) {

                    if (bAvg) {

                        y = ((dev->nValues[i] +
                              dev->nValues[i+1] +
                              dev->nValues[i+2] +
                              dev->nValues[i+3] +
                              dev->nValues[i+4]) *
                            drawing_area->allocation.height) /
                            (dev->nMax * 5);
                    } else {
                        y = (dev->nValues[i] *
                          drawing_area->allocation.height) / dev->nMax;
                    }
                    y = drawing_area->allocation.height - y;
                } else {
                    y = 1;
                }

                if (i == 0) {
                    prevx = x;
                    prevy = y;
                }

                /* --- Draw a line from previous point to current pt. --- */
                gdk_draw_line (g->pixmap,
                               pen,
                               prevx, prevy,
                               x, y);

                /* --- Next previous point is this point. --- */
                prevx = x;
                prevy = y;
            }
        } else {

            /* --- Should never occur. --- */
            printf ("it's NULL (%s)\n", szName);
        }
    }
```

```
/*
 * configure_event
 *
 * Called when the drawing area is created and every
 * time it's resized.
 * Create a new backing pixmap of the appropriate size
 */
static gint configure_event (GtkWidget *widget, GdkEventConfigure *event)
{
    if (g == NULL) {
        g = NewGraphics ();
    }

    /* --- Free the pixmap --- */
    if (g->pixmap) {
        gdk_pixmap_unref (g->pixmap);
    }

    /* --- Create a new pixmap --- */
    g->pixmap = gdk_pixmap_new (widget->window,
                               widget->allocation.width,
                               widget->allocation.height,
                               -1);

    /* --- If we don't have our pens yet --- */
    if (penBlack == NULL) {

        /* --- Get our colorful pens. --- */
        penBlack = GetPen (NewColor (0, 0, 0));
        penRed = GetPen (NewColor (0xffff, 0, 0));
        penBlue = GetPen (NewColor (0, 0, 0xffff));
        penGreen = GetPen (NewColor (0, 0xffff, 0));
        penGray = GetPen (NewColor (0x9000, 0x9000, 0x9000));
    }

    /* --- Clear it out --- */
    gdk_draw_rectangle (g->pixmap,
                        widget->style->white_gc,
                        TRUE,
                        0, 0,
                        widget->allocation.width,
                        widget->allocation.height);

    return TRUE;
}
```

```
/*
 * expose_event
 *
 * Redraw the screen using the pixmap
 */
static gint expose_event (GtkWidget *widget, GdkEventExpose *event)
{
  /* --- Copy it right over. --- */
  gdk_draw_pixmap (widget->window,
          widget->style->fg_gc[GTK_WIDGET_STATE (widget)],
          g->pixmap,
          event->area.x, event->area.y,
          event->area.x, event->area.y,
          event->area.width, event->area.height);

  return FALSE;
}


/*
 * quit
 *
 * Quit the application
 */
void quit ()
{
    gtk_exit (0);
}



/*
 * CreateDrawingArea
 *
 * Create the drawing area widget and return it.
 */
GtkWidget *CreateDrawingArea ()
{
    /* --- Create the drawing area --- */
    drawing_area = gtk_drawing_area_new ();

    /* --- Give it a nice size --- */
    gtk_drawing_area_size (GTK_DRAWING_AREA (drawing_area), 200, 200);

    /* --- Make it visible --- */
    gtk_widget_show (drawing_area);
```

```
/* --- We need the expose_event and the configure_event --- */
gtk_signal_connect (GTK_OBJECT (drawing_area), "expose_event",
        (GtkSignalFunc) expose_event, NULL);
gtk_signal_connect (GTK_OBJECT(drawing_area),"configure_event",
        (GtkSignalFunc) configure_event, NULL);

/* --- Call the function every 2 seconds. --- */
gtk_timeout_add (2000, UpdateAndRepaint, drawing_area);

/* --- Return widget so it can be placed on the screen. --- */
return (drawing_area);
}
```

# Summary

Combining the GDK with the drawing area widget enables you to create complicated applications that involve graphics. The GDK has routines for drawing simple shapes in a drawing area widget. The use of double buffering in a drawing area can eliminate flicker in an application but takes a little additional work. Applications displaying graphical information should always use double buffering to try to eliminate flicker.

# 11

# Styles, Colors, Fonts, Cursors, and Referencing

Sᴛʏʟᴇꜱ ɪɴꜰʟᴜᴇɴᴄᴇ ʜᴏᴡ ᴀ ᴡɪᴅɢᴇᴛ ɪꜱ ᴅʀᴀᴡɴ using both colors and fonts. Each style consists of several colors and a single font. Styles are part of GTK+, but colors and fonts are part of the Graphics Drawing Kit (GDK). Although colors are part of the GDK, GTK+ has a color selection dialog box that can be used in applications to allow users to select colors. Likewise, the fonts have a GTK+ font selection dialog box for those applications that need it. These dialog box widgets are similar to the file selection dialog box and provide a common user interface for developers who want to enable users to select colors and fonts. The GDK also provides the capability to change the mouse cursor to a built-in cursor or a custom cursor. References help GTK+ keep track of widgets that are in use. GTK+ frees widgets that it thinks are no longer in use, and you want to prevent this action at certain times.

## Styles (Colors and Fonts)

Every widget in GTK+ has a style that determines how it is to be drawn on the screen. The basic style consists of a color scheme and a font. Applications in GTK+ typically share the same style, which is why all the widgets use the same color scheme and use the same fonts. A widget can have its own unique style, but it's not necessarily a good idea to give every widget a unique style. Using many styles on a page to display widgets can distract from the application, especially if the widgets have different colors. It's best to limit the styles to a few (or one) and spend the time working on the application's functionality.

Although only one font is defined in a style, the style can have many colors. A widget can be in several modes: NORMAL, ACTIVE, PRELIGHT, SELECTED, and INSENSITIVE. Each mode can have a unique color scheme.

| | |
|---|---|
| NORMAL | The way the object is normally drawn. |
| ACTIVE | The object is *active*—for a button, the ACTIVE state is while the button is pressed down. |
| PRELIGHT | Usually means that the mouse is moving over the widget. This color tells the user to click on the item. |
| SELECTED | Item has been selected. |
| INSENSITIVE | Widget has been made insensitive (not selectable). This mode is also called "disabled" in Microsoft speak. |

Each mode has a set of colors defined to express the mode that the widget is in. You can see this feature by looking at the button widget. The button widget is normally in the NORMAL mode. As the mouse cursor moves over the button widget, the widget goes into PRELIGHT mode, which causes the button to be displayed in the PRELIGHT colors. If the button is pressed, the button is displayed in the ACTIVE colors for the widget. Not all widgets support every mode.

## Colors

Colors are defined as `GdkColor`. The color consists of a red, green, blue (RGB) value that determines its contribution to the color.

```
/* --- Red defined as - lot of red, no green, no blue --- */
GdkColor color = {0, 0xffff, 0x0000, 0x0000};
```

After the `GdkColor` structures have been created, the color should be allocated from the system using the `gdk_color_alloc` function. The `gdk_color_alloc` tries to match the color with the colors that the hardware can support. The function expects a colormap and a color, but if you're using only a few colors, you can use the system colormap by passing in the value returned from the `gdk_colormap_get_system` function. After they are allocated, the colors can be used to create new styles with more (ahem) interesting colors.

## Using Styles

The default style for the application can be retrieved using the `gtk_widget_get_default_style` function. It's bad practice to tinker with this style directly, but you can make a copy of it to manipulate. The `gtk_style_copy` function makes a copy of a style so that it can be modified. The structure of `GdkStyle` contains an array of foreground colors (`fg`), an array of background colors (`bg`), and an array of text colors (`text`) that define the style's colors. To modify the button so that it displays white text on black, you could do the following:

```
/* --- Define the colors --- */
GdkColor white = {0, 0xffff, 0xffff, 0xffff};
GdkColor black = {0, 0x0000, 0x0000, 0x0000};

/* --- Allocate the colors --- */
gdk_color_alloc (gdk_colormap_get_system (), &white);
gdk_color_alloc (gdk_colormap_get_system (), &black);

/* --- Get default style --- */
defstyle = gtk_widget_get_default_style ();

/* --- Make a copy for ourselves. --- */
style = gtk_style_copy (defstyle);

/* --- Modify the color --- */
style->fg[NORMAL] = white;
style->text[NORMAL] = white;
style->bg[NORMAL] = black;
```

After the style is created, it can be used to change the style on any existing widget. The `gtk_widget_set_style` function sets the style of an existing widget. This function sets the style of the widget passed into the `gtk_widget_set_style` function, but does not set the style of any children widgets if it is a container. A function can use the `gtk_container_foreach` to change a widget's style and all the children within the widget like this:

```
void SetStyleRecursively (GtkWidget *widget, gpointer data)

{
    GtkStyle *style;

    /* --- Get the style --- */
    style = (GtkStyle *) data;

    /* --- Set the style of the widget --- */
    gtk_widget_set_style (widget, style);

    /* --- If it might have children widgets --- */
    if (GTK_IS_CONTAINER (widget)) {

        /* --- Set all the children's styles too. --- */
        gtk_container_foreach (GTK_CONTAINER (widget),
                        SetStyleRecursively, style);
    }
}
```

Instead of changing the style of widgets after they have been created, you can easily change the styles that widgets are created with. The `gtk_widget_push_style` function sets the current style for all widget creations. Any widget created after the `gtk_widget_push_style` gets the style that was "pushed." When done, the `gtk_widget_pop_style` should be called to remove that style from the stack. Because the styles are implemented in a stack, multiple styles could be on the stack at any time, but only the style on top is used. If the top style is popped using the `gtk_widget_pop_style`, then the next style in the stack becomes the style that widgets are created with. The `"style_set"` signal gets sent to the widget after the widget's style has been changed.

This example shows how the styles can be used to change color of buttons or to modify the default style for widget creation. The program shows six buttons—the first four are placed within the dialog box in a particular color scheme. (Hint: Christmas color scheme is green and red.) The fifth button causes all the buttons to change color. The last button has all its styles modified so that it starts out with a different color. In fact, moving the mouse over the button shows that the PRELIGHT is a yellow—not the default. (Clicking on the Buttons Go Wild button replaces the startup style with something else.) The missing piece here is the `CallButton` function, which is included in another file. It pops up a dialog box and displays a message (see Figure 11.1). You can take a look at the source for it, but this is the critical piece.

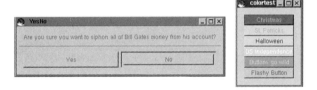

**Figure 11.1**   Color modification dialog box and result.

```
/*
 * File: button.c
 * Auth: Eric Harlow
 *
 * Show how to modify styles - specifically colors
 *
 * --- NORMAL, PRELIGHT, ACTIVE, INSENSITIVE, SELECTED
 */

#include <gtk/gtk.h>
#include <stdlib.h>

GtkWidget *button;
GtkStyle *styleRed;
```

```
/*
 * --- Define colors
 */
GdkColor red = {0, 0xffff, 0x0000, 0x0000};
GdkColor blue = {0, 0x0000, 0x0000, 0xffff};
GdkColor green = {0, 0x0000, 0xffff, 0x0000};
GdkColor yellow = {0, 0xffff, 0xffff, 0x0000};
GdkColor purple = {0, 0xffff, 0x0000, 0xffff};
GdkColor orange = {0, 0xffff, 0x9999, 0x0000};
GdkColor cyan = {0, 0x0000, 0xffff, 0xffff};
GdkColor black = {0, 0x0000, 0x0000, 0x0000};
GdkColor white = {0, 0xffff, 0xffff, 0xffff};

/* --- Create a list of colors to use for the
 *       random color button.
 */
GdkColor colorlist[] = {
    {0, 0xffff, 0x0000, 0x0000},
    {0, 0x0000, 0x0000, 0xffff},
    {0, 0x0000, 0xffff, 0x0000},
    {0, 0xffff, 0xffff, 0x0000},
    {0, 0xffff, 0x0000, 0xffff},
    {0, 0xffff, 0x9999, 0x0000},
    {0, 0x0000, 0xffff, 0xffff},
    {0, 0x0000, 0x0000, 0x0000},
    {0, 0xffff, 0xffff, 0xffff}
};

/* --- Calculate number of buttons. --- */
static int numColors = sizeof (colorlist) / sizeof (GdkColor);

/* --- Create styles for the dialog windows --- */
GtkStyle *styleChristmas;
GtkStyle *styleHalloween;
GtkStyle *styleStPatricks;
GtkStyle *styleUSIndependence;

/* --- vbox for the buttons --- */
GtkWidget *vbox;

/*
 * CreateColorfulStyle
 *
 * Create a style using the colors passed in.
 * Set the foreground color, the text color, and the
 * background color.  Note that this makes all the
```

```
 * states be the same color.
 *
 * fg - foreground color
 * text - text color
 * bg - background color
 */
GtkStyle *CreateColorfulStyle (GdkColor fg,
                               GdkColor text,
                               GdkColor bg)
{
    GtkStyle *defstyle;
    GtkStyle *style;
    int i;

    /* --- Get the default style --- */
    defstyle = gtk_widget_get_default_style ();

    /* --- Make a copy of it. --- */
    style = gtk_style_copy (defstyle);

    /* --- Set the colors for each state --- */
    for (i = 0; i < 5; i++) {

        /* --- Set the colors for the style --- */
        style->fg[i] = fg;
        style->text[i] = text;
        style->bg[i] = bg;
    }

    /* --- All done, here's new style --- */
    return (style);
}


/*
 * RandomStyle
 *
 * Create a random style using the list of colors
 * above.  There is no checking to see if the colors
 * would be a bad choice, like having background color the
 * same as the foreground color.
 */
GtkStyle *RandomStyle ()
{
    GtkStyle *style;
```

```
    /* --- Create a randomly colored style --- */
    style = CreateColorfulStyle (
                colorlist[random () % numColors],
                colorlist[random () % numColors],
                colorlist[random () % numColors]);

    return (style);
}


/*
 * CreateFunkyStyles
 *
 * Create styles for the buttons.  Each style has a different set of
 * colors that will be assigned to buttons to make each have a different
 * color.
 */
void CreateFunkyStyles ()
{
    /* --- Red on green --- */
    styleChristmas = CreateColorfulStyle (red, red, green);

    /* --- Orange on black --- */
    styleHalloween = CreateColorfulStyle (orange, orange, black);

    /* --- Green on white --- */
    styleStPatricks = CreateColorfulStyle (green, green, white);

    /* --- red and white on blue --- */
    styleUSIndependence = CreateColorfulStyle (red, white, blue);
}



/*
 * CloseApp
 *
 * Shut down GTK.
 */
void CloseApp (GtkWidget *widget, gpointer gdata)
{
    gtk_main_quit ();
}



/*
 * button_was_clicked
 *
```

```
 * event handler called when the button is clicked.
 */
void ButtonClicked (GtkWidget *widget, gpointer gdata)
{
    GtkStyle *style;

    /* --- Get the style from the callback --- */
    style = (GtkStyle *) gdata;

    /* --- Push colorful new style - now it's the default --- */
    gtk_widget_push_style (style);

    /* --- Show dialog using fancy style --- */
    CallButton (widget, (gpointer) 2);

    /* --- Remove the style. --- */
    gtk_widget_pop_style ();
}



/*
 * StyleSet
 *
 * Prints a message when the widget's style is modified.
 */
void StyleSet (GtkWidget *widget, gpointer data)
{

    printf ("Style set\n");
}



/*
 * SetStyleRecursively
 *
 * Set the widget's style to the style (data) and make sure
 * that all the children (if it's a container) are also set
 * to that particular style.
 */
void SetStyleRecursively (GtkWidget *widget, gpointer data)
{
    GtkStyle *style;

    /* --- Get the style --- */
    style = (GtkStyle *) data;
```

```
    /* --- Set the style of the widget --- */
    gtk_widget_set_style (widget, style);

    /* --- If it may have children widgets --- */
    if (GTK_IS_CONTAINER (widget)) {

        /* --- Set all the children's styles too. --- */
        gtk_container_foreach (GTK_CONTAINER (widget),
                               SetStyleRecursively, style);
    }
}


/*
 * WildButton
 *
 * Create a wildly colored button using the color table we
 * defined.
 */
void WildButton (GtkWidget *widget, gpointer data)
{
    GtkStyle *style;

    /* --- Pick a random style --- */
    style = RandomStyle ();

    /* --- Set the style of the widget --- */
    SetStyleRecursively (widget, (gpointer) style);
}


/*
 * ColorizeButtons
 *
 * Set the color of the children widgets to a wild (and random)
 * style.
 */
ColorizeButtons (GtkWidget *widget, gpointer data)
{
    /* --- All children get their style reset --- */
    gtk_container_foreach (GTK_CONTAINER (vbox), WildButton, NULL);
}
```

```
/*
 * CreateColorDialogButton
 *
 * Create a button in the vbox.  The style is going to be
 * associated with the button in the callback so that the
 * dialog created when the button is pressed is in the
 * style.
 */
CreateColorDialogButton (GtkWidget *vbox, char *label, GtkStyle *style)
{
    GtkWidget *button;

    /* --- Create a button with a label --- */
    button = gtk_button_new_with_label (label);

    /* --- Set up the style in the callback of the "clicked" --- */
    gtk_signal_connect (GTK_OBJECT (button), "clicked",
                GTK_SIGNAL_FUNC (ButtonClicked), (gpointer) style);

    /* --- Set up the style in the callback of the "style_sheet" --- */
    gtk_signal_connect (GTK_OBJECT (button), "style_sheet",
                GTK_SIGNAL_FUNC (StyleSet), (gpointer) style);

    /* --- The vbox contains the button. --- */
    gtk_box_pack_start (GTK_BOX (vbox), button, FALSE, FALSE, 0);

    /* --- Make the button visible --- */
    gtk_widget_show (button);
}




/*
 * CreateColorizeButton
 *
 * Create a button that changes all the button colors.
 */
void CreateColorizeButton (GtkWidget *vbox, char *label)
{
    GtkWidget *button;

    /* --- Create a button --- */
    button = gtk_button_new_with_label (label);

    /* --- Set up the signal handler --- */
    gtk_signal_connect (GTK_OBJECT (button), "clicked",
```

```
                    GTK_SIGNAL_FUNC (ColorizeButtons), NULL);

    /* --- The main window contains the button. --- */
    gtk_box_pack_start (GTK_BOX (vbox), button, FALSE, FALSE, 0);

    /* --- Make the button visible --- */
    gtk_widget_show (button);
}


/*
 * CreateFlashyButton
 *
 */
void CreateFlashyButton (GtkWidget *vbox, char *label)
{
    GtkStyle *defstyle;
    GtkStyle *style;

    defstyle = gtk_widget_get_default_style ();
    style = gtk_style_copy (defstyle);

    style->fg[GTK_STATE_NORMAL] = purple;
    style->text[GTK_STATE_NORMAL] = purple;
    style->bg[GTK_STATE_NORMAL] = cyan;

    style->fg[GTK_STATE_PRELIGHT] = green;
    style->text[GTK_STATE_PRELIGHT] = green;
    style->bg[GTK_STATE_PRELIGHT] = blue;

    style->fg[GTK_STATE_ACTIVE] = orange;
    style->text[GTK_STATE_ACTIVE] = orange;
    style->bg[GTK_STATE_ACTIVE] = yellow;

    gtk_widget_push_style (style);

    /* --- Create a new button --- */
    button = gtk_button_new_with_label (label);

    /* --- The main window contains the button. --- */
    gtk_box_pack_start (GTK_BOX (vbox), button, FALSE, FALSE, 0);

    /* --- Make the button visible --- */
    gtk_widget_show (button);

    /* --- Remove the style so it's not the default style --- */
```

```
        gtk_widget_pop_style ();
}


/*
 * main
 *
 * Program begins here
 */
int main (int argc, char *argv[])
{
    GtkWidget *window;

    /* --- Initialize gtk, handle command-line parameters --- */
    gtk_init (&argc, &argv);

    /* --- Create a window in gtk - window is NOT visible yet. --- */
    window = gtk_window_new (GTK_WINDOW_TOPLEVEL);

    gtk_signal_connect (GTK_OBJECT (window), "destroy",
                GTK_SIGNAL_FUNC (CloseApp), NULL);

    /* --- Put some room around the objects in container --- */
    gtk_container_border_width (GTK_CONTAINER (window), 15);

    vbox = gtk_vbox_new (FALSE, 0);

    /* --- Allocate the styles --- */
    CreateFunkyStyles ();

    /* --- Create buttons --- */
    CreateColorDialogButton (vbox, "Christmas", styleChristmas);
    CreateColorDialogButton (vbox, "St. Patricks", styleStPatricks);
    CreateColorDialogButton (vbox, "Halloween", styleHalloween);
    CreateColorDialogButton (vbox, "US Independence",
➥styleUSIndependence);

    CreateColorizeButton (vbox, "Buttons go wild");

    CreateFlashyButton (vbox, "Flashy Button");

    /* --- Now, make the window visible --- */
    gtk_widget_show (vbox);
    gtk_container_add (GTK_CONTAINER (window), vbox);
    gtk_widget_show (window);
```

```
/* --- This is the event loop in gtk.  Wait for "quit" --- */
gtk_main ();

/* --- Exit status code. --- */
return 0;
}
```

## The Color Selection Dialog Box

The color selection dialog box provides a standard way for a user to select a color. It is similar to the way the file selection dialog box provides a standard interface for users to select files. The color selection dialog box has several widgets to help the user pick a color (see Figure 11.2).

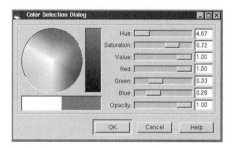

**Figure 11.2**  Color selection widget.

The color selection dialog box is created with the `gtk_color_selection_dialog_new` function. The OK and Cancel buttons on the dialog box can have callbacks on them to handle the button events.

```
/* --- New dialog box --- */
window = gtk_color_selection_dialog_new ("Color Selection Dialog");

/* --- Want to know when 'ok' button pressed --- */
gtk_signal_connect (
        GTK_OBJECT (GTK_COLOR_SELECTION_DIALOG (window)->ok_button),
        "clicked",
        GTK_SIGNAL_FUNC (OkButtonClicked),
        colorInfo);

/* --- Destroy dialog box when "cancel" is clicked --- */
gtk_signal_connect_object (
      GTK_OBJECT (GTK_COLOR_SELECTION_DIALOG (window)->cancel_button),
        "clicked",
        GTK_SIGNAL_FUNC(gtk_widget_destroy),
        GTK_OBJECT (window));
```

The "color_changed" signal indicates when the color has changed in the dialog box. The policy that indicates when to send the update messages is affected by the gtk_color_selection_set_update_policy function. The policies are GTK_UPDATE_CONTINUOUS, GTK_UPDATE_DISCONINUOUS, and GTK_UPDATE_DELAYED.

GTK_UPDATE_CONTINUOUS sends updates continuously as the color changes in the dialog box. GTK_UPDATE_DISCONTINUOUS updates when the mouse button is released. GTK_UPDATE_DELAYED sends the update when the mouse is released or when the mouse has stopped moving within the color circle for a period of time.

```
/* --- Want to know when the color changes --- */
gtk_signal_connect (
    GTK_OBJECT (GTK_COLOR_SELECTION_DIALOG (window)->colorsel),
    color_changed,
    GTK_SIGNAL_FUNC (ColorSelectionChanged),
    Window);

/* --- Need to know immediately when the color changes --- */
/* --- flood with messages - we got a fast machine --- */
gtk_color_selection_set_update_policy (
    GTK_COLOR_SELECTION (GTK_COLOR_SELECTION_DIALOG (window)->colorsel),
    GTK_UPDATE_CONTINUOUS);
```

When a signal handler needs to know the current color in the dialog box, the handler goes through several steps. First, the signal handler needs to get the colorsel member of the color dialog box. Second, an array of color values (defined as gdoubles) has to be retrieved. These values are from zero to one, so they'll have to be converted to the 0-0xffff range by multiplying them by 0xffff. Besides defining the colors, the value returned can also have the opacity of the color defined. Opacity can be configured by the gtk_color_selection_set_opacity function, and it will create additional widgets in the color selection widget to handle the opacity. The opacity is defined by the fourth value in the array.

```
GtkColorSelection *colorsel;
gdouble dacolor[4];

/* --- Get the color window to ask for the color --- */
colorsel = GTK_COLOR_SELECTION (cs->colorsel);

/* --- Get the color values in the widget --- */
gtk_color_selection_get_color (colorsel, dacolor);

/* --- color is a GdkColor --- */
color->red = dacolor[0] * 0xffff;
color->green = dacolor[1] * 0xffff;
```

```
    color->blue = dacolor[2] * 0xffff;

    /* --- Opacity would be dacolor[3] if we set it in the dialog box ---*/

    /* --- Color is now retrieved for use --- */
```

These elements can be put together to illustrate how to use the color selection dialog box to change the color of a widget. The following program allows the user to pick a new color for the button by clicking on the button and selecting a new color. When the OK button is pressed, the style of the button is modified to include the new color. The example consists of two files—colorbutton.c and colordiag.c.

### *colorbutton.c*

The colorbutton.c file creates the main window, controls the button, and changes the color.

```
/*
 * File: colorbutton.c
 *
 */
#include <gtk/gtk.h>
#include <stdlib.h>

GtkWidget *button;
GtkWidget *vbox;

/*
 * CreateBackgroundStyle
 *
 * Create a style using the colors passed in.
 * Set the foreground color, the text color, and the
 * background color.  Note that this makes all the
 * states the same color.
 *
 * fg - foreground color
 * text - text color
 * bg - background color
 */
GtkStyle *CreateBackgroundStyle (GdkColor bg)
{
    GtkStyle *defstyle;
    GtkStyle *style;
    int i;

    /* --- Get the default style --- */
    defstyle = gtk_widget_get_default_style ();
```

```
            /* --- Make a copy of it. --- */
            style = gtk_style_copy (defstyle);

            /* --- Set the colors for each state --- */
            for (i = 0; i < 5; i++) {

                /* --- Set the colors for the style --- */
                style->bg[i] = bg;
            }

            /* --- All done, here's new style --- */
            return (style);
        }


        /*
         * NewStyle
         *
         * Create a random style using the list of colors
         * above.  There is no checking to see whether the colors
         * would be a bad choice.
         */

        GtkStyle *NewStyle (GdkColor c)
        {
            GtkStyle *style;

            /* --- Create a style from the color --- */
            style = CreateBackgroundStyle (c);

            /* --- Return the style --- */
            return (style);
        }


        /*
         * CloseAppWindow
         *
         * Close down the application
         */
        gint CloseAppWindow (GtkWidget *widget, gpointer gdata)
        {
            g_print ("Quitting...\n");
            gtk_main_quit ();
            return (FALSE);
```

```
}


/*
 * SetStyleRecursively
 *
 * Set the style on the current widget and on any
 * children widgets.
 */
void SetStyleRecursively (GtkWidget *widget, gpointer data)
{
    GtkStyle *style;

    /* --- Get the style --- */
    style = (GtkStyle *) data;

    /* --- Set style on current widget --- */
    gtk_widget_set_style (widget, style);

    /* --- If it has other widgets --- */
    if (GTK_IS_CONTAINER (widget)) {

        /* --- Set the style on those widgets too --- */
        gtk_container_foreach (GTK_CONTAINER (widget),
                        SetStyleRecursively, style);
    }
}


/*
 * button_was_clicked
 *
 * event handler called when the button is clicked.
 * We can do this because the color dialog box is modal here
 * and doesn't return until a color is retrieved.
 */
void ButtonClicked (GtkWidget *widget, gpointer gdata)
{
    GtkStyle *style;
    GdkColor color;

    /* --- Call the color dialog box to get a color --- */
    GetDialogColor (&color);

    /* --- Create a style based on the color --- */
    style = NewStyle (color);
```

```
        /* --- Set the style of the widget based on that new style */
        SetStyleRecursively (widget, (gpointer) style);
}


/*
 * CreateButton
 *
 * Create a button and add it to the vbox. Set up the
 * event handler to "ButtonClicked"
 */
CreateButton (GtkWidget *vbox, char *label)
{
    GtkWidget *button;

    /* --- Create a button --- */
    button = gtk_button_new_with_label (label);

    gtk_signal_connect (GTK_OBJECT (button), "clicked",
                GTK_SIGNAL_FUNC (ButtonClicked), NULL);

    /* --- The main window contains the button.  --- */
    gtk_box_pack_start (GTK_BOX (vbox), button, FALSE, FALSE, 0);

    /* --- Make the button visible --- */
    gtk_widget_show (button);
}



/*
 * main
 *
 * Program begins here.
 */
int main (int argc, char *argv[])
{
    GtkWidget *window;

    /* --- Initialize gtk, handle command-line parameters --- */
    gtk_init (&argc, &argv);

    /* --- Create a window --- */
    window = gtk_window_new (GTK_WINDOW_TOPLEVEL);

    /* --- Need to know when window closes --- */
    gtk_signal_connect (GTK_OBJECT (window), "delete_event",
```

```
                    GTK_SIGNAL_FUNC (CloseAppWindow), NULL);

    /* --- Put some room around objects in the container --- */
    gtk_container_border_width (GTK_CONTAINER (window), 15);

    /* --- Create vertical packing box --- */
    vbox = gtk_vbox_new (FALSE, 0);

    /* --- Create a button --- */
    CreateButton (vbox, "Pick Color");

    /* --- Now, make the window visible --- */
    gtk_widget_show (vbox);
    gtk_container_add (GTK_CONTAINER (window), vbox);
    gtk_widget_show (window);

    /* --- Do not return until "quit" --- */
    gtk_main ();

    /* --- Exit status code. --- */
    return 0;
}
```

### colordiag.c

The colordiag.c file displays the color dialog box and returns a color to the caller.

```
/*
 * File: colordiag.c
 *
 * Show the color dialog box to allow someone to pick
 * a color for the button.
 */
#include <gtk/gtk.h>


/*
 * Structure to eliminate global variables
 */
typedef struct  {

    GtkWidget *dialog;
    GdkColor *color;

} typColorDialogInfo;
```

```
/*
 * CloseDialog
 *
 * Close the modal dialog box using the gtk_main_quit because it
 * was made modal by the gtk_main function.  Also release
 * the grab and free the memory.
 */
void CloseDialog (GtkWidget *w, typColorDialogInfo *di)
{
    gtk_main_quit ();
    gtk_grab_remove (w);
    g_free (di);
}



/*
 * OkButtonClicked
 *
 * Get the color currently selected in the dialog box and
 * get the rgb components out.  Set the GdkColor in the
 * colorInfo structure to those values.
 */
void OkButtonClicked (GtkWidget *w,
                typColorDialogInfo *colorInfo)
{
    GtkColorSelectionDialog *cs;
    GtkColorSelection *colorsel;
    gdouble color[4];

    /* --- Get the dialog box and the color --- */
    cs = (GtkColorSelectionDialog *) colorInfo->dialog;
    colorsel = GTK_COLOR_SELECTION (cs->colorsel);

    /* --- Get the color and assign it to the GdkColor --- */
    gtk_color_selection_get_color (colorsel, color);
    colorInfo->color->red = color[0] * 0xffff;
    colorInfo->color->green = color[1] * 0xffff;
    colorInfo->color->blue = color[2] * 0xffff;

    /* --- Destroy the dialog box --- */
    gtk_widget_destroy (GTK_WIDGET (cs));
}

/*
 * ColorSelectionChanged
 *
 * Notified when the color has changed within the dialog box.
 */
```

```
void ColorSelectionChanged (GtkWidget *w,
                            GtkColorSelectionDialog *cs)
{
    GtkColorSelection *colorsel;
    gdouble color[4];

    /* --- Get the color from the selection --- */
    colorsel = GTK_COLOR_SELECTION (cs->colorsel);
    gtk_color_selection_get_color (colorsel, color);

g_print ("The color has been changed!\n");
}



/*
 * GetDialogColor
 *
 * Display a modal dialog box and get the user to select a
 * color that can be sent back to the user.
 */
void GetDialogColor (GdkColor *color)
{
    static GtkWidget *window = NULL;
    typColorDialogInfo *colorInfo;

    /* --- New dialog box --- */
    window = gtk_color_selection_dialog_new ("Color Selection Dialog");

    /* --- Allocate memory for the colorinfo and populate it --- */
    colorInfo = g_malloc (sizeof (typColorDialogInfo));
    colorInfo->dialog = window;
    colorInfo->color = color;

    gtk_color_selection_set_opacity (
        GTK_COLOR_SELECTION (GTK_COLOR_SELECTION_DIALOG (window)-
➥>colorsel),
        TRUE);

    gtk_color_selection_set_update_policy (
        GTK_COLOR_SELECTION (GTK_COLOR_SELECTION_DIALOG (window)-
➥>colorsel),
        GTK_UPDATE_CONTINUOUS);

    /* --- Want to know when window is destroyed --- */
```

```
        gtk_signal_connect (GTK_OBJECT (window), "destroy",
                            GTK_SIGNAL_FUNC (CloseDialog),
                            colorInfo);

        /* --- Want to know when color changes --- */
        gtk_signal_connect (
            GTK_OBJECT (GTK_COLOR_SELECTION_DIALOG (window)->colorsel),
            "color_changed",
            GTK_SIGNAL_FUNC (ColorSelectionChanged),
            window);

        /* --- Want to know when 'ok' button pressed --- */
        gtk_signal_connect (
            GTK_OBJECT (GTK_COLOR_SELECTION_DIALOG (window)->ok_button),
            "clicked",
            GTK_SIGNAL_FUNC (OkButtonClicked),
            colorInfo);

        /* --- Destroy dialog box when "cancel" is clicked --- */
        gtk_signal_connect_object (
            GTK_OBJECT (GTK_COLOR_SELECTION_DIALOG (window)->cancel_button),
            "clicked",
            GTK_SIGNAL_FUNC(gtk_widget_destroy),
            GTK_OBJECT (window));

        /* --- Show window --- */
        gtk_widget_show (window);

        /* --- Grab --- */
        gtk_grab_add (window);

        /* --- This makes it modal in a loop until quit is called --- */
        gtk_main ();
    }
```

## Fonts

The font can be modified in a similar way that the color is modified except that only one font exists across all the modes. The font can be loaded by name or by using the font selection dialog box (see Figure 11.3). Using a new font without using the font selection dialog box requires knowing the font name and using the `gtk_font_load` function. After the font is loaded, the style's font field can be set.

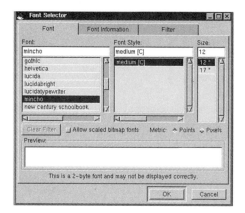

**Figure 11.3**   Font Selector dialog box.

```
/* --- Load up the font --- */
    font = gdk_font_load (szFont);

    /* --- This style uses the new font --- */
    style->font = font;
```

But now the problem becomes how to determine the valid font names for the system. To display all the available fonts on the system, the XListFonts function in Xlib can is used. This function expects a pattern (among other fields) that determines which fonts are returned in the list of font names. To match all the available fonts, a pattern of -* is used. The * matches anything (such as the file system) and would match any fonts. The fonts have names that look like some of these fonts. (These were some of the fonts on my system.)

```
-adobe-courier-medium-r-normal--8-80-75-75-m-50-iso8859-1
-adobe-helvetica-bold-o-normal--10-100-75-75-p-60-iso8859-1
-daewoo-gothic-medium-r-normal--16-120-100-100-c-160-ksc5601.1987-0
-daewoo-mincho-medium-r-normal--24-170-100-100-c-240-ksc5601.1987-0
-isas-fangsong ti-medium-r-normal--16-160-72-72-c-160-gb2312.1980-0
-isas-song ti-medium-r-normal--24-240-72-72-c-240-gb2312.1980-0
-jis-fixed-medium-r-normal--24-230-75-75-c-240-jisx0208.1983-0
-misc-fixed-bold-r-normal--13-120-75-75-c-80-iso8859-1
-adobe-times-medium-i-normal--12-120-75-75-p-63-iso8859-1
```

This short program shows all the fonts available on your system:

```
/*
 * File: DisplayFonts.c
 *
 * Show all fonts available on the system.
 *
 * Needs to be run from an X Window display.
 */
```

```c
#include <gtk/gtk.h>
#include <gdk/gdkx.h>
#include <X11/Xlib.h>

/*
 * If they have more than this many fonts, they have
 * too many fonts anyway.
 */
#define MAX_FONTS 30000

/*
 * main.c
 *
 */
int main (int argc, char *argv[])
{
    int nFonts;
    char **szaFontNames;
    int i;

    /* --- Initialize GTK+.  Needed for the GDK_DISPLAY call --- */
    gtk_init (&argc, &argv);

    /* --- Get the font names --- */
    szaFontNames = XListFonts (GDK_DISPLAY (), "*", MAX_FONTS, &nFonts);

    /* --- Check number retrieved --- */
    if (nFonts == MAX_FONTS) {

        /* --- They have a lot of fonts on their system. --- */
        printf ("Many fonts on your system.  Not displaying all.");
    }

    /* --- Display all the fonts --- */
    for (i = 0; i < nFonts; i++) {

        /* --- Get the name --- */
        printf ("%s\n", szaFontNames[i]);
    }

    /* --- Clean up. --- */
    XFreeFontNames (szaFontNames);
}
```

You can modify the color selection dialog box example to pick a font for the button from the font selection dialog box. The example is nearly identical to the color selection dialog box example except that instead of picking the color of the button, the user selects the font. The dialog box returns a font name that is used with `gtk_font_load` to load the font and update the style of the button. Figure 11.3 showed the Font Selector dialog box in use. Note that the font is not necessarily an English font.

```c
/*
 * File: fontbutton.c
 *
 */
#include <gtk/gtk.h>
#include <stdlib.h>

GtkWidget *button;
GtkWidget *vbox;

gchar *GetFont ();


/*
 * NewStyle
 *
 * Create a new style with the font passed in.
 */

GtkStyle *NewStyle (GdkFont *f)
{
    GtkStyle *style;
    GtkStyle *defstyle;
    int i;

    /* --- Get the default style --- */
    defstyle = gtk_widget_get_default_style ();

    /* --- Make a copy of it. --- */
    style = gtk_style_copy (defstyle);

    style->font = f;

    /* --- return the style --- */
    return (style);
}
```

```
/*
 * CloseAppWindow
 *
 * Close down the application
 */
gint CloseAppWindow (GtkWidget *widget, gpointer gdata)
{
    g_print ("Quitting...\n");
    gtk_main_quit ();
    return (FALSE);
}



/*
 * SetStyleRecursively
 *
 * Set the style on the current widget and on any
 * children widgets.
 */
void SetStyleRecursively (GtkWidget *widget, gpointer data)
{
    GtkStyle *style;

    /* --- Get the style --- */
    style = (GtkStyle *) data;

    /* --- Set style on current widget --- */
    gtk_widget_set_style (widget, style);

    /* --- If it has other widgets --- */
    if (GTK_IS_CONTAINER (widget)) {

        /* --- Set the style on those widgets too --- */
        gtk_container_foreach (GTK_CONTAINER (widget),
                            SetStyleRecursively, style);
    }
}



/*
 * button_was_clicked
 *
 * event handler called when the button is clicked.
 * We can do this because the font dialog box is modal here
 * and doesn't return until a font is retrieved.
 */
```

```
void ButtonClicked (GtkWidget *widget, gpointer gdata)
{
    GtkStyle *style;
    GdkColor color;
    char *szFont;
    GdkFont *font;

    /* --- Call the font dialog box to get a font --- */

    szFont = GetFont ();

    printf ("GetFont=%s\n", szFont);
    font = gdk_font_load (szFont);
    g_free (szFont);

    /* --- Create a style based on the font --- */

    style = NewStyle (font);

    /* --- Set the style of the widget based on that new style
*/
    SetStyleRecursively (widget, (gpointer) style);
}


/*
 * CreateButton
 *
 * Create a button and add it to the vbox. Set up the
 * event handler to "ButtonClicked"
 */
CreateButton (GtkWidget *vbox, char *label)
{
    GtkWidget *button;

    /* --- Create a button --- */
    button = gtk_button_new_with_label (label);

    gtk_signal_connect (GTK_OBJECT (button), "clicked",
                GTK_SIGNAL_FUNC (ButtonClicked), NULL);

    /* --- The main window contains the button.  --- */
    gtk_box_pack_start (GTK_BOX (vbox), button, FALSE, FALSE, 0);

    /* --- Make the button visible --- */
    gtk_widget_show (button);
}
```

```
/*
 * main
 *
 * Program begins here.
 */
int main (int argc, char *argv[])
{
    GtkWidget *window;

    /* --- Initialize gtk, handle command-line parameters --- */
    gtk_init (&argc, &argv);

    /* --- Create a window --- */
    window = gtk_window_new (GTK_WINDOW_TOPLEVEL);

    /* --- Need to know when window closes --- */
    gtk_signal_connect (GTK_OBJECT (window), "delete_event",
              GTK_SIGNAL_FUNC (CloseAppWindow), NULL);

    /* --- Put some room around objects in the container --- */
    gtk_container_border_width (GTK_CONTAINER (window), 15);

    /* --- Create vertical packing box --- */
    vbox = gtk_vbox_new (FALSE, 0);

    /* --- Create buttons --- */
    CreateButton (vbox, "Pick Font");
    CreateButton (vbox, "The fox jumped over the lazy dog");

    /* --- Now, make the window visible --- */
    gtk_widget_show (vbox);
    gtk_container_add (GTK_CONTAINER (window), vbox);
    gtk_widget_show (window);

    /* --- Do not return until "quit" --- */
    gtk_main ();

    /* --- Exit status code. --- */
    return 0;
}
```

The code that creates a modal font dialog box follows. This code requires the
GetFont function to be called and returns the font name in a gchar * that should be
freed when it's not needed.

```c
/*
 * File: gfontsel.c
 *
 * Front end to the font dialog box.  Creates a modal window
 * to select a font.  Use the GetFont () function to pick a name.
 *
 */

#include <gtk/gtk.h>
#include "gtkfontsel.h"

gchar *szFontName = NULL;

/*
 * OkClicked
 *
 * Ok button was clicked
 */
void OkClicked (GtkWidget *widget, GtkWidget *fontsel)
{

    /* --- Typecast to correct type --- */
    GtkFontSelectionDialog *fsd = GTK_FONT_SELECTION_DIALOG (fontsel);

    /* --- Get the font name --- */
    szFontName = gtk_font_selection_dialog_get_font_name (fsd);

    /* --- Display the font name --- */
    printf ("Ok clicked - %s\n", szFontName);

    /* --- Destroy the font selection window --- */
    gtk_widget_destroy (fontsel);
}


/*
 * Quit
 *
 * Quit from the program
 */
void Quit (GtkWidget *widget, gpointer data)
{
    gtk_main_quit ();
}
```

```
/*
 * GetFont
 *
 * Show the font selection dialog box to allow user to
 * pick a font.  Return a gchar * with the font
 * name.
 */
gchar *GetFont ()
{
    GtkWidget *widget;
    GtkFontSelectionDialog *fontsel;
    szFontName = NULL;

    /* --- Create the font selection dialog box --- */
    widget = gtk_font_selection_dialog_new ("Font Selector");

    /* --- Typecast to correct type --- */
    fontsel = GTK_FONT_SELECTION_DIALOG (widget);

    /* --- Callback for the clicked button --- */
    gtk_signal_connect (GTK_OBJECT (fontsel->ok_button), "clicked",
                        GTK_SIGNAL_FUNC (OkClicked), fontsel);

    /* --- Callback for the cancel button --- */
    gtk_signal_connect_object (GTK_OBJECT (fontsel->cancel_button),
➥"clicked",
                                GTK_SIGNAL_FUNC (gtk_widget_destroy),
                                GTK_OBJECT (fontsel));

    /* --- Destroy signal --- */
    gtk_signal_connect (GTK_OBJECT (fontsel), "destroy",
                        GTK_SIGNAL_FUNC (Quit), fontsel);


    /* --- Show the dialog box --- */
    gtk_widget_show (widget);

    /* --- Modal - wait until destroyed --- */
    gtk_main ();

    /* --- Return the font name --- */
    return (szFontName);
}
```

# Cursors

Cursors can be used to provide feedback to the user. You can see the cursor change when it moves over an input field (the I-beam cursor) or when resizing a window (arrow cursor). This feedback can be important at times. Fortunately, GTK+ comes with a full set of built-in cursors. The entire list can be seen in the GDK directory of the GTK+ installation. The gdkcursors.h has definitions for the built-in cursors that you can use. Some examples are the GDK_ARROW and GDK_CLOCK. A built-in cursor is created using the gdk_cursor_new function and passing in the identifier of the built-in cursor. This cursor can be assigned to a window, not a widget. However, it's easy enough to get the window that the widget is associated with, using the window member of the widget.

```
/* --- Create a new cursor --- */
cursor = gdk_cursor_new (GDK_CROSS);

/* --- Assign cursor to the button --- */
gdk_window_set_cursor (button->window, cursor);
```

Easy enough, except that the number of cursors that are built into GTK+ are limited. Suppose you want to create a custom cursor? A custom cursor can be created with xpm data just as the button icons were created. The trick here is that the images must use three colors: one for the foreground, one for the background, and one for the transparent color. The xpm data must be converted to two GtkBitmaps—one for the foreground and one for the background. After the conversion, a cursor is easily created. For example, take the following xpm image:

```
static char * cursor_hand[] = {
"32 32 3 1",
"        c None",
".       c #000000",
"+       c #FFFFFF",
"                                ",
"                                ",
"                 ...            ",
"                .+++.  ...       ",
"                .+++. .+++.  ... ",
"        ...     .+++. .+++. .+++.",
"       .+++.    .+++. .+++. .+++.",
"       .+++.    .+++. .+++. .+++.",
"       .+++.    .+++. .+++. .+++.",
"        .+++. .+++..+++. .+++.   ",
"        .+++..+++..+++. .+++.    ",
"         .+++.+++..+++..+++.     ",
"       ...  .+++++++++++++++.    ",
"      .+++. .+++++++++++++++.    ",
"      .++++..+++++++++++++++.    ",
```

```
"    ..+++++++++++++++++.        ",
"      .+++++++++++++++++.        ",
"      .+++++++++++++++++.        ",
"       ..+++++++++++++++.        ",
"         .+++++++++++++.          ",
"         .+++++++++++.            ",
"           ..........             ",
"                                  ",
"                                  ",
"                                  ",
"                                  ",
"                                  ",
"                                  ",
"                                  ",
"                                  ",
"                                  ",
"                                  ",
"                                "};
```

Here you have a three-color image of a hand that is 32 pixels wide by 32 pixels high. The colors defined in the image are actually ignored. Using this data, you can extract the foreground and mask images using a function taken from the gnumeric. (Don't you just love open-source software?) This function takes the xpm data and returns two bitmaps—one being the foreground image and the other being the mask image.

```
void
create_bitmap_and_mask_from_xpm (GdkBitmap **bitmap,
                                 GdkBitmap **mask,
                                 gchar **xpm)
{
        int height, width, colors;
        char pixmap_buffer [(32 * 32)/8];
        char mask_buffer [(32 * 32)/8];
        int x, y, pix;
        int transparent_color, black_color;

        sscanf (xpm [0], "%d %d %d %d", &height, &width, &colors, &pix);

        g_assert (height == 32);
        g_assert (width  == 32);
        g_assert (colors == 3);

        transparent_color = ' ';
        black_color = '.';

        for (y = 0; y < 32; y++){
                for (x = 0; x < 32;){
                        char value = 0, maskv = 0;
```

```
        for (pix = 0; pix < 8; pix++, x++){
            if (xpm [4+y][x] != transparent_color){
                maskv |= 1 << pix;

                if (xpm [4+y][x] != black_color){
                    value |= 1 << pix;
                }
            }
        }
        pixmap_buffer [(y * 4 + x/8)-1] = value;
        mask_buffer [(y * 4 + x/8)-1] = maskv;
    }
}
*bitmap = gdk_bitmap_create_from_data (NULL, pixmap_buffer,
    32, 32);
*mask   = gdk_bitmap_create_from_data (NULL, mask_buffer,
    32, 32);
}
```

You can now use this function to create a cursor. Of course, the cursor has to be created with the gdk_cursor_new_from_pixmap function instead of the gdk_cursor_new function. This function requires the image and mask data, the foreground and background colors, and the cursor hot point. The *hot point* is the position in the cursor that indicates where the cursor click occurs. For the standard arrow cursor, the hot point usually points to the upper left (0, 0), whereas a hand might have the hot point under the index finger, depending on how it's drawn.

```
GdkBitmap *bitmap;
GdkBitmap *mask;
GdkColor white = {0, 0xffff, 0xffff, 0xffff);
GdkColor black = {0, 0x0000, 0x0000, 0x0000);

/* --- Convert the image data (above) to usable bitmaps --- */
create_bitmap_and_mask_from_xpm (&bitmap, &mask, cursor_hand);

/* --- Create the cursor using the images --- */
cursor = gdk_cursor_new_from_pixmap (
            bitmap, mask, &white, &black, 8, 8);

/* --- Now assign this hand cursor to the window --- */
gdk_window_set_cursor (button->window, cursor);
```

This example uses black and white for the cursor colors, but the colors used in the cursor can be anything—but you get to use only two. I could have made the hand orange with a magenta border by passing in different colors to the gdk_cursor_new_from_pixmap function. Although it is possible to create hideous color combinations using the cursor, it's usually best to stick to black and white.

Here is a complete example showing three buttons—one has a custom hand as the cursor, one uses a built-in cross as a cursor, and the final example uses a gunsight that is blue and red. The last example illustrates that the cursor can be something other than black and white.

```
/*
 * File: cursors.c
 * Auth: Eric Harlow
 *
 * Illustration of how to change cursors
 */

#include <gtk/gtk.h>

static char * cursor_hand[] = {
"32 32 3 1",
"      c None",
".     c #000000",
"+     c #FFFFFF",
"                                ",
"                                ",
"                ...             ",
"              .+++.  ...        ",
"              .+++. .+++.  ...  ",
"       ...    .+++. .+++. .+++. ",
"     .+++.    .+++. .+++. .+++. ",
"     .+++.    .+++. .+++. .+++. ",
"      .+++.   .+++. .+++. .+++. ",
"      .+++. .+++..+++. .+++.    ",
"      .+++..+++..+++. .+++.     ",
"       .+++.+++..+++..+++.      ",
"     ...  .+++++++++++++++.     ",
"    .+++. .+++++++++++++++.     ",
"    .++++..+++++++++++++++.     ",
"     ..+++++++++++++++++++.     ",
"      .+++++++++++++++++++.     ",
"      .+++++++++++++++++.       ",
"       ..+++++++++++++++.       ",
"        .+++++++++++++.         ",
"         .++++++++++.           ",
"           ..........           ",
"                                ",
"                                ",
"                                ",
"                                ",
"                                ",
"                                ",
"                                ",
```

```
"                                ",
"                                ",
"                                ",
"                                "};

static char * cursor_sight[] = {
"32 32 3 1",
"       c None",
".      c #000000",
"+      c #FF0000",
"                                ",
" .............................. ",
" .            +               . ",
" .            +               . ",
" .          +++++             . ",
" .            +               . ",
" .        +++++++++++         . ",
" .            +               . ",
" .          +++++             . ",
" .            +               . ",
" .        +++++++++++         . ",
" .    +    +    +    +    +    . ",
" .    +    +  +++++  +    +    . ",
" .  + + + +  +  +  +  + + + +  . ",
" .  + + + +  +  +  +  + + + +  . ",
" .+++++++++++++++++++++++++++. ",
" .  + + + +  +  +  +  + + + +  . ",
" .  + + + +  +  +  +  + + + +  . ",
" .    +    +  +++++  +    +    . ",
" .    +    +    +    +    +    . ",
" .        +++++++++++         . ",
" .            +               . ",
" .          +++++             . ",
" .            +               . ",
" .        +++++++++++         . ",
" .            +               . ",
" .          +++++             . ",
" .            +               . ",
" .            +               . ",
" .............................. ",
"                                ",
"                                ",
"                                "};

GdkColor white = {0, 0xffff, 0xffff, 0xffff};
GdkColor black = {0, 0x0000, 0x0000, 0x0000};
```

```
GdkColor red = {0, 0xffff, 0x0000, 0x0000};
GdkColor blue = {0, 0x0000, 0x0000, 0xffff};


void
create_bitmap_and_mask_from_xpm (GdkBitmap **bitmap, GdkBitmap **
➥mask, gchar **xpm)
{
        int height, width, colors;
        char pixmap_buffer [(32 * 32)/8];
        char mask_buffer [(32 * 32)/8];
        int x, y, pix;
        int transparent_color, black_color;

        sscanf (xpm [0], "%d %d %d %d", &height, &width, &colors, &pix);

        g_assert (height == 32);
        g_assert (width  == 32);
        g_assert (colors == 3);

        transparent_color = ' ';
        black_color = '.';

        for (y = 0; y < 32; y++){
                for (x = 0; x < 32;){
                        char value = 0, maskv = 0;

                        for (pix = 0; pix < 8; pix++, x++){
                                if (xpm [4+y][x] != transparent_color){
                                        maskv |= 1 << pix;

                                        if (xpm [4+y][x] != black_color){
                                                value |= 1 << pix;
                                        }
                                }
                        }
                        pixmap_buffer [(y * 4 + x/8)-1] = value;
                        mask_buffer [(y * 4 + x/8)-1] = maskv;
                }
        }
        *bitmap = gdk_bitmap_create_from_data (NULL, pixmap_buffer,
➥32, 32);
        *mask   = gdk_bitmap_create_from_data (NULL, mask_buffer,
➥32, 32);
}
```

```
/*
 * CloseAppWindow
 *
 * Shut down GTK+ when user closes window
 */
gint CloseAppWindow (GtkWidget *widget, gpointer *data)
{
    gtk_main_quit ();
    return (FALSE);
}


/*
 * CreateTable
 *
 * Creates a top-level window with several options.  Because
 * this is going to be done many times, it's best just made
 * into a function.
 */
CreateTable (char *szTitle, gint xoptions, gint yoptions)
{
    GtkWidget *window;
    GtkWidget *button;
    GtkWidget *handButton;
    GtkWidget *sightButton;
    GtkWidget *crossButton;
    GtkWidget *table;
    GdkBitmap *bitmap;
    GdkBitmap *mask;
    GdkCursor *cursor;

    /* --- Create the top-level window --- */
    window = gtk_window_new (GTK_WINDOW_TOPLEVEL);

    /* --- Give the window a title. --- */
    gtk_window_set_title (GTK_WINDOW (window), szTitle);

    gtk_signal_connect (GTK_OBJECT (window), "delete_event",
                        GTK_SIGNAL_FUNC (CloseAppWindow), NULL);

    /* --- Give the window a border --- */
    gtk_container_border_width (GTK_CONTAINER (window), 10);

    /* --- Create a 4x4 table --- */
    table = gtk_table_new (2, 2, TRUE);

    handButton = gtk_button_new_with_label ("Hand");
    gtk_table_attach (GTK_TABLE (table), handButton, 0, 1, 0, 1,
                      xoptions, yoptions, 0, 0);
```

```
        gtk_widget_show (handButton);

        crossButton = gtk_button_new_with_label ("Cross");
        gtk_table_attach (GTK_TABLE (table), crossButton, 0, 1, 1, 2,
                          xoptions, yoptions, 0, 0);
        gtk_widget_show (crossButton);

        sightButton = gtk_button_new_with_label ("Gun sight");
        gtk_table_attach (GTK_TABLE (table), sightButton, 1, 2, 0, 1,
                          xoptions, yoptions, 0, 0);
        gtk_widget_show (sightButton);

        /* --- Add the table to the window --- */
        gtk_container_add (GTK_CONTAINER (window), table);

        /* --- Make the table visible --- */
        gtk_widget_show (table);

        /* --- Make the window visible --- */
        gtk_widget_show (window);

        create_bitmap_and_mask_from_xpm (&bitmap, &mask, cursor_hand);
        cursor = gdk_cursor_new_from_pixmap (bitmap, mask, &white, &black,
    ➥16, 8);

        gdk_window_set_cursor (handButton->window, cursor);

        create_bitmap_and_mask_from_xpm (&bitmap, &mask, cursor_sight);
        cursor = gdk_cursor_new_from_pixmap (bitmap, mask, &red, &blue,
    ➥16, 16);

        gdk_window_set_cursor (sightButton->window, cursor);

        cursor = gdk_cursor_new (GDK_CROSS);
        gdk_window_set_cursor (crossButton->window, cursor);
}


/*
 * --- Main.
 *
 * Program begins here.
 *
 * Rather than duplicate code, the CreateTable function is
 * called.  It does the work for us - all we do is pass in
 * how we want the window to appear.
 */
int main (int argc, char *argv[])
```

```
{
    /* --- GTK initialization --- */
    gtk_init (&argc, &argv);

    /* --- No flags set --- */
    CreateTable ("Nothing", 0, 0);

    /* --- Start the gtk loop. --- */
    gtk_main ();

    exit (0);
}
```

# References

Everything in GTK+ involves allocating items. Styles are created or duplicated from existing ones. Widgets are created, and fonts are loaded and assigned to styles. Repeating this process over a long period would surely suck up all your computer's memory—that is, unless you had an easy way to keep track of it. GTK+ keeps track of its memory use by using references to the objects.

A reference to an object is what prevents it from being destroyed. Every time someone takes an object (say, a font) and associates it with another GTK+ object using the GTK+ routines, the object has its reference count updated upward. Every time the referencing object is destroyed, GTK+ takes all the objects that it is referencing and decrements the reference count of those objects. If the reference count is zero, GTK+ assumes that the object is no longer needed and the object is freed.

Most of this work is transparent and is usually not a problem for small applications. Larger applications start to have problems with memory leaks if you're not careful. When widgets are created, they start out with a reference count of zero. When they're assigned to a container in some fashion, the reference count is incremented to indicate that the container is referencing the widget. If the container is destroyed, the container decrements the reference count of all the widgets it references—everything in the container. If that count is zero for any of the widgets, they're destroyed. This action makes sense because the widget should no longer be used at this point. Someone can prevent the widget from being destroyed by incrementing its reference count. By doing so, when the container is destroyed, the widget is still around. Of course, it's useless unless you actually store the widget pointer somewhere to use it.

Items that are not widgets are treated slightly differently. When created, they automatically start out with a reference count of one. These items usually represent styles, pixmaps, or some other reusable data that you want to allocate once and reuse throughout the life of the program. You don't want the application to suddenly destroy a style you created just because the last widget that was using it was destroyed. However, single-use items are frequently dereferenced after a creation like this:

```
/* --- Create pixmap from the data --- */
pixmap = gdk_pixmap_create_from_xpm_d (
                main_window->window,
                &mask, NULL, (gchar **) xpm_data);

/* --- Create a pixmap widget --- */
widget = gtk_pixmap_new (pixmap, NULL);

/* --- Don't need the pixmap any more. --- */
gdk_pixmap_unref (pixmap);
```

Here, the dereferencing of the pixmap normally destroys the pixmap, but the widget is referencing the pixmap as a result of the `gtk_pixmap_new` function. The pixmap will be dereferenced when the widget is destroyed, and if the reference count of the pixmap drops to zero, the pixmap will also be destroyed.

## Summary

Styles consist of fonts and colors that help define what the widgets look like. Styles can be modified individually, or they can be made the default style for future widget creation. GTK+ also has a built-in set of cursors that can be used to modify the cursor within a widget—and you can easily create custom cursors to supplement the built-in cursors. Objects in GTK+ use referencing to keep track of their use and free the objects when the reference count is zero.

# 12

# Molecule Viewer Using GDK

**U**SING THREE-DIMENSIONAL GRAPHICS TO DISPLAY information is always an interesting topic to discuss. In this chapter, you build a `.pdb` file viewer to view a molecule in a drawing widget and use the Graphics Drawing Kit (GDK) to display the molecule (see Figure 12.1). This chapter makes use of some three-dimensional math to display the molecule. If you're not familiar with the math, you can still pick up concepts—just ignore the matrix multiplication. If you're interested in learning more about three-dimensional math, many good books discuss the theory of three-dimensional computer graphics.

In addition to displaying the molecule, you also add code to allow the user to rotate the molecule. Options such as displaying the molecule in color and displaying the molecule with the atom text are also added to the application. To make the molecule rotate smoothly, this application uses double buffering.

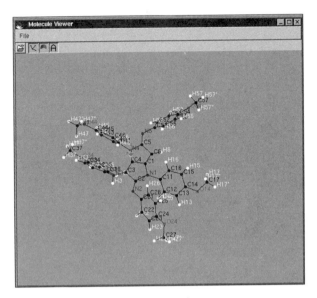

Figure 12.1    Molecule Viewer.

# File Format

To display the .pdb files, you must first be able to read them in and understand the format that describes them. The .pdb file format is quite complex and is designed for displaying complicated molecules. However, we are quite content to ignore much of the information stored in the .pdb file. The only items of concern are the atom names, atom positions, and the connections between the atoms. The relevant .pdb files are broken into two parts—the first part describes the atoms, and the second part (optional) describes the bonds between the atoms. The official description for the atoms is quite complicated:

```
Record Format

COLUMNS   DATA TYPE       FIELD       DEFINITION
-------------------------------------------------------------------
  1 -  6  Record name     "ATOM  "
  7 - 11  Integer         serial      Atom serial number.
 13 - 16  Atom            name        Atom name.
 17       Character       altLoc      Alternate location indicator.
 18 - 20  Residue name    resName     Residue name.
 22       Character       chainID     Chain identifier.
 23 - 26  Integer         resSeq      Residue sequence number.
 27       AChar           iCode       Code for insertion of residues.
 31 - 38  Real(8.3)       x           Orthogonal coordinates for X in
                                        Angstroms.
 39 - 46  Real(8.3)       y           Orthogonal coordinates for Y in
                                        Angstroms.
```

| 47 - 54 | Real(8.3) | z | Orthogonal coordinates for Z in Angstroms. |
|---|---|---|---|
| 55 - 60 | Real(6.2) | occupancy | Occupancy. |
| 61 - 66 | Real(6.2) | tempFactor | Temperature factor. |
| 73 - 76 | LString(4) | segID | Segment identifier, left-justified. |
| 77 - 78 | LString(2) | element | Element symbol, right-justified. |
| 79 - 80 | LString(2) | charge | Charge on the atom. |

The important pieces of the molecule are the "Record name," "Atom," and the three-dimensional position (x, y, z).

The second part of the .pdb file is optional and contains the information required to see the atom bonds. The CONECT lines describe a molecule and all the molecule numbers that it has a bond with. The first number after the CONECT is the first atom index, and the other atoms on the line are the atoms that have a bond with the first atom. An average .pdb file with the bonds in it looks like this:

```
ATOM       1 O11       1      2.227    3.257    9.904
ATOM       2 O12       1      4.387    2.116   10.202
ATOM       3 O13       1      3.470    2.116    8.123
ATOM       4 N1        1      1.032    3.192   13.498
ATOM       5 C1        1      1.135    4.580   13.046
ATOM       6 C2        1      1.192    2.116   12.739
ATOM       7 C3        1      0.762    2.796   14.797
ATOM       8 C3'       1      0.507    3.783   15.877
ATOM       9 C11       1      2.759    4.526    9.626
ATOM      10 C12       1      4.372    2.116   11.603
ATOM      11 C13       1      2.451    2.116    7.171
ATOM      12 B1        1      3.078    2.116    9.530
ATOM      13 N1*       1      1.032    1.041   13.498
ATOM      14 C3*       1      0.762    1.437   14.797
ATOM      15 O11*      1      2.227    0.976    9.904
ATOM      16 C1*       1      1.135   -0.347   13.046
ATOM      17 C3'*      1      0.507    0.450   15.877
ATOM      18 C11*      1      2.759   -0.293    9.626
TER
CONECT     1     9    12
CONECT     2    10    12
CONECT     3    11    12
CONECT     4     5     6     7
CONECT     5     4
CONECT     6     4    13
CONECT     7     4     8    14
CONECT     8     7
CONECT     9     1
CONECT    10     2
CONECT    11     3
CONECT    12     1     2     3    15
CONECT    13     6    14    16
CONECT    14     7    13    17
CONECT    15    12
CONECT    16    13
CONECT    17    14
```

Take a look at the first line in the file. The line begins with ATOM to indicate that this line is going to describe an atom. The next character, 1, is the index of the atom.

The atoms should be sequential. The 011 is the name of the atom—in this case the 0 is probably for oxygen. The position of the atom is stored in the last three numbers on the line. They should be the x, y, and z position of the atom in the structure.

```
ATOM       1 011         1      2.227   3.257   9.904
```

The atoms end with a line labeled TER, and the bonds will follow. The bonds start with the CONECT string and contain an atom number and the atoms that it has a bond with. For instance, the first line of the bonds is the following:

```
CONECT    1    9   12
```

This line indicates that atom 1 should be connected to atoms 9 and 12. Atoms do not need to have bonds, but they usually do.

## Data Structures

The data structure for the atom (typAtom) stores the atom name with two sets of coordinates and a list of atoms that it has bonds with. Atom structures have two sets of coordinates because the original coordinates are stored as well as the "translated" coordinates. The translated coordinates are required because the object is going to be rotated around the axis—and as the object is rotated, the atoms appear to be in a different position in the three-dimensional space. This new position is the translated position and is computed every time the molecule is moved. The translated position reflects the position at which the atom should be shown. Because every atom can have a bond with one or more atoms, the typAtom structure below stores those bonds in a GSList.

```
typedef struct {
    char *szName;        /* --- Molecule name--- */
    double x;            /* --- Original coordinates--- */
    double y;            /*
    double z;            /*
    double tx;           /* --- Translated coordinates--- */
    double ty;           /*
    double tz;           /*
    GSList *bondList;    /* --- Atoms it has a bond with--- */
} typAtom;
```

The bonds describe a relationship between two atoms so that a link can be drawn between them. In addition, a flag speeds up the drawing. The bond should be drawn only once for each pair of molecules.

```
typedef struct {
    typAtom *atom1;      /* --- First atom in the bond --- */
    typAtom *atom2;      /* --- Second atom in the bond --- */
    int bPainted;        /* --- painted --- */
} typBond;
```

Both the atoms and the bonds are stored in a static array. (I could have made it more dynamic, but that would mean more work.) The arrays make the atoms easy to deal with when drawing.

# Painting in Three Dimensions

Because the molecule is a three-dimensional structure, you should try to draw the molecule to provide the illusion of three dimensions. One way to do so is not to make blatant mistakes when drawing the molecule. A blatant mistake would be to draw the molecules without regard to their apparent z-depth. This condition can cause the atoms that are further away to appear above the atoms that are closer to the viewer. You can fix this problem by sorting the atoms by their translated z-depth after they have been translated into their new position. By first drawing the atoms that are far away, you guarantee that the atoms that are closest to the viewer are on top and not overwritten by the distant atoms. The painter's algorithm paints the distant items first and covers them with the nearest items.

# Source Code

All the code that deals with the molecules (with the exception of the matrix math code) is in the `molecule.c` file. Reading, painting, and other molecule manipulations go in the file. By modularizing the code this way, the molecule code can be placed within another application easily. Because most of the new code is in the `molecule.c` file, we can go through the key modules and discuss the functionality of each in turn.

## *ReadMolecule*

The main routine to load in the file has to parse two parts. First the atoms are read in and the names and coordinates of the atoms are pulled from the file. Then the bonds have to be read in and added to the atom data structure as well as the bond array. The `ReadMolecule` is called when the application starts up and defaults to an existing molecule. The `ReadMolecule` may be called by the File→Open menu choice, which allows other `.pdb` files to be read in. When a new file is loaded, some of the data (such as the matrices) need to be reset. The `ReadMolecule` routine also forces a repaint to occur after the molecule is read.

```
/*
 * ReadMolecule
 *
 * Read in a .pdb molecule with the given filename.
 * Store the information in the data structures
 * defined.
 */
void ReadMolecule (char *sFilename)
{
    FILE *fp;
    char buffer[120];
    float x, y, z;
    int nIndex1;
    int nIndex2;
    char szName[120];
    char *sTmp;
```

```
typAtom *atom;
char szTmp[20];

Init3d ();

nAtoms = 0;
nBonds = 0;

/* --- Reset matrices if reading in new file --- */
if (mat) {
    unit (mat);
    unit (amat);
    unit (tmat);
}

nMoleculeRadius = 2;

/* --- Open the file for reading --- */
fp = fopen (sFilename, "r");

/* --- Read in a line from the file --- */
while (fgets (buffer, sizeof (buffer), fp)) {

    /* --- Why it's an 'atom' --- */
    if (strncmp (buffer, "ATOM", 4) == 0) {

        /* --- Read in the atom based on the known file
         *      structure
         */
        strncpy (szName, &buffer[12], 4);
        szName[4] = 0;
        strncpy (szTmp, &buffer[30], 8);
        szTmp[8] = 0;
        x = atof (szTmp);
        strncpy (szTmp, &buffer[38], 8);
        szTmp[8] = 0;
        y = atof (szTmp);
        strncpy (szTmp, &buffer[46], 8);
        szTmp[8] = 0;
        z = atof (szTmp);

        /* --- Atoms are base 1 - index first. --- */
        nAtoms++;

        /* --- Populate the data structure --- */
        atom = &atomlist[nAtoms];
        atom->x = x;
        atom->y = y;
        atom->z = z;
        atom->szName = strdup (szName);
        atom->bondList = NULL;
        sortindex[nAtoms-1] = nAtoms;

    /* --- Does this describe a bond? --- */
    } else if (strncmp (buffer, "CONECT", 6) == 0) {
```

```
              /* --- Get the first bond atom --- */
              sTmp = GetNextValue (&buffer[6], &nIndex1);

              /* --- Get the next bond atom --- */
              while (sTmp = GetNextValue (sTmp, &nIndex2)) {

                  /* --- This bond is this nIndex1 to nIndex2 --- */
                  bondlist[nBonds].atom1 = &atomlist[nIndex1];
                  bondlist[nBonds].atom2 = &atomlist[nIndex2];

                  /* --- Of course the atom should know which
                   *     bonds it is a part of.
                   */
                  atomlist[nIndex1].bondList =
                      g_slist_append (atomlist[nIndex1].bondList,
                                     &bondlist[nBonds]);

                  /* --- Both atoms should know... --- */
                  atomlist[nIndex2].bondList =
                      g_slist_append (atomlist[nIndex2].bondList,
                                     &bondlist[nBonds]);

                  /* --- Just another bond... James Bond. --- */
                  nBonds++;
              }
          }
      }

      /* --- Find bounding box --- */
      FindBB ();

      /* --- Sort the molecules --- */
      SortMolecules (atomlist, sortindex);

      MoleculeRepaint ();
}
```

## FindBB

The bounding box is a three-dimensional box that would fit the molecule you are trying to display. The FindBB routine calculates that bounding box and allows you to scale the object to fit within the screen.

```
/*
 * FindBB
 *
 * Find the minimum bounding box that would fit all the
 * atoms in the molecule
 */
void FindBB ()
{
    int        i;
    typAtom    *atom;

    /* --- At first, the box consisted of a single atom --- */
```

```
/* --- Atoms start at 1 --- */
atom = &atomlist[1];

xmin = atom->x;
xmax = atom->x;

ymin = atom->y;
ymax = atom->y;

zmin = atom->z;
zmax = atom->z;

/* --- Then we added a whole bunch of them --- */
for (i = 2; i <= nAtoms; i++) {

    atom = &atomlist[i];
    if (atom->x < xmin) xmin = atom->x;
    if (atom->x > xmax) xmax = atom->x;
    if (atom->y < ymin) ymin = atom->y;
    if (atom->y > ymax) ymax = atom->y;
    if (atom->z < zmin) zmin = atom->z;
    if (atom->z > zmax) zmax = atom->z;
}

/* --- And now we have our bounding box. --- */
}
```

## Sorting the Atoms

Because the molecule needs to be painted from the farthest atom to the closest atom
to deliver a good three-dimensional image, the atoms must be sorted based on their
translated z-position. The actual z-position cannot be used because the user could have
rotated the molecule and the rotated molecule is the one that the viewer sees. After
sorting, the closer atoms will be painted last and will appear to be on top—just like
the three-dimensional image we perceive and call real life. Rather than actually sort
the atoms, the index to the atoms is sorted. Moving integers around in the array is
much quicker than moving structures.

```
/*
 * SortMolecules
 *
 * Call the sorting function
 */
void SortMolecules (typAtom *atomlist, int *sortindex)
{
    QSortMolecules (atomlist, sortindex, 0, nAtoms-1);
}

/*
 * QSortMolecules
 *
 * This is just a quicksort of the atoms in the molecule.
 *
```

```
 * Note: Rather than sort the atomlist itself, the sortindex
 * is the item being sorted.  Manipulating integers is just
 * quicker than moving structures around in memory - especially
 * because we have to do this in real time over and over again.
 *
 * atomlist - list of atoms to sort
 * sortlist - index of indexes.
 */
void QSortMolecules (typAtom *atomlist, int *sortindex, int lo0, int hi0)
{
    int     nTmp;
    int     lo = lo0;
    int     hi = hi0;
    int     mid;

    if (hi0 > lo0) {

        mid = atomlist[sortindex[(lo0 + hi0) / 2]].tz;

        while (lo <= hi) {

            while (lo < hi0 && atomlist[sortindex[lo]].tz < mid) {
                lo++;
            }

            while (hi > lo0 && atomlist[sortindex[hi]].tz > mid) {
                hi--;
            }

            if (lo <= hi) {

                nTmp = sortindex[lo];
                sortindex[lo] = sortindex[hi];
                sortindex[hi] = nTmp;
                lo++;
                hi--;
            }
        }
        if (lo0 < hi) QSortMolecules (atomlist, sortindex, lo0, hi);
        if (lo < hi0) QSortMolecules (atomlist, sortindex, lo, hi0);
    }
}
```

## TransformPoints

The TransformPoints routine applies a matrix to all the atoms in the molecule. This action has the effect of rotating the image and scaling it to fit the screen. The actual calculation of the matrix is done elsewhere.

```
/*
 * TransformPoints
 *
 * Take the atoms and rotate them to their displayed
 * position so they can be drawn.
 *
```

```
 * mat - The matrix used to calculate the new atom position
 */
void TransformPoints (typMatrix3D *mat)
{
    int    i;

    for (i = 1; i <= nAtoms; i++) {

        Transform (mat, &atomlist [i]);
    }
}
```

## *paint*

The paint routine does not actually do any painting, but is called by anyone who needs to do the painting. The actual painting is done by the DrawMolecule routine, but before it can be called, the matrix that calculates the object's rotation needs to be calculated and applied to every atom. Then the molecule can be drawn.

```
/*
 * paint
 *
 * paint the molecule on the screen, well, at
 * least to the background.  Most of this routine
 * works on getting the matrices correct before calling
 * the routine that does the real painting.
 */
void paint (typGraphics *g)
{
    double xfac;
    double f1;
    double f2;

    /* --- What's the range (delta x, delta y, delta z) --- */
    double xw = xmax - xmin;
    double yw = ymax - ymin;
    double zw = zmax - zmin;

    /* --- Make sure everything is allocated --- */
    Init3d ();

    /* --- Calculate the factor to scale the molecule --- */
    if (yw > xw) xw = yw;
    if (zw > xw) xw = zw;
    f1 = nScreenWidth / xw;
    f2 = nScreenHeight / xw;
    xfac = .7 * (f1 < f2 ? f1 : f2);

    /* --- First make the matrix the unit matrix --- */
    unit (mat);

    /* --- Translate it around the origin.  This moves the
     *     molecule to be centered around the axis as we're
     *     moving it based on the half of the bounding box width.
     */
```

```
    translate (mat, -(xmin + xmax) / 2,
                    -(ymin + ymax) / 2,
                    -(zmin + zmax) / 2);

    /* --- Rotate the image around the axis.  amat is the
     *      matrix that represents how much to rotate the
     *      molecule.
     */
    mult (mat, amat);

    /* --- Scale the molecule based on the screen width --- */
    scale3 (mat, xfac, -xfac, 16 * xfac / nScreenWidth);

    /* --- Translate molecule based on screen width and height --- */
    translate (mat, nScreenWidth / 2, nScreenHeight / 2, 10);

    /* --- Calculate the new position of all the points --- */
    TransformPoints (mat);

    /* --- Draw the molecule based on translated coordinates --- */
    DrawMolecule (g);
}
```

## Drawing the Bonds

The bonds can be drawn when each atom is drawn because you know which bonds
belong to which atoms. However, this method causes each bond to be drawn twice,
which is not desirable. You can also draw the bonds either before or after you draw the
atoms, but both cases will ruin the three-dimensional effect you're trying to achieve
with the molecule. A better approach is to draw the bond with the most distant atom
it's associated with. This solution draws the bond once, and the bond does not cover
the atom that is closer to the viewer.

The molecule is drawn in the DrawMolecule function. The atoms are drawn using
the sortindex array, which is the array that gets sorted. Using the sortindex array
causes the drawing to occur based on the distance from the viewer. The bPainted flag
keeps track of the bonds that have been painted. After a bond has been painted, it is not
painted again (no sense in wasting CPU time) for this frame. The bonds are painted
along with the associated atoms to deliver a decent three-dimensional effect.

```
/*
 * DrawMolecule
 *
 * Draw the molecule.  'nuff said.
 */
void DrawMolecule (typGraphics *g)
{
    int nIndex;
    int nDiameter;
    typBond *bond;
    GSList *list;
    typAtom *atom;
    int i;
    GdkGC *pen;
```

```
/* --- Make sure everything's ready --- */
Init3d ();

/* --- Sort the molecules --- */
SortMolecules (atomlist, sortindex);

/* --- Get the molecule diameter --- */
nDiameter = nMoleculeRadius + nMoleculeRadius;

/* --- If we're showing bonds --- */
if (ShowLines()) {

    /* --- Clear out the flag that indicates that this
     *     particular bond has been painted.
     */
    for (i = 0; i < nBonds; i++) {

        bondlist[i].bPainted = FALSE;
    }
}

/* --- Display all the atoms in the list --- */
for (i = 0; i < nAtoms; i++) {

    /* --- Use the sort list - draw from farthest back
     *     moving up.
     */
    nIndex = sortindex[i];

    /* --- Get the atom the index refers to --- */
    atom = &atomlist[nIndex];

    /* --- This atom has a color --- */
    pen = GetAtomColor (atom);

    /* --- Draw a circle with the atom color --- */
    gdk_draw_arc (g->pixmap, pen, TRUE,
                atom->tx - 3, atom->ty - 3, 7, 7, 0, 360 * 64);

    /* --- If they want labels --- */
    if (ShowLabels ()) {

        /* --- Show the label --- */
        if (atom->szName) {
            gdk_draw_string (g->pixmap, font,
                        pen, atom->tx + 5, atom->ty,
                        atom->szName);
        }
    }

    /* --- If they want lines (bonds) --- */
    if (ShowLines()) {

        /* --- Show all bonds for this atom --- */
        for (list = atom->bondList; list; list = list->next) {

            /* --- Get the bond from the list --- */
```

```
                    bond = (typBond *) list->data;

                    /* --- If it hasn't been painted yet --- */
                    if (bond->bPainted == FALSE) {

                        /* --- Paint the bond (draw the line) --- */
                        DrawBond (g, bond->atom1, bond->atom2);

                        /* --- Bond marked as painted --- */
                        bond->bPainted = TRUE;
                    }
                }
            }
        }

}
```

The DrawBond function connects two atoms with a single line. Note that the line is drawn using the translated coordinates.

```
/*
 * DrawBond
 *
 * Draw a bond between these two atoms.
 *
 * g - our data structure that has information used to draw
 * atom1 - first atom in the bond pair
 * atom2 - second atom in the bond pair.
 */
void DrawBond (typGraphics *g, typAtom *atom1, typAtom *atom2)
{
    gdk_draw_line (g->pixmap, penBlack,
                   (int) (atom1->tx),
                   (int) (atom1->ty),
                   (int) (atom2->tx),
                   (int) (atom2->ty));

}
```

## Atom Colors

The atoms are displayed using colors if the color toolbar button has been selected. If the color toolbar is not selected, the atom is displayed in black. If the color toolbar is pressed, then the atom is displayed in color and that color depends on the name of the atom in the file. For instance, if the name begins with *n,* then the molecule is probably a nitrogen atom and the GdkGC is returned with a blue pen.

```
/*
 * GetAtomColor
 *
 * Gets the color of the atom based on some of the
 * characteristics of the atom.
 *
 * The molecules are either drawn black or drawn in
 * color depending on a flag set by a toolbar button.
```

```
     *
     * If the flag is set...
     * If the name begins with a 'C' (carbon) then we draw
     * it in black.  If the name begins with 'N' (nitrogen)
     * then we draw it in blue.  If the name begins with 'O'
     * (oxygen) then we draw in in red.  Everything else is
     * drawn in gray.
     *
     * atom - atom to have its color chosen
     */
    GdkGC *GetAtomColor (typAtom *atom)
    {
        char szName[10];

        /* --- Don't know the name. --- */
        if (atom->szName == NULL) {
            return (penBlack);
        }

        /* --- Don't show colors --- */
        if (!ShowRGB ()) {
            return (penBlack);
        }

        GetAtomName (szName, atom);

        if (!strcmp (szName, "CL")) {
            return (penGreen);
        } else if (!strcmp (szName, "C")) {
            return (penBlack);
        } else if (!strcmp (szName, "S")) {
            return (penYellow);
        } else if (!strcmp (szName, "P")) {
            return (penOrange);
        } else if (!strcmp (szName, "N")) {
            return (penBlue);
        } else if (!strcmp (szName, "O")) {
            return (penRed);
        } else if (!strcmp (szName, "H")) {
            return (penWhite);
        } else {
            return (penDarkGray);
        }
    }
```

## configure_event

The configure_event initializes the structures. Because it's called when the widget is created or resized, the configure_event allocates the background pixmap to the size of the widget.

```
    /*
     * configure_event
     *
     * Create a new backing pixmap of the appropriate size
```

```
    */
static gint configure_event (GtkWidget *widget, GdkEventConfigure *event)
{
    /* --- Structure doesn't exist? --- */
    if (g == NULL) {

        /* --- Create one --- */
        g = NewGraphics ();
    }

    /* --- Existing pixmap?  --- */
    if (g->pixmap) {

        /* --- Free it --- */
        gdk_pixmap_unref (g->pixmap);
    }

    /* --- Create a new pixmap --- */
    g->pixmap = gdk_pixmap_new (widget->window,
                                widget->allocation.width,
                                widget->allocation.height,
                                -1);

    /* --- Get height and width to clear screen --- */
    nScreenWidth = widget->allocation.width;
    nScreenHeight = widget->allocation.height;

    /* --- Create a new pixmap --- */
    gdk_draw_rectangle (g->pixmap,
                        widget->style->white_gc,
                        TRUE,
                        0, 0,
                        widget->allocation.width,
                        widget->allocation.height);

    /* --- Redraw molecule --- */
    MoleculeRepaint ();

    return TRUE;
}
```

### expose_event

The expose_event is invoked when an area on the screen needs to be updated. For this application, the expose_event only copies the background pixmap onto the drawable widget. Therefore, the expose_event is very fast.

```
/*
 * expose_event
 *
 * Called when an area on the screen has been exposed
 * and we have to repaint it.  The area is repainted from
 * the background area we have.
 */
static gint expose_event (GtkWidget *widget, GdkEventExpose *event)
```

```
    {
        gdk_draw_pixmap(widget->window,
                widget->style->fg_gc[GTK_WIDGET_STATE (widget)],
                g->pixmap,
                event->area.x, event->area.y,
                event->area.x, event->area.y,
                event->area.width, event->area.height);

        return FALSE;
    }
```

## *MoleculeRepaint*

The MoleculeRepaint function is called when something requires that the molecule be redrawn. The background pixmap is cleared, the molecule is drawn on it, and the expose_event is called to copy the background pixmap into the window.

```
    /*
     * MoleculeRepaint
     *
     * Called when the user uses the mouse to move the
     * molecule.  This causes the molecule to be repainted on
     * the screen.
     */
    void MoleculeRepaint ()
    {
        GdkRectangle  update_rect;

        Init3d ();

        /* --- clear pixmap --- */
        gdk_draw_rectangle (g->pixmap,
                        penGray,
                        TRUE,
                        0, 0,
                        drawing_area->allocation.width,
                        drawing_area->allocation.height);

        /* --- Draw molecule in the background --- */
        paint (g);

        /* --- The whole screen --- */
        update_rect.x = 0;
        update_rect.y = 0;
        update_rect.width = drawing_area->allocation.width;
        update_rect.height = drawing_area->allocation.height;

        /* --- Call the expose event - which copies the background
         *     into the widget
         */
        gtk_widget_draw (drawing_area, &update_rect);
    }
```

The molecule is drawn on a background pixmap every time the user manipulates the picture using the mouse. The only difference between this program and the double-buffered-clock application in Chapter 10, "Graphics Drawing Kit," is that the redraw of the clock was caused by a timer that caused the widget to redraw every second. In this program, the painting of the molecule to the background pixmap occurs when the user drags the mouse.

## Creating the Drawing Area

The `CreateDrawingArea` function is called by the `frontend.c` code that creates the application. This single block of code encapsulates everything required to create the molecule drawing area without needing to worry about the application. You can insert this function into any program without making changes. The drawing area listens for the `expose_event` so that the window can be painted, and it listens for the `configure_event` so that much of the configuration of the background pixmap will be configured and ready to be painted on. You need to listen to the `motion_notify_event` so that you know when the user drags the molecule around with the mouse. However, just using `gtk_signal_connect` with `motion_notify_event` causes a problem. Under GTK+, the low-level GDK events are not sent to the application unless they're explicitly told to send those events.

You can use the `gtk_widget_set_events` function and pass in one of the following values:

- `GDK_EXPOSURE_MASK`
- `GDK_POINTER_MOTION_MASK`
- `GDK_POINTER_MOTION_HINT_MASK`
- `GDK_BUTTON_MOTION_MASK`
- `GDK_BUTTON1_MOTION_MASK`
- `GDK_BUTTON2_MOTION_MASK`
- `GDK_BUTTON3_MOTION_MASK`
- `GDK_BUTTON_PRESS_MASK`
- `GDK_BUTTON_RELEASE_MASK`
- `GDK_KEY_PRESS_MASK`
- `GDK_KEY_RELEASE_MASK`
- `GDK_ENTER_NOTIFY_MASK`
- `GDK_LEAVE_NOTIFY_MASK`
- `GDK_FOCUS_CHANGE_MASK`
- `GDK_STRUCTURE_MASK`
- `GDK_PROPERTY_CHANGE_MASK`
- `GDK_PROXIMITY_IN_MASK`
- `GDK_PROXIMITY_OUT_MASK`

For this application, you want the GTK_POINTER_MOTION_MASK that informs you that the mouse has moved. But there is a small problem: The mouse events occur frequently when the user moves the mouse. If the machine is not fast enough to respond to the mouse events or the processing takes too long, the mouse events start to queue up. For example, this situation would occur if you had to draw a very large molecule that required a lot of processing power to compute and draw. In this case, the processing and drawing would continue even after the user stops moving the mouse (to clear out the event queue)—not a good thing to show. (To see this problem in action, comment out the GTK_POINTER_MOTION_HINT_MASK and, on a slow machine, move one of the complicated molecules very quickly with colors, bonds, and labels showing. Keep moving the molecule for a few seconds and then stop.) A better way is to use the mouse hints.

Normally, every mouse movement generates an event that can queue up and cause the application to appear sluggish as the application struggles to clear the queue of mouse-movement events. A better way is to use the GTK_POINTER_MOTION_HINT_MASK, which allows the application to respond to mouse events at the application's pace. The mouse-movement events do not queue up as the mouse moves; instead, a single mouse event is queued to indicate that the mouse has moved. Because the hint flag has been set, no information is provided in the event about where the mouse has moved. Instead, the application needs to query the current mouse position using the gdk_window_get_pointer function.

The difference between using normal mouse-movement events and using hints can be seen in a simple example. Suppose you write an application (say, a molecule viewer) that draws significantly more-complicated models with three-dimensional shading on the atoms. It works great on your whiz-bang, 600MHz, dual-processor machine—so you decide to make it available to the public on your Web page. A user with a 16MHz, 386SX computer downloads the viewer, hoping to analyze some complicated models. Now, suppose you had written the application using the standard mouse-movement events. Your whiz-bang machine needs 1/100 of a second to draw the model as you rotate it with the mouse. Everything works fine as you drag the model this way and that way. On the 386, however, the model takes 20 seconds to paint, and while the machine is painfully trying to draw the molecule, the user decides to drag the mouse around wondering why the molecule hasn't finished painting. After 20 seconds, the molecule finally gets painting, but guess what? There are (ahem) hundreds of mouse-movement events in the queue. Even if the user does nothing more, each of those events causes the molecule to repaint, theoretically tying up the machine for minutes while they are processed. However, if the application uses mouse hints instead of mouse-movement events, when the painting is complete, only a single event would be in the queue to indicate that the mouse has moved. A query would indicate where the mouse was, and it could be processed. Of course, this example is extreme, and anyone doing 3D graphics on a 386 is a nut.

Next, to detect the fact that the user has pressed or released the mouse button, you need to set the GDK_BUTTON_PRESS_MASK and GTK_BUTTON_RELEASE_MASK flags.

Changes to the event mask to get these low-level events must be done before the widget is realized. The best time to set the mask for any widget is immediately after the widget has been created. This example shows how to create and configure a drawing area to receive the mouse-movement events.

```
GtkWidget *CreateDrawingArea ()
{
    GtkWidget *window;

    /* --- Create a top-level window --- */
    window = gtk_window_new (GTK_WINDOW_TOPLEVEL);

    /* --- Create the drawing area  --- */
    drawing_area = gtk_drawing_area_new ();

    /* --- Set the size --- */
    gtk_drawing_area_size (GTK_DRAWING_AREA (drawing_area), 300, 300);

    /* --- Make drawing area visible --- */
    gtk_widget_show (drawing_area);

    /* --- Signals used to handle background pixmap --- */
    gtk_signal_connect (GTK_OBJECT (drawing_area), "expose_event",
                        (GtkSignalFunc) expose_event, NULL);
    gtk_signal_connect (GTK_OBJECT(drawing_area),"configure_event",
                        (GtkSignalFunc) configure_event, NULL);

    /* --- Need to know about mouse movements. --- */
    gtk_signal_connect (GTK_OBJECT (drawing_area), "motion_notify_event",
                        (GtkSignalFunc) motion_notify, NULL);

    /* --- Events to listen for --- */
    gtk_widget_set_events (drawing_area, GDK_EXPOSURE_MASK
                            | GDK_LEAVE_NOTIFY_MASK
                            | GDK_BUTTON_PRESS_MASK
                            | GDK_POINTER_MOTION_MASK
                            | GDK_POINTER_MOTION_HINT_MASK);

    return (drawing_area);
}
```

To see the difference the mouse hints make, you can remove the GDK_POINTER_MOTION_HINT_MASK from the gtk_widget_set_events call. Of course, you have to use a very complicated molecule, or a slow machine, to see the mouse events queue up.

## motion_notify

The motion_notify function detects mouse motion and retrieves the molecule to be redrawn. The mouseDrag function is called to rotate the molecule. The prevx and prevy positions keep track of the previous position of the mouse. The previous mouse position calculates the direction in which the mouse has been dragged. By knowing the direction the mouse was dragged, you can build a matrix with the information and rotate the molecule. Of course, this function handles both hints and normal mouse-movement events.

If the drawing area is configured with hints, then event->is_hint will be true and the mouse position will be queried every time the motion_notify event is called.

```
/*
 * motion_notify
 *
 * Called when the user moves the mouse on the screen
 */
gint motion_notify (GtkWidget *widget, GdkEventMotion *event)
{
    int x, y;
    GdkModifierType state;

    /* --- If it's a hint... (combining several events) --- */
    if (event->is_hint) {

        /* --- Get new position --- */
        gdk_window_get_pointer (event->window, &x, &y, &state);
    } else {

        /* --- Get new position --- */
        x = event->x;
        y = event->y;
        state = event->state;
    }

    /* --- If the mouse button is down --- */
    if (state & GDK_BUTTON1_MASK && g->pixmap != NULL) {

        /* --- Calculate the mouse drag effect on the
         *     molecule.
         */
        mouseDrag (x, y);
    }

    /* --- Keep track of the position of the mouse --- */
    prevx = x;
    prevy = y;

    return TRUE;
}
```

## mouseDrag

The mouseDrag function recomputes the matrix that rotates the molecule. Recall that every atom has a position (x, y, z) that was read in from the .pdb file and a translated position that is used to draw the molecule. The two come together as follows. The molecule is rotated by multiplying the original atom position by the atom matrix (amat) to get the new translated positions. The atom matrix is adjusted to reflect the mouse movement. A new matrix is created (tmat) and is adjusted to reflect the mouse dragging on the x- and y-axes. This new matrix is then multiplied by the atom matrix that causes the atom matrix to reflect the mouse dragging changes. The original matrix coordinates are pumped through the atom matrix to generate the translated atom positions.

The `MoleculeRepaint` function is then called to redraw the screen with the molecule at the new angle using the atom matrix.

```
/*
 * mouseDrag
 *
 * Calculate the new rotation of the molecule based on how
 * the user drags the mouse over the molecule.
 *
 * x - x position of mouse
 * x - y position of mouse
 */
int mouseDrag (int x, int y)
{

    /* --- Calculate the x difference --- */
    double xtheta = (prevy - y) * (360.0f / nScreenWidth);

    /* --- Calculate the y difference --- */
    double ytheta = (x - prevx) * (360.0f / nScreenHeight);

    /* --- Unit matrix --- */
    unit (tmat);

    /* --- Rotate by the -x- the mouse moved --- */
    xrot (tmat, xtheta);

    /* --- Rotate by the -y- the mouse moved --- */
    yrot (tmat, ytheta);

    /* --- Combine into existing rotation to get new rotation --- */
    mult (amat, tmat);

    /* --- Redraw with new rotation --- */
    MoleculeRepaint ();

    return TRUE;
}
```

## frontend.c

The `frontend.c` code has functions for building the main screen, putting up the toolbar and menu, and handling the main events (toolbar buttons, menus, and so on). This code is nearly the same as in the previous modules; several changes give the molecule viewer a unique menu and toolbar.

```
/*
 * File: frontend.c
 * Auth: Eric Harlow
 *
 * GUI front end to the molecule viewer.
 *
 */

#include <sys/stat.h>
```

```
#include <unistd.h>
#include <errno.h>
#include <gtk/gtk.h>

/* ------------------------- */
/* --- Function prototypes --- */
/* ------------------------- */
void MoleculeRepaint ();
void MoleculeShowLines (int bValue);
void ReadMolecule (char *);
GtkWidget *CreateDrawingArea ();
static void CreateMainWindow ();
void CreateToolbar (GtkWidget *vbox_main);
void SetToolbarButton (char *szButton, int nState);
void SelectMenu (GtkWidget *widget, gpointer data);
void DeSelectMenu (GtkWidget *widget, gpointer data);
void SetMenuButton (char *szButton, int nState) ;
GtkWidget *CreateWidgetFromXpm (GtkWidget *window, gchar **xpm_data);
GtkWidget *CreateMenuItem (GtkWidget *menu,
                           char *szName,
                           char *szAccel,
                           char *szTip,
                           GtkSignalFunc func,
                           gpointer data);
GtkWidget *CreateMenuCheck (GtkWidget *menu,
                            char *szName,
                            GtkSignalFunc func,
                            gpointer data);
GtkWidget *CreateSubMenu (GtkWidget *menubar, char *szName);
GtkWidget *CreateBarSubMenu (GtkWidget *menu, char *szName);


/* --------------------- */
/* --- Global variables --- */
/* --------------------- */
GtkWidget            *win_main;
GtkTooltips          *tooltips;
GtkAcceleratorTable *accelerator_table;
GtkWidget            *toolbar;
GtkWidget            *tool_lines;
GtkWidget            *tool_rgb;
GtkWidget            *tool_labels;


/*
 * --- Bitmap for "open"
 */
static const gchar *xpm_open[] = {
"16 16 4 1",
"  c None",
"B c #000000000000",
"Y c #FFFFFFFF0000",
"y c #999999990000",
"                ",
"          BBB   ",
"  BBBBB  B  BB ",
```

```
"   BYYYB        BB ",
" BYYYYYBBBBB       ",
" BYYYYYYYYYB       ",
" BYYYYYYYYYB       ",
" BYYYYYYYYYB       ",
" BYYBBBBBBBBBBB    ",
" BYYByyyyyyyyyB    ",
" BYByyyyyyyyyB     ",
" BYByyyyyyyyyB     ",
" BByyyyyyyyyB      ",
" BByyyyyyyyyB      ",
" BBBBBBBBBBB       ",
"                   "
};

/*
 * --- Bitmap for "lines"
 */
static const char *xpm_lines[] = {
"16 16 2 1",
"  c None",
"B c #000000000000",
"                   ",
"                   ",
"   BB        BB    ",
"   BB        BB    ",
"    B        B     ",
"    B       B      ",
"     B     B       ",
"     B    B        ",
"      B B          ",
"      BB           ",
"      BBBB         ",
"          BB       ",
"           BBB     ",
"            BB     ",
"                   ",
"                   "
};

/*
 * --- Bitmap for "color"
 */
static const char *xpm_rgb[] = {
"16 16 4 1",
"  c None",
"R c #FF0000",
"G c #00FF00",
"B c #0000FF",
"                   ",
"     BBBRRR        ",
"    BBBBBRRRRR      ",
"   BBBBBBBRRRRRR    ",
"   BBBBBBBRRRRRR    ",
"   BBBBBBBRRRRRR    ",
" BBBBBBBRRRRRRR ",
```

```
"  BBBBBBBRRRRRRR  ",
"  BBBBBGGGGRRRRR  ",
"  BBBGGGGGGGGGRRR ",
"   GGGGGGGGGGGGG  ",
"   GGGGGGGGGGGGG  ",
"   GGGGGGGGGGGGG  ",
"    GGGGGGGGGG    ",
"       GGGGGGG    ",
"                  ",
};


/*
 * --- Bitmap for "Labels"
 */
static const char *xpm_labels[] = {
"16 16 4 1",
"  c None",
"R c #FF0000",
"G c #00FF00",
"B c #000000",
"                  ",
"         BB       ",
"       BBBBBB     ",
"      BBB  BBB    ",
"     BB      BB   ",
"     BB      BB   ",
"    BB        BB  ",
"    BB        BB  ",
"     BBBBBBBBBBB  ",
"     BBBBBBBBBBB  ",
"    BB        BB  ",
"    BB        BB  ",
"    BB        BB  ",
"    BB        BB  ",
"    BB        BB  ",
"                  ",
};


/*
 * EndProgram
 *
 * Exit from the program
 */
void EndProgram ()
{
    gtk_main_quit ();
}


/*
 * main
 *
 * --- Program begins here
 */
```

```c
int main(int argc, char *argv[])
{
    /* --- Initialize GTK+ --- */
    gtk_init (&argc, &argv);

    /* --- Initialize tooltips --- */
    tooltips = gtk_tooltips_new ();

    /* --- Create window(s) --- */
    CreateMainWindow ();

    /* --- Read in the default molecule --- */
    ReadMolecule ("molecule.pdb");

    /* --- Main event handling loop --- */
    gtk_main();

    return 0;
}

/*
 * ShowLabels
 *
 * Is the "Show Labels" toolbar button pressed in to
 * indicate that the user wants to display the
 * atom labels?
 */
int ShowLabels ()
{

    return (GTK_TOGGLE_BUTTON (tool_labels)->active);
}

/*
 * ShowRGB
 *
 * Is the "Show RGB" button on the toolbar pressed in?
 * This indicates whether the atoms should be displayed
 * in single color or multicolor mode.
 */
int ShowRGB ()
{

    return (GTK_TOGGLE_BUTTON (tool_rgb)->active);
}


/*
 * ShowLines
 *
 * Indicates whether the lines should be drawn between
 * the atoms to show the bonds.
 */
int ShowLines ()
{
```

```
            return (GTK_TOGGLE_BUTTON (tool_lines)->active);
      }

      /*
       * FileOpen
       *
       * Open a pdb file for displaying
       */
      void FileOpen (GtkWidget *widget, gpointer data)
      {
            GetFilename ("Open Molecule", ReadMolecule);
      }

      /*
       * CreateMainWindow
       *
       * Create the main window and the menu/toolbar associated with it
       */
      static void CreateMainWindow ()
      {
            GtkWidget *widget;
            GtkWidget *vbox_main;
            GtkWidget *menubar;
            GtkWidget *menu;
            GtkWidget *menuitem;
            GtkWidget *menufont;
            GtkWidget *toolbar;
            GtkWidget *button;

            /* --- Create the top window and size it --- */
            win_main = gtk_window_new(GTK_WINDOW_TOPLEVEL);
            gtk_widget_set_usize(win_main, 360, 260);
            gtk_window_set_title (GTK_WINDOW (win_main), "Menu test");
            gtk_container_border_width (GTK_CONTAINER (win_main), 0);

            /* --- Create accel table --- */
            accelerator_table = gtk_accelerator_table_new();
            gtk_window_add_accelerator_table(GTK_WINDOW(win_main),
      ➥accelerator_table);

            /* --- Top-level window should listen for the destroy --- */
            gtk_signal_connect (GTK_OBJECT (win_main), "destroy",
                        GTK_SIGNAL_FUNC(EndProgram), NULL);

            /* --- Create v-box for menu, toolbar --- */
            vbox_main = gtk_vbox_new (FALSE, 0);

            /* --- Put up v-box --- */
            gtk_container_add (GTK_CONTAINER (win_main), vbox_main);

            gtk_widget_show (vbox_main);
            gtk_widget_show (win_main);

            /* --- Menu bar --- */
            menubar = gtk_menu_bar_new ();
            gtk_box_pack_start (GTK_BOX (vbox_main), menubar, FALSE, TRUE, 0);
```

```
    gtk_widget_show (menubar);

    /* ---------------- */
    /* --- File menu --- */
    /* ---------------- */

    menu = CreateBarSubMenu (menubar, "File");

    menuitem = CreateMenuItem (menu, "Open", "^O",
                    "Open an existing item",
                    GTK_SIGNAL_FUNC (FileOpen), "open");

    menuitem = CreateMenuItem (menu, NULL, NULL,
                    NULL, NULL, NULL);

    menuitem = CreateMenuItem (menu, "Quit", "",
                    "What's more descriptive than quit?",
                    GTK_SIGNAL_FUNC (EndProgram), "quit");

    /* --- Create the toolbar --- */
    CreateToolbar (vbox_main);

    widget = CreateDrawingArea ();
    gtk_box_pack_start (GTK_BOX (vbox_main), widget, TRUE, TRUE, 0);
}


/*
 * CreateToolbar
 *
 * Create the toolbar with the specified toolbar
 * options.
 */
void CreateToolbar (GtkWidget *vbox_main)
{
  GtkWidget *widget;

    /* --- Create the toolbar and add it to the window --- */
    toolbar = gtk_toolbar_new (GTK_ORIENTATION_HORIZONTAL,
➥GTK_TOOLBAR_ICONS);
    gtk_box_pack_start (GTK_BOX (vbox_main), toolbar, FALSE, TRUE, 0);
    gtk_widget_show (toolbar);

    /* --- Create "open" button --- */
    gtk_toolbar_append_item (GTK_TOOLBAR (toolbar),
                        "Open Dialog", "Open dialog", "",
                        CreateWidgetFromXpm (vbox_main, (gchar **)
➥xpm_open),
                        (GtkSignalFunc) FileOpen,
                        NULL);

    /* --- Little gap --- */
    gtk_toolbar_append_space (GTK_TOOLBAR (toolbar));


    tool_lines = gtk_toolbar_append_element (GTK_TOOLBAR (toolbar),
```

```
                                    GTK_TOOLBAR_CHILD_TOGGLEBUTTON,
                                    NULL,
                                    "Lines", "Lines", "Lines",
                                    CreateWidgetFromXpm (vbox_main, (gchar **)
    ➥xpm_lines),
                                    (GtkSignalFunc) MoleculeRepaint,
                                    NULL);

        tool_rgb = gtk_toolbar_append_element (GTK_TOOLBAR (toolbar),
                                    GTK_TOOLBAR_CHILD_TOGGLEBUTTON,
                                    NULL,
                                    "Color", "Color", "Color",
                                    CreateWidgetFromXpm (vbox_main, (gchar **)
    ➥xpm_rgb),
                                    (GtkSignalFunc) MoleculeRepaint,
                                    NULL);

        tool_labels = gtk_toolbar_append_element (GTK_TOOLBAR (toolbar),
                                    GTK_TOOLBAR_CHILD_TOGGLEBUTTON,
                                    NULL,
                                    "Labels", "Labels", "Labels",
                                    CreateWidgetFromXpm (vbox_main, (gchar **)
    ➥xpm_labels),
                                    (GtkSignalFunc) MoleculeRepaint,
                                    NULL);


    }
```

## *matrix3d.c*

The matrix3d.c code has the functions required to do the matrix multiplication. For a better understanding of three-dimensional math, please get a book that focuses on the topic. (A book on linear algebra should explain matrix multiplication, as do many books that cover 3D graphics.) The code is included here for completeness.

```
/*
 * File: matrix3d.c
 * Auth: Eric Harlow
 *
 * Converted from a Java Matrix 3d class file.
 */

#include "atom.h"
#include "matrix3d.h"
#include <math.h>


static double pi = 3.14159265;

/*
 * NewMatrix3D
 *
 * Create a new matrix
 */
```

```c
typMatrix3D *NewMatrix3D ()
{
    typMatrix3D *mat;

    mat = (typMatrix3D *) g_malloc (sizeof (typMatrix3D));

    unit (mat);

    return (mat);
}
/*
 * scale
 *
 * Scale the object
 */
void scale (typMatrix3D *mat, double f)
{
    mat->xx *= f;
    mat->xy *= f;
    mat->xz *= f;
    mat->xo *= f;
    mat->yx *= f;
    mat->yy *= f;
    mat->yz *= f;
    mat->yo *= f;
    mat->zx *= f;
    mat->zy *= f;
    mat->zz *= f;
    mat->zo *= f;
}


/*
 * scale3
 *
 * Scale each direction by a different factor
 */
void scale3 (typMatrix3D *mat, double xf, double yf, double zf)
{
    mat->xx *= xf;
    mat->xy *= xf;
    mat->xz *= xf;
    mat->xo *= xf;
    mat->yx *= yf;
    mat->yy *= yf;
    mat->yz *= yf;
    mat->yo *= yf;
    mat->zx *= zf;
    mat->zy *= zf;
    mat->zz *= zf;
    mat->zo *= zf;
}
```

```
/*
 * translate
 *
 * Translate the point represented by the matrix by (x, y, z)
 */
void translate (typMatrix3D *mat, double x, double y, double z)
{
    mat->xo += x;
    mat->yo += y;
    mat->zo += z;
}

/*
 * yrot
 *
 * Add in a y rotation of angle (theta) to the matrix.
 */
void yrot (typMatrix3D *mat, double theta)
{
    double ct;
    double st;
    double Nxx;
    double Nxy;
    double Nxz;
    double Nxo;
    double Nzx;
    double Nzy;
    double Nzz;
    double Nzo;

    theta *= (pi / 180);
    ct = cos (theta);
    st = sin (theta);

    Nxx = (double) (mat->xx * ct + mat->zx * st);
    Nxy = (double) (mat->xy * ct + mat->zy * st);
    Nxz = (double) (mat->xz * ct + mat->zz * st);
    Nxo = (double) (mat->xo * ct + mat->zo * st);

    Nzx = (double) (mat->zx * ct - mat->xx * st);
    Nzy = (double) (mat->zy * ct - mat->xy * st);
    Nzz = (double) (mat->zz * ct - mat->xz * st);
    Nzo = (double) (mat->zo * ct - mat->xo * st);

    mat->xo = Nxo;
    mat->xx = Nxx;
    mat->xy = Nxy;
    mat->xz = Nxz;
    mat->zo = Nzo;
    mat->zx = Nzx;
    mat->zy = Nzy;
    mat->zz = Nzz;
}
```

```c
/*
 * xrot
 *
 * Add in an x rotation of angle (theta) to the matrix.
 */
void xrot (typMatrix3D *mat, double theta)
{
    double ct;
    double st;
    double Nyx;
    double Nyy;
    double Nyz;
    double Nyo;
    double Nzx;
    double Nzy;
    double Nzz;
    double Nzo;

    theta *= (pi / 180);
    ct = cos (theta);
    st = sin (theta);

    Nyx = (double) (mat->yx * ct + mat->zx * st);
    Nyy = (double) (mat->yy * ct + mat->zy * st);
    Nyz = (double) (mat->yz * ct + mat->zz * st);
    Nyo = (double) (mat->yo * ct + mat->zo * st);

    Nzx = (double) (mat->zx * ct - mat->yx * st);
    Nzy = (double) (mat->zy * ct - mat->yy * st);
    Nzz = (double) (mat->zz * ct - mat->yz * st);
    Nzo = (double) (mat->zo * ct - mat->yo * st);

    mat->yo = Nyo;
    mat->yx = Nyx;
    mat->yy = Nyy;
    mat->yz = Nyz;
    mat->zo = Nzo;
    mat->zx = Nzx;
    mat->zy = Nzy;
    mat->zz = Nzz;
}


/*
 * zrot
 *
 * Add in a z rotation of angle (theta) to the matrix.
 */
void zrot (typMatrix3D *mat, double theta)
{
    double ct;
    double st;
    double Nyx;
    double Nyy;
    double Nyz;
    double Nyo;
```

```
    double Nxx;
    double Nxy;
    double Nxz;
    double Nxo;

    theta *= (pi / 180);
    ct = cos(theta);
    st = sin(theta);

    Nyx = (double) (mat->yx * ct + mat->xx * st);
    Nyy = (double) (mat->yy * ct + mat->xy * st);
    Nyz = (double) (mat->yz * ct + mat->xz * st);
    Nyo = (double) (mat->yo * ct + mat->xo * st);

    Nxx = (double) (mat->xx * ct - mat->yx * st);
    Nxy = (double) (mat->xy * ct - mat->yy * st);
    Nxz = (double) (mat->xz * ct - mat->yz * st);
    Nxo = (double) (mat->xo * ct - mat->yo * st);

    mat->yo = Nyo;
    mat->yx = Nyx;
    mat->yy = Nyy;
    mat->yz = Nyz;
    mat->xo = Nxo;
    mat->xx = Nxx;
    mat->xy = Nxy;
    mat->xz = Nxz;
}

/*
 * mult
 *
 * Multiply the first matrix by the second matrix.
 * The first matrix has the new value.
 */
void mult (typMatrix3D *mat, typMatrix3D *rhs)
{
    double lxx = mat->xx * rhs->xx +
                 mat->yx * rhs->xy +
                 mat->zx * rhs->xz;
    double lxy = mat->xy * rhs->xx +
                 mat->yy * rhs->xy +
                 mat->zy * rhs->xz;
    double lxz = mat->xz * rhs->xx +
                 mat->yz * rhs->xy +
                 mat->zz * rhs->xz;
    double lxo = mat->xo * rhs->xx +
                 mat->yo * rhs->xy +
                 mat->zo * rhs->xz + rhs->xo;

    double lyx = mat->xx * rhs->yx +
                 mat->yx * rhs->yy +
                 mat->zx * rhs->yz;
    double lyy = mat->xy * rhs->yx +
                 mat->yy * rhs->yy +
                 mat->zy * rhs->yz;
```

```
          double lyz = mat->xz * rhs->yx +
                       mat->yz * rhs->yy +
                       mat->zz * rhs->yz;
          double lyo = mat->xo * rhs->yx +
                       mat->yo * rhs->yy +
                       mat->zo * rhs->yz + rhs->yo;

          double lzx = mat->xx * rhs->zx +
                       mat->yx * rhs->zy +
                       mat->zx * rhs->zz;
          double lzy = mat->xy * rhs->zx +
                       mat->yy * rhs->zy +
                       mat->zy * rhs->zz;
          double lzz = mat->xz * rhs->zx +
                       mat->yz * rhs->zy +
                       mat->zz * rhs->zz;
          double lzo = mat->xo * rhs->zx +
                       mat->yo * rhs->zy +
                       mat->zo * rhs->zz + rhs->zo;

      mat->xx = lxx;
      mat->xy = lxy;
      mat->xz = lxz;
      mat->xo = lxo;

      mat->yx = lyx;
      mat->yy = lyy;
      mat->yz = lyz;
      mat->yo = lyo;

      mat->zx = lzx;
      mat->zy = lzy;
      mat->zz = lzz;
      mat->zo = lzo;
}


/*
 * unit
 *
 * Make the matrix a unit matrix
 */
void unit (typMatrix3D *mat)
{
    mat->xo = 0;
    mat->xx = 1;
    mat->xy = 0;
    mat->xz = 0;
    mat->yo = 0;
    mat->yx = 0;
    mat->yy = 1;
    mat->yz = 0;
    mat->zo = 0;
    mat->zx = 0;
    mat->zy = 0;
    mat->zz = 1;
```

```
}

/*
 * Transform
 *
 * Translate the atom's coordinates into the tranlated
 * coordinates.
 */
void Transform (typMatrix3D *mat, typAtom *atom)
{
    double lxx = mat->xx, lxy = mat->xy, lxz = mat->xz, lxo = mat->xo;
    double lyx = mat->yx, lyy = mat->yy, lyz = mat->yz, lyo = mat->yo;
    double lzx = mat->zx, lzy = mat->zy, lzz = mat->zz, lzo = mat->zo;

    double x = atom->x;
    double y = atom->y;
    double z = atom->z;

    atom->tx = (x * lxx + y * lxy + z * lxz + lxo);
    atom->ty = (x * lyx + y * lyy + z * lyz + lyo);
    atom->tz = (x * lzx + y * lzy + z * lzz + lzo);
}
```

### Remainder of the Code

The remainder of the code was taken from the previous chapters. The `misc.c` code comes from Chapter 5, "Menus, Toolbars, and Tooltips," and helps build the menus and toolbar. The `filesel.c` code is from Chapter 6, "More Widgets: Frames, Text, Dialog Boxes, File Selection Dialog Box, Progress Bar." These modules required few (if any) changes to get them to work here. Changes were made to `filesel.c` to make it more generic; it can now be used many times (a sign of modular code, I do believe).

## Summary

The molecule viewer is a more complicated example of an application created with GDK. The molecule viewer shows how user interaction works in a drawing area widget with the GDK. The viewer uses mouse events to rotate the object. This chapter covered some of the low-level events so you can respond to a user who is manipulating the molecule with the mouse.

# 13

# Sprites and Animation

T HE GRAPHICS DRAWING KIT (GDK) CAN do more than just draw lines and boxes. With a little help, it can also perform tasks such as animation that can be used for games. GDK is not a high-performance library for writing games, so writing a game such as Doom or Quake is probably not a good idea. However, games that don't have heavy performance requirements can use GDK.

## Animation

Animation in computer games is achieved by rapidly moving images around on the screen. The images can be spaceships, people, or anything else that can represent the player and computer. These movable images are sometimes called *sprites*.

Animation works best when the images on the screen do not flicker. The best way to prevent flicker is to use double buffering (recall the clock example in Chapter 10, "Graphics Drawing Kit"). The animated sequences in this chapter use pixmaps because the format is familiar and because you can easily draw them with transparent areas on a background.

These animated sequences involve three steps. The first step is to clear the background and draw the background scenery. The second step is to draw the images that are going to be animated. The third step is to transfer the painted scene to the window so it can be displayed.

## Using Sprites

To do the animation, you first need to define a sprite as an .xpm image from which you can get a displayable pixmap and a mask. The mask defines the area into which you want to draw. Although the images are rectangular, you don't want to draw the entire rectangle on the background. A better approach is to mask out the image area so that you don't draw where you don't have image data.

A man walking can be generated with three images—feet together, left foot forward, and right foot forward. You can use the image with the feet together twice as the transition between the left foot forward and the right foot forward and between the right foot forward and the left foot forward. The man is carrying a book in one hand to demonstrate the swing of his arm in motion. The images that you can use are as follows:

```
static char *xpm_standright[] = {
"24 24 4 1",
"  c None",
"X c #FFFFFF",
". c #000000",
"b c #0000FF",
"        ......          ",
"        .XXXXX.         ",
"        .XXXXX.XX.      ",
"        .XXXXXXXX.      ",
"        .XXXXX.         ",
"          .XX.          ",
"          .XXXX.        ",
"          .X.XX.        ",
"          .X.XX.        ",
"          .X.XX.        ",
"          .X.XX.        ",
"          .X.XX.        ",
"          .X.XX.        ",
"          .b..          ",
"          .bb.          ",
"          .bb.          ",
"          .bb.          ",
"          .bb.          ",
"          .bb.          ",
"          .bb.          ",
"          .bb...        ",
"          .XXXX.        ",
"          .XXXX.        ",
"          .....         ",
};
```

```
static char *xpm_walkright1[] = {
"24 24 4 1",
"  c None",
"X c #FFFFFF",
". c #000000",
"b c #0000FF",
"       ......           ",
"       .XXXXXX.         ",
"       .XXXXX.XX.       ",
"       .XXXXXXXX.       ",
"       .XXXXXX.         ",
"        .XX.            ",
"        .XXXX.          ",
"        .XXXX.          ",
"        .X.XX.X.        ",
"        .X.XX.X..       ",
"      .X..XX..XX.       ",
"      .X..XX.XXXX.      ",
"      . .XX..XX.        ",
"         .bb. ..        ",
"          ..b.          ",
"         .b..b.         ",
"         .b..b.         ",
"        .b. .b.         ",
"        .b.  .b.        ",
"        .b.  .b.        ",
"        .b.  .b...      ",
"        .XXX. .XXX.     ",
"        .XXX. .XXX.     ",
"         ...   ...      ",
};


static char *xpm_walkright2[] = {
"24 24 4 1",
"  c None",
"X c #FFFFFF",
". c #000000",
"b c #0000FF",
"       ......           ",
"       .XXXXXX.         ",
"       .XXXXX.XX.       ",
"       .XXXXXXXX.       ",
"       .XXXXXX.         ",
"        .XX.            ",
"        .XXXX.          ",
```

```
"      .XXXX.        ",
"      .X.XX.X.      ",
"      ..X.XX.X.     ",
"      .XX. XX..X.   ",
"      .XXXX.XX..X.  ",
"      .XX..XX. .    ",
"      .. .bb.       ",
"        .b..        ",
"        .b..b.      ",
"        .b..b.      ",
"       .b. .b.      ",
"       .b.  .b.     ",
"      .b.   .b.     ",
"      .b..  .b..    ",
"      .XXX. .XXX.   ",
"      .XXX. .XXX.   ",
"       ...  ...     ",
};
```

You can store the images in a sprite data structure defined as

```
typedef struct {

    char **xpm_data;
    GdkPixmap *pixmap;
    GdkBitmap *mask;

} typSprite;
```

where the `xpm_data` is the image `.xpm` pixmap data and the pixmap and mask are the results of a call to `gdk_pixmap_create_from_xpm_d`. The man walking would have a `typSprite` array with the preceding images in an array, and the pixmap and mask parts of the structure initialized to `NULL`.

```
/*
 * Man walking
 */
typSprite walk[] =  {
    { xpm_standright, NULL, NULL },
    { xpm_walkright1, NULL, NULL },
    { xpm_standright, NULL, NULL },
    { xpm_walkright2, NULL, NULL },
    { NULL, NULL, NULL }
};
```

The sprite array defines a series of images and the sequence in which they should be displayed. The `typActor` structure defines where the image is on the screen, which image is displayed in the sequence, and the size of the image, assuming that all the sprites in a sequence are the same size.

```
typedef struct {

    int seq;
    int x;
    int y;
    int height;
    int width;
    int nSequences;
    typSprite *sprites;

} typActor;
```

## Loading the Images

The LoadPixmaps function associates the typActor with the typSprite so that the
actor can keep track of the sprite that's being displayed and where it is on the screen.
You call the pixmap with the window, the actor, and the array of sprites that is going
to be displayed for the actor. Here, the walk sprite array is associated with the actor
and initialized.

```
LoadPixmaps (window, &man, walk);
```

The code for the LoadPixmaps function converts each .xpm data image into pixmap
and mask data. The sprite array is stored in the typActor structure, and the typActor is
initialized with the number of sprites in the sequence and the size of the sprites.

```
void LoadPixmaps (GtkWidget *widget,
                  typActor *actor,
                  typSprite *sprites)
{

    int i = 0;

    /* --- Get every sequence --- */
    while (sprites[i].xpm_data) {

        /* --- Convert xpm data to pixmap & mask --- */
        sprites[i].pixmap = gdk_pixmap_create_from_xpm_d (
                            widget->window,
                            &sprites[i].mask,
                            NULL,
                            sprites[i].xpm_data);
        i++;
    }

    /* --- Get sprite height and width --- */
```

```
    GetWidthHeight (sprites[0].xpm_data, &actor->width,
                    &actor->height);

    /* --- Initialize sprite information --- */
    actor->seq = 0;
    actor->nSequences = i;
    actor->sprites = sprites;
}
```

## Displaying the Images

After all the actors have been associated with sprites, the animation is ready to begin.
Like the other double-buffered examples, the repaint routine draws on the background.
When the drawing is finished, the background image is copied to the drawing area.

```
gint Repaint (gpointer data)

{
    GtkWidget*     drawing_area = (GtkWidget *) data;
    GdkRectangle   update_rect;
    static offset = 0;
    int nTop;

    /* --- clear pixmap (background image) --- */
    gdk_draw_rectangle (pixmap,
            drawing_area->style->black_gc,
            TRUE,
            0, 0,
            drawing_area->allocation.width,
            drawing_area->allocation.height);

    /* --- Draw road --- */
    gdk_draw_rectangle (pixmap,
            drawing_area->style->white_gc,
            TRUE,
            50, 0,
            100,
            drawing_area->allocation.height);

    /*
     * Draw lines on the road
     */

    /* --- Figure out where first line should be --- */
    offset++;
```

```
    if ((offset - GAP_LEN) >= 0) {
        offset -= (LINE_LEN + GAP_LEN);
    }

    /* --- Draw the lines all the way down the road --- */
    nTop = offset;
    do {
        gdk_draw_rectangle (pixmap,
            drawing_area->style->black_gc,
            TRUE,
            100, nTop, 5, LINE_LEN);
        nTop += LINE_LEN + GAP_LEN;
    } while (nTop < drawing_area->allocation.height);

    /* --- Draw each of these images --- */
    SequenceSprite (drawing_area, &bike, 3);
    SequenceSprite (drawing_area, &man, 2);
    SequenceSprite (drawing_area, &woman, 2);
    SequenceSprite (drawing_area, &police, 0);
    SequenceSprite (drawing_area, &ball1, 2);
    SequenceSprite (drawing_area, &car1, 3);

    /* --- The whole screen needs to be updated --- */
    update_rect.x = 0;
    update_rect.y = 0;
    update_rect.width = drawing_area->allocation.width;
    update_rect.height = drawing_area->allocation.height;

    /* --- So update it --- */
    gtk_widget_draw (drawing_area, &update_rect);
}
```

The SequenceSprite function draws each animated image on the background and uses the gdk_draw_pixmap to draw the image. Normally, drawing the image on the background would draw a rectangular area to draw the images (see Figure 13.1).

Fortunately, you can get rid of the non–image data by using the mask returned from the gdk_pixmap_create_from_xpm_d function. The mask is created from the colors in the .xpm data. The color None is the only color not used when creating the mask and becomes transparent in the mask. The gdk_gc_set_clip_mask function sets the mask to be used for the gdk_draw_pixmap function. The mask needs to be positioned where the image is going to be drawn using the gdk_gc_set_clip_origin function. Using these two functions eliminates the square around the image when it is drawn on the page (see Figure 13.2).

**Figure 13.1** Sprites without transparency.    **Figure 13.2** Sprites with transparency.

The SequenceSprite function takes the actor and updates the actor's position on the screen by adding the distance (nDist) to its -x- value and draws it on the screen. The drawing here can use the mask or not—the bUseMask flag indicates whether the sprite should be drawn with or without the mask. Drawing without the mask causes the images to be drawn with a big rectangle around them (refer to Figure 13.2). Of course, if the image was drawn with the clipping mask, the clipping mask should be set to NULL after the image is drawn and the mask is no longer needed. Here's the full sequence sprite function.

```
SequenceSprite (GtkWidget *drawing_area, typActor *actor, int nDist)
{
    GdkGC *gc;

    /* --- Move the actor along --- */
    actor->x += nDist;

    /* --- Too far over, reset position --- */
    if (actor->x > drawing_area->allocation.width) {
        actor->x = 0;
    }

    /* --- Use the next image for the actor --- */
    actor->seq++;

    /* --- Use 0 if at the end --- */
    if (actor->seq >= actor->nSequences) {
        actor->seq = 0;
    }

    /* --- Get foreground color --- */
    gc = drawing_area->style->fg_gc[GTK_STATE_NORMAL];
```

```
    if (bUseMask) {

        /* --- Set the clipping of the sprites --- */
        gdk_gc_set_clip_mask (gc, actor->sprites[actor->seq].mask);

        /* --- Set the origin of the clipping --- */
        gdk_gc_set_clip_origin (gc, actor->x, actor->y);
    }

    /* --- Copy pixmap to the window, properly clipped --- */
    gdk_draw_pixmap (pixmap,
        drawing_area->style->fg_gc[GTK_STATE_NORMAL],
        actor->sprites[actor->seq].pixmap,
        0, 0,
        actor->x, actor->y,
        actor->width, actor->height);

    if (bUseMask) {

        /* --- Clear the clipping mask --- */
        gdk_gc_set_clip_mask (gc, NULL);
    }
}
```

## Entire Code

The entire animation demo follows. It takes several animated sequences and moves them across the window. Most of the sprites are a series of pixmaps that are used to make the images appear like they're in motion. The man walking in the image looks like he's taking steps as he moves, and the cyclist looks like he's peddling his bike to move forward. The ball sprite illustrates a sprite that has transparent areas within the object. As the ball moves over the background and other sprites, the other objects can be seen through the holes in the ball.

```
/*
 * Auth: Eric Harlow
 * Linux application development
 *
 * Demo of sprites.
 */

#include <gtk/gtk.h>
#include <time.h>

#include "man.h"
#include "woman.h"
```

```
#include "ball.h"
#include "driver.h"
#include "police.h"
#include "bike.h"


#define LINE_LEN 20
#define GAP_LEN 15

/*
 * Our sprite data structure
 */
typedef struct {

    char **xpm_data;
    GdkPixmap *pixmap;
    GdkBitmap *mask;

} typSprite;

/*
 * Here's the actor. Actor consists of one or more
 * sprites.
 */
typedef struct {

    int seq;
    int x;
    int y;
    int height;
    int width;
    int nSequences;
    typSprite *sprites;

} typActor;

/*
 * Man walking
 */
typSprite walk[] =  {
    { xpm_standright, NULL, NULL },
    { xpm_walkright1, NULL, NULL },
    { xpm_standright, NULL, NULL },
    { xpm_walkright2, NULL, NULL },
    { NULL, NULL, NULL }
};
```

```
/*
 * Man on a bike
 */
typSprite sprite_bike[] = {
    { xpm_bike1, NULL, NULL },
    { xpm_bike2, NULL, NULL },
    { xpm_bike3, NULL, NULL },
    { NULL, NULL, NULL }
};


/*
 * Woman walking
 */
typSprite sprite_woman[] =  {
    { xpm_womanr, NULL, NULL },
    { xpm_womanwalkr1, NULL, NULL },
    { xpm_womanr, NULL, NULL },
    { xpm_womanwalkr2, NULL, NULL },
    { NULL, NULL, NULL }
};


/*
 * Police car
 */
typSprite sprite_police[] = {
    { xpm_police1, NULL, NULL },
    { xpm_police2, NULL, NULL },
    { NULL, NULL, NULL }
};


/*
 * Partially transparent ball.
 */
typSprite sprite_ball[] = {
    { xpm_ball1, NULL, NULL },
    { NULL, NULL, NULL }
};

/*
 * Car
 */
typSprite sprite_car[] = {
    { xpm_car1, NULL, NULL },
```

```
      { xpm_car1, NULL, NULL },
      { NULL, NULL, NULL }
};


/*
 * Here are the stars of the production
 */
typActor man;
typActor bike;
typActor woman;
typActor police;
typActor ball1;
typActor car1;

/* --- Backing pixmap for drawing area --- */
static GdkPixmap *pixmap = NULL;

/* --- Flag to use mask --- */
static int bUseMask = TRUE;

/*
 * Prototypes.
 */
void GetWidthHeight (gchar **xpm, int *width, int *height);


/*
 * LoadPixmaps
 *
 * Load the actor's pixmaps, get the sprite information
 * from the xpm data and initialize the actor animation
 * information.
 */
void LoadPixmaps (GtkWidget *widget, typActor *actor, typSprite *sprites)
{

    int i = 0;

    /* --- Get every sequence --- */
    while (sprites[i].xpm_data) {

        /* --- Convert .xpm data to pixmap & mask --- */
        sprites[i].pixmap = gdk_pixmap_create_from_xpm_d (
                            widget->window,
                            &sprites[i].mask,
```

```
                                    NULL,
                                    sprites[i].xpm_data);
          i++;
      }

      /* --- Get sprite height and width --- */
      GetWidthHeight (sprites[0].xpm_data, &actor->width, &actor->height);

      /* --- Initialize sprite information --- */
      actor->seq = 0;
      actor->nSequences = i;
      actor->sprites = sprites;
}


/*
 * SequenceSprite
 *
 * Move to the next sprite in the sequence and
 * draw it with the mask
 */
SequenceSprite (GtkWidget *drawing_area, typActor *actor, int nDist)
{
      GdkGC *gc;

      actor->x += nDist;
      if (actor->x > drawing_area->allocation.width) {
          actor->x = 0;
      }

      /* --- Use the next image for the actor --- */
      actor->seq++;

      /* --- Use 0 if at the end --- */
      if (actor->seq >= actor->nSequences) {
          actor->seq = 0;
      }

      /* --- Get foreground color --- */
      gc = drawing_area->style->fg_gc[GTK_STATE_NORMAL];

      if (bUseMask) {

          /* --- Set the clipping of the sprites --- */
          gdk_gc_set_clip_mask (gc, actor->sprites[actor->seq].mask);
```

```
                /* --- Set the origin of the clipping --- */
                gdk_gc_set_clip_origin (gc, actor->x, actor->y);
        }

        /* --- Copy pixmap to the window, properly clipped --- */
        gdk_draw_pixmap (pixmap,
                drawing_area->style->fg_gc[GTK_STATE_NORMAL],
                actor->sprites[actor->seq].pixmap,
                0, 0,
                actor->x, actor->y,
                actor->width, actor->height);

        if (bUseMask) {

            /* --- Clear the clipping mask --- */
            gdk_gc_set_clip_mask (gc, NULL);
        }
}


/*
 * Repaint
 *
 * data - widget to repaint
 */
gint Repaint (gpointer data)
{
    GtkWidget*    drawing_area = (GtkWidget *) data;
    GdkRectangle  update_rect;
    static offset = 0;
    int nTop;

    /* --- clear pixmap (background image) --- */
    gdk_draw_rectangle (pixmap,
            drawing_area->style->black_gc,
            TRUE,
            0, 0,
            drawing_area->allocation.width,
            drawing_area->allocation.height);

    /* --- Draw road --- */
    gdk_draw_rectangle (pixmap,
            drawing_area->style->white_gc,
            TRUE,
            50, 0,
            100,
            drawing_area->allocation.height);
```

```
    /*
     * Draw lines on the road
     */

    /* --- Figure out where first line should be. --- */
    offset++;
    if ((offset - GAP_LEN) >= 0) {
        offset -= (LINE_LEN + GAP_LEN);
    }

    /* --- Draw the lines all the way down the road --- */
    nTop = offset;
    do {
        gdk_draw_rectangle (pixmap,
                drawing_area->style->black_gc,
                TRUE,
                100, nTop, 5, LINE_LEN);
        nTop += LINE_LEN + GAP_LEN;
    } while (nTop < drawing_area->allocation.height);

    /* --- Draw each of these images --- */
    SequenceSprite (drawing_area, &bike, 3);
    SequenceSprite (drawing_area, &man, 2);
    SequenceSprite (drawing_area, &woman, 2);
    SequenceSprite (drawing_area, &police, 0);
    SequenceSprite (drawing_area, &ball1, 2);
    SequenceSprite (drawing_area, &car1, 3);

    /* --- The whole screen needs to be updated --- */
    update_rect.x = 0;
    update_rect.y = 0;
    update_rect.width = drawing_area->allocation.width;
    update_rect.height = drawing_area->allocation.height;

    /* --- So update it --- */
    gtk_widget_draw (drawing_area, &update_rect);
}

/*
 * configure_event
 *
 * Create a new backing pixmap of the appropriate size
 * Of course, this is called whenever the window is
 * resized.  We have to free up things we allocated.
 */
static gint configure_event (GtkWidget *widget, GdkEventConfigure *event)
{
```

```
        /* --- Free background if we created it --- */
        if (pixmap) {
            gdk_pixmap_unref (pixmap);
        }

        /* --- Create a new pixmap with new size --- */
        pixmap = gdk_pixmap_new (widget->window,
                    widget->allocation.width,
                    widget->allocation.height,
                    -1);

        return TRUE;
}

/*
 * expose_event
 *
 * When the window is exposed to the viewer or
 * the gdk_widget_draw routine is called, this
 * routine is called.  Copies the background pixmap
 * to the window.
 */
gint expose_event (GtkWidget *widget, GdkEventExpose *event)
{

        /* --- Copy pixmap to the window --- */
        gdk_draw_pixmap (widget->window,
            widget->style->fg_gc[GTK_WIDGET_STATE (widget)],
            pixmap,
            event->area.x, event->area.y,
            event->area.x, event->area.y,
            event->area.width, event->area.height);

        return FALSE;
}


/*
 * quit
 *
 * Get out of the application
 */
void quit ()
{
    gtk_exit (0);
}
```

```
/*
 * GetWidgthHeight
 *
 * Get the widget and height for the xpm data
 *
 */
void GetWidthHeight (gchar **xpm, int *width, int *height)
{

        sscanf (xpm [0], "%d %d", width, height);
}



/*
 * main
 *
 * Program begins here.
 */
int main (int argc, char *argv[])
{
    GtkWidget *window;
    GtkWidget *drawing_area;
    GtkWidget *vbox;

    /* --- Initialize GTK+ --- */
    gtk_init (&argc, &argv);

    if (argc > 1) {
        bUseMask = FALSE;
    }

    /* --- Create the top-level window --- */
    window = gtk_window_new (GTK_WINDOW_TOPLEVEL);

    vbox = gtk_hbox_new (FALSE, 0);
    gtk_container_add (GTK_CONTAINER (window), vbox);
    gtk_widget_show (vbox);

    gtk_signal_connect (GTK_OBJECT (window), "destroy",
                GTK_SIGNAL_FUNC (quit), NULL);

    /* --- Create the drawing area  --- */
    drawing_area = gtk_drawing_area_new ();
    gtk_drawing_area_size (GTK_DRAWING_AREA (drawing_area), 200, 300);
    gtk_box_pack_start (GTK_BOX (vbox), drawing_area, TRUE, TRUE, 0);
```

```
        gtk_widget_show (drawing_area);

        /* --- Signals used to handle backing pixmap --- */
        gtk_signal_connect (GTK_OBJECT (drawing_area), "expose_event",
                    (GtkSignalFunc) expose_event, NULL);
        gtk_signal_connect (GTK_OBJECT(drawing_area),"configure_event",
                    (GtkSignalFunc) configure_event, NULL);

        /* --- Show the window --- */
        gtk_widget_show (window);

        /* --- Repaint every so often --- */
        gtk_timeout_add (100, Repaint, drawing_area);

        /* --- Load all these sprites --- */
        LoadPixmaps (window, &man, walk);
        LoadPixmaps (window, &bike, sprite_bike);
        LoadPixmaps (window, &woman, sprite_woman);
        LoadPixmaps (window, &police, sprite_police);
        LoadPixmaps (window, &ball1, sprite_ball);
        LoadPixmaps (window, &car1, sprite_car);

        /* --- Position them --- */
        bike.x = 30;
        bike.y = 60;

        man.x = 50;
        man.y = 60;

        man.x = 60;
        man.y = 60;

        police.x = 60;
        police.y = 90;

        ball1.x = 0;
        ball1.y = 90;

        car1.x = 0;
        car1.y = 120;

        /* --- Call gtk-main loop --- */
        gtk_main ();

        return 0;
}
```

# Video Games

GDK can do more than simple animation. You can use the information in the previous section to create the basics for a game modeled after the 1980s video arcade game Defender. For those too young to remember, Defender was a game where the hero flew around a planet keeping his people from being plucked by the invading aliens. The aliens would attempt to pick up the people from the surface of the planet and carry them to the top of the screen, at which point the aliens would mutate. The mutation would destroy the person carried to the top and create a deadlier alien.

I had to recreate the game mostly from memory (I could not find a local arcade that carried what would be considered an antique in the video game world). I also had to eliminate some of the original features (because of space limitations): There is no scoring, and some of the aliens from the original game are missing. The purpose here is to illustrate the capabilities of the GDK in a short game that can be extended. (As always, the extension is left as an exercise.)

## Games with GTK+/GDK

For this program, you use some of what you learned about sprites and animation to write the framework of a game. The animation in Defender is similar to the animation you did earlier except that now the player controls one of the sprites and the computer controls the behavior of the other sprites and the interaction between all the sprites. As you can probably tell, you can use GTK+ and GDK to create games that are more elaborate than this simple version of Defender.

The real video game is much more complex, but this example illustrates that GTK+ can be used for a video game with a fairly low impact on CPU, especially on newer hardware. (In other words, on a Pentium 133 the game ran well with low CPU usage. It probably wouldn't play very well on either a 386 or a 486SX-16.)

## Game Breakdown

There are several factors to consider when creating a game: Game input, graphics, artificial intelligence, special effects, collisions, level enhancements, and scoring are just some of the items you might add when writing this type of game. We aren't going to consider all these factors. For instance, this version of Defender does not implement scoring and does not have game levels. Progressively harder game levels are necessary for a *real* game: Without variety and challenge, the game suffers a quick death in the discount bin.

### Input

The keyboard is one input device that everyone should have available, so it is the device that players use for this game. The game has movement (left, right, up, and down) and the capability to fire at the aliens (see Figure 13.3). The movement can be done with the arrow keys, and the firing can be done with the Spacebar, but it's never quite that easy.

Writing games is different from writing applications. With a game, you have to know which keys are pressed at all times. For instance, a player could be holding down a direction key and tapping the Spacebar at the same time to shoot down an alien. This technique won't work with GTK+ by default, because the last key that was pressed is the one sent to the application. If the user holds down the key, it will repeat. If other keys were already down when a new key is pressed, those other keys are ignored.

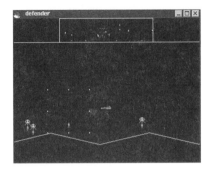

**Figure 13.3**   Some landers are grabbing humans—one lander has exploded, dropping a human.

### Tracking the Keypresses

You can get around the keypress problem by using the `"key_press_event"` signal and the `"key_release_event"` signal. When a key is pressed, the `"key_press_event"` signal is sent, and when a key is released, the `"key_release_event"` is sent. Well…not quite. The `"key_release_event"` is not sent by default, so just putting a callback on it won't work. To make sure you get the event, the `gtk_widget_set_events` function needs to be called with `GDK_KEY_RELEASE_MASK`. This step causes the `"key_release_event"` to be sent to the window. GTK+ masks out these "minor" signals, so you have to tell GTK+ that you really want them.

### Repeating Keys

The repeating keys aren't necessary here, although the only effect on the application of holding down multiple keys is to cause unnecessary processing of the keys and weird keystroke combinations. The `gdk_key_repeat_disable` function turns off the repeating keys in the application. After the function is called, any key gets only one `"key_press_event"` when it's pressed, even if the user holds down the key. The problem with the `gdk_key_repeat_disable` function is that its effects are global—not just to the game, but to all applications that are running. To prevent the game from affecting other applications the `gtk_key_repeat_disable` function is enabled within the application's `"focus_in_event"` that indicates the game has the focus. Should the focus leave the game for another application, the `"focus_out_event"` callback makes a call to the `gdk_key_repeat_restore` function, which enables the key to repeat when the user leaves the game to work on that spreadsheet when the boss walks by.

## Graphics

The game has several graphical elements: a radar screen that shows all the units in the game, the main screen where most of the action occurs, sprites for each game piece, and some special effects. Each unit in the game is a pixmap loaded from .xpm data within the application. The game is double buffered to provide smooth animation. For every frame of the game, the entire screen is redrawn. First the background is cleared, next the units that are on screen are drawn, and then the radar is drawn— showing all the units. When all the drawing has been completed, the image is transferred from the background to the drawing area widget.

The graphics in the main screen are drawn from pixmaps. The graphics in the radar, however, are drawn using colorful dots. Each color represents a different unit so that, after a while, spotting the various units is easy. Even the missiles that the aliens fire and the explosions show up in the radar!

## Artificial Intelligence (AI)

Every unit in the game has its own priorities. The AI in this game is primitive but accomplishes the task of making it a challenge, especially when more units are added—and you can actually lose the game. (The collision detection for the player is disabled.)

The game has only two units with AI, and they each try to accomplish specific tasks. The landers, which search for people to pick up, are programmed to move horizontally until they find someone. When the landers are directly above a human on the surface, they drop down and try to bring the person to the top of the screen where they (the aliens) can turn into mutants (see Figure 13.4). The mutants hunt down the player—they are programmed to move in a somewhat random fashion, but always toward the player.

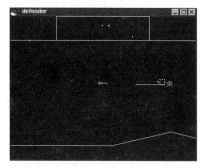

**Figure 13.4**  The hero shoots a pair of mutants—one is killed, and the other is about to die.

The AI for the mutant has one of four outcomes to move in the -x- direction—move away from the player, stay at the location, move toward the player, or move toward the player in a big leap. Fifty percent of the time, the mutant is moving toward the player. The mutant can still hop backward in the chaotic motion, but over the long term, the mutant moves toward the hero. The movement along the -y- direction is similar, but occurs only if the hero is in sight. Otherwise, the movement along the y-axis is random. The movement is programmed in the `AIModule` function. Each unit has a chance of firing at the player when he's within range. The mutants, of course, have a higher chance of firing.

## Game Internals

The game needs to keep track of all the specific units as well as their positions in the world. The game sprites and the mountains are the most important items to keep track of. The sprites are always moving in the game, and although the mountains don't move, they *appear* to move as the hero flies around. Their position (relative to the hero) is changing, and the mountains that get drawn on the screen change as the hero moves horizontally. Because the world "wraps around," the code for computing distances and directions between units is a little complex. To make things simple, all units use the same data structure, although they don't all use every field.

### Data Structures

The two basic data structures are the `typSprite` data structure and the `typUnit`. The `typSprite` contains the pixmap information including the sprite mask, height, and width. The `typUnit` data structure contains the information about all the units in the game. The player, the aliens, the missiles, and even the explosions are just `typUnits`. The `typUnit` stores the unit type (`LANDER`, `MUTANT`, `MISSILE`, `EXPLOSION`, and so on), the coordinates of the unit, velocity, life, and chance of firing on the player. The *life* aspect of the specific units probably needs a little explaining.

The life of most objects is *forever*, or at least until the object gets blasted, but some units have a life expectancy. For instance, missiles fired from the aliens eventually "die," so they're given a life that's decremented as the missile moves away from the alien…until the life reaches zero and it disappears. Explosions are similar to missiles in that they also have a life expectancy—except that the explosions are really eight small sprites thrown in many directions to simulate an explosion. A linked list (`GList *`) keeps track of all units except for the player/hero. Thus the linked list contains the aliens, the missiles, and all eight pieces of every explosion.

### Mountains

The mountains are generated to show motion when the aliens or people are not visible on the screen or have been destroyed. Mountains act as a reference point in the game to help simulate motion. They are generated by creating random peaks (x, y) and then use the peaks to build a list of points that make up the mountains' peaks and valleys.

### Calculations

Because the game is a virtual world going from 0 to X_RANGE and back to 0, a few additional steps are required when calculating distance or direction. Assume X_RANGE is 2000. If the player's x value is 1999 and an enemy's x value is 1, the distance between them is not 1998, but rather 2 because the world scrolls from 1999 back to 0.

### Data Types

Now that you have an understanding of what the program is supposed to do, let's go through it. The data types and graphics are covered first, followed by the implementation code.

## *defender.h*

```
/*
 * Directions the player can move.
 */
enum {
    MOVE_LEFT,
    MOVE_RIGHT,
    MOVE_UP,
    MOVE_DOWN
};


/*
 * The cast of characters in the game.
 */
enum {
  HERO,      /* --- player --- */
  PERSON,    /* --- people on the surface --- */
  LANDER,    /* --- alien trying to pluck people --- */
  MUTANT,    /* --- alien that took person to top and mutated --- */
  MISSILE,   /* --- alien shoots at player --- */
  LASER,     /* --- player shoots at alien --- */
  EXPLOSION /* --- somebody goes kaboom --- */

};


/*
 * Data structure used by all game units.
 */
typedef struct unit {

    int bDestroy;             /* --- Scheduled to be destroyed --- */
```

```
    int direction;        /* --- Which direction is unit going? --- */
    int type;             /* --- Unit type --- */
    float pctFiring;      /* --- Chance of firing on player --- */
    float x;              /* --- Position --- */
    float y;              /* --- Position --- */
    float vx;             /* --- Velocity --- */
    float vy;             /* --- Velocity --- */
    int life;             /* --- Life left --- */
    struct unit *lockunit; /* --- Units locked to it --- */

} typUnit;



typedef struct {

    int x;
    int y;

} typPoint;



typedef struct {

    typPoint start;
    typPoint peak;
    typPoint end;

} typMountain;



/*
 * The sprites used to draw the units on the screen
 */
typedef struct {

    char **xpm_data;      /* --- Original xpm data --- */
    GdkPixmap *pixmap;    /* --- Pixmap --- */
    GdkBitmap *mask;      /* --- Pixmap mask --- */
    int height;           /* --- Height of sprite --- */
    int width;            /* --- Width of sprite --- */

} typSprite;
```

***mutant.h***

The mutant.h contains the graphics for all the characters in the game.

```
/*
 * Graphics for all the characters in the
 * defender-like game.
 */

static char * xpm_missile[] = {
"2 2 2 1",
"      c None",
"X     c #ffffff",
"XX",
"XX",
};


static char * xpm_mutant[] = {
"16 12 4 1",
"      c None",
"b     c #8888ff",
"r     c #FF3366",
"G     c #00AA00",
"      bbbr       ",
"    rrbbbrrr     ",
"   GrrbbbrrrG    ",
"  GGr  rr  rGG   ",
"  GGr  rr  rGG   ",
"  GGrrrrrrrrGG   ",
"   GGrrrrrrGG    ",
"    GGGrrGGG     ",
"    GG rr GG     ",
"   GG  rr  GG    ",
"  GG   rr   GG   ",
" GG    rr    GG  ",
};


static char * xpm_lander[] = {
"16 12 4 1",
"      c None",
"y     c #ffaa00",
"g     c #88FF88",
"G     c #009900",
"     yyyy        ",
"    GGyyyyGG     ",
```

```
"    GGGGggGGGG    ",
"  GGG  gg  GGG   ",
"  GGG  gg  GGG   ",
"  GGGgggggGGG    ",
"    GGGggggGGG   ",
"     GGGGGGGG    ",
"    GG GG GG     ",
"    GG GG GG     ",
"  GG    GG    GG ",
" GG     GG     GG ",
};

static char * xpm_ship1 [] = {
"22 7 4 1",
"  c None",
"x c #777777",
"p c #ff66ff",
"o c #cccccc",
"    x                 ",
"   xxx                ",
"  xxxxx               ",
"xxxxxxxxxxxxxpp        ",
"xxxxxxxxxxxxxxxxxxoo  ",
"pppppxxooxxxxxxxxooo",
"  pppppxxoo            "
};


static char * xpm_ship2 [] = {
"22 7 4 1",
"  c None",
"x c #777777",
"p c #ff66ff",
"o c #cccccc",
"                x    ",
"               xxx   ",
"              xxxxx  ",
"      ppxxxxxxxxxxxxx",
" ooxxxxxxxxxxxxxxxxx",
"oooxxxxxxxxxooxxpppppp",
"            ooxxppppp "
};


static char * xpm_man[] = {
"6 10 4 1",
```

```
"        c None",
"y       c #ffaa00",
"p       c #CC00CC",
"P       c #FF44FF",
"   pp   ",
"   yP   ",
"  yPPP  ",
"  PPPP  ",
"  PPPP  ",
"  PPPP  ",
"   pp   ",
"   pp   ",
"   pp   ",
"   pp   ",
};
```

### animate.c

The code in animate.c does not have any of the game logic. It's concerned with creating the window and event processing. The underlying logic could be any game; it
just happens to be a Defender clone in this case.

```
/*
 * Auth: Eric Harlow
 * File: animate.c
 *
 * Linux application development
 *
 * Defender game.
 */

#include <gtk/gtk.h>
#include <gdk/gdkkeysyms.h>
#include "defender.h"


/* --- Backing pixmap for drawing area  --- */
GdkPixmap *pixmap = NULL;


/*
 * DisplaySprite
 *
 * Display the sprite on the drawing_area at the prescribed
 * coordinates.  Use a mask so that we do not draw the
 * invisible area - it should be transparent.
 *
```

```
 * drawing_area - where to draw the sprite
 * sprite - the sprite to draw
 * x, y - position to draw the sprite.
 */
void DisplaySprite (GtkWidget *drawing_area, typSprite *sprite, int x,
➥int y)
{
    GdkGC *gc;
    int midx, midy;

    /* --- Get gc of the normal style --- */
    gc = drawing_area->style->fg_gc[GTK_STATE_NORMAL];

    /* --- Set up the clip mask and origin --- */
    gdk_gc_set_clip_mask (gc, sprite->mask);
    gdk_gc_set_clip_origin (gc, x, y);

    /* --- Copy pixmap to the window --- */
    gdk_draw_pixmap (pixmap,
         drawing_area->style->fg_gc[GTK_STATE_NORMAL],
         sprite->pixmap,
         0, 0, x, y,
         sprite->width, sprite->height);

    /* --- Clear the clip mask when done. --- */
    gdk_gc_set_clip_mask (gc, NULL);
}



/*
 * Repaint
 *
 * data - widget to repaint
 */
gint Repaint (gpointer data)
{
    GtkWidget*   drawing_area = (GtkWidget *) data;
    GdkRectangle  update_rect;
    static offset = 0;                  -
    int nTop;

    /* --- Draw the game on the background. --- */
    DrawScreen (pixmap, drawing_area);

    /* --- Copy background to screen --- */
```

```
        update_rect.x = 0;
        update_rect.y = 0;
        update_rect.width = drawing_area->allocation.width;
        update_rect.height = drawing_area->allocation.height;

        /* --- Copy the background to the foreground --- */
        gtk_widget_draw (drawing_area, &update_rect);

        return TRUE;
}


/*
 * configure_event
 *
 * Create a new backing pixmap of the appropriate size.
 * Of course, this is called whenever the window is
 * resized.  We have to free up things we allocated.
 */
static gint configure_event (GtkWidget *widget, GdkEventConfigure *event)
{
        /* --- Free background if we created it --- */
        if (pixmap) {
                gdk_pixmap_unref (pixmap);
        }

        /* --- Create a new pixmap with new size --- */
        pixmap = gdk_pixmap_new (widget->window,
                        widget->allocation.width,
                        widget->allocation.height,
                        -1);

        return TRUE;
}



/*
 * GotFocus
 *
 * Called when the window gets the focus.  This is necessary
 * because the keys repeat themeselves and block out other
 * keys when pressed at the same time.  The only way around
 * this is to disable that behavior and handle the key "up"
 * and "down" ourselves.  Of course, this change is global
 * across all applications, so we should set it only when we
 * have the focus.
 */
static gint GotFocus (GtkWidget *widget, gpointer data)
```

```
{
    gdk_key_repeat_disable ();
}

/*
 * LostFocus
 *
 * See GotFocus.  Because the change is global, we should
 * restore the repeat so that other applications aren't
 * messed up.
 */
static gint LostFocus (GtkWidget *widget, gpointer data)
{
    gdk_key_repeat_restore ();
}


/*
 * KeyPress
 *
 * Hey, a keypress.  Add the key to the list of
 * keys currently being pressed.
 */
static gint KeyPress (GtkWidget *widget, GdkEventKey *event)
{

    AddKey (event);
}

/*
 * KeyRelease
 *
 * Hey, they let go of a keypress.  Remove the
 * key from the list of keys that is currently
 * being pressed.
 */
static gint KeyRelease (GtkWidget *widget, GdkEventKey *event)
{
    RemoveKey (event);
}

/*
 * expose_event
 *
 * When the window is exposed to the viewer or
 * the gdk_widget_draw routine is called, this
```

```
 * routine is called.  Copies the background pixmap
 * to the window.
 */
gint expose_event (GtkWidget *widget, GdkEventExpose *event)
{

    /* --- Copy pixmap to the window --- */
    gdk_draw_pixmap (widget->window,
        widget->style->fg_gc[GTK_WIDGET_STATE (widget)],
        pixmap,
        event->area.x, event->area.y,
        event->area.x, event->area.y,
        event->area.width, event->area.height);

    return FALSE;
}


/*
 * GetPen
 *
 * Get a pen using the GdkColor passed in.  The "pen"
 * (just a GdkGC) is created and returned ready for
 * use.
 */
GdkGC *GetPen (GdkColor *c)
{
    GdkGC *gc;

    /* --- Create a gc --- */
    gc = gdk_gc_new (pixmap);

    /* --- Set the foreground to the color --- */
    gdk_gc_set_foreground (gc, c);

    /* --- Return it. --- */
    return (gc);
}


/*
 * NewColor
 *
 * Create and allocate a GdkColor with the color
 * specified in the parameter list.
 */
```

```
GdkColor *NewColor (long red, long green, long blue)
{
    /* --- Get the color --- */
    GdkColor *c = (GdkColor *) g_malloc (sizeof (GdkColor));

    /* --- Fill it in. --- */
    c->red = red;
    c->green = green;
    c->blue = blue;

    gdk_color_alloc (gdk_colormap_get_system (), c);

    return (c);
}


/*
 * quit
 *
 * Get out of the application
 */
void quit ()
{
    gtk_exit (0);
}



/*
 * main
 *
 * Program begins here.
 */
int main (int argc, char *argv[])
{
    GtkWidget *window;
    GtkWidget *drawing_area;
    GtkWidget *vbox;

    StartGame ();

    gtk_init (&argc, &argv);

    window = gtk_window_new (GTK_WINDOW_TOPLEVEL);
    /*--- Don't allow window to be resized ---*/
    gtk_window_set_policy (GTK_WINDOW(WINDOW), FALSE, FALSE, TRUE);
    vbox = gtk_hbox_new (FALSE, 0);
    gtk_container_add (GTK_CONTAINER (window), vbox);
```

```
   gtk_widget_show (vbox);

   gtk_signal_connect (GTK_OBJECT (window), "destroy",
               GTK_SIGNAL_FUNC (quit), NULL);

   /* --- Create the drawing area  --- */
   drawing_area = gtk_drawing_area_new ();
   gtk_drawing_area_size (GTK_DRAWING_AREA (drawing_area), 400,
➡GetGameHeight ());
   gtk_box_pack_start (GTK_BOX (vbox), drawing_area, TRUE, TRUE, 0);

   gtk_widget_show (drawing_area);

   gtk_widget_set_events (window, GDK_KEY_RELEASE_MASK);

   /* --- Signals used to handle backing pixmap --- */
   gtk_signal_connect (GTK_OBJECT (drawing_area), "expose_event",
               (GtkSignalFunc) expose_event, NULL);
   gtk_signal_connect (GTK_OBJECT (drawing_area), "configure_event",
               (GtkSignalFunc) configure_event, NULL);

   /* --- Focus signals --- */
   gtk_signal_connect (GTK_OBJECT (window), "focus_in_event",
               (GtkSignalFunc) GotFocus, NULL);
   gtk_signal_connect (GTK_OBJECT (window), "focus_out_event",
               (GtkSignalFunc) LostFocus, NULL);

   /* --- Key press signals --- */
   gtk_signal_connect (GTK_OBJECT (window), "key_press_event",
               (GtkSignalFunc) KeyPress, NULL);
   gtk_signal_connect (GTK_OBJECT (window), "key_release_event",
               (GtkSignalFunc) KeyRelease, NULL);

   /* --- Show the window --- */
   gtk_widget_show (window);

   /* --- Repaint every second --- */
   gtk_timeout_add (100, Repaint, drawing_area);

   LoadImages (window);

   /* --- Call gtk-main loop --- */
   gtk_main ();

   return 0;
}
```

```
/*
 * GetWidthHeight
 *
 * Get the height and width of the pixmap from the xpm data.
 */
void GetWidthHeight (gchar **xpm, int *width, int *height)
{

        sscanf (xpm [0], "%d %d", width, height);

}
```

### keys.c

The file keys.c keeps track of which keys are pressed, and handles calling the appropriate movement and firing functions based on the keys that are being pressed.

```
/*
 * Auth: Eric Harlow
 * File: keys.c
 * Developing Linux Applications
 */


#include <gtk/gtk.h>
#include <gdk/gdkkeysyms.h>
#include "defender.h"


/*
 * Movement
 */
int keyLeft = 0;
int keyRight = 0;
int keyUp = 0;
int keyDown = 0;

/*
 * Firing
 */
int keyFire = 0;

/*
 * AddKey
 *
 * Add the key to the keys that are being kept
 * track of.  We only keep track of a few of the keys,
 * and we ignore the rest.
```

```
    */
void AddKey (GdkEventKey *event)
{
switch (event->keyval) {

        /* --- Left arrow --- */
        case GDK_Left:
            keyLeft = TRUE;
            break;

        /* --- Right arrow --- */
        case GDK_Right:
            keyRight = TRUE;
            break;

        /* --- Up arrow --- */
        case GDK_Up:
            keyUp = TRUE;
            break;

        /* --- Down arrow --- */
        case GDK_Down:
            keyDown = TRUE;
            break;

        /* --- Space --- */
        case ' ':
            keyFire = TRUE;
            break;

        /* --- Ignore the rest --- */
        default:
            break;
    }
}


/*
 * RemoveKey
 *
 * If we're keeping track of a key and the key
 * goes up, we flag it as not being pressed.
 */
void RemoveKey (GdkEventKey *event)
{
    switch (event->keyval) {
```

```
            case GDK_Left:
                keyLeft = FALSE;
                break;

            case GDK_Right:
                keyRight = FALSE;
                break;

            case GDK_Up:
                keyUp = FALSE;
                break;

            case GDK_Down:
                keyDown = FALSE;
                break;

            case ' ':
                keyFire = FALSE;
                break;

            default:
                break;
        }
    }


/*
 * HandleKeysPressed
 *
 * When it comes time to move everyone, this
 * routine is called to move/fire based on the
 * keys that are currently pressed.
 */
void HandleKeysPressed ()
{

    /*
     * Try and move in each direction
     */
    if (keyLeft) {
        HeroMove (MOVE_LEFT);
    }

    if (keyRight) {
        HeroMove (MOVE_RIGHT);
    }
```

```
    if (keyUp) {
        HeroMove (MOVE_UP);
    }

    if (keyDown) {
        HeroMove (MOVE_DOWN);
    }

    /*
     * Try and fire.
     *
     * Of course, once we fire, we clear the flag so
     * the player has to hit the key for multiple shots.
     * Otherwise they could just hold down the key.
     */
    if (keyFire) {

        /* --- Zap --- */
        HeroFire ();

        /* --- Oh my, key is good for only one shot --- */
        keyFire = FALSE;
    }
}
```

### defender.c

This file is the main module for all the game logic and drawing. It doesn't care about the front end at all—just about painting the drawing area that makes up the game space.

```
/*
 * File: defender.c
 * Auth: Eric Harlow
 *
 * Sort of like the 1980s game Defender, but not a
 * complete version.
 *
 */

#include <gtk/gtk.h>
#include "defender.h"
#include "defproto.h"
#include "mutant.h"
#include "math.h"

/*
 * How many people and aliens should the game start
```

```
 * out with?
 */
#define START_ALIENS 10
#define START_PEOPLE 10


/*
 * These are for the acceleration of the player/hero, the
 * effect of friction to slow him down, and the maximum
 * velocity that can be attained.
 */
#define FRICTION .5
#define MAX_SPEED 16
#define ACCELERATION 3.5


/*
 * Of course, the laser has to be configurable too.  The
 * laser beam has a speed (how fast it travels out) and
 * a length (primarily for show).
 */
#define LASER_LENGTH 60
#define LASER_SPEED 60


/*
 * Range of the game.
 */
#define X_RANGE 2000


/*
 * How high the mountain peaks are.
 */
#define MAX_PEAK 150


/*
 * The number of mountain peaks generated.
 */
#define NUM_PEAKS 10


/*
 * --- Trigger happiness
 *
 * The mutants are much more trigger happy than the landers
 * are.
 */
#define LANDER_TRIGGER_PCT 3
#define MUTANT_TRIGGER_PCT 6
```

```
/*
 * During an explosion, we use eight sprites spiraling away
 * from where the item exploded.  These are the eight
 * directions.
 */
int x_exp[] = {1, 1, 0, -1, -1, -1, 0, 1};
int y_exp[] = {0, 1, 1, 1, 0, -1, -1, -1};




/*
 * How big is the radar screen?
 */
#define RADAR_WIDTH 200
#define RADAR_HEIGHT 50

/*
 * How big are other things in the screen?
 */
#define GAME_HEIGHT 220
#define BOTTOM_HEIGHT 30
#define PERSON_HEIGHT (RADAR_HEIGHT+GAME_HEIGHT+7)

/*
 * Colors used for drawing
 */
GdkGC *penGreen = NULL;
GdkGC *penWhite = NULL;
GdkGC *penPurple = NULL;
GdkGC *penRed = NULL;

/*
 * Variables used in calculations
 */
int nShipAdjustment;
int nRelativeAdjustment;
int nScreenWidth;

/*
 * Define the sprites for the cast of characters.
 */
typSprite sprite_man[1]    = { { xpm_man, NULL, NULL, 0, 0 } };
typSprite sprite_ship1[1]  = { { xpm_ship1, NULL, NULL, 0, 0 } };
typSprite sprite_ship2[1]  = { { xpm_ship2, NULL, NULL, 0, 0 } };
typSprite sprite_lander[1] = { { xpm_lander, NULL, NULL, 0, 0 } };
typSprite sprite_mutant[1] = { { xpm_mutant, NULL, NULL, 0, 0 } };
```

```
typSprite sprite_missile[1] = { { xpm_missile, NULL, NULL, 0, 0 } };

/*
 * The ship could be pointing left or right (sprite_ship1,
 * sprite_ship2) - however, sprite_ship is what's used to
 * draw it.  If the ship changes direction, then this
 * should also be adjusted.
 */
typSprite *sprite_ship = sprite_ship1;


/*
 * List of mountain peaks.
 */
GList *terrainList = NULL;

/*
 * All the units in the game.
 */
GList *unitList = NULL;

/*
 * The hero.
 */
typUnit *hero = NULL;


/*
 * Prototypes.
 */
GdkColor *NewColor (long red, long green, long blue);
GdkGC *GetPen (GdkColor *c);
void GetWidthHeight (gchar **xpm, int *width, int *height);
void DisplaySprite (GtkWidget *drawing_area, typSprite *sprite, int x,
→int y);


/*
 * UnitScreenX
 *
 * Convert the unit's X coordinates to screen coordinates
 * relative to the hero's coordinates.
 */
int UnitScreenX (typUnit *unit)
{
    int xPos;
```

```
    /* --- Adjust -x- if out of range --- */
    if (unit->x < 0) {
        unit->x += X_RANGE;
    } else if (unit->x > X_RANGE) {
        unit->x -= X_RANGE;
    }

    /* --- Make it relative --- */
    xPos = (int) (unit->x - nRelativeAdjustment);

    /* --- Readjust -x- if out of range --- */
    if (xPos < 0) xPos += X_RANGE;
    if (xPos > X_RANGE) xPos -= X_RANGE;

    return (xPos);
}


/*
 * ScreenX
 *
 * Take the game -x- value and convert it to the screen
 * -x- value.
 */
int ScreenX (int x)
{
    int xPos;

    /* --- Adjust if out of range --- */
    if (x < 0) {

        x += X_RANGE;

    } else if (x > X_RANGE) {

        x -= X_RANGE;
    }

    /* --- Make it absolute --- */
    xPos = (int) (x - nRelativeAdjustment);

    /* --- Readajust if out of range --- */
    if (xPos < (-(X_RANGE - nScreenWidth) / 2)) {

        xPos += X_RANGE;
```

```
    } else if (xPos > ((X_RANGE - nScreenWidth) / 2)) {

        xPos -= X_RANGE;
    }

    return (xPos);
}


/*
 * GameX
 *
 * Take a screen -x- value and convert it to the
 * game coordinate -x- value.
 */
int GameX (int x)
{
    int xPos;

    /* --- Relative to the hero --- */
    xPos = (int) (x + nRelativeAdjustment);

    /* --- Make sure it's not out of range --- */
    if (xPos < 0) xPos += X_RANGE;
    if (xPos > X_RANGE) xPos -= X_RANGE;

    return (xPos);
}


/*
 * Move
 *
 * Move a unit in the X direction by vx (velocity in x) and
 * in the Y direction by vy.
 */
void Move (typUnit *unit)
{

    /* --- Move the unit --- */
    unit->y += unit->vy;
    unit->x += unit->vx;

    /* --- But keep it within the world --- */
    if (unit->x < 0) unit->x += X_RANGE;
    if (unit->x > X_RANGE) unit->x -= X_RANGE;
```

```
}


/*
 * LoadPixmaps
 *
 * Load the image into the sprite.
 */
void LoadPixmaps (GtkWidget *widget, typSprite *sprites)
{

    /* --- Create a pixmap from the xpm data --- */
    sprites->pixmap = gdk_pixmap_create_from_xpm_d (
                            widget->window,
                            &sprites->mask,
                            NULL,
                            sprites->xpm_data);

    /* --- Get the width and height --- */
    GetWidthHeight (sprites->xpm_data,
                    &sprites->width,
                    &sprites->height);

}

/*
 * LoadImages
 *
 * Load up the images so that we can display them in the
 * game and configure the colors.
 */
void LoadImages (GtkWidget *window)
{
    /* --- Load up the images --- */
    LoadPixmaps (window, sprite_man);
    LoadPixmaps (window, sprite_ship1);
    LoadPixmaps (window, sprite_ship2);
    LoadPixmaps (window, sprite_lander);
    LoadPixmaps (window, sprite_mutant);
    LoadPixmaps (window, sprite_missile);

    /* --- Get the colors defined --- */
    penRed = GetPen (NewColor (0xffff, 0x8888, 0x8888));
    penGreen = GetPen (NewColor (0, 0xffff, 0));
    penPurple = GetPen (NewColor (0xffff, 0, 0xffff));
    penWhite = GetPen (NewColor (0xffff, 0xffff, 0xffff));
```

```
    }


    /*
     * CreateHero
     *
     * Create the typUnit for the player and initialize
     * it with the player settings.
     */
    typUnit *CreateHero ()
    {
        /* --- Allocate the memory --- */
        hero = g_malloc (sizeof (typUnit));

        /* --- Initialize player information --- */
        hero->bDestroy = FALSE;
        hero->direction = 1;
        hero->type = HERO;
        hero->x = 0;
        hero->y = 150;
        hero->vx = 0;
        hero->vy = 0;
        hero->lockunit = NULL;

        /* --- Return object. --- */
        return (hero);
    }



    /*
     * HeroFire
     *
     * Our hero is opening fire!  Create a laser shot
     * and add it to the global list of units.
     */
    void HeroFire ()
    {
        typUnit *laser;

        /* --- Create the laser --- */
        laser = (typUnit *) g_malloc (sizeof (typUnit));

        /* --- The direction is the same as the spaceship --- */
        laser->direction = hero->direction;

        laser->type = LASER;
```

```
    /*
     * Move the starting point of the laser in front of the
     * spaceship.
     */
    if (laser->direction > 0) {
        laser->x = hero->x + (sprite_ship->width / 2);
    } else {
        laser->x = hero->x - (sprite_ship->width / 2);
    }
    laser->y = hero->y + 4;

    laser->vx = LASER_SPEED * hero->direction;
    laser->vy = 0;
    laser->lockunit = NULL;
    laser->bDestroy = 0;

    /* --- Laser bolt lasts through two movements. --- */
    laser->life = 2;

    /* --- Add the laser to the list of units --- */
    unitList = g_list_append (unitList, laser);
}


/*
 * HeroMove
 *
 * Move the player in the direction specified.
 */
void HeroMove (int direction)
{
    switch (direction) {

        case MOVE_UP:
            hero->y -= 3;
            break;

        case MOVE_DOWN:
            hero->y += 3;
            break;

        case MOVE_LEFT:
            /*
             * Make sure the ship is pointing in the
             * correct direction.
             */
```

```
                    sprite_ship = sprite_ship2;
                    hero->direction = -1;

                    /* --- Speed up the ship --- */
                    hero->vx -= ACCELERATION;
                    break;

                case MOVE_RIGHT:
                    /*
                     * Make sure the ship is pointing in the
                     * correct direction.
                     */
                    sprite_ship = sprite_ship1;
                    hero->direction = 1;

                    /* --- Speed up the ship --- */
                    hero->vx += ACCELERATION;
                    break;
        }
}


/*
 * ApplyFriction
 *
 * Slow down gradually and make sure the player cannot go
 * into warp speed by holding down the acceleration.
 */
void ApplyFriction ()
{
    /* --- Slow ship down --- */
    if (hero->vx > FRICTION) {
        hero->vx -= FRICTION;
    } else if (hero->vx < -FRICTION) {
        hero->vx += FRICTION;
    } else {

        /* --- Speed less than friction, we stop --- */
        hero->vx = 0;
    }

    /* --- Don't let the maximum speed be exceeded --- */
    if (hero->vx > MAX_SPEED) hero->vx = MAX_SPEED;
    if (hero->vx < -MAX_SPEED) hero->vx = -MAX_SPEED;
}
```

```
/*
 * CreatePerson
 *
 * Create the little people on the planet.
 */
typUnit *CreatePerson ()
{
    typUnit *person;

    /* --- Allocate the memory --- */
    person = g_malloc (sizeof (typUnit));

    /* --- Initialize the person --- */
    person->bDestroy = FALSE;
    person->direction = 0;
    person->type = PERSON;
    person->x = rand () % X_RANGE;
    person->y = PERSON_HEIGHT;
    person->vx = 0;
    person->vy = 0;
    person->lockunit = NULL;

    return (person);
}




/*
 * PlacePeople
 *
 * Create people randomly and place them on the screen
 */
void PlacePeople ()
{
    int i;
    typUnit *person;

    /* --- Create all the little people --- */
    for (i = 0; i < START_PEOPLE; i++) {

        /* --- Create a person --- */
        person = CreatePerson ();

        /* --- Add it to the list of units --- */
        unitList = g_list_append (unitList, person);
    }
```

```
}


/*
 * CreateAlien
 *
 * Create an alien lander
 */
typUnit *CreateAlien ()
{
    typUnit *alien;

    /* --- Get the memory --- */
    alien = g_malloc (sizeof (typUnit));

    /* --- Initialize the structure --- */
    alien->bDestroy = FALSE;
    alien->pctFiring = LANDER_TRIGGER_PCT;
    alien->type = LANDER;
    alien->x = rand () % X_RANGE;
    alien->y = rand () % 50 + RADAR_HEIGHT ;
    alien->vx = 0;
    alien->vy = 0;
    alien->lockunit = NULL;

    return (alien);
}


/*
 * CreateMissile
 *
 * Missiles are what the aliens fire.  They are given
 * a fixed direction and last a limited amount of time
 * before they disappear.
 */
typUnit *CreateMissile (typUnit *alien, typUnit *hero)
{
    float flength;
    typUnit *missile;

    /* --- Allocate the memory --- */
    missile = (typUnit *) g_malloc (sizeof (typUnit));

    /* --- Initialize the structure --- */
    missile->bDestroy = FALSE;
```

```
    missile->pctFiring = 0;
    missile->type = MISSILE;
    missile->x = alien->x;
    missile->y = alien->y;

    /* --- Calculate missile velocity --- */
    missile->vx = (float) DistanceBetween (missile, hero) *
                             Direction (missile, hero);
    missile->vy = (float) (hero->y - alien->y);

    /*
     * Adjust missile velocity
     */
    flength = sqrt (missile->vx * missile->vx + missile->vy * missile-
➡>vy);
    if (flength < .1) flength = .1;
    flength /= 3;
    missile->vx /= flength;
    missile->vy /= flength;

    missile->lockunit = NULL;

    /*
     * --- This missile has a life; when it goes to zero,
     *     it gets destroyed.
     */
    missile->life = 60;

    return (missile);
}


/*
 * AddExplosion
 *
 * A unit was destroyed - we create an explosion at the
 * unit's location
 */
void AddExplosion (typUnit *unit)
{
    typUnit *frag;
    int i;

    /* --- Creating eight fragments --- */
    for (i = 0; i < 8; i++) {
```

```
        /* --- Create a fragment of the explosion --- */
        frag = (typUnit *) g_malloc (sizeof (typUnit));

        /* --- Initialize the fragment --- */
        frag->bDestroy = FALSE;
        frag->pctFiring = 0;
        frag->type = EXPLOSION;
        frag->x = unit->x;
        frag->y = unit->y;

        /* --- Moves quite fast --- */
        frag->vx = x_exp[i] * 5;
        frag->vy = y_exp[i] * 5;

        frag->lockunit = NULL;

        /* --- Short life --- */
        frag->life = 20;

        /* --- Add it to the list of units --- */
        unitList = g_list_append (unitList, frag);
    }
}


/*
 * PlaceAliens
 *
 * Create the aliens.
 */
void PlaceAliens ()
{
    int i;
    typUnit *alien;

    /* --- Create each of the aliens --- */
    for (i = 0; i < START_ALIENS; i++) {

        /* --- Create one alien --- */
        alien = CreateAlien ();

        /* --- Add it to the units list --- */
        unitList = g_list_append (unitList, alien);
    }
}
```

```
/*
 * DistanceBetween
 *
 * Calculate the distance between two units - but
 * only use the X direction to calculate the distance.
 * The distance is not just the difference between
 * the units X coordinates, but because the world
 * wraps around, we have to consider the fact that
 * the distance between 1 and X_RANGE - 1 is not
 * (X_RANGE-1) - 1
 */
int DistanceBetween (typUnit *u1, typUnit *u2)
{
    int nDistance;
    int nDistance2;

    /* --- Figure out which is greater --- */
    if (u1->x < u2->x) {

        /* --- Calculate distance both ways --- */
        nDistance = u2->x - u1->x;
        nDistance2 = X_RANGE + u1->x - u2->x;

    } else {
        /* --- Calculate distance both ways --- */
        nDistance = u1->x - u2->x;
        nDistance2 = X_RANGE + u2->x - u1->x;
    }

    /* --- Pick smaller of the distances --- */
    return ((nDistance < nDistance2) ? nDistance : nDistance2);
}


/*
 * Direction
 *
 * What is the -x- directory between the two units?
 * It's either going to be -1, 1, or 0.
 */
int Direction (typUnit *u1, typUnit *u2)
{
    int nDistance;
    int nDistance2;

    if (u1->x < u2->x) {
```

```
            /* --- Distance each way --- */
            nDistance = u2->x - u1->x;
            nDistance2 = X_RANGE + u1->x - u2->x;

        } else {
            /* --- Distance each way --- */
            nDistance2 = u1->x - u2->x;
            nDistance = X_RANGE + u2->x - u1->x;
        }

        /* --- Direction depends on closer distance --- */
        return ((nDistance < nDistance2) ? 1 : -1);
    }




    /*
     * AttemptFiring
     *
     * Have the alien fire at the hero.
     */
    void AttemptFiring (typUnit *unit)
    {
        typUnit *missile;

        /* --- Close enough to shoot at --- */
        if (DistanceBetween (hero, unit) < (nScreenWidth / 2)) {

            /* --- Random chance - less than unit's chance --- */
            if ((rand () % 100) < unit->pctFiring) {

                /* --- Create the missle going after the hero --- */
                missile = CreateMissile (unit, hero);

                /* --- Add to the list of units --- */
                unitList = g_list_append (unitList, missile);
            }
        }
    }



    /*
     * AIModule
     *
     * Contains the logic for each of the units to move.
     * Some units like landers are looking for people to
```

```
 * pick up.  Mutuants hunt down the player.  Missiles
 * just go until they die, etc.
 */
void AIModule (typUnit *unit)
{
    typUnit *tmp;
    int bestdist = 50000;
    typUnit *closest = NULL;
    GList *node;

    /*
     * Alien lander AI logic
     */
    if (unit->type == LANDER) {

        /* --- if the alien's locked on a person --- */
        if (unit->lockunit) {

            /* --- Move it up --- */
            closest = unit->lockunit;
            unit->y -= .5;
            closest->y -= .5;

            /* --- If alien's made it to the top --- */
            if (unit->y - (sprite_lander[0].height / 2) < RADAR_HEIGHT) {

                /* --- Assimilate human! --- */
                unit->y = RADAR_HEIGHT + (sprite_lander[0].height / 2);
                unit->type = MUTANT;
                unit->pctFiring = MUTANT_TRIGGER_PCT;
                unit->lockunit = NULL;
                closest->bDestroy = TRUE;
            }

            return;
        }

        /* --- Any people nearby to snatch? --- */
        for (node = unitList; node; node = node->next) {

            tmp = (typUnit *) node->data;
            if (tmp->type == PERSON && tmp->lockunit == NULL) {

                /* --- Look for a closer person --- */
                if (DistanceBetween (unit, tmp) < bestdist) {
                    closest = tmp;
```

```
                    bestdist = DistanceBetween (unit, tmp);
              }
         }
    }

    /* --- We're locked onto a target --- */
    if (bestdist <= 1) {

         /* --- Scootch it over a bit --- */
         unit->vx = 0;
         unit->x = closest->x;

         /*
          * --- Check for a lock... ---
          */

         if ((unit->y + (sprite_lander[0].height / 2) + .8) <
             (closest->y - (sprite_man[0].height / 2))) {

              /* --- Come down on it. --- */
              unit->y += .5;

         } else if ((unit->y + (sprite_lander[0].height / 2)) >
             (closest->y - (sprite_man[0].height / 2))) {

              unit->y -= .5;
         } else {

              /* --- Lock it in --- */
              unit->lockunit = closest;
              closest->lockunit = unit;
              closest->life = 20;
         }

    /* --- Anything in reasonable range? --- */
    } else if (bestdist < 20) {

         /* --- Move towards it --- */
         unit->vx = Direction (unit, closest);
         unit->x += unit->vx;
    } else {

         /*
          * --- Nothing nearby.  Move in a random direction.
          */
         if (unit->vx == 0) {
```

```
              if ((rand () % 2) == 0) {
                  unit->vx = 1;
              } else {
                  unit->vx = -1;
              }
          }
          unit->x += unit->vx;
      }

      /*
       * See if there is anything worth shooting at.
       */
      AttemptFiring (unit);

  /*
   * Mutant AI logic
   */
  } else if (unit->type == MUTANT) {

      /*
       * --- Let's go crazy.  Mutant moves almost randomly, yet
       *     slowly towards the player.
       */
      unit->vx = Direction (unit, hero) * ((rand () % 4) + 1);
      unit->vy = rand () % 5 - 2;

      /*
       * If the hero is within smelling distance, move towards
       * player in the -y- direction.
       */
      if (DistanceBetween (unit, hero) < 200) {
          if (unit->y < hero->y) unit->vy++;
          if (unit->y > hero->y) unit->vy--;
      }

      /* --- Finally move the unit --- */
      Move (unit);

      /* --- Let the mutant attempt firing --- */
      AttemptFiring (unit);

  /*
   * --- Missiles and explosions
   */
  } else if ((unit->type == MISSILE) ||
             (unit->type == EXPLOSION)) {
```

```
            /* --- These have a life.  Decrement it. --- */
            unit->life --;

            /* --- Move it. --- */
            Move (unit);

            /* --- When it reaches zero, destroy it --- */
            if (unit->life <= 0) {
                unit->bDestroy = TRUE;
            }

        /*
         * Person AI
         */
        } else if (unit->type == PERSON) {

            /*
             * Only time person moves by itself is when it's falling
             * from the sky after the alien carrying it has been shot.
             */
            if (unit->lockunit == NULL && unit->y < PERSON_HEIGHT) {

                /* --- Move it down --- */
                unit->y += 2;
            }
        }
    }
}


/*
 * GetSprite
 *
 * Get the sprite for the unit.
 */
typSprite *GetSprite (typUnit *unit)
{
    typSprite *sprite;

    /* --- Get sprite --- */
    switch (unit->type) {

        case HERO:
            sprite = sprite_ship;
            break;

        case PERSON:
```

```
                    sprite = sprite_man;
                    break;

            case LANDER:
                    sprite = sprite_lander;
                    break;

            case MUTANT:
                    sprite = sprite_mutant;
                    break;

            case MISSILE:
            case EXPLOSION:
                    sprite = sprite_missile;
                    break;

            default:
                    sprite = NULL;
                    break;
        }
        return (sprite);
}


/*
 * AnyoneBetween
 *
 * Is any unit between these coordinates?  Used by the
 * laser when computing if anything has been hit.
 */
typUnit *AnyoneBetween (int x1, int y1, int x2, int y2)
{
        GList *node;
        typUnit *unit;
        typUnit *closestUnit = NULL;
        int closestX;
        typSprite *sprite;
        int screenX;

        /* --- Check each unit --- */
        for (node = unitList; node; node = node->next) {

                unit = (typUnit *) node->data;

                /* --- If it's a bad guy --- */
                if ((unit->type == LANDER) ||
```

```
                        (unit->type == PERSON) ||
                        (unit->type == MUTANT)) {

                    /* --- Get sprite and screen position --- */
                    screenX = UnitScreenX (unit);
                    sprite = GetSprite (unit);

                    /* --- If we have a sprite --- */
                    if (sprite) {

                        /* --- If in range using -x- --- */
                        if ((screenX >= x1 && screenX <= x2) ||
                            (screenX <= x1 && screenX >= x2)) {

                            /* --- And in range using -y- --- */
                            if ((unit->y - (sprite->height / 2) < y1) &&
                                unit->y + (sprite->height / 2) > y1) {

                                /*
                                 * Haven't found a unit or this one
                                 * is closer.
                                 */
                                if ((closestUnit == NULL) ||
                                    (abs (x1 - screenX) < abs (x1 - closestX)))
                                {

                                    /* --- This is closest so far --- */
                                    closestUnit = unit;
                                    closestX = screenX;
                                }
                            }
                        }
                    }
                }
            }
        }

        return (closestUnit);
    }


    /*
     * UnitTop
     *
     * Calculate the maximum height of the unit based on the
     * radar screen and the sprite size.
     */
```

```
int UnitTop (typUnit *unit)
{
    typSprite *sprite;

    /* --- Get the sprite --- */
    sprite = GetSprite (unit);

    /* --- Add 1/2 sprite size to radar size. --- */
    return (RADAR_HEIGHT + (sprite[0].height / 2));
}


/*
 * UnitBottom
 *
 * Calculate how low the unit can appear on the screen.
 * It's partially based on the unit's size.
 */
int UnitBottom (typUnit *unit)
{
    typSprite *sprite;

    sprite = GetSprite (unit);
    return (GetGameHeight () - (sprite[0].height / 2));
}



void AdjustSpriteHeight (typUnit *unit)
{
    typSprite *sprite;
    int nTop;
    int nBottom;

    /* --- Get the sprite for the unit --- */
    sprite = GetSprite (unit);
    if (sprite == NULL) return;

    /* --- Calculate the top and bottom range of unit --- */
    nTop = UnitTop (unit);
    nBottom = UnitBottom (unit);

    /* --- Don't let them go too high or too low --- */
    if (unit->y < nTop) {
        unit->y = nTop;
```

```
        } else if (unit->y > nBottom) {
            unit->y = nBottom;
        }
    }



    /*
     * DisplayOtherUnits
     *
     * Display all the units on the screen. First, we need
     * to move the units to their new positions.
     * Some of this is done in the AI module.
     *
     */
    void DisplayOtherUnits (GdkPixmap *pixmap, GtkWidget *drawing_area)
    {
        typUnit *unit;
        typUnit *unitHit;
        GList *node;
        int xPos;
        int xPosEnd;
        typSprite *sprite;

        /* --- Each unit in the list --- */
        for (node = unitList; node; node = node->next) {

            /* --- Get the unit --- */
            unit = (typUnit *) node->data;

            /*
             * --- Run the AI module on it to move it ---
             */
            AIModule (unit);

            /*
             * If the unit was destroyed by the AI,
             * don't draw the unit.
             */
            if (unit->bDestroy) {
                continue;
            }

            /*
             * If there's no sprite for the unit,
             * we can't draw it now, can we?
             */
```

```
    sprite = GetSprite (unit);
    if (sprite == NULL) continue;

    /* --- Where on the screen is it going? --- */
    xPos = UnitScreenX (unit);

    /* --- Make sure unit doesn't go out of bounds --- */
    AdjustSpriteHeight (unit);

    /* --- Finally draw unit --- */
    DisplaySprite (drawing_area, sprite,
                (int) (xPos - sprite[0].width / 2),
                (int) (unit->y - sprite[0].height / 2));
}

/*
 * --- Once everyone is painted, fire the lasers.
 */

for (node = unitList; node; node = node->next) {

    unit = (typUnit *) node->data;

    /* --- If this is a laser --- */
    if (unit->type == LASER) {

        /* --- Get starting and ending positions --- */
        xPos = ScreenX ((int) unit->x);
        xPosEnd = xPos + LASER_LENGTH * unit->direction;

        /* --- See if anything was hit --- */
        unitHit = AnyoneBetween ((int) xPos, (int) unit->y,
                                (int) xPosEnd, (int) unit->y);
        if (unitHit) {

            /* --- Something was hit --- */

            /* --- Laser shot only goes this far --- */
            xPosEnd = UnitScreenX (unitHit);

            /* --- Destroy the unit --- */
            unitHit->bDestroy = TRUE;
            unit->bDestroy = TRUE;

            /* --- Special effects of destruction --- */
            AddExplosion (unitHit);
```

```
            }

            /* --- Draw the laser --- */
            gdk_draw_line (pixmap, penWhite,
                           xPos, unit->y,
                           xPosEnd,
                           unit->y);

            /* --- Get real coordinates of laser --- */
            unit->x = GameX (xPosEnd);

            /* --- If laser has gone too far... --- */
            if (DistanceBetween (unit, hero) > nScreenWidth / 2) {

                /* --- Destroy it --- */
                unit->bDestroy = TRUE;
            }
        }
    }
}


/*
 * Terrain functions
 *
 */


/*
 * MountainCompare
 *
 * Compare function for sorting the mountain peaks.
 */
gint MountainCompare (typMountain *m1, typMountain *m2)
{
    return (m1->start.x - m2->start.x);
}


/*
 * AddMountain
 *
 * Add a mountain peak to the list we use to keep track
 * of the mountain peaks.
 */
```

```
GList *AddMountain (GList *mountainList, int peakx, int peaky)
{
    typMountain *node;

    node = (typMountain *) g_malloc (sizeof (typMountain));
    node->start.x = peakx - peaky;
    node->start.y = 0;
    node->peak.x = peakx;
    node->peak.y = peaky;
    node->end.x = peakx + peaky;
    node->end.y = 0;

    return (g_list_insert_sorted (mountainList, node, MountainCompare));
}


/*
 * AddPoint
 *
 * Add a mountain peak at (x, y)
 */
GList *AddPoint (GList *terrainList, int x, int y)
{
    typPoint *p;

    /* --- Allocate the memory --- */
    p = (typPoint *) g_malloc (sizeof (typPoint));

    /* --- Initialize the point --- */
    p->x = x;
    p->y = y;

    /* --- Add the point to the list --- */
    terrainList = g_list_append (terrainList, p);

    return (terrainList);
}


/*
 * GenerateTerrain
 *
 * Create random mountain peaks that are used to generate
 * the background terrain.
 */
 void GenerateTerrain ()
```

```
{
    int peakx;
    int peaky;
    GList *mountainList = NULL;
    GList *node;
    typMountain *prevMountain;
    typMountain *mtn;
    int i;

    /* --- Compute the peaks --- */
    for (i = 0; i < NUM_PEAKS; i++) {
        peakx = rand () % X_RANGE;
        peaky = rand () % MAX_PEAK;

        mountainList = AddMountain (mountainList, peakx, peaky);
    }

    prevMountain = NULL;

    terrainList = AddPoint (terrainList, 0, 0);

    /* --- Compute the lines based on the peaks --- */
    for (node = mountainList; node; node = node->next) {

        mtn = (typMountain *) node->data;

        /* --- First mountain --- */
        if (prevMountain == NULL) {
            terrainList = AddPoint (terrainList, mtn->start.x, mtn-
➥>start.y);
            terrainList = AddPoint (terrainList, mtn->peak.x, mtn-
➥>peak.y);
            prevMountain = mtn;

        /* --- Don't cross paths --- */
        } else if (prevMountain->end.x < mtn->start.x) {

            terrainList = AddPoint (terrainList,
                                    prevMountain->end.x,
                                    prevMountain->end.y);
            terrainList = AddPoint (terrainList, mtn->start.x, mtn-
➥>start.y);
            terrainList = AddPoint (terrainList, mtn->peak.x, mtn-
➥>peak.y);
            prevMountain = mtn;
```

```
            /* --- Previous mountain eats this one --- */
        } else if (prevMountain->end.x > mtn->end.x) {

            /* --- Do nothing yet --- */
        } else {

            /* --- Mountains intersect --- */
            terrainList = AddPoint (terrainList,
                                    (prevMountain->end.x + mtn->start.x)
➥/ 2,
                                    (prevMountain->end.x - mtn->start.x)
➥/ 2);
            terrainList = AddPoint (terrainList, mtn->peak.x, mtn-
➥>peak.y);
            prevMountain = mtn;
        }
    }
    terrainList = AddPoint (terrainList,
                                prevMountain->end.x,
                                prevMountain->end.y);
    terrainList = AddPoint (terrainList, X_RANGE, 0);
}



void StartGame ()
{
    unitList = NULL;

    /* --- Create our hero's ship --- */
    hero = CreateHero ();

    /* --- Generate the map --- */
    GenerateTerrain ();

    /* --- Place the people --- */
    PlacePeople ();

    /* --- Place aliens --- */
    PlaceAliens ();
}

/*
 * DrawMountainSlope
 *
 * Draw the mountains in the background of the game.
```

```
 */
void DrawMountainSlope (GdkPixmap *pixmap,
                        typPoint *lastPt,
                        typPoint *pt,
                        int nTop,
                        int nBottom)
{
    int x1;
    int x2;
    int nStart;
    int nEnd;
    int nHeight;

    nHeight = nBottom - nTop;
    nStart = hero->x - (nScreenWidth / 2);
    nEnd = hero->x + (nScreenWidth / 2);

    x1 = ScreenX (lastPt->x);
    x2 = ScreenX (pt->x);

    if ((x2 < 0) ||
        (x1 > nScreenWidth)) {

        /* --- Do nothing --- */

    } else {

        /* --- Draw point --- */
        gdk_draw_line (pixmap, penWhite,
                ScreenX (lastPt->x),
                (int) (nBottom - ((lastPt->y * nHeight) / MAX_PEAK)),
                ScreenX (pt->x),
                (int) (nBottom - ((pt->y * nHeight) / MAX_PEAK)));
    }
}


void DrawMountains (GdkPixmap *pixmap,
                    GtkWidget *drawing_area,
                    int nTop, int nBottom)
{
    typPoint *lastPt;
    typPoint *pt;
    GList *node;

    lastPt = NULL;
```

```
    /* --- Where is the viewpoint from? --- */
    for (node = terrainList; node; node = node->next) {

        /* --- Get the point. --- */
        pt = (typPoint *) node->data;

        if (lastPt) {

            DrawMountainSlope (pixmap, lastPt, pt, nTop, nBottom);
        }
        lastPt = pt;
    }
}


void CalculateAdjustments (GtkWidget *drawing_area)
{
    nShipAdjustment = (drawing_area->allocation.width / 2);
    nRelativeAdjustment = hero->x - nShipAdjustment;
}


/*
 * DrawAllUnits
 *
 * Draw all the units
 */
void DrawAllUnits (GdkPixmap *pixmap,
            GtkWidget *drawing_area)
{
    /*
     * Move and display the hero
     */
    ApplyFriction ();
    Move (hero);

    /* --- Keep him in-bounds. --- */
    AdjustSpriteHeight (hero);

    DisplaySprite (drawing_area, sprite_ship,
                nShipAdjustment - (sprite_ship->width / 2),
                (int) hero->y - (sprite_ship->height / 2));
    /*
     * Move and display everyone else
     */
    DisplayOtherUnits (pixmap, drawing_area);
```

```
    }


    /*
     * DrawRadar
     *
     * Draw all the units on the radar screen.  Of course, the
     * radar screen has to be drawn and then the units have to
     * have their points converted to "radar" coordinates and
     * little dots are drawn on the screen in different colors
     * to reflect the type of each unit in the game.
     */
    void DrawRadar (GdkPixmap *pixmap, GtkWidget *drawing_area)
    {
        int    nLeft;
        GList *node;
        typUnit *unit;
        int x, y;
        int nMin;
        int newx, newy;

        /* --- Get radar coordinates --- */
        nLeft = (drawing_area->allocation.width - RADAR_WIDTH) / 2;
        nMin = hero->x - (X_RANGE / 2);

        /* --- Clear out the rectangle --- */
        gdk_draw_rectangle (pixmap, drawing_area->style->white_gc,
                            FALSE,
                            nLeft, 0, RADAR_WIDTH, RADAR_HEIGHT);


        /*
         * --- Display all the units
         */
        for (node = unitList; node; node = node->next) {

            unit = (typUnit *) node->data;
            x = unit->x;
            y = unit->y;

            if (x > hero->x + (X_RANGE / 2)) {

                x -= X_RANGE;

            } else if (x < hero->x - (X_RANGE / 2)) {

                x += X_RANGE;
```

```
        }

        /* --- Convert -x- to radar coordinates --- */
        newx = (x - nMin) * RADAR_WIDTH / X_RANGE;

        /* --- Convert -y- to radar coordinates --- */
        newy = ((y - RADAR_HEIGHT) * (RADAR_HEIGHT - 6) / GAME_HEIGHT) +
2;

        switch (unit->type) {

            case PERSON:
                gdk_draw_rectangle (pixmap, penPurple,
                        TRUE, nLeft + newx-1, newy-1, 2, 2);
                break;

            case LANDER:
                gdk_draw_rectangle (pixmap, penGreen,
                        TRUE, nLeft + newx-1, newy-1, 2, 2);
                break;

            case MUTANT:
                gdk_draw_rectangle (pixmap, penRed,
                        TRUE, nLeft + newx-1, newy-1, 2, 2);
                break;

            case MISSILE:
            case EXPLOSION:
                gdk_draw_rectangle (pixmap, penWhite,
                        TRUE, nLeft + newx, newy, 1, 1);
                break;
        }
    }

    /*
     * --- Put the hero on the screen too.
     */

    /* --- Convert -x- to radar coordinates --- */
    newx = (hero->x - nMin) * RADAR_WIDTH / X_RANGE;

    /* --- Convert -y- to radar coordinates --- */
    newy = ((hero->y - RADAR_HEIGHT) * (RADAR_HEIGHT - 6) / GAME_HEIGHT)
+ 2;

    gdk_draw_rectangle (pixmap, penWhite, TRUE,
```

```
                              nLeft + newx-1, newy-1, 2, 2);
}


/*
 * DrawScreen
 *
 * This does a lot of work.  It draws the background and
 * all the units, as well as the radar.  This routine is
 * essentially the main loop that gets called by the
 * timer every update frequency.
 */
void DrawScreen (GdkPixmap *pixmap, GtkWidget *drawing_area)
{
    /* --- Move player based on keys pressed --- */
    HandleKeysPressed ();

    /* --- Get the screen width --- */
    nScreenWidth = drawing_area->allocation.width;

    /* --- Figure out the offset of the player --- */
    CalculateAdjustments (drawing_area);

    /* --- Clear pixmap (background image) --- */
    gdk_draw_rectangle (pixmap,
            drawing_area->style->black_gc,
            TRUE,
            0, 0,
            drawing_area->allocation.width,
            drawing_area->allocation.height);

    /* --- Draw top border and radar screen --- */
    gdk_draw_line (pixmap, drawing_area->style->white_gc,
                0, RADAR_HEIGHT,
                drawing_area->allocation.width,
                RADAR_HEIGHT);

    /* --- Oh those high peaks --- */
    DrawMountains (pixmap, drawing_area,
                drawing_area->allocation.height - 65,
                drawing_area->allocation.height - BOTTOM_HEIGHT);

    /* --- Draw the characters --- */
    DrawAllUnits (pixmap, drawing_area);

    /* --- Draw the units on the radar --- */
```

```
    DrawRadar (pixmap, drawing_area);

    /* --- Look for collisions --- */
    CollisionCheck ();

    /* --- Clean up those that got destroyed --- */
    FreeDestroyedUnits ();
}



/*
 * CollisionCheck
 *
 * Hero suffers a collision?  Check for a collision
 * but don't really do anything.  This isn't really
 * a game, but rather a demo on how this could be done.
 */
void CollisionCheck ()
{
    GList *node;
    typSprite *sprite;
    int hero_x;
    int unit_x;
    typUnit *unit;

    /* --- See if anything collides with the hero. --- */
    for (node = unitList; node; node = node->next) {

        /* --- Get the unit --- */
        unit = (typUnit *) node->data;

        /* --- Get the unit's sprite --- */
        sprite = GetSprite (unit);

        if (sprite == NULL) continue;

        /* --- Eliminate non-collisions --- */
        if (hero->y + (sprite_ship->height / 2) <
            unit->y - (sprite->height / 2)) continue;

        if (hero->y - (sprite_ship->height / 2) >
            unit->y + (sprite->height / 2)) continue;

        hero_x = UnitScreenX (hero);
        unit_x = UnitScreenX (unit);
```

```
            if (hero_x + (sprite_ship->width / 2) <
                unit_x - (sprite->width / 2)) continue;

            if (hero_x - (sprite_ship->width / 2) >
                unit_x + (sprite->width / 2)) continue;

            /* --- Hero collides here since everything failed. --- */
        }
    }


/*
 * GetGameHeight
 *
 * Get the height of the game.
 */
int GetGameHeight ()
{

    return (RADAR_HEIGHT + GAME_HEIGHT + BOTTOM_HEIGHT);
}


/*
 * FreeDestroyedUnits
 *
 * The units are just marked as being destroyed.  This
 * routine goes through the list and removes all the units
 * that are marked as destroyed and frees up any memory
 * they're using.
 */
void FreeDestroyedUnits ()
{
    GList *node;
    GList *next;
    typUnit *unit;

    node = unitList;
    while (node) {

        next = node->next;

        unit = (typUnit *) node->data;

        /* --- If it's to be destroyed --- */
        if (unit->bDestroy) {
```

```
        /* --- Remove from the list of units --- */
        unitList = g_list_remove (unitList, unit);

        /* --- If unit was locked to another --- */
        if (unit->lockunit) {

            /* --- Remove lock to this unit --- */
            unit->lockunit->lockunit = NULL;
        }
        g_free (unit);
    }

    node = next;
    }
}
```

# Summary

You can use GTK+ with the GDK to create both animated graphics and video games. The performance of games within GTK+ is good for basic video games, even on slow machines. More complicated video games require faster hardware and probably a faster library.

# IV

# Extending GTK+

# 14

# Trees, *Clists*, and Tabs

THE GtkTree, GtkCList, AND GtkNotebook ARE MORE interesting widgets than the common entry widgets. These three widgets show some of the power of developing applications using GTK+ widgets. The widgets provide an object-oriented interface and make developing applications with widgets easy. The three widgets discussed here are among the more useful widgets in GTK+, but many others are available.

## Tree Widget

The tree widget (GtkTree) displays hierarchical information: a set of directories or perhaps a family tree showing your parents, their parents, and so on. Trees allow the entire hierarchy of items to be viewed, or items can be collapsed into their parent items within the tree.

Figure 14.1 shows an example of the GtkTree widget with a list box widget to display directories and files. Only directories are displayed within the tree on the left. The subdirectories of each directory within the tree are displayed as leaf nodes that can be collapsed into the parent node. The list box displays the files within a directory when it is selected in the tree. You'll create the following program as you learn about the tree widget.

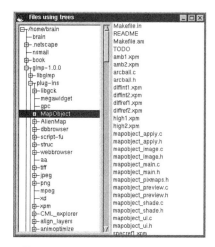

**Figure 14.1**   Tree widget in action.

## Tree Creation

You can use the `gtk_tree_new` function to create the `GtkTree` widget. The tree that is created is initially empty and needs to be populated. To create a leaf node, use the `gtk_tree_item_new_with_label` function and pass in the name of the leaf node. After the leaf node is created, it needs to be assigned to a parent node. The parent can be the `GtkTree` widget (for a top-level node) or another leaf node. Here you create a `GtkTree` widget and add a top-level node to it.

```
/* --- Create the tree --- */
tree = gtk_tree_new();

/* --- Create a leaf node --- */
leaf = gtk_tree_item_new_with_label ("Top level leaf!");

/* --- Add item to the tree --- */
gtk_tree_append (GTK_TREE (tree), leaf);

/* --- Don't forget to make tree and leaves visible --- */
gtk_widget_show (leaf);
gtk_widget_show (tree);
```

Now you can add some leaves to the tree, but adding the data that makes up the leaves requires several steps. First, you create a new `GtkTree`, using the `gtk_tree_new` function. Next, you mark the tree as a subtree and assign it a parent tree item, using the `gtk_tree_item_set_subtree` function. Then you can add elements into the subtree by using the same functions you used to add elements into the tree.

```
/* --- Create a new tree item --- */
subtree = gtk_tree_new ();

/* --- Make the leaf a parent to the subtree --- */
gtk_tree_item_set_subtree (GTK_TREE_ITEM (leaf), subtree);

/* --- Create a new leaf --- */
new_leaf = gtk_tree_item_new_with_label ("leaf");

/* --- Add new leaf to the subtree --- */
gtk_tree_append (GTK_TREE (subtree), new_leaf);

/* --- Make new leaf visible --- */
gtk_widget_show (new_leaf);
```

The `gtk_tree_append` function is only one of the functions available to add items to a GtkTree. You can also use the `gtk_tree_prepend` function, which inserts at the beginning of a tree, or the `gtk_tree_insert` function to insert an item at any position within the tree.

```
/* --- Add an item at the beginning of a tree --- */
gtk_tree_prepend (GTK_TREE (tree) leaf);

/* --- Add an item at beginning using insert --- */
gtk_tree_insert (GTK_TREE (tree), leaf, 0);

/* --- Add to end of tree using insert --- */
gtk_tree_insert (GTK_TREE (tree), leaf, -1);

/* --- Insert after the second element --- */
gtk_tree_insert (GTK_TREE (tree), leaf, 2);
```

To remove items in the tree, you can use the `gtk_tree_remove_item` function. When the item is removed from the tree, all the leaf nodes of that item are also removed.

```
/* --- Remove the leaf from the tree --- */
gtk_tree_remove_item (tree, leaf);
```

To clear a tree of leaf nodes, you can use the `gtk_tree_clear_items` function. The start and end leaf positions are passed in as indicators of which items are to be deleted. To remove all children:

```
/* --- Remove all children from tree --- */
gtk_tree_clear_items (tree, 0, -1);
```

## Tree Signals

The `GtkTree` widget has some custom signals of its own. The `"SELECTION_CHANGED"`, `"SELECT_CHILD"`, and `"UNSELECT_CHILD"` signals are sent to the `GtkTree` widget to indicate the state of selected items. The tree items get the `"COLLAPSE_TREE"` and `"EXPAND_TREE"` signals.

## Building the File Viewer

Given the information introduced here, you can start building the file viewer. The file viewer consists of a `GtkTree` widget and a list box widget placed side by side within the application window. First, the main function needs to create the application window.

```
/*
 * main
 *
 * Program begins here
 */
int main (int argc, char *argv[])
{
    GtkWidget *window;
    GtkWidget *table;

    /* --- GTK initialization --- */
    gtk_init (&argc, &argv);

    /* --- Create the top window --- */
    window = gtk_window_new (GTK_WINDOW_TOPLEVEL);

    /* --- Give the window a title --- */
    gtk_window_set_title (GTK_WINDOW (window), "Files using trees");

    /* --- Set the window size --- */
    gtk_widget_set_usize (window, 250, 250);

    /* --- You should always remember to connect the delete_event
     *     to the main window.
     */
    gtk_signal_connect (GTK_OBJECT (window), "delete_event",
                        GTK_SIGNAL_FUNC (delete_event), NULL);

    gtk_widget_show (window);

    /* --- Create the tree  --- */
    CreateTree (window);

    gtk_main ();

    exit (0);
}
```

The `CreateTree` function creates a horizontal packing box so the `GtkTree` widget and the list box widget can be placed side by side. The `GtkTree` widget is placed in a scrolled window so that if the items in the tree are expanded and they exceed the height of the widget being displayed, the user can scroll around in the list using the scroll bars provided by the scrolled window. The `getcwd` function gets the current working directory from the system so that it can be displayed at the root of the `GtkTree` widget. This information tells the user the full path of the directory for the tree widget. The directory information is passed into the `CreateSubTree` function for it to populate the `GtkTree` with all the directories.

```
/*
 * CreateTree
 *
 * Create the tree that shows the file structure.
 *
 * window - parent window
 */
static void CreateTree (GtkWidget *window)
{
    char buffer[MAX_PATH];
    GtkWidget *box1;
    GtkWidget *scrolled_win;
    GtkWidget *tree;
    GtkWidget *leaf;
    GtkWidget *item1, *item2, *item3;
    GtkWidget *tree1, *tree2, *tree3;
    GtkWidget *item;

    /* --- Vertical box --- */
    box1 = gtk_hbox_new (FALSE, 0);
    gtk_container_add (GTK_CONTAINER (window), box1);
    gtk_widget_show (box1);

    /* --- Create scrolled window for the tree --- */
    scrolled_win = gtk_scrolled_window_new (NULL, NULL);
    gtk_scrolled_window_set_policy (GTK_SCROLLED_WINDOW (scrolled_win),
                                    GTK_POLICY_AUTOMATIC,
➥GTK_POLICY_AUTOMATIC);
    gtk_box_pack_start (GTK_BOX (box1), scrolled_win, TRUE, TRUE, 0);
    gtk_widget_set_usize (scrolled_win, 250, 250);
    gtk_widget_show (scrolled_win);

    /*
     * --- Create root tree widget
     */
    tree = gtk_tree_new();

    /*
     * --- Create list box
```

```
 */
listbox = gtk_list_new ();
gtk_widget_set_usize (listbox, 250, 250);
gtk_box_pack_start (GTK_BOX (box1), listbox, TRUE, TRUE, 0);
gtk_widget_show (listbox);

/* --- Add the tree to the scrolled window --- */
gtk_container_add (GTK_CONTAINER (scrolled_win), tree);

/* --- Make it visible --- */
gtk_widget_show (tree);

/*
 * --- Create root tree item widget (current directory)
 */
leaf = gtk_tree_item_new_with_label (
            getcwd (buffer, sizeof (buffer)));

/* --- Add item to the tree --- */
gtk_tree_append (GTK_TREE (tree), leaf);

/* --- Make it visible --- */
gtk_widget_show (leaf);

/* --- Create a subtree under this item --- */
CreateSubtree (getcwd (buffer, sizeof (buffer)),
            getcwd (buffer, sizeof (buffer)), leaf);

/* --- Make window visible --- */
gtk_widget_show (window);
}
```

The CreateSubtree function gets the directories that are in the path. These directories become leaf nodes to the node that represents the path. For instance, the directory book may have a directory ch1, ch2, and ch3. In this case, the book node of the tree has three children nodes—ch1, ch2, and ch3. The opendir function enables you to scan through the files and directories in any directory. Then you can use the IsDirectory function to figure out whether the item in the directory is a file or a directory. If the item is a directory, it's recursively passed to CreateSubtree to calculate the associated children nodes. Each node has a "select" signal callback so that when you click on a directory, the list box can be populated with all the files in the directory.

```
/*
 * CreateSubtree
 *
 * Adds directories into the tree control and puts in
 * an event handler so that when an item is selected
```

```
 * in the tree, the list box will be populated.
 *
 * szPath - path to add the files from
 */
static void CreateSubtree (char *szPath, char *szDir, GtkWidget* item)
{
    DIR *directory;
    struct dirent *dirEntry;
    struct stat fileStatus;
    GtkWidget* item_subtree = NULL;
    GtkWidget* item_new;
    char buffer[MAX_PATH];
    int nSubDirectories = 0;

    /* --- Read current directory --- */
    directory = opendir (szPath);

    /* --- While we are reading through the directory  --- */
    while (dirEntry = readdir (directory)) {

        /* --- Don't count these as valid directories for display --- */
        if (!strcmp (dirEntry->d_name, "..") ||
            !strcmp (dirEntry->d_name, ".")) {

            /* --- Ignore these directories ("." and "..") --- */
        } else {

            /* --- Create full path --- */
            sprintf (buffer, "%s/%s", szPath, dirEntry->d_name);

            /* --- If this is a directory --- */
            if (IsDirectory (buffer)) {

                if (item_subtree == NULL) {

                    /* --- Create a new tree item --- */
                    item_subtree = gtk_tree_new ();

                    /* --- Add the item to the tree --- */
                    gtk_tree_item_set_subtree (GTK_TREE_ITEM (item),
                                               item_subtree);

                }

                /* --- Create an entry for the file --- */
                item_new = gtk_tree_item_new_with_label
```

```
➥(dirEntry->d_name);

                    /* --- Add item to the tree --- */
                    gtk_tree_append (GTK_TREE (item_subtree), item_new);

                    /* --- Load all of its elements into the tree --- */
                    CreateSubtree (buffer, dirEntry->d_name, item_new);

                    /* --- Make it visible --- */
                    gtk_widget_show (item_new);

                    /* --- Notify when an item is selected --- */
                    gtk_signal_connect (GTK_OBJECT (item_new),
                            "select",
                            GTK_SIGNAL_FUNC (select_item),
                            g_strdup (buffer));

                }
            }
        }

    /* --- All done --- */
    closedir (directory);

    gtk_widget_show (item);
}
```

Here is the IsDirectory function that takes the name of the file/directory and uses stat to see whether the item is a file or a directory.

```
/*
 * IsDirectory
 *
 * Check to see whether the path is a directory or just a file.
 *
 * buffer - full path to check.
 *
 * returns (TRUE) if the path is a directory
 */
int IsDirectory (char *buffer)
{
    struct stat buf;

    if (stat (buffer, &buf) < 0) {

        /* --- Error - ignored --- */
        return (FALSE);
```

```
    }

    /* --- Return whether it is a directory --- */
    return (S_ISDIR (buf.st_mode));
}
```

The select_item function is called whenever an item is clicked in the tree widget. The function displays a short message (for illustration purposes) and calls the PopulateListbox function to display the list of files in the directory.

```
void select_item (GtkWidget *widget, gpointer data)
{
    printf ("item selected %s\n", (char *) data);

    PopulateList box ((char *) data);
}
```

None of the code in the PopulateListbox should need explaining. Given a path, it goes through all the files/directories in the path and populates the list box with a list of all the filenames in the path.

```
/*
 * PopulateListbox
 *
 * Adds the files for the directory into the list box.
 * Only adds files.
 *
 * szPath - path to add the files from
 */
static void PopulateListbox (char *szPath)
{
    DIR *directory;
    struct dirent *dirEntry;
    struct stat fileStatus;
    char buffer[MAX_PATH];

    /* --- Clear the list box --- */
    gtk_list_clear_items (GTK_LIST (listbox),
                          0,
                          g_list_length (GTK_LIST (listbox)->children));

    /* --- Read current directory --- */
    directory = opendir (szPath);

    /* --- While we are reading through the directory --- */
    while (dirEntry = readdir (directory)) {
```

```
                /* --- Don't count these as valid directories for display --- */
                if (!strcmp (dirEntry->d_name, "..") ||
                    !strcmp (dirEntry->d_name, ".")) {

                    /* --- Ignore these directories ("." and "..") --- */
                } else {

                    /* --- Create full path --- */
                    sprintf (buffer, "%s/%s", szPath, dirEntry->d_name);

                    /* --- If this not directory --- */
                    if (!IsDirectory (buffer)) {

                        /* --- Add file to the list box --- */
                        AddListItem (listbox, dirEntry->d_name);
                    }
                }
            }

        /* --- All done --- */
        closedir (directory);
    }
```

The AddListItem function is just a shortcut function to add a string to a list box.

```
    /*
     * AddListItem
     *
     * Add an item to a list box
     *
     * listbox - list box to add the item to
     * text - text string to display in the list box
     */
    void AddListItem (GtkWidget *listbox, char *sText)
    {
        GtkWidget *item;

        /* --- Create list item from data --- */
        item = gtk_list_item_new_with_label (sText);

        /* --- Add item to list box --- */
        gtk_container_add (GTK_CONTAINER (listbox), item);

        /* --- Make it visible --- */
        gtk_widget_show (item);
    }
```

The result is a file viewer application that uses the current directory as a starting point, reads the structure of the file system without going up any levels, and displays the file system tree from the current directory. Clicking on any directory name displays the files in that directory, and the directories can be expanded or collapsed by clicking on the plus or minus characters next to the name of the directory.

# Notebook Widget

The notebook widget (GtkNotebook) makes it possible to display information in several pages where each page can be brought to the front by clicking on a tab that represents the page. Each tab has a description on it to allow the user to identify the page. The tabs can be on the top, bottom, left, or right of the page.

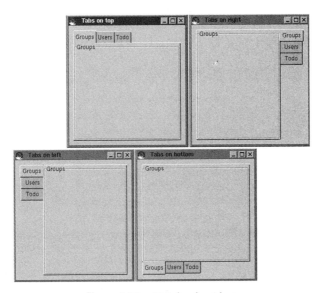

**Figure 14.2**   Notebook widget.

A GtkNotebook is created with the gtk_notebook_new function. Tabs are placed in the GtkNotebook by using the gtk_notebook_set_tab_pos function and passing in one of the position values (GTK_POS_TOP, GTK_POS_BOTTOM, GTK_POS_LEFT, GTK_POS_RIGHT).

```
/* --- Create the notebook --- */
notebook = gtk_notebook_new ();

/* --- Put the tabs along the top of the notebook --- */
gtk_notebook_set_tab_pos (GTK_NOTEBOOK (notebook), GTK_POS_TOP);
```

## Adding and Removing Pages

The GtkNotebook widget is not usable without some pages on it. Pages can be added with the gtk_notebook_append_page function that adds pages to the end of the page list. The gtk_notebook_prepend_page function adds pages to the beginning of the page list, and the gtk_notebook_insert_page can insert a page anywhere in the page list. The widgets passed to these functions need to be created before trying to create the page. This step usually involves creating a label for the tab and some type of container for the child so that other widgets can be placed within it. To remove the pages, you can use gtk_notebook_remove_page.

```
/* --- Create label and container for page --- */
label = gtk_label_new ("First tab");
container = gtk_frame_new ("Public information");

/* --- Add a page to the end of the notebook --- */
gtk_notebook_append_page (notebook, container, label);

/* --- Create label and container for page --- */
label = gtk_label_new ("Last tab");
container = gtk_frame_new ("Secret information");

/* --- Add a page to the end of the notebook --- */
gtk_notebook_prepend_page (notebook, container, label);

/* --- Create label and container for page --- */
label = gtk_label_new ("Middle tab");
container = gtk_frame_new ("Quasi secret information");

/* --- Add a page to the end of the notebook --- */
gtk_notebook_insert_page (notebook, container, label);
```

## Manipulating Pages

You can use the gtk_notebook_current_page function to retrieve the current page and the gtk_notebook_set_page function to set the current page. The gtk_notebook_next_page function and gtk_notebook_prev_page function can go up and down the page list. The gtk_notebook_set_show_tabs can hide or display the GtkNotebook tabs.

```
/* --- Get the current page --- */
nPage = gtk_notebook_current_page (notebook);

/* --- Go to the next page --- */
gtk_notebook_set_page (notebook, nPage + 1);

/* --- Go to the previous page --- */
```

```
gtk_notebook_prev_page (notebook);

/* --- Go to the next page (again) --- */
gtk_notebook_next_page (notebook);

/* --- Hide the tabs from the user --- */
gtk_notebook_set_show_tabs (notebook, FALSE);
```

Hiding the tabs might seem strange at first because the user would not be able to click on the tab to go to the other pages in the notebook, but sometimes having the application control the page that is currently displayed is desirable. This situation is similar to a Microsoft application wizard that walks a user through a complicated procedure. A procedure may require the user to go through 10 steps, and it's usually easier to display one step at a time on a page. When the user has successfully accomplished a step, the application can switch to the next page for the next step.

The program at the end of this chapter has several pages within it to illustrate the use of the GtkNotebook widget within an application.

# The *GtkCList* Widget

The GtkCList widget enables you to view tabular information within a single widget. The widget can have any number of rows and columns of data within it, and the columns can be set to any desired size. The widget is frequently used to view database information where each row within the GtkCList widget is a row within a database, and each column within the GtkCList widget is a field in the database.

The GtkCList widget is created with a fixed number of columns that cannot be changed once it has been set. The GtkCList widget must be destroyed and re-created if the number of columns in the widget changes. The GtkCList widget can be created with the gtk_clist_new function by passing in the number of columns needed for the widget, or it can be created by using the gtk_clist_new_with_titles function that also takes an array of titles as a parameter. You can use the gtk_clist_set_column_title function to set or modify the titles.

```
/* --- Create a table with 3 columns --- */
clist = gtk_clist_new (3);

/* --- Give each column a title --- */
gtk_clist_set_column_title (GTK_CLIST, 0, "Id");
gtk_clist_set_column_title (GTK_CLIST, 1, "Name");
gtk_clist_set_column_title (GTK_CLIST, 2, "Address");
```

The shorter version of the preceding code follows.

```
/* --- Define the titles --- */
char *szTitles[] = { "Id", "Name", "Address"};

/* --- Create the clist with titles all in one shot --- */
Clist = gtk_clist_new_with_titles (3, szTitles);
```

## Add Data into *GtkCList*

Information can be appended in the GtkCList with the gtk_clist_append function. It takes the GtkCList and an array of strings as the parameters. The array should be the number of columns that are in the GtkCList.

```
/* --- Adding a row of static data --- */
char *szData = {"0123", "Eric", "123 Main St."};

/* --- Add the row of data to the clist --- */
gtk_clist_append (GTK_CLIST (clist), szData);
```

In addition to appending data to the GtkCList, the data can also be inserted at any position in the GtkCList by using the gtk_clist_insert function and passing in the index of where to insert the row.

```
/* --- Inserting a row of static data --- */
char *szData = {"0123", "Eric", "123 Main St."};

/* --- Insert the data after row 10 --- */
gtk_clist_insert (GTK_CLIST (clist), 10, szData);
```

After the text has been added to the GtkCList, it can be modified with the gtk_clist_set_text function. The gtk_clist_get_text function takes a pointer to a string (a char **) and populates it with the data in a particular row and column. If the pointer is NULL, the GTKCList widget is not populated. The function returns a nonzero value if it succeeds in populating the pointer. The text is not a copy and should not be directly modified.

```
char *data;

/* --- Change the data in an existing row/column --- */
gtk_clist_set_text (GTK_CLIST (clist), 3, 1, "Joe");

/* --- Get the text --- */
gtk_clist_get_text (GTK_CLIST (clist), 3, 1, &data);
```

## Removing Rows

The rows can be removed from the GtkCList by using the gtk_clist_remove function and passing in the index of the row to remove. However, when removing all the items in the GtkCList, a faster method is to call gtk_clist_clear, which removes all the items from the GtkCList.

```
/* --- Remove first row --- */
gtk_clist_remove (CLIST (clist), 0);

/* --- Remove all the items from the list --- */
gtk_clist_clear (CLIST (clist));
```

## Speeding Up Insertion and Deletion

Just as the text widget can have lots of data added to it, the `GtkCList` is a prime candidate for the display of large sets of data, especially database files. To help speed up the process of adding and modifying information in the `GtkCList` widget, the `GtkCList` can be frozen, like the text widget, to prevent the updating of the data until the insertions or modifications to the `GtkCList` widget have been completed. The `gtk_clist_freeze` function prevents updates to the widget from occurring until the corresponding `gtk_clist_thaw` function is called.

```
/* --- Freeze the widget --- */
gtk_clist_freeze (CLIST (clist));

/* --- Do some processing --- */

/* --- Unfreeze the list --- */
gtk_clist_thaw (CLIST (clist));
```

## Title Characteristics

The title bar in the `GtkCList` has a few properties that can be modified for the application. For example, you can decide whether you even want to display the titles. The `gtk_clist_column_titles_hide` function hides the title bar; the `gtk_clist_column_titles_show` function shows the title bar. Instead of a title, the `GtkCList` can display a widget. The `gtk_clist_set_column_widget` function allows the placement of any widget in the title bar and is a good way to display graphical images for the title bar.

```
/* --- Hide the title bars --- */
gtk_clist_column_titles_hide (GTK_CLIST (clist));

/* --- Make the titles visible --- */
gtk_clist_column_titles_show (GTK_CLIST (clist));

/* --- Put a previously created pixmap in as the title --- */
gtk_clist_set_column_widget (GTK_CLIST (clist), 1, pixmap_widget);
```

## Column and Row Parameters

It's going to be necessary to manually adjust the width of the columns when the `GtkCList` is created. The `GtkCList` has no idea how wide to make the columns and just guesses at the column width using the title width. You can use the `gtk_clist_set_column_width` function to set the width of any column in the clist. You can also set the row height by using the `gtk_clist_set_row_height` function, but unless you're changing the font that the `GtkCList` is being displayed in or adding large graphics to the `GtkCList`, setting the row height shouldn't be necessary. The row height can be changed by using the `gtk_clist_set_row_height` function.

```
/* --- Set the width of the column to 100 pixels --- */
gtk_clist_set_column_width (GTK_CLIST (clist), 0, 100);
```

```
/* --- Change the row height for the images --- */
gtk_clist_set_row_height (GTK_CLIST (clist), 25);
```

The data in the columns can also be adjusted to align left, right, or be centered. The gtk_clist_set_column_justification function takes the widget and column as well as a GtkJustification. The valid values for the GtkJustification are GTK_JUSTIFY_LEFT, GTK_JUSTIFY_RIGHT, GTK_JUSTIFY_CENTER, and GTK_JUSTIFY_FILL.

### Graphics in a *GtkCList*

So far we've only covered the display of textual information. Staring at row after row of text and numbers can be quite dreary at times, so the GtkCList also supports the insertion of pixmaps into a row. The pixmap is inserted with gtk_clist_set_pixmap and can be queried with the gtk_clist_get_pixmap function. It's important to note that when the textual information is added with an insert or an append function, the columns that display the pixmaps should have the text set to NULL. Otherwise, the pixmaps do not display.

```
/* --- Give the item a pixmap --- */
gtk_clist_set_pixmap (GTK_CLIST (clist), row, col, pix, mask);
```

```
/* --- Take a look at the existing pixmap --- */
gtk_clist_get_pixmap (GTK_CLIST (clist), row, col, &pix, &mask);
```

# Creating an Application

The following application uses both the GtkNotebook widget and the GtkCList widget to display the log file from an Apache Web server. The log files are broken down into three notebook pages. The first page displays the traffic by the hour of the day (see Figure 14.3). This information enables you to determine whether the bandwidth is adequate for peak periods. The second page shows traffic by day, starting from the beginning of the log file. This information enables you to look for traffic trends— perhaps an ad placed on one of the sites caused traffic to spike for the few days that it was running. Did you notice the traffic increase? Probably not.

The third page shows the traffic generated by the user. This application treats the home page as a separate user page.

Each GtkCList is going to feature a pixmap to graphically display the traffic, whether it's by hour, by day, or by user. This information allows the user to quickly spot problems—like the new user running an X-rated site from his home page. It's a lot quicker to look at graphics than it is to scan rows of numbers for the information.

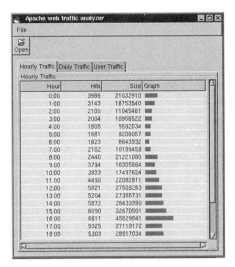

**Figure 14.3**   Traffic by hour.

Many of the files for this project were used before. One of the themes here has been code reuse. The files `misc.c`, `progressbar.c`, and `filesel.c` have already been covered. `Frontend.c` has been slightly modified to cover the different front end. The primary files for this project are the log parser (`parselog.c`), the GtkNotebook/clist display (`Notebook.c`), and the graphical pixmap generator (`bitmaps.c`).

The pixmaps displayed in the table are unique because they're generated on-the-fly. Rather than use static pixmap data, the pixmap data is generated by a routine that allocates and generates a pixmap based on the size of the horizontal bar that is to be displayed. A horizontal graphics bar is easy to automatically generate, and is more flexible than creating static pixmap data. We can easily change the size of resolution of the graph by modifying the routine that generates the pixmap data. However, if we had to use static images, we'd spend a lot of time editing all the possible pixmap combinations that make up the bar graphs.

## *logtypes.h*

The `logtypes.h` file defines the data structures used within the application. Each structure is defined to store the specific set of data that you need to track.

The `typTimeStamp` stores the date and time of a hit to a Web page.

```
typedef struct {

    int year;
    int month;
    int day;
```

```
    int hours;
    int minutes;
    int seconds;

} typTimeStamp;
```

The `typHit` stores all the information about a Web site hit, or impression.

```
typedef struct {

    char *sIp;
    char *sUser;
    char *sDate;
    char *sCmd;
    char *sURL;
    int nResult;
    int nSize;
    typTimeStamp date;

} typHit;
```

The `typStat` stores all the hits and bytes transferred for a URL.

```
typedef struct {

    char *sURL;
    long nHits;
    long nSize;

} typStat;
```

The `typDate` keeps track of a date for the analysis by date.

```
typedef struct {

    int year;
    int month;
    int day;

} typDate;
```

The `typDateInfo` record stores the hits and bytes transferred for a particular date.

```
typedef struct {

    long nHits;
    long nSize;
    typDate *date;

} typDateInfo;
```

## *parselog.c*

For the data to be displayed, it has to be read in and summarized. The information is stored in a `Gtree`, so the lookup and retrieval of the information is quick. An access log contains many rows of data, and you need quick access to the information that is going to be updated. Every record from the access log is read in, parsed, and stored as a hit. The hit is then sent to the various functions that summarize the information, using the information in the hit. For instance, if the hit was for a particular user's page on a particular day, the hit would be added to that user's summary information as well as the daily summary information. When the parsing of the log file is completed, the `GtkCList` uses the summary information to display the log file.

```c
/*
 * File: parselog.c
 * Auth: Eric Harlow
 *
 * Parse an Apache log file and summarize information.
 */

#include <stdio.h>
#include <string.h>
#include <sys/types.h>
#include <sys/stat.h>
#include <unistd.h>
#include <time.h>
#include <gtk/gtk.h>
#include "logtypes.h"


/*
 * Define data for the storage of hourly information.
 */
long timeOfDayHits[24];
long timeOfDaySize[24];

/*
 * Define trees to store the different types of data.
 */
GTree *fileTree = NULL;
GTree *dateTree = NULL;
GTree *userTree = NULL;

void ParseLine (char *buffer);

#define MONTHS 12
char *sValidMonths[] = { "Jan", "Feb", "Mar", "Apr", "May", "Jun",
                         "Jul", "Aug", "Sep", "Oct", "Nov", "Dec" };
```

```
/*
 * Date2Str
 *
 * Convert the date to a string.
 * date - date to convert
 * buffer - char* big enough to hold the date/time
 */
void Date2Str (typTimeStamp *date, char *buffer)
{
    sprintf (buffer, "%d/%d/%d %d:%d:%d ",
                           date->month,
                           date->day,
                           date->year,
                           date->hours,
                           date->minutes,
                           date->seconds);
}



/*
 * ConvertDate
 *
 * Convert the date from a format of 30/Feb/1999:11:42:23
 * which is how the date was stored in my Apache log files.
 */
void ConvertDate (char *sDate, typTimeStamp *date)
{
    char sMonth[33];
    int i;

    /* --- Break down the date into its components --- */
    sscanf (sDate, "%d/%3c/%d:%d:%d:%d", &date->day,
                              sMonth,
                              &date->year,
                              &date->hours,
                              &date->minutes,
                              &date->seconds);

    /* --- Convert the string date into a numeric --- */
    for (i = 0; i < MONTHS; i++) {

        /* --- Is this the month? --- */
        if (!strncasecmp (sValidMonths[i], sMonth, strlen
 ➥(sValidMonths[i]))) {
            date->month = i + 1;
            break;
```

```
            }
        }
}


/*
 * ParseLog
 *
 * Parse the log file and organize the data in the log file into
 * a format that can be interpreted by a user.
 *
 * sFile - File to read.
 */
void ParseLog (char *sFile)
{
    FILE *fp;
    char buffer[350];
    long nFileLen = 0;
    struct stat fileStatus;

    /* --- Alloc trees and init data --- */
    Init ();

    /* --- Get filename --- */
    stat (sFile, &fileStatus);
    nFileLen = fileStatus.st_size;

    /* --- Open le file <--- that's French, you know --- */
    fp = fopen (sFile, "r");

    /* --- Make sure we opened *something* --- */
    if (fp) {

        /* --- Show the progress bar --- */
        StartProgress ();

        /* --- While we have data --- */
        while (!feof (fp)) {

            /* --- Update the progress bar with information --- */
            UpdateProgress (ftell (fp), nFileLen);

            /* --- Read a line from the file --- */
            fgets (buffer, sizeof (buffer), fp);

            /* --- If not end of file --- */
```

```
            if (!feof (fp)) {

                /* --- Parse the data --- */
                ParseLine (buffer);
            }
        }

        /* --- Done - don't need progress bar --- */
        EndProgress ();

        /* --- Close the file --- */
        fclose (fp);
    }
}


/*
 * ParseLine
 *
 * Parse the line retrieved from the log file and break it
 * down into its components and update the stats being
 * kept.
 */
void ParseLine (char *buffer)
{

    char *sUnknown;
    char *sNull;
    char *sDate;
    char output[88];
    typHit hit;

    /* --- Get basic information --- */
    hit.sIp = strtok (buffer, " ");
    sUnknown = strtok (NULL, " ");
    hit.sUser = strtok (NULL, " ");

    /* --- Extract the date --- */
    sDate = strtok (NULL, "]");
    sDate++;

    /* --- Convert the date string --- */
    ConvertDate (sDate, &hit.date);

    /* --- Get file, size, status --- */
    sNull = strtok (NULL, "\");
```

```
    hit.sCmd = strtok (NULL, "\");
    hit.nResult = atoi (strtok (NULL, " "));
    hit.nSize = atoi (strtok (NULL, " "));

    /* --- Page was an error --- */
    if (hit.nResult == 404) return;

    /* --- Convert back to string --- */
    Date2Str (&hit.date, output);

    sUnknown = strtok (hit.sCmd, " ");
    hit.sURL = strtok (NULL, " ");

    /* --- Valid URL--- */
    if (hit.sURL) {

        /* --- Update the stats --- */
        UpdateStats (&hit);
    }
}



/*
 * UpdateStats
 *
 * Update information about the "hit"
 * Currently keep stats on:
 *      The time of day that the hit occurred on.
 *      The traffic occurring on each of the days.
 *      The traffic associated with user's Web sites.
 */
UpdateStats (typHit *hit)
{
    /* --- Update hourly stats --- */
    timeOfDayHits[hit->date.hours]++;
    timeOfDaySize[hit->date.hours] += hit->nSize;

    /* --- Update this information --- */
    TrackFiles (hit);
    TrackDates (hit);
    TrackUsers (hit);
}
```

```
/*
 * TrackUsers
 *
 * Track traffic to the user's sites.
 */
TrackUsers (typHit *hit)
{
    char *sURL;
    typStat *stat;
    char *sUser;

    /* --- Bad data --- */
    if (hit->sURL == NULL || strlen (hit->sURL) == 0) return;

    /* --- Get first part of the path --- */
    sUser = strtok (&hit->sURL[1], "/");

    if (sUser == NULL) return;

    /* --- If it's a user site --- */
    if (sUser[0] == '~') {

        /* --- Get the name --- */
        sUser = &sUser[1];

    /* --- If ~ was encoded as %7E --- */
    } else if (!strcmp (sUser, "%7E")) {

        /* --- Get the name --- */
        sUser = &sUser[3];
    } else {

        /* --- Not a user, belongs to main site --- */
        sUser = "*ROOT";
    }

    /* --- See if the user exists in the tree --- */
    stat = g_tree_lookup (userTree, sUser);

    /* --- If user does not exist --- */
    if (stat == NULL) {

        /* --- Make space for the user --- */
        stat = g_malloc (sizeof (typStat));

        /* --- Populate fields --- */
```

```
        stat->sURL = strdup (sUser);
        stat->nHits = 0;
        stat->nSize = 0;

        /* --- Insert user into tree --- */
        g_tree_insert (userTree, stat->sURL, stat);
    }

    /* --- Update hit count for user --- */
    stat->nHits ++;
    stat->nSize += hit->nSize;
}


/*
 * TrackFiles
 *
 * Keep track of hit counts on individual files
 */
TrackFiles (typHit *hit)
{
    char *sURL;
    typStat *stat;

    /* --- Look up the URL in the tree --- */
    stat = g_tree_lookup (fileTree, hit->sURL);

    /* --- If the URL is not found --- */
    if (stat == NULL) {

        /* --- Create a node for the URL --- */
        stat = g_malloc (sizeof (typStat));

        /* --- Populate the node --- */
        stat->sURL = strdup (hit->sURL);
        stat->nHits = 0;
        stat->nSize = 0;

        /* --- Add the node to the tree --- */
        g_tree_insert (fileTree, stat->sURL, stat);
    }

    /* --- Update the file hit count --- */
    stat->nHits ++;
    stat->nSize = hit->nSize;
}
```

```
/*
 * TrackDates
 *
 * Track the traffic that occurs on any given date.
 */
TrackDates (typHit *hit)
{
    char *sURL;
    typStat *stat;
    typDate date;
    typDate *newdate;
    typDateInfo *info;

    /* --- Get the date of the hit --- */
    date.year = hit->date.year;
    date.month = hit->date.month;
    date.day = hit->date.day;

    /* --- Look up the date --- */
    info = g_tree_lookup (dateTree, &date);

    /* --- If no data for the date? --- */
    if (info == NULL) {

        /* --- Create field to hold date information --- */
        info = g_malloc (sizeof (typDateInfo));
        newdate = g_malloc (sizeof (typDate));

        /* --- Populate fields --- */
        *newdate = date;

        info->nHits = 0;
        info->nSize = 0;
        info->date = newdate;

        /* --- Add date info to the tree --- */
        g_tree_insert (dateTree, newdate, info);
    }

    /* --- Update date hit count --- */
    info->nHits ++;
    info->nSize += hit->nSize;
}
```

```
/*
 * CompareStrings
 *
 * Function to compare two strings for a tree callback.
 * Could have just passed strcmp into the tree function
 * but may want to change the comparision in the future.
 */
gint CompareStrings (gpointer g1, gpointer g2)
{
    return (strcmp ((char *) g1, (char *) g2));
}



/*
 * CompareDates
 *
 * Compare two dates and return negative value if first date is
 * less than the second date, positive value if first date is
 * greater than the second date, and zero if the two dates are
 * the same.
 */
gint CompareDates (gpointer g1, gpointer g2)
{
    typDate *d1 = (typDate *) g1;
    typDate *d2 = (typDate *) g2;

    /* --- Year has highest priority --- */
    if (d1->year == d2->year) {

        /* --- Years are same, what about months? --- */
        if (d1->month == d2->month) {

            /* --- Return difference between days --- */
            return (d1->day - d2->day);
        } else {

            /* --- Months are different - calculate delta --- */
            return (d1->month - d2->month);
        }
    } else {

        /* --- Years are different - calc delta --- */
        return (d1->year == d2->year);
    }
}
```

```
/*
 * GetHitsForHour
 *
 * Function to return the the number of hits for a given
 * time of day.
 */
GetHitsForHour (int nHours, long *hits, long *size)
{
    /* --- If the clock is out of range --- */
    if (nHours < 0 || nHours > 23) {

        *hits = 0;
        *size = 0;

    } else {
        *hits = timeOfDayHits[nHours];
        *size = timeOfDaySize[nHours];
    }
}


/*
 * Init
 *
 * Initialize data so that the log file can be read in.
 * Create trees necessary to store the log data.
 */
int Init ()
{
    int i;

    /* --- Create the trees that will store the information --- */
    fileTree = g_tree_new (CompareStrings);
    dateTree = g_tree_new (CompareDates);
    userTree = g_tree_new (CompareStrings);

    /* --- Clear out the hits by hour --- */
    for (i = 0; i < 24; i++) {
        timeOfDayHits[i] = 0;
        timeOfDaySize[i] = 0;
    }
}


/*
 * FreeURLs
 *
```

```
 * Free the memory associated with the URLs.
 * This is a traverse callback
 */
gint FreeURLs (gpointer key, gpointer value, gpointer data)
{
    typStat *info;

    info = (typStat *) value;
    free (info->sURL);
    g_free (info);
    return (0);
}



/*
 * FreeDates
 *
 * Free information allocated to keep track of the
 * traffic by date.  This is a traverse callback.
 */
gint FreeDates (gpointer key, gpointer value, gpointer data)
{
    typDateInfo *info;

    info = (typDateInfo *) value;
    g_free (info->date);
    g_free (info);
    return (0);
}




/*
 * FreeResources
 *
 * Free the memory used in the tree nodes and then free the
 * trees.
 */
FreeResources ()
{
    /* --- Free data stored in the tree --- */
    g_tree_traverse (userTree, FreeURLs, G_IN_ORDER, NULL);
    g_tree_traverse (dateTree, FreeDates, G_IN_ORDER, NULL);
    g_tree_traverse (fileTree, FreeURLs, G_IN_ORDER, NULL);

    /* --- Free the trees --- */
```

```
        g_tree_destroy (userTree);
        g_tree_destroy (dateTree);
        g_tree_destroy (fileTree);

        /* --- Clear pointers --- */
        userTree = NULL;
        dateTree = NULL;
        fileTree = NULL;
}
```

## *bitmaps.c*

The GtkCList displays a graph that reflects the traffic for the site, day, or hour. Rather than create several .xpm files for the pixmaps, it's quicker just to have the code generate the .xpm data dynamically.

This approach also makes it easy to change the width of the graph. Rather than redraw the graph, you can change how wide the graphs should be. Note that because this graph is horizontal, the pixmap image data is the same for each row of the pixmap. You can take advantage of this situation by reusing the same string for each row in the pixmap.

```
#include <gtk/gtk.h>
#include <strings.h>


/*
 * CreateBarBitmap
 *
 * Create a pixmap with the characteristics desired.
 *
 * height - height to make the pixmap
 * width - width to make the pixmap
 * size - how big the bar should be
 * sColor - color of the filled-in area
 */
char **CreateBarBitmap (int height, int width, int size, char *sColor)
{
    char **sBitmap;
    char *newbuffer;
    char buffer[88];
    int i;

    /* --- Create the room for the data --- */
    sBitmap = g_malloc ((height + 1 + 2) * sizeof (gchar *));

    /* --- Create pixmap header - height/width/colors/#chars --- */
```

```
    sprintf (buffer, "%d %d 2 1", width, height);
    sBitmap[0] = g_strdup (buffer);

    /* --- Define the "none" color --- */
    sBitmap[1] = g_strdup ("  c None");

    /* --- Define the filled-in color --- */
    sprintf (buffer, "X c %s", sColor);
    sBitmap[2] = g_strdup (buffer);

    /* --- Fill in the buffer with the size --- */
    strcpy (buffer, " ");
    for (i = 0; i < size; i++) {

        strcat (buffer, "X");
    }

    /* --- Leave the remainder not filled in --- */
    while (i < width) {
        strcat (buffer, " ");
        i++;
    }

    /* --- Pad with blank --- */
    strcat (buffer, " ");

    /* --- Copy the string --- */
    newbuffer = g_strdup (buffer);

    /* --- Make it the data for all the strings --- */
    for (i = 3; i < height+3; i++) {
        sBitmap[i] = newbuffer;
    }

    /* --- Return the creation --- */
    return (sBitmap);
}


/*
 * FreeBarBitmap
 *
 * Free all the memory that was allocated to create the
 * bitmap.
 */
FreeBarBitmap (char **bitmap)
```

```
{
    g_free (bitmap[0]);
    g_free (bitmap[1]);
    g_free (bitmap[2]);
    g_free (bitmap[3]);
    g_free (bitmap);
}
```

## Notebook.c

After the data is loaded into the trees, these routines create and display the data within each of the GtkCList widgets. The widgets are created on separate pages, and the user is allowed to change the tabs to see information on the other pages. The data in the GtkCList widgets is created by traversing the tree in order. The textual information (date, user, hits, and so on) is displayed, and the maximum traffic is calculated. After the textual information is displayed and the maximum is calculated, the tree for the display is traversed a second time to display the graphs. The maximum traffic is necessary because the graphs are relative to the largest value and cannot be displayed until the maximum value is calculated.

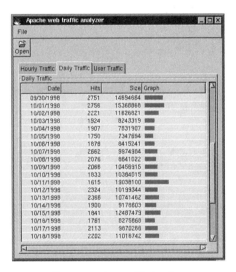

**Figure 14.4**  Traffic by day.

```
/*
 * Auth: Eric Harlow
 * File: Notebook.c
 *
 * Create a sample notebook application
```

```
     */


#include <gtk/gtk.h>
#include "logtypes.h"


extern GTree *dateTree;
extern GTree *userTree;

GtkWidget *hourlyPage = NULL;
GtkWidget *dailyPage = NULL;
GtkWidget *userPage = NULL;
GtkWidget *hourlyCList = NULL;
GtkWidget *dailyCList = NULL;
GtkWidget *userCList = NULL;


typedef struct {
    GtkWidget *widget;
    long nMaxSize;
    long row;
} typGraphInfo;

/*
 * Titles displayed on the clist for the various pages
 */
char *szHourlyTitles[] = {"Hour", "Hits", "Size", "Graph"};
char *szDailyTitles[] = {"Date", "Hits", "Size", "Graph"};
char *szUserTitles[] = {"User", "Hits", "Size", "Graph"};

#define NUM_GRAPHS 21
GdkPixmap *pixmapGraph [NUM_GRAPHS];
GdkBitmap *mask[NUM_GRAPHS];

char **CreateBarBitmap (int height, int width, int size, char *sColor);


/*
 * GeneratePixmaps
 *
 * Generate the pixmaps for all the sizes of horizontal bars
 * that are supported.
 */
GeneratePixmaps (GtkWidget *widget)
{
    int i;
```

```
        gchar **pixmap_d;
        GdkColor *transparent = NULL;

        /* --- For each possible graph --- */
        for (i = 0; i < NUM_GRAPHS; i++) {

            /* --- Get the data for the graph --- */
            pixmap_d = CreateBarBitmap (9, 65, i * 3, "#ff0000");

            /* --- Create a pixmap --- */
            pixmapGraph[i] = gdk_pixmap_create_from_xpm_d (
                        widget->window,
                        &mask[i], NULL,
                        (gpointer) pixmap_d);

            /* --- Free the data --- */
            FreeBarBitmap (pixmap_d);
        }
    }



    /*
     * AddPage
     *
     * Add a page to the notebook
     *
     * notebook - existing notebook
     * szName - name to give to the new page
     */
    GtkWidget *AddPage (GtkWidget *notebook, char *szName)
    {
        GtkWidget *label;
        GtkWidget *frame;

        /* --- Create a label from the name --- */
        label = gtk_label_new (szName);
        gtk_widget_show (label);

        /* --- Create a frame for the page --- */
        frame = gtk_frame_new (szName);
        gtk_widget_show (frame);

        /* --- Add a page with the frame and label --- */
        gtk_notebook_append_page (GTK_NOTEBOOK (notebook), frame, label);

        return (frame);
    }
```

```
/*
 * CreateNotebook
 *
 * Create a new notebook and add pages to it.
 *
 * window - window to create the notebook in.
 */
void CreateNotebook (GtkWidget *window)
{
    GtkWidget *widget;
    GtkWidget *box1;
    GtkWidget *notebook;

    /* --- Create the notebook --- */
    notebook = gtk_notebook_new ();

    /* --- Listen for the switch page event --- */
    gtk_signal_connect (GTK_OBJECT (notebook), "switch_page",
                        GTK_SIGNAL_FUNC (PageSwitch), NULL);

    /* --- Make sure tabs are on top --- */
    gtk_notebook_set_tab_pos (GTK_NOTEBOOK (notebook), GTK_POS_TOP);

    /* --- Add notebook to vbox --- */
    gtk_box_pack_start (GTK_BOX (window), notebook, TRUE, TRUE, 0);

    /* --- Give notebook a border --- */
    gtk_container_border_width (GTK_CONTAINER (notebook), 10);

    /* --- Add pages to the notebook --- */
    hourlyPage = AddPage (notebook, "Hourly Traffic");
    dailyPage = AddPage (notebook, "Daily Traffic");
    userPage = AddPage (notebook, "User Traffic");

    /* --- Show everything --- */
    gtk_widget_show_all (window);
}


/*
 * PopulatePages
 *
```

```
 * Populates the pages on the notebook with the information.
 * Populates the hourly page, daily page, and the user page.
 *
 * Frees the data used to generate the page when done.
 */
PopulatePages ()
{
    /* --- Free clist data if already used --- */
    if (userCList) {
        gtk_clist_clear (GTK_CLIST (userCList));
    }
    if (hourlyCList) {
        gtk_clist_clear (GTK_CLIST (hourlyCList));
    }
    if (dailyCList) {
        gtk_clist_clear (GTK_CLIST (dailyCList));
    }

    /* --- Populate each of the fields --- */
    PopulateHourly ();
    PopulateDaily ();
    PopulateUser ();

    /* --- Free the resources generated by parselog --- */
    FreeResources ();
}



/*
 * PopulateHourly
 *
 * Populates the clist with the hourly information.
 * Assumes that the trees are fully populated with
 * data ready to be picked.
 */
PopulateHourly ()
{
    gchar *strValue[4];
    int i;
    int ix;
    long hits;
    long size;
    gchar buffer0[88];
    gchar buffer1[88];
    gchar buffer2[88];
```

```
long nMaxSize = 0;

/* --- Here's the array used to insert into clist --- */
strValue[0] = buffer0;
strValue[1] = buffer1;
strValue[2] = buffer2;

/* --- This is NULL because it's a pixmap --- */
strValue[3] = NULL;

/* --- If clist not created yet... --- */
if (hourlyCList == NULL) {

    /* --- Create the clist with four columns --- */
    hourlyCList = gtk_clist_new_with_titles (4, szHourlyTitles);

    /* --- Make sure titles are visible --- */
    gtk_clist_column_titles_show (GTK_CLIST (hourlyCList));

    /* --- Set the column widths --- */
    gtk_clist_set_column_width (GTK_CLIST (hourlyCList), 0, 80);
    gtk_clist_set_column_width (GTK_CLIST (hourlyCList), 1, 80);
    gtk_clist_set_column_width (GTK_CLIST (hourlyCList), 2, 80);
    gtk_clist_set_column_width (GTK_CLIST (hourlyCList), 3, 40);

    /* --- Set the justification on each of the columns --- */
    gtk_clist_set_column_justification (GTK_CLIST (hourlyCList),
                            0, GTK_JUSTIFY_RIGHT);
    gtk_clist_set_column_justification (GTK_CLIST (hourlyCList),
                            1, GTK_JUSTIFY_RIGHT);
    gtk_clist_set_column_justification (GTK_CLIST (hourlyCList),
                            2, GTK_JUSTIFY_RIGHT);

    /* --- Add the clist to the correct page --- */
    gtk_container_add (GTK_CONTAINER (hourlyPage), hourlyCList);
}

/* --- Generate a row for each hour of the day --- */
for (i = 0; i < 24; i++) {

    /* --- Show the time - like 3:00 --- */
    sprintf (strValue[0], "%d:00", i);

    /* --- Get # of hits for that hour --- */
    GetHitsForHour (i, &hits, &size);
```

```
        /* --- Display hit count and byte count --- */
        sprintf (strValue[1], "%ld", hits);
        sprintf (strValue[2], "%ld", size);

        /* --- Add the data to the clist --- */
        gtk_clist_append (GTK_CLIST (hourlyCList), strValue);

        /* --- Keep track of max byte count --- */
        if (size > nMaxSize) {
            nMaxSize = size;
        }
    }


    /*
     * Now that the clist is generated, we need to go back
     * and add the horizontal graph to the clist.  Couldn't do
     * it earlier because we didn't know the max.
     */

    /* --- Every hour of the day --- */
    for (i = 0; i < 24; i++) {

        /* --- Get hits for the hour --- */
        GetHitsForHour (i, &hits, &size);

        /* --- Calculate how big graph should be --- */
        ix = (size * NUM_GRAPHS-1) / nMaxSize;

        /* --- Display that graph in the clist --- */
        gtk_clist_set_pixmap (GTK_CLIST (hourlyCList),
                i, 3, (GdkPixmap *) pixmapGraph[ix], mask[ix]);
    }

    /* --- Show the clist --- */
    gtk_widget_show_all (GTK_WIDGET (hourlyCList));
}



/*
 * ShowDateInfo
 *
 * Show information about the traffic on a particular
 * day.  Dumps the information into the clist that
 * represents the daily graph.
```

```
 *
 * This is called by the tree traverse callback!
 */
gint ShowDateInfo (gpointer key, gpointer value, gpointer data)
{
    char *strValue[4];
    typDateInfo *dateInfo;
    long *pnMax;
    char buffer0[88];
    char buffer1[88];
    char buffer2[88];
    int i;

    /* --- Get info passed it --- */
    dateInfo = (typDateInfo *) value;
    pnMax = (long *) data;

    /* --- Set up structures to populate clist --- */
    strValue[0] = buffer0;
    strValue[1] = buffer1;
    strValue[2] = buffer2;
    strValue[3] = NULL;

    /* --- Fill in the date in the first column --- */
    sprintf (strValue[0], "%02d/%02d/%4d", dateInfo->date->month,
                                           dateInfo->date->day,
                                           dateInfo->date->year);

    /* --- Fill in the hits and byte count --- */
    sprintf (strValue[1], "%ld", dateInfo->nHits);
    sprintf (strValue[2], "%ld", dateInfo->nSize);

    /* --- Append the data into the clist --- */
    gtk_clist_append (GTK_CLIST (dailyCList), strValue);

    /* --- Keep track of the maximum value --- */
    if (*pnMax < dateInfo->nSize) {

        *pnMax = dateInfo->nSize;
    }

    /* --- 0 => keep on trucking --- */
    return (0);
}
```

```
/*
 * ShowUserInfo
 *
 * Shows information about a user (no graphs) but keeps track
 * of the maximum byte count so that the graphs can be generated.
 *
 * This is called as the traverse tree callback.
 */
gint ShowUserInfo (gpointer key, gpointer value, gpointer data)
{
    char *strValue[4];
    typStat *info;
    long *pnMax;
    char buffer0[88];
    char buffer1[88];
    char buffer2[88];
    int i;

    /* --- Get information passed in --- */
    info = (typStat *) value;
    pnMax = (long *) data;

    /* --- Buffers to append data --- */
    strValue[0] = buffer0;
    strValue[1] = buffer1;
    strValue[2] = buffer2;
    strValue[3] = NULL;

    /* --- Update the URL in first column --- */
    sprintf (strValue[0], "%s", info->sURL);

    /* --- Update bytes and size in next column --- */
    sprintf (strValue[1], "%ld", info->nHits);
    sprintf (strValue[2], "%ld", info->nSize);

    /* --- Add the data to the clist --- */
    gtk_clist_append (GTK_CLIST (userCList), strValue);

    /* --- Keep track of the maximum size --- */
    if (info->nSize > *pnMax) {
        *pnMax = info->nSize;
    }

    return (0);
}
```

```
/*
 * DisplayGraph
 *
 * Display the daily graph in the clist.
 *
 * Called as a tree traverse callback.
 */
gint DisplayGraph (gpointer key, gpointer value, gpointer data)
{
    int ix;
    typGraphInfo *graphInfo = (typGraphInfo *) data;
    typDateInfo *dateInfo = (typDateInfo *) value;

    /* --- Figure out which graph to display based on size --- */
    ix = (dateInfo->nSize * NUM_GRAPHS-1) / graphInfo->nMaxSize;

    /* --- Set the pixmap in the clist to this one --- */
    gtk_clist_set_pixmap (GTK_CLIST (graphInfo->widget),
                          graphInfo->row, 3, pixmapGraph[ix], mask[ix]);

    /* --- Next row to display --- */
    graphInfo->row++;

    /* --- Continue... --- */
    return (0);
}




/*
 * PopulateDaily
 *
 * Populates the clist with the data from the tree.
 * Assumes that the data in the tree has been fully
 * populated.
 */
PopulateDaily ()
{
    gchar *strValue[4];
    int i;
    long hits;
    long size;
    long nMaxDaily;
    gchar buffer0[88];
    gchar buffer1[88];
    gchar buffer2[88];
```

```
int nRow = 0;
typGraphInfo graphInfo;

/* --- Create the table --- */
strValue[0] = buffer0;
strValue[1] = buffer1;
strValue[2] = buffer2;

/* --- NULL - graphic is going here --- */
strValue[3] = NULL;

/* --- If the clist has not been created yet... --- */
if (dailyCList == NULL) {

    /* --- Create the clist --- */
    dailyCList = gtk_clist_new_with_titles (4, szDailyTitles);

    /* --- Make sure titles are being shown --- */
    gtk_clist_column_titles_show (GTK_CLIST (dailyCList));

    /* --- Set the column widths --- */
    gtk_clist_set_column_width (GTK_CLIST (dailyCList), 0, 80);
    gtk_clist_set_column_width (GTK_CLIST (dailyCList), 1, 80);
    gtk_clist_set_column_width (GTK_CLIST (dailyCList), 2, 80);

    /* --- Set the column justifications --- */
    gtk_clist_set_column_justification (GTK_CLIST (dailyCList),
                                        0, GTK_JUSTIFY_RIGHT);
    gtk_clist_set_column_justification (GTK_CLIST (dailyCList),
                                        1, GTK_JUSTIFY_RIGHT);
    gtk_clist_set_column_justification (GTK_CLIST (dailyCList),
                                        2, GTK_JUSTIFY_RIGHT);

    /* --- Add the clist to the notebook page --- */
    gtk_container_add (GTK_CONTAINER (dailyPage), dailyCList);
}

/* --- set max to zero --- */
nMaxDaily = 0;

/*
 * --- Traverse tree and display the textual information
 *     while gathering the maximum so that the graph can
 *     be displayed
 */
g_tree_traverse (dateTree, ShowDateInfo, G_IN_ORDER, &nMaxDaily);
```

```
    /* --- Information for displaying of the graph --- */
    graphInfo.nMaxSize = nMaxDaily;
    graphInfo.widget = dailyCList;
    graphInfo.row = 0;

    /* --- Re-traverse the tree and display graphs --- */
    g_tree_traverse (dateTree, DisplayGraph, G_IN_ORDER, &graphInfo);

    /* --- Show the clist now --- */
    gtk_widget_show_all (GTK_WIDGET (dailyCList));
}



/*
 * DisplayUserGraph
 *
 * Display the graph for each user.
 * This is called from a traverse tree - it's a callback with the
 * data passed into it.
 *
 * value - contains information about this user's activity
 * data - contains information about the graph, incl. widget and max
 */
gint DisplayUserGraph (gpointer key, gpointer value, gpointer data)
{
    int ix;
    typGraphInfo *graphInfo = (typGraphInfo *) data;
    typStat *statInfo = (typStat *) value;

    /* --- How big should the graph be? --- */
    ix = (long) (((double) statInfo->nSize * NUM_GRAPHS-1) /
                       graphInfo->nMaxSize);

    /* --- Set the pixmap to an appropriate size --- */
    gtk_clist_set_pixmap (GTK_CLIST (graphInfo->widget),
                       graphInfo->row, 3, pixmapGraph[ix], mask[ix]);

    /* --- Go to the next row --- */
    graphInfo->row++;

    return (0);
}



/*
 * PopulateUser
```

```
 *
 * Populate the user graph with the information about each user's
 * Web site traffic.  The display is created in two parts.  The
 * first part displays the text data and computes the necessary
 * values for the second part to display the graph.
 */
PopulateUser ()
{
    gchar *strValue[4];
    int i;
    long hits;
    long size;
    gchar buffer0[88];
    gchar buffer1[88];
    gchar buffer2[88];
    int nRow = 0;
    long nMax;
    typGraphInfo graphInfo;

    /* --- Buffered values --- */
    strValue[0] = buffer0;
    strValue[1] = buffer1;
    strValue[2] = buffer2;
    strValue[3] = NULL;

    /* --- If there's no user clist yet --- */
    if (userCList == NULL) {

        /* --- Create the clist with titles --- */
        userCList = gtk_clist_new_with_titles (4, szUserTitles);

        /* --- Show titles --- */
        gtk_clist_column_titles_show (GTK_CLIST (userCList));

        /* --- Show width of columns --- */
        gtk_clist_set_column_width (GTK_CLIST (userCList), 0, 80);
        gtk_clist_set_column_width (GTK_CLIST (userCList), 1, 80);
        gtk_clist_set_column_width (GTK_CLIST (userCList), 2, 80);

        /* --- Justify columns --- */
        gtk_clist_set_column_justification (GTK_CLIST (userCList),
                                      0, GTK_JUSTIFY_LEFT);
        gtk_clist_set_column_justification (GTK_CLIST (userCList),
                                      1, GTK_JUSTIFY_RIGHT);
        gtk_clist_set_column_justification (GTK_CLIST (userCList),
                                      2, GTK_JUSTIFY_RIGHT);
```

```
        /* --- Add clist to page --- */
        gtk_container_add (GTK_CONTAINER (userPage), userCList);
    }

    /* --- Traverse the tree to show text info and get max --- */
    nMax = 0;
    g_tree_traverse (userTree, ShowUserInfo, G_IN_ORDER, &nMax);

    /* --- Populate structure for graphical tree traversal --- */
    graphInfo.nMaxSize = nMax;
    graphInfo.widget = userCList;
    graphInfo.row = 0;

    /* --- Display graphs --- */
    g_tree_traverse (userTree, DisplayUserGraph, G_IN_ORDER, &graphInfo);

    gtk_widget_show_all (GTK_WIDGET (userCList));
}
```

# Summary

You can now use more complicated widgets to make more interesting applications. The GtkTree widget displays information best described as being in a tree. The branches can be viewed, or they can be collapsed for viewing only the information that you want to see. The GtkNotebook widget is good for displaying multiple pages of user-driven or application-driven information. By hiding the tabs on the GtkNotebook widget, the widget becomes application driven. The GtkCList widget is great for displaying multiple columns of information, usually from a database. Text and graphics can be mixed in the widget to make ordinary information more pleasant to view.

# 15

# Creating Your Own Widgets

$A$T SOME POINT IN DEVELOPMENT, THE EXISTING widgets will probably fall short: perhaps a game needs a radar screen widget or an application needs to display many graphs. While GTK+ has a large set of widgets included, it is impossible to develop a set of widgets that meet everyone's development needs. Fortunately, GTK+ provides an interface that enables developers to extend the standard widget set.

## Understanding Widgets

One of the best ways to learn how to create new widgets is to read the readily available source code for GTK+. It is a great learning tool when you have questions about how something was done. This chapter uses examples from GTK+ to illustrate how widgets are created.

GTK+ was designed in an object-oriented manner. However, because it was implemented in C and C is not an objected-oriented language, creating widgets that adhere to the object-oriented nature of GTK+ requires some knowledge. Fortunately, after the widget is created, using it in an object-oriented manner is quite easy—it's just going to be a little difficult to actually understand all the tricks that went into its making. Widgets are created with two files. One is the actual code that creates and defines the widget, and the other is a header file that defines the data structures and prototypes for the widget.

## Inheriting Behavior

Widgets can be based on an existing widget, or they can be created from scratch. Basing the widget on an existing widget makes the coding easier if the widget already implements much of the behavior. The GtkToggleButton uses the GtkButton as its base and inherits the GtkButton's behaviors because the GtkButton already implements much of what the toggle button would need to code. The behavior specific to the toggle button is added to override the button behavior.

## Creating from Scratch

You can also create widgets from scratch, but this approach requires more work. Most widgets created from scratch use the GtkWidget as the base widget, which provides a minimal base to which the developer can add new functionality. A few widgets derive their base functionality from GtkMisc.

Compared to widgets that are based on the GtkWidget, GtkMisc-based widgets are less resource intensive because they do not have an associated X Window; instead they use the parent's X Window to perform drawing. However, because GtkMisc-based widgets don't have an X Window associated with them, they have some limitations. For instance, the GtkLabel cannot receive mouse events. To get labels to receive mouse events, they have to be placed within a GtkEventBox. Labels can be derived from GtkMisc because it's a display-only widget and doesn't usually have to handle any mouse interaction.

# Examining How Widgets Work

Widgets should use other widgets as a base whenever possible to leverage the coding of other developers and to reduce code bloat. This part of the chapter looks at the sections of an existing widget and dissects the code to understand the different pieces of a widget. Most of the examples here are from the button widget, but they should be similar to any widget.

## *include* File

The widget include defines the data structures necessary for the widget as well as prototypes for the widget functions. An important feature of the include is that include files can't be included multiple times; to avoid this problem, the widget header files use a unique identifier mark to signify their presence. In addition, the include files might be used with C++, so they should mark the C routines as C routines for the linker. The Gtk_button.h starts this way:

```
#ifndef __GTK_BUTTON_H__
#define __GTK_BUTTON_H__
```

```
#include <gdk/gdk.h>
#include <gtk/gtkcontainer.h>


#ifdef __cplusplus
extern "C" {
#pragma }
#endif /* __cplusplus */

/*
 *
 * include file stuff goes here.
 *
 */
```

The `include` file should end with the code that corresponds to the top of the file.

```
#ifdef __cplusplus
}
#endif /* __cplusplus */


#endif /* __GTK_BUTTON_H__ */
```

Of course, the `GTK_BUTTON_H` definition should be changed to your own label if you're creating a widget.

### Macros

The header file also has to define macros to be used by the new widget. We frequently use macros like `GTK_BUTTON` to convert a `GtkWidget` to a `GtkButton`, and this macro and others are defined next. The button widget defines three macros:

```
#define GTK_BUTTON(obj)    (GTK_CHECK_CAST ((obj), GTK_TYPE_BUTTON,
➥GtkButton))
#define GTK_BUTTON_CLASS(klass)         (GTK_CHECK_CLASS_CAST ((klass),
➥GTK_TYPE_BUTTON, GtkButtonClass))
#define GTK_IS_BUTTON(obj)              (GTK_CHECK_TYPE ((obj),
➥GTK_TYPE_BUTTON))
```

In this case, `GTK_TYPE_BUTTON` is defined as

```
#define GTK_TYPE_BUTTON                 (gtk_button_get_type ())
```

The `GTK_BUTTON` here is used throughout the programs that use the `GtkButton`, but the other two macros are used primary by the internal `Gtk_Button` widget code.

### Data Structures

The next step is to determine which data structures are required. For this step, you need to figure out which signals to use and which data to keep within the structures. The `GtkButton` needs a small structure.

```
struct _GtkButton
{
  GtkContainer container;

  GtkWidget *child;

  guint in_button : 1;
  guint button_down : 1;
};
```

This GtkButton structure defines the local data used by each button. The first item in the structure must be the widget that the current widget is derived from. In this case, it's the GtkContainer widget. The remaining data is for use by the button.

The button class also needs to be created. Just as the button widget has local data and information, the class needs to store class information that's common to all widgets of the particular type, such as available signals. The class for a button looks like this:

```
struct _GtkButtonClass
{
  GtkContainerClass parent_class;

  void (* pressed)  (GtkButton *button);
  void (* released) (GtkButton *button);
  void (* clicked)  (GtkButton *button);
  void (* enter)    (GtkButton *button);
  void (* leave)    (GtkButton *button);
};
```

Note that here, too, the parent class is defined first in the structure followed by a list of function pointers. The parent class structure must be defined first in the new widget class structure. These pointers are treated as virtual functions in C and are populated when the widget is created. But if another widget uses the GtkButton as a base class (like GtkToggleButton), it can modify these functions to change the behavior of the button. You also need to typedef these structures without the underscores.

```
typedef struct _GtkButton      GtkButton;
typedef struct _GtkButtonClass GtkButtonClass;
```

## Prototypes

The final part of the header defines any prototypes to be used by the applications. At a minimum, the prototype should define the *new* widget function and whatever functions are needed to manipulate the widget. The GtkButton widget has the following defined:

```
GtkType   gtk_button_get_type   (void);
GtkWidget* gtk_button_new        (void);
```

```
GtkWidget* gtk_button_new_with_label (const gchar *label);
void       gtk_button_pressed         (GtkButton *button);
void       gtk_button_released        (GtkButton *button);
void       gtk_button_clicked         (GtkButton *button);
void       gtk_button_enter           (GtkButton *button);
void       gtk_button_leave           (GtkButton *button);
```

## C Implementation Code

The C file is a bit more complicated than the header. Fortunately, much of the code can be copied (with some modifications) from existing widgets. The first step is to enumerate the signals that are going to be defined by the widget. (Do not include signals that are already defined in the widget that is used as the base widget.) The GtkButton widget defines the following signals followed by the LAST_SIGNAL indicator:

```
enum {
  PRESSED,
  RELEASED,
  CLICKED,
  ENTER,
  LEAVE,
  LAST_SIGNAL
};
```

However, the GtkToggleButton, which uses the GtkButton as its base class, only has to define any new signals that are specific to the toggle button. The toggle button needs to add a "toggled" signal, so it defines its new signals as

```
enum {
  TOGGLED,
  LAST_SIGNAL
};
```

Every widget needs to have a get_type function that provides GTK+ with information about the widget. The information is packed into a GtkTypeInfo structure and passed to Gtk_type_unique to uniquely identify the new widget. The GtkTypeInfo requires the following information:

- Widget's name
- Object size (for example, how big is a GtkButton?)
- Class size (for example, how big is a GtkButtonClass?)
- Class initialization function
- Object initialization function
- Set argument function
- Get argument function

For the button, this structure is defined as follows:

```
GtkTypeInfo button_info =
      {
        "GtkButton",
        sizeof (GtkButton),
        sizeof (GtkButtonClass),
        (GtkClassInitFunc) gtk_button_class_init,
        (GtkObjectInitFunc) gtk_button_init,
        (GtkArgSetFunc) gtk_button_set_arg,
        (GtkArgGetFunc) NULL,
      };
```

This structure is passed to the Gtk_type_unique function with the parent class's type to generate a unique ID for the widget. This ID should be generated only once, and the value returned is saved. It is to be used whenever the get_type function is called for the button. The entire code for the get_type function looks something like this:

```
GtkType
gtk_button_get_type (void)
{
   static GtkType button_type = 0;

   /* --- If ID not generated yet --- */
   if (!button_type)
     {
       GtkTypeInfo button_info =
       {
         "GtkButton",
         sizeof (GtkButton),
         sizeof (GtkButtonClass),
         (GtkClassInitFunc) gtk_button_class_init,
         (GtkObjectInitFunc) gtk_button_init,
         (GtkArgSetFunc) gtk_button_set_arg,
         (GtkArgGetFunc) NULL,
       };

       button_type = gtk_type_unique (gtk_container_get_type (),
                                      &button_info);
     }

     return button_type;
}
```

The next step is to define the gtk_button_class_init and gtk_button_init functions.

### Class Initialization

The class_init function defined in the get_type function is called to create the widget's class structure. The widget's class structure defines the information common to all the widgets of this type. The information includes defining new signals and redefining (overriding) old signals. New button signals are added by having a static array of the signals defined as

```
static guint button_signals[LAST_SIGNAL] = { 0 };
```

The LAST_SIGNAL was defined as part of the signal enumeration. The array will have to be populated with the widget's signal identifiers. The signal identifiers are generated by calling the gtk_signal_new function.

The class initialization for the button is broken down into a few sections. The more important pieces of code are summarized below. The first part is concerned with getting the parental information from the widget class structure.

```
static void gtk_button_class_init (GtkButtonClass *klass)
{
  GtkObjectClass *object_class;
  GtkWidgetClass *widget_class;
  GtkContainerClass *container_class;

  object_class = (GtkObjectClass*) klass;
  widget_class = (GtkWidgetClass*) klass;
  container_class = (GtkContainerClass*) klass;

  parent_class = gtk_type_class (gtk_container_get_type ());
```

The next step is to create the new signals. The button_signals array was created earlier. Now it must be populated with the signals. Each signal is created with the gtk_signal_new function and put in the array-enumerated index as the position within the array. The gtk_signal_new function is defined as

```
gint gtk_signal_new (const gchar *name,
                     GtkSignalRunType run_type,
                     GtkType object_type,
                     gint function_offset,
                     GtkSignalMarshaller marshaller,
                     GtkType return_val,
                     gint nparams,
                     [parameter types]);
```

The "pressed" and "clicked" signals vary only in the name and signal offset. They're using the default marshaller and have zero parameters.

```
button_signals[PRESSED] =
    gtk_signal_new ("pressed",
                    GTK_RUN_FIRST,
                    object_class->type,
```

```
                              GTK_SIGNAL_OFFSET (GtkButtonClass, pressed),
                              gtk_signal_default_marshaller,
                              GTK_TYPE_NONE, 0);

        button_signals[CLICKED] =
            gtk_signal_new ("clicked",
                              GTK_RUN_FIRST,
                              object_class->type,
                              GTK_SIGNAL_OFFSET (GtkButtonClass, clicked),
                              gtk_signal_default_marshaller,
                              GTK_TYPE_NONE, 0);
```

The signals then need to be added to the object class.

```
gtk_object_class_add_signals (object_class, button_signals, LAST_SIGNAL);
```

The widget also can choose to override any of the signals in any of the parent classes. Here the button chooses to override many widget signals and some of the container signals.

```
        widget_class->activate_signal = button_signals[CLICKED];
        widget_class->map = gtk_button_map;
        widget_class->unmap = gtk_button_unmap;
        widget_class->realize = gtk_button_realize;
        widget_class->draw = gtk_button_draw;
        widget_class->draw_focus = gtk_button_draw_focus;
        widget_class->draw_default = gtk_button_draw_default;
        widget_class->size_request = gtk_button_size_request;
        widget_class->size_allocate = gtk_button_size_allocate;
        widget_class->expose_event = gtk_button_expose;
        widget_class->button_press_event = gtk_button_button_press;
        widget_class->button_release_event = gtk_button_button_release;
        widget_class->enter_notify_event = gtk_button_enter_notify;
        widget_class->leave_notify_event = gtk_button_leave_notify;
        widget_class->focus_in_event = gtk_button_focus_in;
        widget_class->focus_out_event = gtk_button_focus_out;
        container_class->add = gtk_button_add;
        container_class->remove = gtk_button_remove;
        container_class->foreach = gtk_button_foreach;
```

Finally, the button's signals are populated. The `"clicked"` signal is set to NULL because the widget doesn't care about the signal, although developers may care about the signal when they are programming with the button widget.

```
        klass->pressed = gtk_real_button_pressed;
        klass->released = gtk_real_button_released;
        klass->clicked = NULL;
        klass->enter = gtk_real_button_enter;
        klass->leave = gtk_real_button_leave;
    }
```

## Emitting Signals

Signals can be emitted in GTK+ by using the `gtk_signal_emit` function or the `gtk_signal_emit_by_name` function. Usually, `gtk_signal_emit` is used within the widget because it has access to the signal table and knows the signal ID. The `gtk_signal_emit_by_name` uses the name instead of the signal ID and is primarily used outside the widget. The code for the `GtkButton` has a `gtk_button_clicked` function that can be called to emit the `"clicked"` signal. All it does is call the `gtk_signal_emit` function.

```
Void gtk_button_clicked (GtkButton *button)
{
    gtk_signal_emit (GTK_OBJECT (button), button_signals[CLICKED]);
}
```

When you want the event to occur so that the callback can handle the event, you can use the `gtk_signal_emit_by_name` function.

```
gtk_signal_emit_by_name (GTK_OBJECT (button), "changed");
```

When a signal is emitted, it's propagated to all the signal handlers. The propagation can be stopped by using the `gtk_signal_emit_stop_by_name` function in one of the signal handlers. Stopping a signal comes in handy when you want to filter the signals being propagated by a widget. For instance, you might want to filter certain keys from being typed into the widget. You could create a `"key_press_event"` callback that calls the `gtk_signal_emit_stop_by_name` function to prevent the other signal handlers from getting the `"key_press_event"` signal when certain keys are pressed.

### The *init* Function

The `init` function initializes a button instance for use. This step involves the initialization of data in the button's data structure and sometimes creating other widgets. The `GtkButton` `init` function is quite simple because all it does is perform some initialization:

```
static void gtk_button_init (GtkButton *button)
{
  GTK_WIDGET_SET_FLAGS (button, GTK_CAN_FOCUS);

  button->child = NULL;
  button->in_button = FALSE;
  button->button_down = FALSE;
}
```

Other widgets may be a bit more complicated to initialize. The `GtkFileSelection` is quite a bit more complicated because when the widget is created, it has to create all the children widgets that are within the dialog box. The list box widgets and the button widgets are created within the file selection dialog box, making it (the dialog box) much more complicated. If you're creating a simple widget, then your initialization function will look more like the `GtkButton`'s widget.

# Creating a Widget

After the data structures, class initialization, and widget initialization code have been written, the final major step is to write the code that allows the developer to create the widget. For the GtkButton, there are two functions—Gtk_button_new and Gtk_button_new_with_label. The Gtk_button_new creates a widget by getting the type and creating a new instance of that type. That part of the code is standard for creating a widget.

```
GtkWidget*
gtk_button_new (void)
{
   return GTK_WIDGET (gtk_type_new (gtk_button_get_type ()));
}
```

The more interesting code is for creating the button with a label. Notice how much this looks like standard GTK+ code. The code creates a button and a label and puts the label in the button—this code could have been written in an application and required no knowledge of the internals of the GtkButton. It built upon what was already created.

```
GtkWidget*
gtk_button_new_with_label (const gchar *label)
{
   GtkWidget *button;
   GtkWidget *label_widget;

   button = gtk_button_new ();
   label_widget = gtk_label_new (label);
   gtk_misc_set_alignment (GTK_MISC (label_widget), 0.5, 0.5);

   gtk_container_add (GTK_CONTAINER (button), label_widget);
   gtk_widget_show (label_widget);

   return button;
}
```

## Creating a Graphing Widget

Creating a widget from scratch isn't trivial—but neither is it particularly complicated. The great part about having the source code to GTK+ available is that its many widgets provide a great wealth of knowledge that you can leverage when creating new widgets. To see how to create a widget from scratch, you can create a very simple graphing widget that displays simple graphs. When thinking about creating a widget from scratch, try to understand its similarities to other widgets. In the case of the graphing widget, you can use the drawing area widget as a model because it provides a minimal set of functions required to perform drawing. You can expand on the knowledge you gain by studying the drawing area widget to create the graphing widget.

**Figure 15.1**   The graphing widget.

## The Header File

The small header file for the graphing widget simply describes the minimum required to get the widget going. The widget stores the graph data in an array called `values` in the widget data structure as well as the number of graph data elements.

```
/*
 * File: gtkgraph.h
 * Auth: Eric Harlow
 */
#ifndef __GTK_GRAPH_H__
#define __GTK_GRAPH_H__


#include <gdk/gdk.h>
#include <gtk/gtkvbox.h>


#ifdef __cplusplus
extern "C" {
#endif /* __cplusplus */


/*
 * --- Macros for conversion and type checking
 */
#define GTK_GRAPH(obj) \
   GTK_CHECK_CAST (obj, gtk_graph_get_type (), GtkGraph)
#define GTK_GRAPH_CLASS(klass) \
   GTK_CHECK_CLASS_CAST (klass, gtk_graph_get_type, GtkGraphClass)
#define GTK_IS_GRAPH(obj) \
   GTK_CHECK_TYPE (obj, gtk_graph_get_type ())

/*
 * --- Defining data structures
 */
```

```
typedef struct _GtkGraph                GtkGraph;
typedef struct _GtkGraphClass    GtkGraphClass;

/*
 * Here's the graph data
 */
struct _GtkGraph
{
    GtkWidget vbox;

    gint *values;
    gint num_values;
};


/*
 * Here's the class data
 */
struct _GtkGraphClass
{
  GtkWidgetClass parent_class;
};


/*
 * Function prototypes
 */
GtkWidget* gtk_graph_new (void);
void gtk_graph_size (GtkGraph *graph, int size);
void gtk_graph_set_value (GtkGraph *graph, int index, int value);


#ifdef __cplusplus
}
#endif /* __cplusplus */


#endif /* __GTK_GRAPH_H__ */
```

### Graph Code

The graph code defines the graphing widget as inheriting from GtkWidget. The graphing widget needs to override the widget code for the draw, expose, realize, and size_request for the graph to take control over its behavior. The GtkGraph also overrides the object destroy signal to free memory allocated before calling the parent class destroy callback. The two functions used to populate the graph are Gtk_graph_size, to set the number of bar graphs, and `Gtk_graph_set_value`, to set the value of a particular bar element. The actual meat of the code is in the `draw` function. The `draw` function for the graph widget is going to be called `gtk_graph_draw`. This will perform the display of the widget when required. Here's the code:

```
/*
 * File: GtkGraph.c
 * Auth: Eric Harlow
 *
 * Simple gtk graphing widget
 */

#include <string.h>
#include <stdlib.h>
#include <stdio.h>
#include <gtk/gtk.h>
#include "gtkgraph.h"

static GtkWidgetClass *parent_class = NULL;

/*
 * forward declarations:
 */
static void gtk_graph_class_init (GtkGraphClass *class);
static void gtk_graph_init (GtkGraph *graph);
static void gtk_graph_realize (GtkWidget *widget);
static void gtk_graph_draw (GtkWidget *widget, GdkRectangle *area);
static void gtk_graph_size_request (GtkWidget *widget,
                                    GtkRequisition *req);
static gint gtk_graph_expose (GtkWidget *widget, GdkEventExpose *event);
static void gtk_graph_destroy (GtkObject *object);


/*
 * gtk_graph_get_type
 *
 * Internal class. Used to define the GtkGraph class to GTK+
 */
guint gtk_graph_get_type (void)
{
  static guint graph_type = 0;

    /* --- If not created yet --- */
    if (!graph_type) {

        /* --- Create a graph_info object --- */
        GtkTypeInfo graph_info =
```

```
              {
                "GtkGraph",
                sizeof (GtkGraph),
                sizeof (GtkGraphClass),
                (GtkClassInitFunc) gtk_graph_class_init,
                (GtkObjectInitFunc) gtk_graph_init,
                (GtkArgSetFunc) NULL,
                (GtkArgGetFunc) NULL,
              };

        /* --- Tell GTK+ about it - get a unique identifying key --- */
        graph_type = gtk_type_unique (gtk_widget_get_type (),
➥&graph_info);
    }
    return graph_type;
}



/*
 * gtk_graph_class_init
 *
 * Override any methods for the graph class that are needed for
 * the graph class to behave properly.  Here, the functions that
 * cause painting to occur are overridden.
 *
 * class - object definition class.
 */
static void gtk_graph_class_init (GtkGraphClass *class)
{
    GtkObjectClass *object_class;
    GtkWidgetClass *widget_class;

    /* --- Get the widget class --- */
    object_class = (GtkObjectClass *) class;
    widget_class = (GtkWidgetClass *) class;
    parent_class = gtk_type_class (gtk_widget_get_type ());

    /* --- Override object destroy --- */
    object_class->destroy = gtk_graph_destroy;

    /* --- Override these widget methods --- */
    widget_class->realize = gtk_graph_realize;
    widget_class->draw = gtk_graph_draw;
    widget_class->size_request = gtk_graph_size_request;
    widget_class->expose_event = gtk_graph_expose;
}
```

```
/*
 * gtk_graph_init
 *
 * Called each time a graph item gets created.
 * This initializes fields in our structure.
 */
static void gtk_graph_init (GtkGraph *graph)
{
    GtkWidget *widget;

    widget = (GtkWidget *) graph;

    /* --- Initial values --- */
    graph->values = NULL;
    graph->num_values = 0;
}


/*
 * gtk_graph_new
 *
 * Create a new GtkGraph item
 */
GtkWidget* gtk_graph_new (void)
{
  return gtk_type_new (gtk_graph_get_type ());
}


/*
 * gtk_graph_realize
 *
 * Associate the widget with an X Window.
 *
 */
static void gtk_graph_realize (GtkWidget *widget)
{
  GtkGraph *darea;
  GdkWindowAttr attributes;
  gint attributes_mask;

  /* --- Check for failures --- */
  g_return_if_fail (widget != NULL);
  g_return_if_fail (GTK_IS_GRAPH (widget));

  darea = GTK_GRAPH (widget);
```

```
    GTK_WIDGET_SET_FLAGS (widget, GTK_REALIZED);

    /* --- attributes to create the window --- */
    attributes.window_type = GDK_WINDOW_CHILD;
    attributes.x = widget->allocation.x;
    attributes.y = widget->allocation.y;
    attributes.width = widget->allocation.width;
    attributes.height = widget->allocation.height;
    attributes.wclass = GDK_INPUT_OUTPUT;
    attributes.visual = gtk_widget_get_visual (widget);
    attributes.colormap = gtk_widget_get_colormap (widget);
    attributes.event_mask = gtk_widget_get_events (widget) |
➥GDK_EXPOSURE_MASK;

    /* --- We're passing in x, y, visual and colormap values --- */
    attributes_mask = GDK_WA_X | GDK_WA_Y | GDK_WA_VISUAL |
➥GDK_WA_COLORMAP;

    /* --- Create the window --- */
    widget->window = gdk_window_new (gtk_widget_get_parent_window (widget),
                                     &attributes, attributes_mask);
    gdk_window_set_user_data (widget->window, darea);

    widget->style = gtk_style_attach (widget->style, widget->window);
    gtk_style_set_background (widget->style, widget->window,
➥GTK_STATE_NORMAL);
}

/*
 * gtk_graph_size
 *
 * Custom method to set the size of the graph.
 */
void gtk_graph_size (GtkGraph *graph, int size)
{
    g_return_if_fail (graph != NULL);
    g_return_if_fail (GTK_IS_GRAPH (graph));

    graph->num_values = size;
    graph->values = g_realloc (graph->values, sizeof (gint) * size);
}

/*
 * gtk_graph_set_value
 *
 * Custom method to set the size.
 */
```

```
void gtk_graph_set_value (GtkGraph *graph, int index, int value)
{
    g_return_if_fail (graph != NULL);
    g_return_if_fail (GTK_IS_GRAPH (graph));
    g_return_if_fail (index < graph->num_values && index >= 0);

    graph->values[index] = value;
}



/*
 * gtk_graph_draw
 *
 * Draw the widget.  Draws the widget based on the
 * number of values in the bar graph.
 */
static void gtk_graph_draw (GtkWidget *widget, GdkRectangle *area)
{
    GtkGraph *graph;
    int width;
    int height;
    int column_width;
    int max = 0;
    int i;
    int bar_height;

    /* --- Check for obvious problems --- */
    g_return_if_fail (widget != NULL);
    g_return_if_fail (GTK_IS_GRAPH (widget));

    /* --- Make sure it's a drawable widget --- */
    if (GTK_WIDGET_DRAWABLE (widget)) {

        graph = GTK_GRAPH (widget);
        if (graph->num_values == 0) {
            return;
        }

        /* --- Get height and width --- */
        width = widget->allocation.width - 1;
        height = widget->allocation.height - 1;

        /* --- Calculate width of the columns --- */
        column_width = width / graph->num_values;
```

```
            /* --- Find the max value --- */
            for (i = 0; i < graph->num_values; i++) {
                if (max < graph->values[i]) {
                    max = graph->values[i];
                }
            }

            /* --- Display each bar graph --- */
            for (i = 0; i < graph->num_values; i++) {

                bar_height = (graph->values[i] * height) / max;

                gdk_draw_rectangle (widget->window,
                                    widget->style->fg_gc[GTK_STATE_NORMAL],
                                    TRUE,
                                    (i * column_width),
                                    height-bar_height,
                                    (column_width-2),
                                    bar_height);
            }
        }
}


/*
 * gtk_graph_size_request
 *
 * How big should the widget be?
 * It can be modified.
 */
static void gtk_graph_size_request (GtkWidget *widget,
                                    GtkRequisition *req)
{

    req->width = 200;
    req->height = 200;
}

/*
 * gtk_graph_expose
 *
 * The graph widget has been exposed and needs to be painted.
 *
 */
static gint gtk_graph_expose (GtkWidget *widget, GdkEventExpose *event)
{
```

```
    GtkGraph *graph;

    /* --- Do error checking --- */
    g_return_val_if_fail (widget != NULL, FALSE);
    g_return_val_if_fail (GTK_IS_GRAPH (widget), FALSE);
    g_return_val_if_fail (event != NULL, FALSE);

    if (event->count > 0) {
        return (FALSE);
    }

    /* --- Get the graph widget --- */
    graph = GTK_GRAPH (widget);

    /* --- Clear the window --- */
    gdk_window_clear_area (widget->window, 0, 0,
                           widget->allocation.width,
                           widget->allocation.height);

    /* --- Draw the graph --- */
    gtk_graph_draw (widget, NULL);
}


/*
 * gtk_graph_destroy
 *
 * Destroy the widget and free up any allocated memory.
 * When done, call the parent destroy to make sure any
 * memory allocated by the parent is freed.
 */
static void gtk_graph_destroy (GtkObject *object)
{

    GtkGraph *graph;

    /* --- Check type --- */
    g_return_if_fail (object != NULL);
    g_return_if_fail (GTK_IS_GRAPH (object));

    /* --- Convert to graph object --- */
    graph = GTK_GRAPH (object);

    /* --- Free memory --- */
    g_free (graph->values);

    /* --- Call parent destroy --- */
```

```
            GTK_OBJECT_CLASS (parent_class)->destroy (object);
    }
```

## Using the Widget

You can now use the graphing widget to display a simple graph on a window. The example creates a graph and populates it with values to be displayed.

```c
/*
 * File: main.c
 * Auth: Eric Harlow
 *
 * Example showing custom widget
 */

#include <gtk/gtk.h>
#include "gtkgraph.h"

/*
 * CloseAppWindow
 *
 * The window is closing down.  Need to shut down GTK+.
 */
gint CloseAppWindow (GtkWidget *widget, gpointer *data)
{
    gtk_main_quit ();

    return (FALSE);
}




/*
 * main - program begins here
 */
int main (int argc, char *argv[])
{
    GtkWidget *window;
    GtkWidget *graph;

    /* --- GTK+ initialization --- */
    gtk_init (&argc, &argv);

    /* --- Create the top-level window --- */
    window = gtk_window_new (GTK_WINDOW_TOPLEVEL);

    gtk_window_set_title (GTK_WINDOW (window), "Bar graph");
```

```
/* --- You should always remember to connect the delete_event
        to the main window. --- */
gtk_signal_connect (GTK_OBJECT (window), "delete_event",
                    GTK_SIGNAL_FUNC (CloseAppWindow), NULL);

/* --- Give the window a border --- */
gtk_container_border_width (GTK_CONTAINER (window), 20);

/*
 * --- Create a graph
 */

/* --- Create a new graph --- */
graph = gtk_graph_new ();

/* --- Show the graph  --- */
gtk_widget_show (graph);

/* --- Set the number of elements in the graph --- */
gtk_graph_size (GTK_GRAPH (graph), 5);

/* --- Set the height of each of the graph elements --- */
gtk_graph_set_value (GTK_GRAPH (graph), 0, 5);
gtk_graph_set_value (GTK_GRAPH (graph), 1, 10);
gtk_graph_set_value (GTK_GRAPH (graph), 2, 15);
gtk_graph_set_value (GTK_GRAPH (graph), 3, 20);
gtk_graph_set_value (GTK_GRAPH (graph), 4, 25);
gtk_widget_draw (graph, NULL);

/*
 * --- Make the main window visible
 */
gtk_container_add (GTK_CONTAINER (window), graph);
gtk_widget_show (window);

gtk_main ();
exit (0);
}
```

# Summary

Creating widgets is easy. Widgets provide applications with an interface much simpler than the widget internals suggest. Widgets can be created by inheriting much of their behavior from existing widgets, or they can be created from scratch. Creating the widgets from scratch requires more work and coding, but allows more flexibility.

# Index

## H

## I-J

# Books for Networking Professionals

## Windows NT Titles

### Windows NT TCP/IP

By Karanjit Siyan
1st Edition
480 pages, $29.99
ISBN: 1-56205-887-8

If you're still looking for good documentation on Microsoft TCP/IP, then look no further—this is your book. *Windows NT TCP/IP* cuts through the complexities and provides the most informative and complete reference book on Windows-based TCP/IP. Concepts essential to TCP/IP administration are explained thoroughly, then related to the practical use of Microsoft TCP/IP in a real-world networking environment. The book begins by covering TCP/IP architecture, advanced installation, and configuration issues, then moves on to routing with TCP/IP, DHCP Management, and WINS/DNS Name Resolution.

### Windows NT DNS

By Michael Masterson, Herman L. Knief, Scott Vinick, and Eric Roul
1st Edition
340 pages, $29.99
ISBN: 1-56205-943-2

Have you ever opened a Windows NT book looking for detailed information about DNS only to discover that it doesn't even begin to scratch the surface? DNS is probably one of the most complicated subjects for NT administrators, and there are few books on the market that really address it in detail. This book answers your most complex DNS questions, focusing on the implementation of the Domain Name Service within Windows NT, treating it thoroughly from the viewpoint of an experienced Windows NT professional. Many detailed, real-world examples illustrate further the understanding of the material throughout. The book covers the details of how DNS functions within NT, then explores specific interactions with critical network components. Finally, proven procedures to design and set up DNS are demonstrated. You'll also find coverage of related topics, such as maintenance, security, and troubleshooting.

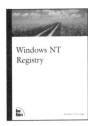

### Windows NT Registry

By Sandra Osborne
1st Edition
564 pages, $29.99
ISBN: 1-56205-941-6

The NT Registry can be a very powerful tool for those capable of using it wisely. Unfortunately, there is very little information regarding the NT Registry, due to Microsoft's insistence that their source code be kept secret. If you're looking to optimize your use of the Registry, you're usually forced to search the Web for bits of information. This book is your resource. It covers critical issues and settings used for configuring network protocols, including NWLink, PTP, TCP/IP, and DHCP. This book approaches the material from a unique point of view, discussing the problems related to a particular component, and then discussing settings, which are the actual changes necessary for implementing robust solutions. There is also a comprehensive reference of Registry settings and commands, making this the perfect addition to your technical bookshelf.

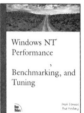

## Windows NT Performance

By Mark Edmead and Paul Hinsberg

1st Edition

288 pages, $29.99

ISBN: 1-56205-942-4

Performance monitoring is a little like preventative medicine for the administrator: No one enjoys a checkup, but it's a good thing to do on a regular basis. This book helps you focus on the critical aspects of improving the performance of your NT system, showing you how to monitor the system, implement benchmarking, and tune your network. The book is organized by resource components, which makes it easy to use as a reference tool.

---

## Windows NT Terminal Server

By Ted Harwood

1st Edition

416 pages, $29.99

ISBN: 1-56205-944-0

It's no surprise that most administration headaches revolve around integration with other networks and clients. This book addresses these types of real-world issues on a case-by-case basis, giving tools and advice on solving each problem. The author also offers the real nuts and bolts of thin client administration on multiple systems, covering such relevant issues as installation, configuration, network connection, management, and application distribution.

---

## Windows NT Security

By Richard Puckett

1st Edition Summer 1999

600 pages, $29.99

ISBN: 1-56205-945-9

Swiss cheese. That's what some people say Windows NT security is like. And they may be right, because they only know what the NT documentation says about implementing security. Who has the time to research alternatives; play around with the features, service packs, hot fixes, and add-on tools; and figure out what makes NT rock solid? Well, Richard Puckett does. He's been researching Windows NT security for the University of Virginia for a while now, and he's got pretty good news. He's going to show you how to make NT secure in your environment, and we mean really secure.

---

## Windows NT Network Management

By Anil Desai

1st Edition Spring 1999

400 pages, $34.99

ISBN: 1-56205-946-7

Administering a Windows NT network is kind of like trying to herd cats—an impossible task characterized by constant motion, exhausting labor, and lots of hairballs. Author Anil Desai knows all about it—he's a Consulting Engineer for Sprint Paranet, and specializes in Windows NT implementation, integration, and management. So we asked him to put together a concise manual of best practices, a book of tools and ideas that other administrators can turn to again and again in managing their own NT networks. His experience shines through as he shares his secrets for reducing your organization's Total Cost of Ownership.

### Planning for Windows 2000

By Eric K. Cone
1st Edition Spring 1999
400 pages, $29.99
ISBN: 0-73570-048-6

Windows 2000 is poised to be one of the largest and most important software releases of the next decade, and you are charged with planning, testing, and deploying it in your enterprise. Are you ready? With this book, you will be. *Planning for Windows 2000* lets you know what the upgrade hurdles will be, informs you how to clear them, guides you through effective Active Directory design, and presents you with detailed rollout procedures. Eric K. Cone gives you the benefit of his extensive experience as a Windows 2000 Rapid Deployment Program member, sharing problems and solutions he's encountered on the job.

### MCSE Core NT Exams Essential Reference

By Matthew Shepker
1st Edition
256 pages, $19.99
ISBN: 0-7357-0006-0

You're sitting in the first session of your Networking Essentials class and the instructor starts talking about RAS and you have no idea what that means. You think about raising your hand to ask about RAS, but you reconsider—you'd feel pretty foolish asking a question in front of all these people. You turn to your handy *MCSE Core NT Exams Essential Reference* and find a quick summary on Remote Access Services. Question answered. It's a couple months later and you're taking your Networking Essentials exam the next day. You're reviewing practice tests and you keep forgetting the maximum lengths for the various commonly used cable types. Once again, you turn to the *MCSE Core NT Exams Essential Reference* and find a table on cables, including all of the characteristics you need to memorize in order to pass the test.

# BackOffice Titles

### Implementing Exchange Server

By Doug Hauger, Marywynne Leon, and William C. Wade III
1st Edition
400 pages, $29.99
ISBN: 1-56205-931-9

If you're interested in connectivity and maintenance issues for Exchange Server, then this book is for you. Exchange's power lies in its ability to be connected to multiple email subsystems to create a "universal email backbone." It's not unusual to have several different and complex systems all connected via email gateways, including Lotus Notes or cc:Mail, Microsoft Mail, legacy mainframe systems, and Internet mail. This book covers all of the problems and issues associated with getting an integrated system running smoothly and addresses troubleshooting and diagnosis of email problems with an eye towards prevention and best practices.

## Exchange Server Administration

By Janice K. Howd
1st Edition Spring 1999
400 pages, $34.99
ISBN: 0-7357-0081-8

OK, you've got your Exchange Server installed and connected, now what? Email administration is one of the most critical networking jobs, and Exchange can be particularly troublesome in large, heterogenous environments. So Janice Howd, a noted consultant and teacher with over a decade of email administration experience, has put together this advanced, concise handbook for daily, periodic, and emergency administration. With in-depth coverage of topics like managing disk resources, replication, and disaster recovery, this is the one reference book every Exchange administrator needs.

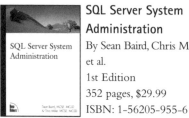

## SQL Server System Administration

By Sean Baird, Chris Miller, et al.
1st Edition
352 pages, $29.99
ISBN: 1-56205-955-6

How often does your SQL Server go down during the day when everyone wants to access the data? Do you spend most of your time being a "report monkey" for your co-workers and bosses? *SQL Server System Administration* helps you keep data consistently available to your users. This book omits the introductory information. The authors don't spend time explaining queries and how they work. Instead they focus on the information that you can't get anywhere else, like how to choose the correct replication topology and achieve high availability of information.

## Internet Information Server Administration

By Kelli Adam, et. al.
1st Edition Fall 1999
300 pages, $29.99
ISBN: 0-73570-022-2

Are the new Internet technologies in Internet Information Server giving you headaches? Does protecting security on the Web take up all of your time? Then this is the book for you. With hands-on configuration training, advanced study of the new protocols in IIS, and detailed instructions on authenticating users with the new Certificate Server and implementing and managing the new e-commerce features, *Internet Information Server Administration* gives you the real-life solutions you need. This definitive resource also prepares you for the release of Windows 2000 by giving you detailed advice on working with Microsoft Management Console, which was first used by IIS.

## SMS Administration

By Wayne Koop and Brian Steck
1st Edition Summer 1999
350 pages, $34.99
ISBN: 0-7357-0082-6

Microsoft's new version of its Systems Management Server (SMS) is starting to turn heads. While complex, it's allowing administrators to lower their total cost of ownership and more efficiently manage clients, applications and support operations. So if your organization is using or implementing SMS, you'll need some expert advice. Wayne Koop and Brian Steck can help you get the most bang for your buck, with insight, expert tips, and real-world examples. Brian and Wayne are consultants specializing in SMS, having worked with Microsoft on one of the most complex SMS rollouts in the world, involving 32 countries, 15 languages, and thousands of clients.

# Unix/Linux Titles

## Solaris Essential Reference

By John Mulligan
1st Edition Spring 1999
350 pages, $19.99
ISBN: 0-7357-0230-7

Looking for the fastest, easiest way to find the Solaris command you need? Need a few pointers on shell scripting? How about advanced administration tips and sound, practical expertise on security issues? Are you looking for trustworthy information about available third-party software packages that will enhance your operating system? Author John Mulligan— creator of the popular Unofficial Guide to Solaris Web site (sun.icsnet.com)— delivers all that and more in one attractive, easy-to-use reference book. With clear and concise instructions on how to perform important administration and management tasks and key information on powerful commands and advanced topics, *Solaris Essential Reference* is the reference you need when you know what you want to do and you just need to know how.

## Linux System Administration

By James T. Dennis
1st Edition Spring 1999
450 pages, $29.99
ISBN: 1-56205-934-3

As an administrator, you probably feel that most of your time and energy is spent in endless firefighting. If your network has become a fragile quilt of temporary patches and workarounds, then this book is for you. For example, have you had trouble sending or receiving your email lately? Are you looking for a way to keep your network running smoothly with enhanced performance? Are your users always hankering for more storage, more services, and more speed? *Linux System Administration* advises you on the many intricacies of maintaining a secure, stable system. In this definitive work, the author addresses all the issues related to system administration, from adding users and managing files permission to Internet services and Web hosting to recovery planning and security. This book fulfills the need for expert advice that will ensure a trouble-free Linux environment.

## Linux Security

By John S. Flowers
1st Edition Spring 1999
400 pages, $29.99
ISBN: 0-7357-0035-4

New Riders is proud to offer the first book aimed specifically at Linux security issues. While there are a host of general UNIX security books, we thought it was time to address the practical needs of the Linux network. In this definitive work, author John Flowers takes a balanced approach to system security, from discussing topics like planning a secure environment to firewalls to utilizing security scripts. With comprehensive information on specific system compromises, and advice on how to prevent and repair them, this is one book that every Linux administrator should have on the shelf.

### Developing Linux Applications

By Eric Harlow
1st Edition
400 pages, $34.99
ISBN: 0-7357-0214-7

We all know that Linux is one of the most powerful and solid operating systems in existence. And as the success of Linux grows, there is an increasing interest in developing applications with graphical user interfaces that really take advantage of the power of Linux. In this book, software developer Eric Harlow gives you an indispensable development handbook focusing on the GTK+ toolkit. More than an overview on the elements of application or GUI design, this is a hands-on book that delves deeply into the technology. With in-depth material on the various GUI programming tools and loads of examples, this book's unique focus will give you the information you need to design and launch professional-quality applications.

### Linux Essential Reference

By David "Hacksaw" Todd
1st Edition Summer 1999
400 pages, $19.99
ISBN: 0-7357-0852-5

This book is all about getting things done as quickly and efficiently as possible by providing a structured organization to the plethora of available Linux information. We can sum it up in one word: VALUE. This book has it all: concise instruction on how to perform key administration tasks; advanced information on configuration; shell scripting; hardware management; systems management; data tasks; automation; and tons of other useful information. All coupled with an unique navigational structure and a great price. This book truly provides groundbreaking information for the growing community of advanced Linux professionals.

# Lotus Notes and Domino Titles

### Domino System Administration

By Rob Kirkland
1st Edition Summer 1999
500 pages, $34.99
ISBN: 1-56205-948-3

Your boss has just announced that you will be upgrading to the newest version of Notes and Domino when it ships. As a Premium Lotus Business Partner, Lotus has offered a substantial price break to keep your company away from Microsoft's Exchange Server. How are you supposed to get this new system installed, configured, and rolled out to all of your end users? You understand how Lotus Notes works—you've been administering it for years. What you need is a concise, practical explanation about the new features, and how to make some of the advanced stuff really work. You need answers and solutions from someone like you, who has worked with the product for years, and understands what it is you need to know. *Domino System Administration* is the answer—the first book on Domino that attacks the technology at the professional level, with practical, hands-on assistance to get Domino running in your organization.

**Lotus Notes and Domino Essential Reference**

By Dave Hatter & Tim Bankes

1st Edition Spring 1999

500 pages, $24.99

ISBN: 0-7357-0007-9

You're in a bind because you've been asked to design and program a new database in Notes for an important client that will keep track of and itemize a myriad of inventory and shipping data. The client wants a user-friendly interface, without sacrificing speed or functionality. You are experienced (and could develop this app in your sleep), but feel that you need to take your talents to the next level. You need something to facilitate your creative and technical abilities, something to perfect your programming skills. Your answer is waiting for you: *Lotus Notes and Domino Essential Reference*. It's compact and simply designed. It's loaded with information. All of the objects, classes, functions, and methods are listed. It shows you the object hierarchy and the overlaying relationship between each one. It's perfect for you. Problem solved.

# Networking Titles

**Cisco Router Configuration and Troubleshooting**

By Pablo Espinosa and Mark Tripod

1st Edition

300 pages, $34.99

ISBN: 0-7357-0024-9

Want the real story on making your Cisco routers run like a dream? Why not pick up a copy of *Cisco Router Configuration and Troubleshooting* and see what Pablo Espinosa and Mark Tripod have to say? They're the folks responsible for making some of the largest sites on the Net scream, like Amazon.com, Hotmail, USAToday, Geocities, and Sony. In this book, they provide advanced configuration issues, sprinkled with advice and preferred practices. You won't see a general overview on TCP/IP—we talk about more meaty issues like security, monitoring, traffic management, and more. In the troubleshooting section, the authors provide a unique methodology and lots of sample problems to illustrate. By providing real-world insight and examples instead of rehashing Cisco's documentation, Pablo and Mark give network administrators information they can start using today.

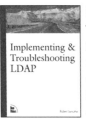

## Implementing and Troubleshooting LDAP

Implementing & Troubleshooting LDAP

By Robert Lamothe
1st Edition Spring 1999
400 pages, $34.99
ISBN: 1-56205-947-5

While there is some limited information available about LDAP, most of it is RFCs, white papers, and books about programming LDAP into your networking applications. That leaves the people who most need information—administrators—out in the cold. What do you do if you need to know how to make LDAP work in your system? You ask Bob Lamothe. Bob is a UNIX administrator with hands-on experience in setting up a corporate-wide directory service using LDAP. Bob's book is NOT a guide to the protocol; rather, it is designed to be an aid to administrators to help them understand the most efficient way to structure, encrypt, authenticate, administer, and troubleshoot LDAP in a mixed network environment. The book shows you how to work with the major implementations of LDAP and get them to coexist.

## Implementing Virtual Private Networks

Implementing Virtual Private Networks

By Tina Bird and Ted Stockwell
1st Edition Spring 1999
300 pages, $29.99
ISBN: 0-73570-047-8

Tired of looking for decent, practical, up-to-date information on virtual private networks? *Implementing Virtual Private Networks*, by noted authorities Dr. Tina Bird and Ted Stockwell, finally gives you what you need—an authoritative guide on the design, implementation, and maintenance of Internet-based access to private networks. This book focuses on real-world solutions, demonstrating how the choice of VPN architecture should align with an organization's business and technological requirements. Tina and Ted give you the information you need to determine whether a VPN is right for your organization, select the VPN that suits your needs, and design and implement the VPN you have chosen.

## Understanding Data Communications, Sixth Edition

Understanding Data Communications Sixth Edition

By Gilbert Held
6th Edition Summer 1999
500 pages, $34.99
ISBN: 0-7357-0036-2

Updated from the highly successful fifth edition, this book explains how data communications systems and their various hardware and software components work. Not an entry-level book, it approaches the material in a textbook format, addressing the complex issues involved in internetworking today. A great reference book for the experienced networking professional, written by noted networking authority, Gilbert Held.

# We Want to Know What You Think

To better serve you, we would like your opinion on the content and quality of this book. Please complete this card and mail it to us or fax it to 317-581-4663.

Name_____

Address _____

City _____State _____Zip _____

Phone _____

Email Address _____

Occupation _____

Operating System(s) that you use _____

What influenced your purchase of this book?
- ❏ Recommendation
- ❏ Table of Contents
- ❏ Magazine Review
- ❏ New Riders' Reputation
- ❏ Cover Design
- ❏ Index
- ❏ Advertisement
- ❏ Author Name

How would you rate the contents of this book?
- ❏ Excellent
- ❏ Good
- ❏ Below Average
- ❏ Very Good
- ❏ Fair
- ❏ Poor

How do you plan to use this book?
- ❏ Quick reference
- ❏ Classroom
- ❏ Self-training
- ❏ Other

What do you like most about this book?
Check all that apply.
- ❏ Content
- ❏ Accuracy
- ❏ Listings
- ❏ Index
- ❏ Price
- ❏ Writing Style
- ❏ Examples
- ❏ Design
- ❏ Page Count
- ❏ Illustrations

What do you like least about this book?
Check all that apply.
- ❏ Content
- ❏ Accuracy
- ❏ Listings
- ❏ Index
- ❏ Price
- ❏ Writing Style
- ❏ Examples
- ❏ Design
- ❏ Page Count
- ❏ Illustrations

What would be a useful follow-up book to this one for you? _____

Where did you purchase this book? _____

Can you name a similar book that you like better than this one, or one that is as good? Why?
_____
_____

How many New Riders books do you own? _____

What are your favorite computer books? _____
_____

What other titles would you like to see us develop? _____
_____

Any comments for us? _____
_____
_____
_____

*Developing Linux Applications, 0-7357-0021-4*

Fold here and tape to mail

- - - - - - - - - - - - - - - - - - - - - - - - - - - - - - - - - - - - - - - - - - - - - - - - - - - - - - - - - - - - - - - - - - - - - - - - - - - - -

New Riders Publishing
201 W. 103rd St.
Indianapolis, IN  46290

# New Riders | How to Contact Us

## Visit Our Web Site

**www.newriders.com**

On our Web site you'll find information about our other books, authors, tables of contents, indexes, and book errata. You can also place orders for books through our Web site.

## Email Us

Contact us at this address:

**newriders@mcp.com**

- If you have comments or questions about this book
- To report errors that you have found in this book
- If you have a book proposal to submit or are interested in writing for New Riders
- If you would like to have an author kit sent to you
- If you are an expert in a computer topic or technology and are interested in being a technical editor who reviews manuscripts for technical accuracy

**newriders-sales@mcp.com**

- To find a distributor in your area, please contact our international department at the address above.

**newriders-pr@mcp.com**

- For instructors from educational institutions who wish to preview New Riders books for classroom use. Email should include your name, title, school, department, address, phone number, office days/hours, text in use, and enrollment in the body of your text along with your request for desk/examination copies and/or additional information.

## Write to Us

New Riders Publishing
201 W. 103rd St.
Indianapolis, IN 46290-1097

## Call Us

Toll-free (800) 571-5840 + 9 + 4557
If outside U.S. (317) 581-3500. Ask for New Riders.

## Fax Us

(317) 581-4663